The Power and the People

This book is about power: the power wielded over others – by absolute monarchs, tyrannical authoritarian regimes and military occupiers – and the power of the people who resist and deny their rulers' claims to that authority by whatever means. The extraordinary events in the Middle East in 2011 offered a vivid example of how nonviolent demonstration can topple seemingly invincible rulers. Drawing on these dramatic events and parallel moments in the modern history of the Middle East, from the violent uprisings in Algeria against the French in the early twentieth century, to revolution in Iran in 1979 and the Palestinian *intifada*, the book considers the ways in which the people have united to unseat their oppressors and fight against the status quo to shape a better future. The book also probes the relationship between power and forms of resistance and how common experiences of violence and repression create new collective identities. Nowhere is this more strikingly exemplified than in the art of the Middle East, its posters and graffiti, and its provocative installations which are discussed in the concluding chapter. This brilliant, yet unsettling, book affords a panoramic view of the twentieth- and twenty-first-century Middle East through occupation, oppression and political resistance.

Charles Tripp is Professor of Politics with reference to the Middle East at the School of Oriental and African Studies, University of London. His many publications include three editions of *A History of Iraq* (2007, 2002, 2000) and *Islam and the Moral Economy: The Challenge of Capitalism* (2006).

The Power and the People

Paths of Resistance in the Middle East

CHARLES TRIPP
University of London

CAMBRIDGE
UNIVERSITY PRESS

CAMBRIDGE UNIVERSITY PRESS
Cambridge, New York, Melbourne, Madrid, Cape Town,
Singapore, São Paulo, Delhi, Mexico City

Cambridge University Press
32 Avenue of the Americas, New York, NY 10013-2473, USA

www.cambridge.org
Information on this title: www.cambridge.org/9780521007269

First published 2013

Printed in the United States of America

A catalog record for this publication is available from the British Library.

Library of Congress Cataloging in Publication Data
Tripp, Charles.
The power and the people : paths of resistance in the Middle East / Charles Tripp.
   p. cm.
Includes bibliographical references and index.
ISBN 978-0-521-80965-8 (hardback) – ISBN 978-0-521-00726-9 (pbk.)
  1. Government, Resistance to – Middle East – History. 2. Protest movements – Middle
East – History. 3. Nonviolence – Middle East – History. 4. Middle East – Politics and
government – 1945– I. Title.
JQ1758.A91T75 2012
322.40956–dc23   2012008620

ISBN 978-0-521-80965-8 Hardback
ISBN 978-0-521-00726-9 Paperback

To my father, Peter Tripp (1921–2010)
and
to my mother, Rosemary Tripp (1922–2012)

When Egypt arose
After they thought it slept
It was to curse hunger and humiliation
And the wrongs it had suffered and its government

Ahmad Fu'ad Negm Letter No 1 from
Tora Prison, *January 1977*

Contents

List of Illustrations and Credits

Because the illustrations are being printed in the text itself, they are reproduced in black and white in this book. However, this fails to do justice to them. In the following list, I have therefore provided a website address for anyone who wishes to see a full-colour reproduction of the image concerned.

Acknowledgements

Anyone looking through these pages will see that I have relied extensively on the scholarship of others. I have acknowledged their many contributions by referring to their works in the text and in the bibliography, but I should stress here that I owe a debt of gratitude to them all. Without the light of their research and their insights into particular aspects of the contentious politics of the Middle East, it would have been extraordinarily difficult to attempt any systematic illumination of the paths of resistance chosen by so many of the region's citizens.

Thanks to them and to my growing familiarity with their works, I was able to develop a few years ago a Masters course at SOAS on 'The Politics of Resistance in the Middle East'. In this lie the origins of the book. However, it was taken a step further when the first cohort of Masters students responded positively and imaginatively to this experimental course in the autumn of 2008. Their questions, the insights they shared, the ideas and the enthusiasm that they brought to the course greatly enriched it and persuaded me that I should build upon it to write this book. So my special thanks go to Mohammed al-Khalifa, Erika Atzori, Philip Bato, Barrie Boles, Catherine Ellis, Tucker George, Zoe Jackman, Vania Kaneva, Luke Massey, Patrick McCluskey, Annalisa Renna, Thomas Rogan, John Samuel, Jennifer Schuster, Lena Sinjab, Sam Southgate, Leila Stockmarr, Michael Whiting and Valerie Yorke. Their successors in 2009–10, 2010–11 and 2011–12 who have taken the same course have been no less imaginative and enthusiastic. I have valued the seminars that have given me the chance to engage with them and to benefit from their critical readings in the subject. Puzzling over some of their questions these past few years has undoubtedly helped to clarify my thoughts, and I am grateful to all of them as well. But I must admit that I feel a particular debt of gratitude to those who set me thinking that there was sufficient coherence in the subject matter for it to become the basis of a book.

During the course of my research and writing, there have been many others who have given me their time, their energy and their advice. To all of them I remain profoundly grateful and would like to mention in particular Ghaith Abdul-Ahad, Johannes Abeling, Etel Adnan, Shiva Balaghi, Li-Chao Chen, Rochelle Davis, Tom Finn, Laura Gribbon, Ramin Haerizadeh, Khosrow Hassanzadeh, John Jurayj, Karima Khalil, Salam Khedher, Louisa MacMillan, Hanaa Malallah, Nicky Nodjoumi, Walid Raad, Laila Shawa, Avi Shlaim, Walid Siti, Vera Tamari, Hale Tenger, Isabelle van den Eynde, Dan Walsh and Moiz Zilberman. My thanks to each of you for the assistance you have given me. I hope that you think the end result was worthy of your help.

I would also like to thank Marigold Acland, my editor at Cambridge University Press, whose enthusiasm helped to set this project in motion and whose constructive and critical readings of the text have, I hope, improved it greatly. Finally, for their support and for their constant encouragement that have helped me in the completion of the manuscript, I owe a debt of gratitude and love to Venetia, Emily and Rhiannon.

Glossary

Alawi	the heterodox sect to which the family of Hafiz al-Asad and many of the senior figures of the Syrian regime since 1970 belong [also known as *nusayri*]
Amazigh (pl. *Imazighen*)	the name adopted across North Africa by much of the Berber population to describe themselves
al-Anfal	the Iraqi Army operation in the Kurdish regions of Iraq 1988–9 that caused an estimated 130,000 deaths and depopulated and devastated large swathes of the Kurdish region
Aouchem	[lit., 'sign' or 'tattoo' (Arabic: *wasm*)] name of artistic movement in Algeria in the 1960s
`ashura	tenth day of the month of Muharram, held in special reverance by Shi`i Muslims, since it commemorates the death of Imam Hussein in 680 AD at Karbala
bai' salam	a contract for the advance sale of specified goods to be delivered later
Basij	volunteer militia organization founded in 1979 following the Iranian revolution

fatwa	a judgment delivered by a recognized Muslim scholar
Fedayeen	*al-fida'iyin* [the redeemers (who sacrifice themselves)] common reference to Palestinian armed guerrilla groups
fiqh	Islamic jurisprudence
habous	*al-habus* – property endowment recognized under Islamic law [also known as *al-waqf*]
hadith	saying or tradition of the Prophet Muhammad
hawala	system of money transfer common in South Asia and the Middle East that depends largely on trust
hawaladar	the agent who organizes the *hawala* transfers
hijab	woman's head covering or veil
hittistes	term used for young urban unemployed in North Africa – 'those who spend their time leaning against the wall [*al-ha'it*]'
hogra	*haqqara* – to hold in contempt. Used in North African states to express the contemptuous attitude of the authorities to their citizens
ijtihad	independent interpretation of an Islamic legal or theological question
infitah	[lit., 'opening'] the opening of the economy to foreign and private capital that began across the Middle East in the 1970s–80s
intifada	[lit., 'shaking off'] the name given to various popular uprisings across the Middle East
intifadat al-aqsa	the uprising in the Occupied Palestinian Territories that began in 2000
intifadat al-safar	the uprising in southern Iraq in 1977

isqat	[lit., 'fall'] referring to women allegedly compromised by unsupervised association with men
jahsh	[lit., 'little donkeys'] derogatory term used against Kurdish tribal irregulars employed by the Iraqi Ba'thist government
Jaish al-Mahdi	[army of the Mahdi] armed organization in the service of Muqtada al-Sadr in post-2003 Iraq
jihad	effort or struggle on behalf of Islam
jihadi	term used to describe those Islamists who believe that such a struggle must be an armed one
kaffiyeh	black-and-white checkered head cloth traditionally worn by rural Palestinian men
mahram	a category of relative in Islamic law so close that marriage is forbidden. Hence, it has come to mean chiefly a close male relative of a woman allowed to escort her when she travels
Majles	[lit., 'assembly'] the short name of the Iranian parliament
Makhzen	[lit., 'the store' or 'storehouse' (*al-makhzan*)] the state or government in Morocco
mizrahim	[lit., 'easterners'] has come to mean mainly Jewish citizens of Israel who immigrated from Arab countries
Moudawana	*mudawwanat al-ahwal al-shakhsiyya* – the term used for the Moroccan Family Code of personal status laws, until its reform in 2004
mudaraba	contract in Islamic law in which a lender invests capital and a borrower invests time, energy and expertise

musharaka	contract in Islamic law in which both the lender and the borrower make a financial investment in a venture
al-Nakba	[lit., 'the catastrophe'] the term used by Palestinians and in the Arab world to refer to the war of 1948 that saw the establishment of the state of Israel on most of the territory of Palestine
peshmerga	[lit., 'those who face death'] term used to refer to Kurdish guerrilla forces
Le Pouvoir	[lit., 'the power'] used in Algeria to refer to the key elite of the security forces and the political establishment
salafi	[lit., 'one who follows the ancestors'] refers to a trend in modern Islamic thought that looks back to the example of the earliest Muslims
shabab	collective term for youth or younger generation
al-Shabbiha	[lit., 'ghosts'] name of the armed militia in Syria largely recruited from the home regions of the al-Asad and allied clans of the ruling elite
shaikh	[lit., 'old man'] honorific for an Islamic scholar, or a tribal chieftain
shari`a	Islamic law
shura	counsel
sumud	steadfastness
tajnis	[lit., 'to confer nationality'] used to describe the process in Bahrain whereby the government has naturalized large numbers of Sunni Muslims, Arab and non-Arab, particularly in the security services
Tamazight	term in common use to describe the increasingly standardized forms of Amazigh/Berber language
umma	(Muslim) community
wali	guardian

waqf	property endowment recognized in Islamic law
al-yafta	banner or sign, used in public spaces for announcements, political slogans and advertising
Yishuv	the Zionist settlement in Palestine during the British Mandate 1917–48

List of Abbreviations

AIS
: Armée Islamique du Salut [Islamic Salvation Army] armed Islamist organization active in Algeria in the 1990s

ALN
: Armée de Libération Nationale [National Liberation Army] the fighting wing of the Algerian national liberation movement against French rule

CPA
: Coalition Provisional Authority – the U.S. government of Iraq from May 2003–June 2004

DFLP
: Democratic Front for the Liberation of Palestine

EFITU
: Egyptian Federation of Independent Trade Unions (formed January 2011)

ETUF
: Egyptian Trade Union Federation (state-run union organization, dissolved August 2011)

Etzel
: Irgun Zvai Leumi (also known as the Irgun) [National Military Organization] – an armed Zionist organization active in Palestine 1930–48

Fatah
: [lit., 'conquest' or 'victory'] Harakat al-Tahrir al-Watani al-Filastini [Palestine National Liberation Movement] founded in 1959 and the principal member of the PLO [Palestine Liberation Organization] after 1969

FFS
: Front des Forces Socialistes [Socialist Forces Front] political party in Algeria formed by Hocine Ait Ahmed in 1963

FIS   Front Islamique du Salut [Islamic Salvation Front]
             Islamist political organization in Algeria founded in
             1989
FJP   Freedom and Justice Party [Hizb al-Hurriyya wa-l-
             `Adala] Egyptian political party formed in 2011 to
             represent the Muslim Brotherhood
FLN   Front de Libération Nationale [National Liberation
             Front] the main organization of the Algerian
             struggle for national liberation against France
FSA   Free Syrian Army [al-Jaish al-Suri al-Hurr] armed
             opposition organization that emerged out of the
             uprising in Syria in 2011
GEB   Groupe d'Etudes Berbères [Group of Berber Studies]
GIA   Groupe Islamique Armé [Islamic Armed Group] armed
             Islamist organization active in Algeria in the 1990s
             particularly
GICM   Groupe Islamique Combattant Marocain
Haganah   [the defence] armed Zionist organization active in
             Palestine 1930–48
Hamas   [lit., 'enthusiasm'] Harakat al-Muqawama al-Islamiyya
             [Islamic Resistance Movement] Islamist political
             and armed organization active in Occupied
             Palestine since the 1980s
Irgun   see Etzel
KDP   Kurdish Democratic Party (in Iraq)
Lehi   Lohami Herut Israel [Fighters for the Freedom of Israel]
             also known as the Stern Gang. Armed Zionist
             organization active in Palestine in the 1940s
MAK   Mouvement de l'Autonomie Kabyle [Kabyle Autonomy
             Movement]
MCB/A   Mouvement Culturel Berbère/Amazigh [Berber/
             Amazigh Cultural Movement]
NDP   National Democratic Party – until 2011 the ruling
             political party in Egypt
NLF   National Liberation Front – one of the two main
             independence organizations in the British colony of
             Aden and the protectorates in the 1960s
NTC   National Transitional Council [al-Majlis al-Watani al-
             Intiqali] – the rebel government formed in Benghazi

	in February 2011 that led the uprising against Qadhafi
OAS	Organisation de l'Armée Secrète [Organization of the Secret Army] armed organization of European settlers in Algeria who wanted to keep Algeria French
OWFI	Organization of Women's Freedom in Iraq
PA	Palestinian Authority – full name al-Sulta al-Filastiniyya al-Wataniyya [Palestinian National Authority] established in the Occupied Palestinian Territories in 1994
Palmach	Plugot Machatz [Strike Force] elite unit of the Haganah [see p. xxii]
PFLP	Popular Front for the Liberation of Palestine
PFWAC	Palestinian Federation of Women's Action Committees
PJD	Parti de la Justice et du Développement [Justice and Development Party] (Morocco)
PLO	Palestine Liberation Organization
PUK	Patriotic Union of Kurdistan
RND	Rassemblement National Démocratique [National Rally for Democracy] political party in Algeria founded in 1997
SCAF	Supreme Council of the Armed Forces (the group of military officers who took over power in Egypt after the fall of President Mubarak in February 2011)
Shas	*Shomrei sfarad* (Sfarad's guards [of the Torah]) political party representing religiously observant Mizrahi and Sephardi Israelis
SNC	Syrian National Council [al-Majlis al-Watani al-Suri] Syrian coalition of opposition forces formed in exile during the Syrian uprising in 2011
UGTT	Union Générale Tunisienne du Travail [The General Tunisian Union of Labour]
UMT	Union Marocaine du Travail [Moroccan Union of Labour]
USFP	Union Socialiste des Forces Populaires [Socialist Union of Popular Forces] (Morocco)
al-Wifaq	Jam`iyyat al-Wifaq al-Watani al-Islamiyya [Islamic National Accord Association] political party in Bahrain

Introduction

In early March 2011, a group of teenagers in the Syrian border town of Dar`a, fired up by the spirit of rebellion that they had seen sweeping across the Arab world, went out one night to paint graffiti on walls in the town. Prominent among the slogans they sprayed was the call that had been reverberating through the Arab world since the uprising in Tunisia in January: '*al-sha`b yurid isqat al-nizam*' [the people want the downfall of the regime]. If they were hoping that the citizens of Dar`a would wake up the next day to be amazed and secretly gratified by their daring, they were right. But they also discovered the danger of such an act and such words in a country that had been ruled under 'emergency laws' for more than forty years. The teenagers were rounded up by the political security police, incarcerated in its grim headquarters and subjected to the beatings and burnings that were part of the routine brutality of the force. When the boys' relatives came to try to find them, they were treated with contempt by the governor and his security officials who told them to forget about the boys and to go home.

This triggered a series of public protests in the town. The arrests, the rumours of torture and finally the contemptuous attitude of the officials were too much to bear. Joined by hundreds of others, the boys' relatives marched through Dar`a demonstrating their anger. Chants and slogans were shouted against the regime, posters of the president, Bashar al-Asad, were defaced, a statue of his father, Hafiz al-Asad, the late president, was toppled and destroyed, the ruling Ba`th party headquarters and the court building were torched, as were the offices of Syriatel, the telecoms company owned by Rami Makhlouf, a first cousin of the president. The Syrian security forces responded by firing into the crowds in an effort to drive them from the streets. A number of people were killed and dozens wounded but were denied access to the town's hospital. Instead, the citizens turned the al-`Umari mosque in the old town into a provisional medical station to treat casualties. This was then raided by the security forces, with further loss of life, including one of the doctors. In all, five people died violently in Dar`a that day.

However, this was just the beginning. In the weeks and months that followed, demonstrations and uprisings spread throughout Syria, met by an increasingly violent response from government security forces that cost the lives of thousands of Syrian citizens. What had begun with the semi-humorous slogan 'Your time is up, Doctor' (referring to Bashar al-Asad's training as an ophthalmologist) had become within a matter of weeks 'Butcher of the People! Traitor to Syria!'. In late April, giving an oration at one of the many funerals in Dar`a, a former Syrian MP, Riyadh Saif, proclaimed 'We are all martyrs-to-be for the sake of our rights, of our dignity and for the dignity of the entire nation and the Syrian people!'[1] Appropriately enough, the citizens of Dar`a renamed the square outside the al-`Umari mosque, the scene of such violence, 'Dignity Square' [*midan al-karama*].

This sequence of events not only captures a moment in the unfolding drama of Syria's politics, but also highlights some of the key features of a politics of resistance in action, helping to justify its closer study. Public demonstrations can easily be identified as dramatic signs of dissent and opposition. More than that, however, open protests, their causes and the course they take can shine a piercing light on key features of power itself. Whether in a democratic or in an authoritarian system, such as in Syria, power clothes itself for much of the time in the guise of normality, of routine, of a presence that need not be questioned because it is so much part of the 'natural' order of things. This is not necessarily part of some deep conspiracy. It may be the outcome of everyday conformity, enforced if necessary by the coercive arm of the state, but generally visible only in exceptional circumstances. It is habit that can make power so binding, since people tend to take it and their position within it so much for granted.

It is precisely such a relationship that, for instance, some anarchists of late-nineteenth-century Europe and America tried to rupture. They wanted to startle people out of their complacency through acts of violence that were meant to – and often did – provoke the state to reveal its own capacity for violence, red in tooth and claw, using force to maintain fundamental inequalities.[2] Equally, Marxist revolutionaries have long tried to awaken the working class, to make its members see clearly the true nature of the oppressive system of exploitation that they may have been blinded to by the false gods of nationalism or liberal capitalism.[3] As many have recognized, the hold of any system of power is directly related to the hold it can exercise on people's imagination. The circumstances that begin to create the possibility of self-consciousness, of offering people a chance to 'come out of themselves', are those that can also cause dramatic shifts in power, creating resistance among those who had until then gone along with their own subordination.[4]

In Syria, in 2011, this is what had begun to happen in Dar`a, but also in many other places across the country. The familiarity of the situation that other Syrians saw or were made aware of struck home forcefully, causing them to think again about much that they might have otherwise accepted. Whether this had been through habit, prudence or dissimulation must remain an open question. It is one that has been extensively explored in Lisa Wedeen's notion that for much of the time, when confronted by the bombast of the regime, Syrians act 'as if' they subscribed to its own account of itself and its authority.[5] It was now, however, their opportunity to act in ways that turned conformity on its head. In doing so it was clear, through their choice of targets, both symbolic and actual, that the citizens of Dar`a – and of towns across Syria – had an intimate knowledge not only of the public state, but also of the 'shadow state' in Syria. Resistance in this sense followed the contours of power itself, marked by the very familiarity that had once appeared to breed conformity.

In the case of Dar`a, as elsewhere, this familiarity determined the targets that drew the anger of the demonstrators and also shaped their initial demands. These included not only the immediate release of the group of teenagers responsible for the graffiti, but also the release of all political prisoners, the repeal of the state of emergency laws that had been in force for nearly fifty years, a public enquiry into the deaths of the five who had been killed on the first day of protest, an end to corruption and the repeal of the law governing agricultural lands along the border which placed them effectively under the arbitrary control of the security forces. This mixture of local and national demands indicated that the townspeople knew full well how the two spheres were connected, and were aware of the networks of the 'shadow state' that linked the

Syrian security apparatus and the business enterprises owned by those close to the al-Asad clan. In this respect, the protests and the attacks on symbols of power were acts of resistance against the systems of inclusion and closure that had denied most of the population the chance to decide their own lives.

Here, as elsewhere, resistance thus follows and contests the lines of inclusion and exclusion that are integral to all systems of power. They may be conceded or they may be imposed, just as the criteria they use may be agreed or simply accepted – or they may come to be resented. A politics of resistance in this sense illuminates both the dividing lines of this relationship and the increasingly threadbare rationales used to justify their maintenance. It means more than simply opposition to particular policies, the usual stuff of contentious politics. This is a politics of contention on a more fundamental scale. It goes to the heart of a system of power over others, its principles and the ways that people experience it. All of these factors, including the implementation of policies that consistently disadvantage some, whilst privileging others, can feed into a politics of resistance that takes as its core issue the lines of discrimination themselves.

In the Syrian case, as in the events in Tunisia and Egypt that had inspired so many in Syria, the main divide was between those who were connected with the security and business networks at the summit of the state, and those – the vast majority of the citizenry – who were systematically excluded. It was they who had to suffer the prospects of unemployment and of job discrimination in favour of the children of the elite. As the subjects of unanswerable power, they had no recourse when the 'emergency laws' in all three countries were routinely invoked to maintain order and to give the security apparatus and their business associates immunity from any kind of public scrutiny. Given the origins of much of the ruling elite in Syria among the clans of the Jebel Alawi, it could also give a sectarian sharpness to denunciation of that elite. This had been very much in evidence during the Muslim Brotherhood-led uprisings of the late 1970s. It was also heard occasionally in some of the slogans of 2011 as the violence escalated, particularly in Latakia and Banias, cities with a history of sectarian tension. Nor was the regime itself slow to exploit this social divide. It wanted to portray the protests as driven by sectarian animosity in an effort to 'denationalize' the resistance and to create a climate of fear amongst Syria's religious minorities.

Elsewhere in the region, as in Bahrain and in Israel and the occupied Palestinian territories, resistance has arisen to contest exclusion drawn along sectarian, as well as ethnic lines. In these cases, a political order has been imposed on large numbers of people, ensuring their unequal access to resources, both material and institutional, on the basis of acknowledged and unacknowledged criteria of discrimination. Whether in the episodic uprisings and protest movements among the majority Shi'a of Bahrain, or among the Palestinians under Israeli military occupation, resistance has been more than simply a response to oppressive practices. It has become a way of engaging with, indicting and seeking to change whole systems of power and exclusion, demonstrating a capacity for independent action. By making clear what they were hoping to free themselves from, through many small gestures and acts of resistance, as well as by staging major demonstrations, the resistance movements dredged up and laid bare what have been called the 'capillary' forms of power.[6]

The focus on the politics of resistance in this book is also therefore a way of examining the genealogy of resistance and its potential. Although spectacular and highly visible acts of resistance – demonstrations, protests, riots, insurrections – draw attention to an unbearable situation, as they are intended to do, they do not come out of nowhere. On the contrary, they may be merely the most obvious expression of what happens at the moment when some catalytic event brings to the fore long-simmering resentments. Such an event resonates because the ground has been prepared through stories, poems, songs and a wide array of local acts of defiance and resistance, unseen by the authorities and by outside observers. One of the common themes repeated by participants in the dramatic events of 2011 across the Arab world was the spectacular impact on them and their friends of the evaporation of fear. One of the chants in the streets of Dar'a was 'There is no fear, there is no fear, after today there is no fear'.[7]

This was a sentiment echoed in countless ways from the streets of Tunis, to Cairo's Tahrir Square and to Bahrain's Pearl Roundabout. But the presence of fear – that is, the fear of what the consequences might be of open opposition to an oppressive system of power – is testimony to the fact that such opposition exists, that the exercise of power is resented and that people have ceased to believe that the existing order of things is the proper order of things. In this sense, fear is a symptom of hostility. It is also a perfectly understandable response to the violence of forces of military occupation, or of the national security state. More than that, it indicates that the so-called 'awe of the state' [*haibat al-dawla*] was nothing more than people's recognition that the state could do them harm. This might still shake their faith in their own capacity to act effectively or safely, but it could not suppress the idea of resistance itself. As Khalil Mutran, poet of an earlier generation of nationalist resistance put it, having listed the forms of physical violence that oppressive forces can inflict on the body of the subject:

> 'that is your [only] power –
> And in it is our protection from you. So thank you'.[8]

It could be argued therefore that a politics of resistance follows power in that it too is capillary in nature, branching out in many different ways. It takes not simply the obvious routes of physical resistance, but also follows the paths of the imagination where resistance to power is not only told but also valued – it forms part of the narratives of everyday life that give meaning to encounters with power. It is for this reason that the kinds of practices described as forms of 'everyday resistance' cannot be dismissed as of little relevance to larger, more visible resistance projects. Whether or not they are intended to contribute to such a larger project, their very existence, as the accepted everyday practices of the marginalized and excluded, can prepare the ground in ways that the authorities are unable to detect.[9] Thus novels, plays, poems, films, the visual arts, as well as forms of expression that go beyond such conventions, cannot be dismissed as 'merely' cultural, of little relevance to the kinds of resistance seen in the streets of a country undergoing violent upheaval. On the contrary, the ruthless attention paid to the control of such matters by authorities everywhere, not only in the Middle East, testifies to their own fear of the power of the imagination in stimulating ideas of resistance and in providing it with a ready repertoire.

A study of resistance in all its phases and aspects is therefore also an important way of understanding the reservoirs of images and memories that people draw upon when acting politically. It brings into focus the models that they follow for both imagining and organizing resistance to despised or unwelcome domination. In the events of 2011 in the Middle East, the sight of popular uprisings carried out by people who in many ways – language, religion, youth, culture, music, histories, political subjection – were much like themselves, inspired people from country to country across the Arab world, as well as in Iran. Whether in the Yemeni capital Sana'a, or in the Jordanian capital Amman, or in the provincial cities of Syria or of Egypt or of Libya, the actions, slogans and chants transferred easily from one setting to another, since in some key respects they could be seen to be the same. This explains the resonating power of the calls for the fall of the regime, the songs where the words may have been altered to take in the name of a local hate figure, or indeed the ways of mobilizing to confront the security forces by occupying public space. Of course, events did not and could not play themselves out in the same way in each country, as the inhabitants of Libya, of Syria, of Bahrain and of Yemen have found to their cost. Nevertheless, what was significant in each of these countries was the way in which region-wide repertoires of resistance meshed with the local practices that had long formed common threads, however widely dispersed the workplaces, urban neighbourhoods, villages and provincial towns concerned.

Dramatic as the events of 2011 undoubtedly were, they were also large-scale performances of actions that had been taking place in different countries for a number of years. Thus, despite the immediacy and uncertainty of the factors that caused the demonstrations in Tunisia to have such a momentous effect, they would be difficult to understand without having some insight into the events of the 1980s when riots and demonstrations ripped through Tunisia's cities. Their force and coordination would also be difficult to grasp without some understanding of the effects of Tunisia's much-vaunted neo-liberal economic restructuring on the Tunisian workforce as a whole. Similarly, the capacity of Egyptian workers to organize for civil resistance in 2011 and to believe that it stood a chance of success came out of their struggles of the previous decade. It was then that they had organized themselves outside the reach of their official unions to protest the impact of the economic privatization programmes. Even those Egyptians who had tried openly to contest the dominant order but who had been thwarted, such as the Kifaya movement, or the '6 April' movement, could at least draw upon a repertoire of actions, symbolic and otherwise, that stood them in good stead with the beginning of national protests and demonstrations in January 2011.

In this sense, therefore, to study the politics of resistance is also to study a key component of political power in a field of contention. Understanding the main dynamics of contentious politics means paying attention to the vocabularies that create the basis of new solidarities, the performances that escape and challenge the everyday ordering of power. Even if there is no identifiable movement or cause, or little public sign of it, disenchantment with authority and direct and indirect subversion of power can thrive and, under certain circumstances, coalesce to challenge the material power of regime and state.[10]

In the Middle East in particular, where the focus has often been on the politics of the imperial adventures, the states, regimes and apparatuses of power that have given the landscape of the region some of its distinctive features, resistance has often been portrayed as episodic, rather than systemic. This study hopes to open out the field to examine a variety of political actors and actions that have resisted imposed forms of power. Thus it may take in but is not limited to specific political movements and organizations that have tried to claim exclusive possession of an ineffable quality that makes them the 'essence of resistance'. The case of Hizbullah in Lebanon brings this out. Despite evidence to the contrary, it has tried to identify itself with 'resistance' as if this were a general property. In fact, appropriation of the term, with its many associations, is part of Hizbullah's own myth of power in the game of Lebanese politics. However, resistance, like power itself, is a relation between political actors. That relation changes over time, shaped by the shifting context of political activity and by the seductions of power. Nowhere was this more in evidence than in a speech by the leader of Hizbullah, Hassan Nasrallah, in early December 2011 where he extolled the resistance of Hizbullah and even of the Syrian regime, but poured contempt on the widespread Syrian resistance to that regime.[11]

It should be fairly clear by now how 'resistance' is to be understood in this book and thus the kinds of politics that will be examined under this heading. It will look at activities aimed at contesting and resisting systems of power that people in different places have found increasingly intolerable for a wide variety of reasons. In some settings, this may bring out very public forms of protest and resistance, intended to make those in power reconsider and change specific policies, or indeed the way they exercise power. Whether from the outset, as in Iraq following the U.S.-led invasion of 2003 or in Egypt in 2011, or gradually, as in Bahrain and Syria in the same year, organized resistance may also aim at the complete overthrow of the political regime that has brought the resistance into being through its behaviour.

The methods chosen to make resistance effective, both within a particular country and beyond, will also vary. Spectacular violence, armed uprisings, as well as mass popular demonstrations and the deliberate choice of nonviolent methods have all been much in evidence in the recent political history of the Middle East. They have constituted the fabric and texture of the politics of resistance, reflecting the responses of the particular regime they are challenging. Thus what began as a popular demonstration demanding redress within the framework of the law in Libya in February 2011 became in a matter of days an armed insurrection that tore the country in two and invited foreign military intervention. Conversely, the determination of the assembled protesters in Cairo's Tahrir Square chanting '*Silmiyya! Silmiyya!*' [peaceful, peaceful] to be neither moved nor provoked into responding violently to the attack launched upon them by thousands of riot police and enlisted 'supporters' of President Mubarak confronted the Egyptian armed forces with a very public choice that sealed the fate of the president.

Spectacular violence has also been part of the repertoire of resistance. It has been used to convey messages aimed at recognition of the determination that had led people to desperate acts. In Iraq since 2003, the massacres of Shi`i pilgrims, the destruction of sacred sites, the killings of villagers and members of the security forces and the much-publicized videos of beheadings have sent repeated gruesome signals of an intention to resist the new order that the U.S.-led invasion brought into being. In other places, such as Tunisia and Egypt in 2011, spectacular violence has been turned against the self through public acts of self-immolation, as signals of defiance and despair on the part of those made powerless by the system under which they live. And within branches of the Palestinian and Iraqi resistance movements, these two features have been combined by the suicide bombers who have killed and wounded hundreds, and in doing so have spectacularly annihilated themselves.

Whether the forms of resistance are violent, nonviolent or can be classified as acts of 'rightful resistance', and whether the intention is to reform existing structures of power or radically to reshape them, the qualities shared by much of the varied politics of resistance in this study are both intentional and demanding of public recognition.[12] In that sense, they follow the contours of domination itself. They are also in most instances acts of collective political organization in the sense that they express resistance to subordination by people who find themselves categorized in the same way. At one level, this can mean that citizens are treated as subjects, excluded from the privileges and power enjoyed by the governing elites. The attempt to win recognition of their dignity and thus their rights as citizens has been a central part of widespread resistance politics. This can also apply to those who find themselves disadvantaged and discriminated against as a special category, be they women in Morocco or Iran, Shi`a in Bahrain, Palestinians under Israeli military occupation, or Berbers in Algerian society. This in itself can help to give a collective identity to a politics of resistance where no strong sense of cohesion existed before.

Collective action to redress sensed wrongs and to assert meaningful rights have been integral to the politics of resistance. Uprisings, demonstrations and protests aimed at the removal of the categorical exclusions and the social closure that denies such rights have been a visible, sometimes spectacular aspect of these politics. But this has often been preceded and underpinned by less visible forms of behaviour that may involve resistance to the implications of the wider ordering of power for the individual. Individually or collusively, people devise strategies to ensure that the impact of the exclusions is lessened where possible. Closer to the idea of 'everyday resistance', these forms of subversion create a counterculture of the subaltern. Here the imposed categories, with their association of contempt, are hollowed out and their material effects lessened. Whether this happens in the sphere of property (through pilfering, quiet encroachment and alternative economies) or of education (through alternative forms that escape the dictation of the state) or of culture, broadly defined (through reaffirmation of values that resist the mainstream), all these activities can feed into a politics of resistance.[13] They may not in themselves either lead to or be intended to lead to the more public and spectacular forms of resistance that demand public recognition and aim to overturn the order of power. However, they may prepare the ground for such actions, and feed into the larger stream once other circumstances combine to define a more general and public politics of contention.

Cases such as these, where groups of people have been systematically excluded from the system of power that dominates them, illustrate one of the difficulties apparent in any study of resistance. This is the value-laden association of the term, both because of historical associations and because of the centrality in many traditions of political thought of the right to resist unjust and oppressive power. In the century or so of European imperial domination of the Middle East, resistance was seen as both a religious and a national duty. It took on the heroic associations of a struggle against alien forces that had unleashed disruptive violence on the peoples of the region. The same idea was taken up by many during and after the years of the Cold War. It was then that American power was seen as the ruthless carrier of a neo-colonialism that tried to dominate the peoples of the region because of the value of their oil or their part in the global strategic balance. For instance, the positive associations of the term resistance became integral to the struggle between the Palestinians and Israel and in the attitudes to the conflict taken by different parties. It became a defining element in the self-representation of a group like Hizbullah in Lebanon, projecting itself as standing at the forefront of resistance to Israel and to U.S. hegemony in the Middle East.

Even without this wider resonance of resistance to global hegemonic power, attitudes to resistance within particular states have largely depended upon how people feel about the incumbent regime. Thus in Iraq after 2003, the term 'the resistance' [*al-muqawama*] was appropriated as a badge of honour by all the varied groups fighting not only U.S. and allied military occupation, but also the Iraqi governments that emerged out of the slow process of state reconstruction after 2004. For their part, it was noticeable that the Iraqi security forces avoided the word, using a variety of terms – terrorists, *jihadi*, *salafi*, Ba'thists, reactionaries, agents – to describe the forces that challenged them and the government they served. Precisely because *al-muqawama* had taken on such positive overtones, it was a difficult term to use about those who had you in their sights. Similarly, because of the strong historical and circumstantial association with the idea of resisting power that was by definition oppressive, retrograde and unyielding, the term resistance took on unmistakably positive overtones in many parts of the Middle East. Like the terms 'revolution' and 'revolutionary', there was a strong presumption that it could not be associated with reactionary or oppressive goals, despite widespread evidence to the contrary.

One way of avoiding such a charged and value-laden set of associations when using the term is to return to the idea of resistance as something that is closely related to, because intimately engaged with, different forms of power wherever they are found. It could therefore be said to be the other side of the relation that constitutes power itself and corresponds to the observation by Michel Foucault that 'Wherever there is power, there is resistance, and yet, or rather by the same token, the latter is never external to power ... [T]he strictly relational character of power's connections ... can only exist as a result of a multiplicity of points of resistance ... These points of resistance are present everywhere in the network of power'.[14] The more contested that power may be, the easier it is to see such contestation as being an identifiable politics of resistance. Where power itself is more conceded, diffuse and less confrontational, then resistance becomes less useful as a term for understanding political struggle and the political lexicon provides other, more appropriate terms. However, this in itself raises another problem that has become apparent both in some of the writings on the politics of resistance, and in the practice of such politics in specific places.

Power certainly breeds resistance, but it may also need resistance, or something it portrays as such, to justify itself. It projects onto those that resist it the antithesis of its own image, the dark side that will erupt unless power can keep it in check. More than a propaganda device, this is a mobilizing idiom common to those who find their own exclusive hold on power challenged. Terrorism, disorder, sectarianism, fanaticism and tribalism have all been projected onto resistance movements across the region as if these terms, rather than their struggle against entrenched and exclusive power, were the most appropriate ways of thinking of them – and dealing with them – as political actors. Thus for Qadhafi in Libya, the citizens who rose up against him and against the practices of his regime in 2011 could be dismissed as fanatical followers of al-Qaʿida. In Bahrain, with Saudi assistance, the civil rights movement was accused of being the dupes of malign foreign forces (Iran) and suppressed accordingly. In Syria, faced by popular uprisings in towns across the country demanding greater rights and freedoms, the government of Bashar al-Asad lost no time in labelling them all as *salafi* and sectarian, as well as agents of unnamed foreign powers determined to sow discord and to impose their will on Syria.

In all these cases, resistance movements were portrayed by those in power as the antitheses of themselves. This was meant to appeal to their own followers, to waverers and to foreign powers who might have been tempted to assist one side or the other. Whatever the designation, these are the binary antitheses that are unmistakably the effect of power itself: 'the other' is projected as a way of denying legitimacy to those who oppose and resist. One of the more poignant themes in the testimonies of Egyptian demonstrators who were seized and ruthlessly interrogated by the security forces in January and February 2011 was their bewilderment at being repeatedly accused of betraying their country by their tormentors. It was perhaps not surprising therefore that some of those involved in the Egyptian protests should have called former president Mubarak himself be tried for treason, as well as for corruption and the abuse of power.[15]

But this raises the question of the degree to which resistance, in shadowing power, also takes on some of its qualities, similarly dividing the world into binary opposites. For much the same strategic and imaginative reasons, a common feature of resistance movements is the portrayal of power, and the figure standing at the apex of power, as the embodiment of all that the resistance is seeking to root out.

The unrelenting call for the president to go has been a marked feature of recent uprisings in the Arab world, just as the call for the downfall and death of the Shah resonated across Iran in 1978. But power is more complex, more widespread and more integrated into the fabric of society than this representation would suggest. So too, as resistance progresses and some of its earlier, obvious targets succumb, the nature of what is being resisted, why and by what means can begin to lack definition. The multilayered structure of power may thwart and complicate resistance. As one Lebanese interlocutor replied realistically enough when asked in 2011 why Lebanon had remained so calm when regional protest movements were gathering strength: 'But in Lebanon [to change anything] we would have to get rid of eighteen Ben Alis'.[16]

Equally, as participants in the Palestinian *intifidat*, as well as those who took part in the Tunisian and Egyptian uprisings, and the initial enthusiasts for resistance in Iraq have all discovered, a project that once appeared straightforward can become increasingly ambiguous. Concessions, even the disappearance of unifying targets and apparent victories, can fragment coalitions that had come together around easily identifiable objectives. This presents a practical challenge to movements of resistance when trying to maintain the kind of momentum that had initially shaken the status quo, forcing change where none had been offered. In Egypt, for instance, those who organized successfully to resist the power of Mubarak and his associates were faced by the challenge of the follow-up in the months after his downfall. Confronted by the ruling military council, but also by more faceless, less easily identified systems of economic and bureaucratic power, continued resistance became a more contentious project in the eyes of some. In these circumstances, those campaigning and demonstrating for extensive and radical change were aware of the danger that '*kifaya!*' [enough!] – the slogan that had been so powerful in signalling resistance to Mubarak's long tenure of power – was now being used against them. Such developments also make the identification of what can be considered and analysed within a framework of the politics of resistance that much harder. And it has, of course, generated within the field of protest and resistance as practice, as well as in the field of its study, disputes about what kinds of activity merit the term 'resistance'.[17]

For all the problems of identification as well as practice, there are some arguments that will serve as unifying threads throughout this study. The examples and illustrations will come from the recent political experiences of peoples across the Middle East, but the arguments themselves have a wider relevance, beyond this particular region. The first of these is the basic contention of the correlation between the forms of power and the forms of resistance. This is not simply a strategic choice of resistance movements. It explains why particular kinds of resistance may seem like a fitting response to those confronted by certain systems of power. It also throws light on the views of those in power and those who would organize to resist them. It may also go some way to explain why particular methods – spectacular violence, nonviolence, quiet encroachment – may be chosen and why they may find general support at particular times and places. These may reflect but not necessarily mimic the ways in which people have experienced power itself.

One of the ethical and political dilemmas that has confronted resistance movements everywhere is that which stems from concern that, in resisting power, they may be imitating not simply its methods but also its way of seeing the world. In fact, for some, this has not been a dilemma so much as a strategic choice, based on calculations of what will work to break the power they confront. As countless historical examples have shown, the longer-term effects of this can be truly disturbing. However, these concerns have also given rise to thoughts about genuine alternatives in the conception of power, as well as in the forms of resistance. Thus the phenomenon of 'leaderless movements' witnessed in a number of places in the Middle East in 2011, together with the determined pursuit of nonviolent methods to bring into being a system of governance based upon the recognition and protection of rights, have been powerful examples of just such a politics of resistance. Deliberately avoiding the kinds of resistance associated with the necessarily conspiratorial political organizations of the past, as well as refusing to be drawn into the use of violence as a short cut to power, movements in Tunisia, Egypt, Syria and Yemen have confronted their regimes. However, as these cases have also demonstrated, it can be a precarious and risky business to maintain such a posture, with no guarantee of success, nor automatic consensus within the resistance that this is the best way to proceed.

In fact, common experiences of power have been central in explaining why resistance can be taken up by large numbers of people, across a country and, as the events of 2011 showed, across a region. This is the second of the three main arguments that run through the book. In Algeria, a very apt term has been used to describe both the attitude of those in power to the Algerian people and thus the cause of their resentment of and resistance to those in authority. '*Hogra*' [contempt] is the powerful word used by many in the country to sum up the nature of the relationship between '*Le Pouvoir*' [the power – referring to the ruling elite] and the people.[18] Other terms may be used in other parts of the Middle East, but the experience of power for many has been much the same, summed up in this withering term and in the kinds of everyday brutalities, humiliations and violations of human dignity that have been so much part of the practice of power. It is for this reason that protests that began in the provinces, in the unconsidered and marginal towns of the interior across the region, became such powerful symbols and cata-lysts of protest. When they brought the struggle to the heart of power in capital cities, they signalled the loss of control by the authorities and threatened to give the lie to the all-seeing, supremely competent state. In many respects – ironically given the origins of the idea in colonial counterinsurgency and its use in North Africa – local resistance can be like *les taches d'huile* [oil spots] which, when they join up, form not the basis of established order but the conflagration of general resistance.[19]

This is not merely a mechanical effect, but the result of local author-ities overreaching themselves and behaving in such a way that they outrage local feelings. Such behaviour cumulatively makes people look at themselves and their relations with those in power in a different light. This in turn causes flashes of recognition elsewhere, making people realize that they are experiencing a similar kind of domination. The familiarity of the predicament and the feeling of common cause can create the organizational and imaginative underpinnings of resistance. However diffuse, resentments and general awareness can be turned into active protest by further measures taken by the authorities – the sudden raising of basic food prices, the blatant and careless rigging of an election, the use of open and disproportionate violence or the humil-iation of someone with whom others can identify. It is when people realize not only that they suffer a common predicament but also that they can have an impact by acting together that a powerful moment of open collective resistance can be created.

It is the contingent nature of this sequence of events that underpins the third main argument. This concerns the timescale necessary to understand a politics of resistance and its effects in any particular place – or perhaps more accurately, the different time frames of its different moments. There are two timescales at work. The first is the immediate impact that any movement of open resistance might have on the forces confronting it. Whether successful or not in achieving its declared objective, such as the toppling of the Shah of Iran in 1978–9, or the overthrow of President Ben Ali of Tunisia in 2011, there is the question of what happens next. Ambiguous outcomes, the fragile coalition of resistance and the loss of focus on a clear target can all contribute to its apparent dissipation amidst waning enthusiasm and a less obvious sense of empowerment. It can be argued that this was the fate of the first Palestinian *intifada* that began in 1987. It was also evident in Tunisia and Algeria in the 1980s and in Egypt after the April 2008 strikes and sit-ins at al-Mahalla al-Kubra and elsewhere.

Nevertheless, it can be argued that, disappointing as some of the immediate outcomes of these collective acts of resistance may have been, they set in motion processes that were to have major significance in the years that followed. Their legacies, although obviously very different, were many. They helped to shape attitudes towards power, the performance of power and indeed the future repertoire of resistance itself. Some have derived from this a pessimistic reading of resistance, arguing that it can never achieve the goals it sets out to achieve, or that, in achieving them, it becomes too beholden to the logic of power that it tried to displace. There are certainly plenty of examples of this across the Middle East, from the Front de Libération Nationale (FLN) in Algeria, the National Liberation Front (NLF) in Aden and other anti-colonial revolutions, to the Islamic Republic of Iran. But it can also encourage a longer view, beyond the immediate short-term outcomes of a process of resistance. A movement that may have informed and inspired thousands can live on in the power of memory. This can provide the repertoires of meaningful resistance in ongoing confrontations with power over many decades.

I hope that this book will help to remind people of these aspects of politics, and in doing so will help them to understand better the ways in which the forms of power are shadowed by the practices of resistance. None of these processes is by any means specific to the Middle East even if the forms they take and the repertoires on which they draw will be specific to the histories of its peoples. It is in this region that some of the most consistent and consistently varied manifestations of a politics of resistance can be seen. This should not be surprising, given the history and persistence of authoritarian, unequal and imposed systems of power across the region. As against this, a politics of resistance has drawn in millions. They have shown this in open demonstrations of defiance, violent and nonviolent. But the peoples of the Middle East have also, through collective organization, through art and through counter-narratives, developed alternative, sideways views of power in ways that suggest the basis for a resistance of the future.

As is common knowledge, 'Middle East' is itself a term originally devised by imperial powers with strategic not merely geographical concerns in mind. Notoriously, it then became a term for classifying the varied peoples and cultures of the region, marginalizing them by making them into a common object of knowledge, spuriously portrayed as fundamentally different to those who were busy subjecting them to new regimes of power. Ironically, and very much in keeping with some of the arguments in this book, whatever its origins, the term 'Middle East' has taken on a new lease of life, appropriated and transformed by those who find themselves so described. It has become a term to describe a field of empathy, resonance and action. This signifies both an internal variety, but also a space in which people's political aspirations, their experiences of power and resistance to power have been shown to share much in common with peoples across the globe. Like them, people in the Middle East have been engaged in struggles to free themselves from the systems that have denied them agency, autonomy and dignity. Many of these systems are indeed 'of' the region itself, but, like power everywhere, they make strenuous, sometimes ruthless efforts to maintain their distance from the people they rule. Military occupation has not simply been a recurrent feature of the region's history. It has been an apt metaphor for the kind of power that has dominated so many of its peoples.

It is therefore perhaps not so surprising that a book on the politics of resistance should still appear to map out the areas of study with this ambivalent term 'Middle East'. In doing so, I do not intend to suggest that all resistance movements in the Middle East are merely parts of some larger 'Middle Eastern' phenomenon, let alone that they differ in some essential way from resistance movements elsewhere. On the contrary, the three main arguments outlined above apply to political resistance as a generic or universal phenomenon. Power as a relation is marked by the particular characteristics of the parties to that relationship. This will vary with the place and the time in which it is exercised. The same applies to resistance. However, power itself as a distinct kind of relationship knows no homeland. Neither does resistance.

Precisely because there is such a wide variety and long history of resistance in the Middle East, matching the variety and depth of domination to which peoples in the region have been subjected, this will not be an encyclopedic account. On the contrary, I intend to examine different forms of resistance, of the spheres in which they take place and to see how that may have developed in various places at various times. Each of these spheres is connected to the other. If I were writing a book about the history and dynamics of political resistance in any particular country, there would be good reason to draw together these connecting threads. In such a case, it would be crucial to analyse the drivers of resistance, the imagination of its possibility, the mutually supportive or corrosive forms it may have taken and the spheres of social life it affected. Analytically, these could be examined separately, but contingently they would need to be looked at through their interactions.

Thus I will provide some cross-references in the book and shall try to show how, for instance, labour resistance in Egypt may have fed into the civil disorder and protest of 2011, or how Palestinian artists have contributed to the larger movement of Palestinian resistance. However, I shall be looking at these aspects for the forms taken by resistance, and thus at the spheres in which they have played themselves out, in part to suggest more generic themes. These themes will highlight the forms of power with which, as concept and political phenomenon, resistance is so intimately entwined. This may be within the fields of the imagination, of the economy, of the state and military occupation, or the social restrictions associated with gender differences. Systems of power provoke their own resistance, and this study will be devoted largely to examining the distinctive forms of resistance that can thereby be brought into being.

Freed from the obligation to reconstruct the path that resistance may have taken over the years in any particular country, I shall use themed chapters to take examples from across the region. The case studies have been chosen to illuminate particular forms of behaviour and the political processes of which they are a part. They are meant to throw light not only on registers of political resistance, but also on some of the unforeseen consequences that may have followed from the choices made by the actors involved. They attempt to bring to the fore distinctive features of a politics of resistance in specific places. But I also hope that they can enhance our understanding of the processes at work, not only in the Middle East, when resistance shadows power.

I

State Capture and Violent Resistance

WHY ARMED RESISTANCE?

A boot repeatedly treading on a face is one of the more disturbing images of the violence at the heart of political power. Used by George Orwell in his novel *1984* to sum up the brutality of a totalitarian regime, it was linked in the story to an equally disturbing image of the violence and moral dilemmas involved in resistance to oppression. When asked about the lengths to which he would go to resist, Winston, the protagonist, admits that he would be willing to throw acid in the face of a child if it would help to break the power of the ruling party. In both cases, the force of the image is in part due to the fact that the victim has a face, is a recognizable person like us, but the perpetrators remain faceless. These are the common currency of governments and of resistance organizations in their portrayals of each other, made all the more plausible by the ferocious violence of which both have been capable.

In the case of the state, the organization of violence has been associated with a physical presence, concentrated in a particular site, the administrative centre, the location of supreme authority and the source of command to the armed forces. It is this aspect of state power and the resistance it provokes that I shall be discussing in this chapter. In the Middle East, as in other parts of the world, these sites are recognizable as magnificent historical relics, such as the Cairo citadel looming over the old city, the all-seeing but unseen spaces of the Topkapi Palace with their views across and around Istanbul, or the towering citadel of Aleppo that dominates the landscape from the summit of its man-made hill at the city's centre.

But they are also present in the infrastructure of the modern state, in the ministries, military barracks, presidential and royal palaces, police headquarters and so forth. Sometimes they are cordoned off in discrete quarters, like the Green Zone in post-2003 Baghdad; sometimes they are on the outskirts, literally within striking distance should the need arise, such as the Bab al-Aziziyya barracks in Tripoli. In some cases, these buildings were inherited from the colonial era when provincial capitals were refashioned into the administrative centres of new territorial states. In others, they are themselves constructed by the highly centralized, authoritarian states that emerged in the Middle East in the latter half of the twentieth century. They provide the image, but also the focus of 'state capture', when one regime displaces another by force. In reality, state power may be highly diffuse – as I shall explore in later chapters – but this particular aspect of the state appeals both to those dedicated to a regime's violent consolidation and to those plotting its violent overthrow.

It is in this context that armed resistance to established power becomes so prominent. Violence may be the dimension of power that people first encounter, rudely awakened by an invading army, or by a newly successful military junta asserting its control. The presence of soldiers and security personnel on the streets, guarding the buildings that house them and the administration that organizes them, as well as the casual violence of countless personal encounters, make this the visible presence of the state. It tends to set limits to open, public space, but by the same token, these same features of the security state become the main targets of insurrectionary violence, at least in its early stages.

THE ROOTS OF RESISTANCE: COLONIAL AND ANTI-COLONIAL VIOLENCE

Across the Middle East, from the nineteenth century onwards, military campaigns have shaped the political order, carving out the modern states that make up the region. Sometimes this was geared explicitly to a European colonial project, as in France's campaigns in Algeria in the 1830s and 1840s, or, some eighty years later, those of Italy in Libya. At other times and places, the rationale had more to do with European imperial control and strategic advantage, as in the British suppression of the local 'piracy' it used as the pretext for establishing a powerful naval presence in the Persian Gulf, or the alleged threat to foreign nationals which Great Britain claimed justified its invasion and occupation of

Egypt in 1882. Most dramatically for the shape of the modern Middle East, the British military campaigns that conquered the remaining Arab provinces of the Ottoman Empire during the First World War were part of a war between rival imperial powers. The inhabitants of the region were largely spectators, although sometimes co-opted by both sides to help in the war effort, usually under false pretences.

Even in those countries that did not directly experience the firepower of European imperial armies, military campaigns were the main method of consolidating territorial control and of gaining international recognition for the newly defined states and their governments. Thus the Turkish republic emerged in 1923 out of a war of national liberation, consolidating the control of the new capital Ankara over the populations of Anatolia, Istanbul and Thrace. In Iran, the commander of the Cossack Brigade and minister of defence, Reza Khan, led his forces on a series of campaigns to reconquer the provinces of the decaying Qajar Empire, pausing only to displace the Qajar dynasty itself and to proclaim himself the first Pahlavi Shah of Iran. In the Arabian peninsula, during the same period, the Najdi Amir, Abd al-Aziz ibn Saud, used the fighting force of the *Ikhwan* to bring as much of the peninsula under his control as he could manage, laying the foundation for the international recognition of the Kingdom of Saudi Arabia in 1932.

In all of these cases, there was no mistaking the brutal force of state making. It allowed invading powers and regional leaders like Ataturk and Ibn Saud to stake out their exclusive control of territory. They went on to found states that demanded submission to new principles of government – republican and nationalist in the case of Turkey, dynastic with Islamic overtones in the case of Saudi Arabia. But violence was intimately bound up with the character of the political order that was being brought so roughly into being. It helped to shape the power that would intimately affect the lives of all those who found themselves within its jurisdiction. For that very reason, it was both exemplary and sometimes demonstratively cruel – and helped to mould the very imagination of what that power could do to those who opposed it.

The Long Algerian War of Independence, 1830–1962

Violent acts provoked a range of violent responses. Those who found themselves in the path of these juggernauts either reacted immediately and ferociously or developed networks and strategies that would lay the groundwork for later resistance. In many respects, this is the story of colonial and imperial rule in the Middle East. The gradual French military occupation of Algeria in the nineteenth century is a good example. As the French forces encroached upon the lands and peoples of an ever-expanding area of North Africa, they met armed resistance. Sometimes this was co-ordinated, but more often it was fragmented, centred on places where there was the greatest potential for organizing against French firepower, or where the threat of colonial rule to property and independence was at its sharpest.

With each armed uprising in areas that the French believed their own use of force had settled, their reprisals became ever more severe. For instance, at Zaatcha in 1849, the French army demolished the oasis town, cut down its palm gardens and killed many of its inhabitants. Gruesomely underlining the message, the French commander, General Herbillon, ordered the decapitation of the rebel leader, Bou Ziyan, and of his teenage son, impaling their heads on posts at the centre of this scene of devastation.[1] In 1871, following the collapse of the last major rebellion of the nineteenth century, that of Muhammad al-Hajj al-Muqrani, the ferocity of the French reprisals cost tens of thousands of Algerian lives. But the French response went beyond this obvious cruelty and led to a fundamental reshaping of Algeria. European settlement was actively encouraged, deepening the colonial enterprise and dispossessing the Algerians of their lands whether or not they had supported the armed uprising. As the French governor of the time stated, echoing the sentiments of the French colonists, his intention was 'not to perpetuate the national identity of the natives ... but to break down the resistance of Arab society'.[2]

Despite the thoroughness and duration of the occupation, this proved to be a doomed endeavour. The occupation only served to reinforce the idea of difference on which resistance is based, suggesting through the open and latent violence of the colonial state the means by which it could be effectively resisted. The savagery of the reprisals by French security forces and by colonial vigilantes that left thousands of Algerians dead after the so-called Sétif revolt of 1945 would eventually produce the FLN (Front de Libération Nationale) and its armed wing, the ALN (Armée de Libération Nationale), in the mid-1950s. As Jean-Paul Sartre observed, 'the son of the colonialist and the son of the Muslim are both the children of the objective violence that defines the system itself'.[3] Thus the very system of colonialism, with its settler privileges and subjection of the native population, was rooted in the initial and sustained violence of French military occupation. Eruptions like the riots and reprisals of 1945 showed the underlying character of the system when opposition dared to show itself.

For Frantz Fanon, it was only when Algerians recognized this and took up arms against the colonizer and the occupier that they would reinscribe themselves as agents into their own history. It was a way of developing the self-recognition that would in turn gain them recognition by the colonizers and others. Armed resistance was thus for Fanon both the outcome of a historical situation grounded in violence and a liberating mechanism. Although he was horrified by it and wary of its long-term effects on those who used it even in a project of self-liberation, Fanon nevertheless saw violence as an inescapable aspect of the situation that colonialism had created in Algeria. It was a step that was necessary but not in the end sufficient for national liberation.[4]

This was indeed the course followed by the FLN as an armed resistance movement. Initially, it targeted the personnel of the security forces and Algerian collaborators, the Algerian holders of public office in the French colonial system. Using spectacular violence to show the chasm that now set nationalist Algerians apart from those who still helped to sustain French rule, the FLN tried to drive home to those Algerians who did not join their ranks the price they would have to pay. The arrests, collective punishments and repression that followed reinforced the opinion of those within the FLN, such as Zirout Yousef, who argued for a widening of the scope of the insurrection to encompass not simply the French security forces and Algerian collaborators, but also the European settler population as a whole. The rationale was that the settlers were the main reason for France's continued occupation of Algeria and were thus instrumental in keeping the colonial system in place. Furthermore, this approach resonated with Fanon's view that while the settlers might dream of the disappearance of the colonized, it was they who were in fact much more strongly positioned to oust the settler minority.[5]

This new direction found its most notorious expression in the Philippeville massacre of August 1955, where nearly 100 French men, women and children were killed in the small mining settlement of El-Halia on a day of widespread attacks on isolated colonial settlements across Algeria. This death toll paled into insignificance compared to the hundreds of Algerians killed in mass reprisals by settler vigilante squads, as well as by the French security forces in the weeks that followed. As Ferhat Abbas said, 'These peasants will kill. But they will also be killed'.[6] This was indeed the logic of mobilization. As the two populations became polarized, the battle lines were drawn up and armed resistance was transformed into a war of national liberation, involving tens of thousands, carrying the fight into the cities and across the frontiers into neighbouring Tunisia.

Despite military setbacks, such as the ruthlessly waged Battle of Algiers of 1956–7, and the decimation of its leadership, the FLN pursued the armed struggle, watchful of the effect as much on international opinion and on the French electorate as on the settler population. The settlers, for all their defiance and bravado, gradually began to realize that they could not rely on the French government to support them unquestioningly. General de Gaulle's famously ambivalent 1958 declaration to the Algerian settlers – 'Je vous ai compris' [I have understood you] – did not necessarily mean that he liked what he now understood. It was this that led, in turn, to the emergence of a settler resistance movement, Organisation de l'Armée Secrète [Organization of the Secret Army] (OAS) responsible for spectacular acts of violence against French officials and the Algerian population in the last years of French rule. This was the last gasp of colonial power. The escalation of the violence and the changing attitude of the French electorate paved the way for the Evian Accords in 1962, establishing the sovereign Algerian Republic and causing the mass exodus of a million or so settlers. Only a few years before, it had seemed that they could dictate policy both to Paris and to the Algerians, but they were now acting out the choice made brutally clear to them by the slogan of the Algerian resistance: 'La valise ou le cercueil' [the suitcase or the coffin].

The FLN had been established some 120 years after the initial French occupation of Algeria and was a product of its time. This was the era of decolonization, when it became feasible to challenge European military might throughout Asia and Africa, as the Vietnamese had shown at Dien Bien Phu in March–May 1954. But one can also link the forms of resistance in the 1950s to a longer history of Algerian resistance to colonial violence. It was not simply that the FLN conjured up the spirit of Abd al-Qadir, the leader of an initially successful guerrilla campaign against the French in the 1830s and 1840s, and transformed him into a national hero. Equally important was the link between the continuing experiences by Algerians of the expropriation, discrimination and violence that lay at the heart of the colonial regime. These had provoked the many outbreaks of armed resistance prior to the repression of the 1870s, and they had smouldered on in the resentments of a people dispossessed, looking to new champions to protect them from the colonial state. Because of the violence of colonialism, armed resistance was a thread woven into the very fabric of the colonial situation itself.

Palestine: Resisting Foreign Occupation, 1920–1948

The same could be said of the resistance encountered by the British army that occupied Palestine during the First World War, laying the basis for the mandate administration and enabling Zionist settlement. General Allenby's proclamation of martial law upon the capture of Jerusalem made it clear that the enemy was identified as the Turks, rather than the Palestinians themselves – 'lest any of you be alarmed by reason of your experience at the hands of the enemy who has retired, I hereby inform you that it is my desire that every person pursue his lawful business without fear of interruption'.[7] This was not exactly a ringing declaration of liberation. It was more a demand that all should accept without protest the new order being imposed upon Palestine.

However, Palestinians already knew of the Balfour Declaration, published one month before, in which the British government had pledged itself to support 'the establishment in Palestine of a national home for the Jewish people'.[8] This had displeased some, like Lord Rothschild, who had wanted a more forceful statement 'that Palestine should be reconstituted as the National Home of the Jewish people'.[9] Nevertheless, for many, it indicated that the British government was about to embark on a project of social engineering that would open up Palestine to Jewish – in the context of the time, that meant European – settlement, threatening radically to transform Palestinian society. Thus, despite Allenby's words, the force of British arms ensured a major 'interruption' in the lives of the Palestinians, promising a future for Palestine that could only be looked upon with fear and apprehension by most of its inhabitants.

It was not long before these fears were translated into violent resistance, initially in the shape of communal riots, targeting both Zionists and Jewish Palestinians. The so-called Wailing Wall riots of 1929 cost the lives of 133 Jews and 116 Arabs in communal violence across the country. They were early signs of Palestinians' fears for their country under British occupation.[10] British reactions to the rising level of communal tension and the occasional outbursts of violence neither allayed these fears nor prevented the deepening of Zionist settlement in Palestine. The riots had not deterred Jews from immigrating, given the growing menace of anti-Semitism in central Europe. If anything, the period saw a strengthening of Zionist settlement, the development of self-governing institutions in the Yishuv and the emergence of the 'divided economy' of Palestine.[11]

It was not surprising, therefore, that Palestinians should have organized armed resistance, both against the British occupiers and against the Jewish settlements built under their protection. Shaikh Izz al-Din al-Qassam's organization – the Black Hand – was set up in 1930 to carry out armed attacks on Jewish settlements and on state infrastructure, such as the railways. Inevitably, this led to clashes with the British security forces and it was in just such a clash that al-Qassam was killed near Jenin in 1935. However, in the years that followed, especially in the aftermath of the Palestinian General Strike of 1936, armed resistance became more organized, joining together small groups throughout the countryside and benefiting from the recruitment of thousands in the polarizing situation of mandatory Palestine. The Peel Commission's recommendation that the country be partitioned as a way out of the impasse only served to increase the violence, graphically illustrating the Palestinians' rejection of the plan.

The armed resistance was strategic in the sense that its organizers were trying to convince the British to abandon the idea of dividing Palestine. But it also came from the growing violence of the situation in which the Palestinians found themselves. Testimonies of villagers who took part in the revolt as teenagers show how combustible was the mixture when family and village bonds of loyalty met coercion and humiliation at the hands of the British security forces. As many of them state, their feelings of outrage and revenge found a ready outlet in armed resistance. This was not necessarily grounded in any larger view of the politics of the situation. Rather, it emerged from the intimacy of the violence they experienced as the repression of 1937–8 affected increasing numbers of Palestinians. Public floggings, house demolitions and collective punishments brought the reality of colonial occupation into the heart of countless remote villages.[12]

In response to the insurgency, the British government had massively reinforced its military presence in the country, deploying it to impress upon the Palestinians the futility of taking up arms against the occupying power. Mass detentions, widespread house demolitions, collective punishments, as well as executions, judicial and non-judicial, and the widespread use of torture, were aimed at countering the insurgency. They were also intended to drive home to the Palestinian population the cost of supporting armed resistance. The effect on many was to provoke them further, but cumulatively the scale of the British military response overwhelmed the resources of the Palestinians and, apart from a few incidents, armed resistance in Palestine was more or less over by the end of 1938.[13]

At the same time, the British authorities had gone even further than before in tolerating the Zionists' development of paramilitary organizations. When the British authorities formed the Jewish Settlement Police, the Jewish Auxiliary Corps and the counter-insurgency Night Squads, they provided training in action for the *Haganah* (the Zionist paramilitary organization, developed initially to protect Jewish settlements), despite its lack of British official recognition. Ironically, together with some of its more radical offshoots, such as *Etzel*, it was to become the core of Zionist armed resistance to British rule in Palestine a few years later when British policy swung once more towards the idea of a unified Palestine with an Arab majority.

In this respect, despite its effective suppression by 1939, the Palestinian resistance had had a profound effect on the British government. It had cost the lives of thousands of Palestinians, as well as of hundreds of Jews and roughly 200 British officials and security forces.[14] However, it did lead the British government to issue the Palestine White Paper of 1939, committing Great Britain to the curtailment of Jewish immigration and to the eventual grant of independence to a unitary Palestinian state with an Arab majority. Nevertheless, as Palestine's post-war history demonstrated, the military and political damage the revolt inflicted on Palestinian society, economy and political leadership had effectively crippled the capacities of Palestinian resistance at a time when the struggle for the country intensified.

In the aftermath of the Holocaust and the Second World War, it was the Jewish community that took up arms against the British. Determined that unlimited Jewish immigration should continue, and that a Jewish state should be established, the paramilitary organizations of the Zionist movement – *Palmach*, *Etzel/Irgun* and *Lehi*/the Stern Gang – tried to hasten British departure from Palestine and to prevent the implementation of the 1939 White Paper. The *Irgun*, in particular, led by Menachem Begin, staged a series of attacks against land registry and tax offices as well as British security forces. Fewer than 200 British forces were killed in the three-year campaign, but it had an effect similar to that of the Arab revolt in Palestine a decade earlier. In trying to suppress the insurgency, the British intensified the repression of the Jewish community, reinforcing Jewish support for even the most extreme resistance organizations. The psychological impact of the relentless campaign of

bombings and assassinations also had an impact on British official thinking and on a British public weary of war. It seemed to underline the
futility of trying to hold Palestine by force, leading Great Britain to
relinquish its mandate to the United Nations, which voted in 1947 to
divide Palestine between an Arab and a Jewish state.[15]

The war that followed in 1948 established the state of Israel on most of
the territory of Palestine. This was accompanied by the dispossession of
some 725,000 Palestinian Arabs who were driven out by Israeli forces or
who fled the fighting in those areas taken by the Israelis. Meanwhile, the
neighbouring Arab states of Egypt and Jordan occupied the remaining
lands of historical Palestine. Faced by the shattering of Palestinian society,
the carving up of Palestinian territory by foreign armies of occupation and
the creation of a large, vulnerable and wholly dependent refugee population, there was little scope for political organization, let alone resistance
by the Palestinians themselves. Individual acts of defiance did take place,
whether surreptitiously, in the attempts by villagers to return to their
homes, or, more spectacularly, in the assassination of King Abdullah of
Jordan in the Haram al-Sharif in Jerusalem in 1951. But systematic armed
resistance only developed later and emerged in the 1960s.

OCCUPYING POWERS: WAR, SETTLEMENT, RESISTANCE AND IDENTITY

The violence of the colonial legacy has continued to shape both the
organization and the imagination of power and resistance in the Middle
East. It laid the groundwork for the despotic and often divided states that
have been so much a part of the region's landscape. It also helped to sow
the seeds of war, most obviously in the case of Israel and Palestine, more
obliquely in the case of Iraq and its turbulent relations with its neighbours.
At the same time, it provided a powerful framework for imagining power,
both among those trying to impose their will on a subject population and
for those trying to resist this very same subjugation. Heroic memories of
battles past, as well as the political provocations and opportunities of the
present, have provided the pretext, the sanction and the sites for the use of
force and its armed resistance well into the twenty-first century.

Palestine: The Emergence and the Purposes of Armed Resistance

The 1967 June war saw Israel occupy all of the territory of mandatory
Palestine, in addition to the Sinai Peninsula and the Golan Heights.

The shock of this event galvanized and transformed Palestinian resistance in the decade that followed. Led by the PLO and its affiliated organizations, armed resistance first took the form of isolated but unnerving acts of violence mainly by *Fatah* against civilian and military Israeli targets. This led to Israeli reprisals, such as the military operation against PLO guerrilla forces in the Jordan valley at Karameh in March 1968. The battle, in which the conventional armed forces of Jordan came to the assistance of the PLO, causing significant Israeli losses, was held up as a triumph for the united Arab forces, leading King Hussein of Jordan to state that 'We may reach the stage where we shall all become fedayeen'.[16]

Despite its morale-boosting effects, the scale of Palestinian and Jordanian losses in the battle showed that any such conventional confrontation would inevitably favour Israel. As for a protracted guerrilla war, Abu Iyad, one of the leaders of the PLO, could still be optimistic in 1969 when he stated that armed force would be used to reach a position where the PLO could move its 'bases into the occupied territories, when the act of organic linkage becomes total, deep and moves effectively among all the posts in the occupied territories'.[17] However, given the demographic and geographical imbalance between the resources at the disposal of the Palestinians and the Israelis in the occupied territories, it was soon apparent that this was not a realistic strategy for armed resistance.

Instead, a different approach developed and became the mark of Palestinian resistance for some decades to come. Echoing Fanon's perspective on Algeria, violence was seen as a way of writing the Palestinians as a nation back into world history. It was a powerful means of gaining recognition, from its targets, from the region, from the international community and from the dispersed and demoralized Palestinians themselves.[18] As countless tracts, films and interviews made clear at the time, to pick up arms as a Palestinian was an act of resistance, not simply in the mechanical sense of resisting the occupying Israeli forces, but also in defiance of the dominant view that denied them the right to any form of collective representation. This view was expressed most succinctly by the Israeli politician Golda Meir who notoriously stated in 1969 that 'there were no such thing as Palestinians ... they did not exist',[19] but it was shared by many others. The emergence of the Palestinian armed resistance was intended to prove them wrong.

Armed resistance was thus one part of a larger revolutionary project outlined at the time by George Habash, leader of the Popular Front for the Liberation of Palestine (PFLP): 'what is missing and this we must at all costs remedy, is revolutionary awareness... We have to train a totally new kind of militant'.[20] For *Fatah*, it was still possible to imagine 'waging a popular war of liberation in which people will participate on a large scale ... the political struggle without the armed struggle cannot achieve the aims of the revolution'.[21] This found expression in the common platform at the meeting of the 7th Palestinian National Council, entitled 'Revolutionary People's war is the fundamental way to liberate Palestine', in which all factions agreed to create a unified military committee 'to further the armed struggle and to go to a new state in the *fidayin* action and in the people's war of liberation' through the arming of the 'Arab masses'.[22]

However, there was still the question of where such resistance could take place. The occupied territories, although idealized as the site for resistance and for mobilization of the Palestinian people, could not offer the terrain or resources necessary for a sustained guerrilla war. For their part, the Jordanian authorities showed in 'Black September' 1970 that they would fight the PLO rather than let Jordan be used as a base for armed resistance to Israel, fearing that the prime target for such activity would be the government of Jordan itself. This led the PLO to establish a base for its forces in the much more porous territories of southern Lebanon, facing Israel, but, crucially, within a state that was powerless to exclude them. Indeed, as one of the founders of the PLO, Shafiq al-Hout, frankly explained, 'The revolution landed in Lebanon because it was a garden without a fence'.[23]

It was from here that Palestinian organizations launched a series of armed attacks, sometimes within Israel, but often beyond, aimed at targets symbolically associated with Israel. Additionally, the spate of hijackings of international aircraft brought world media coverage of their cause. George Habash was clear about their purpose: 'When we hijack a plane it has more effect than if we killed a hundred Israelis in battle ... For decades world opinion ... simply ignored us. At least the world is talking about us now'.[24] As with the FLN in Algeria, the Palestinian resistance organizations had to make a calculation about the identity of their targets and the political effects of violence that could result in the deaths of non-combatants, both Israeli and non-Israeli. Events like the attack on a school bus in Israel in 1970, or the Munich Olympics of 1972 where eleven members of the Israeli team died in a hostage-taking attempt by the Palestinian Group 'Black September', or the attacks on Qiryat Shmona and Ma`alot in 1974 where some forty-five Israelis died provoked international condemnation and brought about Israeli reprisals. However, they and the other incidents at this time also placed the Palestinian cause itself firmly on the international agenda. In doing so, they paved the way for international recognition. Indeed, only eighteen months after the Munich deaths, Yassir Arafat was invited to address the General Assembly of the UN, soon followed by the granting of UN observer status to the PLO.

The cumulative effect on successive Israeli governments was also clear. The largest Israeli military operations against the PLO – Operation Litani in southern Lebanon in 1978 and the Israeli invasion of Lebanon in 1982 – were only in part designed to counter the sporadic, small-scale armed operations across Israel's northern border. They were aimed principally at ending Palestinian resistance in any form, thereby, the Israeli government hoped, ending Palestinian aspirations to independence, paving the way for a redrawing of the map in the Levant. In this sense, the Palestinians had established themselves through armed resistance, however gruesome some of its methods, and however many Palestinians died in the Israeli reprisals. They were now a political problem that could not simply be wished away. Ironically, therefore, although the Lebanon war brought about the expulsion of the PLO from Lebanon and its dispersal around different Arab states, it paved the way for the opening of direct negotiations between the PLO and Israel in the 1990s.

This was not to happen until after the first *intifada*, the Palestinian uprising in the occupied territories (see Chapter 2) that erupted in 1987. Coming out of local frustrations, humiliations and resentments, it demanded a different kind of recognition: that Palestinians living under military occupation should be heard not only by the Israeli authorities but by the increasingly remote PLO leadership. The latter had used the strategy of armed resistance to gain international recognition and a grudging acknowledgement from Israel. For their part, the leadership of the *intifada* deliberately inverted the picture and used unarmed, stone-throwing protestors to face up to the overwhelming armed force of the Israel.

Through the persistence and the courage of the demonstrators, the Israeli authorities were forced to recognize that there was a problem that needed to be addressed in the occupied territories. The security problem was different to that posed by armed resistance. What made it more problematic from the Israeli perspective was the widespread support and solidarity shown for the *intifada* across all sections of Palestinian society, with boycotts, strikes and disruption supplementing the stone throwing and demonstrations in the streets. In addition, the vivid depiction by the international media of unarmed children and youths confronting and often suffering and dying at the hands of heavily armed Israeli soldiers reversed the image that Israel had always tried to project of itself, damaging that image irreparably, especially after the brutalities of the Lebanese war.

In this sense, unarmed resistance had an impact as great as and, in this context, more effective than the armed resistance of previous decades. However, the *intifada* was not wholly without fatal violence on the part of the Palestinians. The killing of informants and collaborators, as in Algeria thirty years before, was part of a recognizable thread within the uprising. Equally, there were fatal attacks on individual Israelis, both civilian and military. Nevertheless, the realization that twenty years of military occupation had neither made Palestinians more accepting of their situation nor Israelis more secure led eventually to direct negotiations between Israel and the PLO and to the signing of the Oslo Accords in 1993.

Despite the optimism, even euphoria that followed the signing of the accords, the return of Arafat and the PLO leadership to Palestine, and the establishment of the Palestine National Authority (PA) in 1994, the reality was that Israel remained overwhelmingly powerful and present, in military control of all Palestinian territory. Only in some of the urban centres was the PA nominally in charge of both civil and security matters. Otherwise, the Israeli military authorities retained control of the occupied territories of the West Bank and the Gaza Strip, managing all roads through an elaborate system of checkpoints, controlling the water supplies and overseeing the inexorable expansion of Israeli settlements and the expropriation of Palestinian land. The lack of progress in negotiations between Israel and the PA thwarted efforts to achieve any resolution of the key issues that mattered so much to the Palestinians generally – such as the final status of Jerusalem, the resolution of the question of the refugees of 1948 and their descendants, the ending of Israeli settlement building and the opening of borders that would be wholly under control of the PA. This gradually undermined the authority of Arafat and the PLO.

Their authority was already being questioned by those Palestinian organizations that regarded the 1993 Oslo Accords as an unwarranted Palestinian capitulation. In particular, the main Islamist political organization active in the occupied territories, *Hamas*, had emerged as a prominent player in Palestinian politics during the *intifada* of the

1980s. It had developed from its grassroots bases, especially in the Gaza Strip, as an uncompromising critic of the PLO and of the Israeli occupying forces. For *Hamas* at this stage, armed struggle for the liberation of all of historical Palestine was still a defining objective, even if it seemed scarcely realistic to many. Its armed wing, the Izz al-Din al-Qassam Brigades, keeping alive the memory of one of the early organizers of Palestinian resistance, was founded towards the end of the *intifada* and led off with attacks on Israeli military targets.

Like the PLO in its initial organization of armed resistance, *Hamas* seemed to be using armed struggle to draw attention to the existence of a substantial section of the Palestinian community that refused to compromise. They were signalling their rejection of the post-Oslo order. As the first *Hamas* communiqué in December 1987 stated: 'Let the reckless settlers beware. Our people know the way of sacrifice and martyrdom and are generous in this regard ... Let them understand that violence breeds nothing but violence and death bestows but death'.[25] This echoed the FLN campaign in the 1950s and 1960s against settlers, and was reinforced by the warning of *Hamas* leader Ahmed Bakr: 'Israel can beat all the Arab armies. However, it can do nothing against a youth with a knife or an explosive charge on his body ... if the Israelis want security, they will have to abandon their settlements'.[26] Although the direct military effect of this campaign on the Israeli military establishment was minimal, the violence did influence the political calculations of the Israeli government under Ariel Sharon. In 2005, he ordered the evacuation of all Israeli forces and the dismantling of all Israeli settlements in the Gaza Strip. In many respects, this decision echoed that taken five years earlier by the government of Ehud Barak to evacuate all Israeli forces from southern Lebanon under the relentless pressure of Hizbullah's guerrilla war of attrition.

Armed resistance was thus clearly a way of communicating with the dominant power. In this context, the use of suicide bombing became a powerful *Hamas* tactic, particularly in the wake of the notorious killing of twenty-nine Palestinians in the mosque of Hebron by an Israeli settler in 1994. Thereafter, the Israeli public in general, not merely its security forces or state infrastructure, became targets of a sustained campaign of violence.[27] In this campaign, the suicide bomb proved to be particularly unnerving, especially with the dramatic increase in the frequency and devastating effects of these bombings after 2000. Some saw this as a way of redressing the imbalance of power. For instance, Fathi al-Shiqaqi of Islamic Jihad claimed that 'martyrdom operations ... are a realistic option in confronting the unequal balance of power. If we are unable to effect a balance of power now, we can achieve a balance of horror'.[28] Equally, Abd al-Karim of the *Fatah*-affiliated Al-Aqsa Martyrs' Brigades saw this tactic as a way of increasing 'losses to Israel to a point at which the Israeli public would demand a withdrawal from the West Bank and the Gaza Strip'.[29]

The suicide-bombing campaign was extraordinarily powerful as a signal of determination, of self-sacrifice, of a war no longer confined to limited engagements between the security forces and the insurgents on terms set by the former. As a member of the Qassam brigades stated in 2001: 'We do not have tanks or rockets, but we have something superior – our exploding Islamic human bombs. In place of a nuclear arsenal, we are proud of our arsenal of believers'.[30] The battle was now carried into the very heart of the Israeli civilian population. They had believed that the overwhelming disparity between their own forces and those of the resistance gave them the reassurance of security. However, the ability of the suicide bomber to get through even the most secure cordon, devastating and disrupting the tranquil surface of everyday life, redoubled the sense of insecurity, placing huge political pressure on Israel's political leadership.

This was dramatically in evidence in 2001–2 when Israeli assassinations of resistance leaders or military strikes against sites of Palestinian resistance were followed almost immediately by retaliatory bombings within Israel itself. For instance, the Israeli assassination of a senior *Hamas* commander, Mahmud Abu Hanud, in November 2001 was followed by a series of *Hamas* bombings, gun attacks and suicide bombs in Haifa, Jerusalem and at the settlement of Immanuel that left nearly forty Israelis dead. Equally, following the March 2002 Israeli air and tank attacks on Gaza, *Hamas* suicide bombers in Jerusalem, Netanya and Haifa claimed nearly sixty lives. The intent was clear from the words of one of the Qassam brigade fighters: 'We are just sending a message [to Israel] to tell them: we can act against you. We can harm your children as you are doing to ours'.[31]

In order to encourage the sense of insecurity, *Hamas* made it harder for the Israeli authorities to profile the suicide bombers. They were recruited from a variety of backgrounds, ages and, after 2002, from women as well as men. In fact, other organizations, such as the Al-Aqsa Martyrs' Brigade had already been recruiting and training women as suicide bombers, both because women were not seen then as a threat by the Israeli security forces and because of the powerful messages which the women themselves and their sponsoring organizations wanted to convey. As one of their number, Andaleeb Takatkeh, stated in her final message: 'I've chosen to say with my body what Arab leaders have failed to say ... My body is a barrel of gunpowder that burns the enemy'.[32] One of the trainers of suicide bombers, Munir al-Makdah, asserted that this form of armed resistance was simply part of the logical progression of resistance itself: '*Jihad* and the resistance begin with the word, then with the sword, then with the stone, then with the gun, then with planting bombs and then transforming bodies into human bombs'.[33]

Hamas and the Palestinians more generally paid a high price for this activity, as Israeli retribution took its toll in human lives. However, the very fact that the suicide bombings continued in the face of this made the message all the more powerful. In fact, by 2000, the logic of this inherently violent situation could be seen in the outbreak of the second – 'Al-Aqsa' – *intifada*. This began with the riots protesting Ariel Sharon's electioneering visit to the Haram al-Sharif in Jerusalem and the Israeli security forces' response that left nearly fifty Palestinians dead and nearly 2,000 injured. The violence and the deaths ensured that this would be a very different kind of uprising to the *intifada* of the 1980s.[34]

Violence escalated on both sides, with a marked imbalance of casualties caused by the overwhelming firepower of the Israeli armed forces compared to that of the Palestinian resistance organizations. As the fighting intensified in the years that followed, the Oslo process disintegrated. Not only *Hamas*, but also the Al-Aqsa Martyrs Brigade of Arafat's *Fatah* organization, as well as the PFLP, the Popular Resistance Committees and Islamic Jihad took up arms again in an unequal struggle with the Israeli security forces. In 2002, Israeli forces reoccupied those areas of the Palestinian territories which they had left in the 1990s. They laid siege to Jenin and bombarded the headquarters of Arafat in Ramallah, al-Muqata`a. Trapped by the Israeli blockade, he remained there until he was evacuated in 2004 for hospital treatment in Paris where he died shortly after his arrival.

For the Palestinians, armed resistance was now driven by a number of motives. Some of these were contradictory and others unrealizable, given the forces at their disposal. *Hamas* and Islamic Jihad, as well as the Popular Resistance Committees, continued to make their mark through attacks on Israeli targets, both military and civilian. As far as the latter were concerned, they appeared to fall into two categories. The first were the civilians connected to the settlements in the occupied territories who, like the settlers in Algeria, enjoyed a privileged existence in terms of resources and protection. They represented the two facets of Israeli settler society: extreme forms of Zionism, whether religious or secular, on the one hand, and economic opportunism provided by subsidized housing on the other. They were seen consequently either as symbolic targets or as people who could be driven out if the deteriorating security situation made it too dangerous to live in the occupied territories. These considerations led to attacks on settlers, particularly on the roads that criss-crossed the occupied territories and to which the settlers had privileged access. In 2000, this resulted in approximately seventeen deaths. It also made Jerusalem a particular site of bombs and attacks. The city, having been annexed by Israel in 1967 and formally designated in the Basic Law of August 1980 'the complete and united . . . capital of Israel', had great symbolic importance but was also a place where Palestinians could operate with relative ease.

The resistance organizations continued their campaign of suicide bombs, car bombs and rockets against civilians inside Israel itself. Given the imbalance in firepower, the Palestinian resistance organizations stood little chance of effectively defending their own populations against Israeli military action. At the same time, Palestinian civilian casualties mounted, since, by their nature, the resistance organizations had to operate within Palestinian towns and villages. Consequently, Israel's strategy of retaliation and targeted assassination caused widespread civilian deaths.[35] Attacks on Israeli civilians were intended to show the Israeli public the price they would pay for the tactics of their armed forces. But for some of the Palestinian organizations, particularly the Islamists, there was also a symbolic dimension. Unlike the PLO, they did not recognize Israel as legitimately occupying the Palestinian territories conquered in 1948. The campaign inside Israel symbolized this rejection and asserted their belief that all of Israel, and its population, were the illegal and unwanted occupiers of Palestinian land.

The effects of this sequence of violent events were felt in 2004–5 when the Al-Aqsa *intifada* more or less came to an end. The change of leadership in the PA with the death of Arafat, and in *Hamas*, with Israel's killing in quick succession in March and April 2004 of Shaikh Ahmad Yassin and of Abd al-Aziz al-Rantissi, did not end the violence. However, the deaths coincided with the initiative of the Israeli prime minister, Ariel Sharon, to withdraw from the Gaza Strip. Implicitly acknowledging the intransigence of the resistance and the failure of Israel's tactics to bring it to an end, he declared in 2004 that Israel would dismantle all settlements in the Gaza Strip, an operation completed by the middle of 2005. Israeli settlers and military forces were withdrawn, but Israel was left in control of the borders, the crossings abutting its own territory, as well as all sea and air access. The move did not therefore signify the end of Israel's control of the Gaza Strip. Nor did it prevent repeated Israeli bombardments of and armed incursions into the area in the years that followed. However, it did encourage the belief, similar to that in Algeria of the 1950s, that foreign settlers would be removed when the home government no longer saw any advantage in protecting them – a calculation made possible by the willingness of the resistance to use armed force.

An earlier acknowledgement of the power of violent resistance had begun in 2002 but gained momentum during these years. This was the construction of a barrier – in some places a concrete wall, in others a system of fences – which was meant to provide a physical means of separating the occupied West Bank from Israel. The inclusion within the barrier of a number of settlements established by Israel on occupied territory seemed to many to suggest that it was as much a means of redrawing the map and of making the future of certain Israeli settlements non-negotiable. Thus the tortuous line of the barrier is 760 km long – roughly twice the length of the 1967 border with the West Bank – and it appropriates more than eight per cent of West Bank territory. Israel had already constructed such a barrier around Gaza to prevent infiltration into Israel by people determined to carry out suicide bombings or other acts of violence.

This had led *Hamas*, Islamic Jihad and others in Gaza to develop rockets which they fired into Israel, causing nearly thirty civilian casualties between 2001 and 2009, as well as some structural damage. Above all, the regular launching of rockets introduced an element of disruption and insecurity in those Israeli towns that were within range – a range that was increased over those years from about 10 km to 40 km, enabling the rockets to fall on towns like Beersheba, Ashdod and Ashkelon. Militarily negligible, the rockets were, however, communicating the very fact of resistance itself. Khaled Mishaal of *Hamas* characterized them in 2009 as 'our cry of protest to the world. Israel and its American and European sponsors want us to be killed in silence. But die in silence we will not'.[36] At the same time, a spokesperson of the PFLP claimed the rockets were 'both a practical and a symbolic representation of our resistance to the occupier', demonstrating that 'so long as one rocket is launched at the occupier, our people, our resistance and our cause is alive'.[37] As with other phases of the campaign of armed resistance, the rockets launched into Israel from Gaza provoked repeated Israeli military incursions into the Gaza Strip, beginning with Operation Summer Rains, not long after the Israeli withdrawal, and leading up to the notorious Operation Cast Lead in the winter of 2008–9. In this campaign, nearly 1,500 Palestinians were killed, hundreds of buildings destroyed and much of the infrastructure crippled.[38]

Prolonged military occupation has produced many forms of resistance. It has been generated by the predicament, but also by the historical memory of the occupied population. In the case of armed resistance, as the Palestinian example shows, the motives have been various – some have been generated by very particular humiliations and brutalities, channelled by organizations with a more strategic view of the leverage that violence can provide and the messages it can communicate. In Palestine, because of the span of time involved, the impression of permanent occupation and the lack of any external restraint on Israel, there has also been a powerful incentive to use violence. It is intended to disrupt, disconcert and so to contest the status quo. But it also comes out of the violence that underpins the occupation itself, exemplified in continuing dispossession, land appropriation, building demolitions and restrictions that favour the occupying power.

Iraq: Resistance to Foreign Occupation After 2003

Armed resistance in Algeria and Palestine had their roots in a long experience of colonial violence and occupation. Iraq had also had its share of colonial conquest and armed insurrections in the twentieth century. Most memorably, the British conquest of Mesopotamia during the First World War and the founding of the Iraqi state had been carried out by British force of arms. It had also provided the arena and the targets for the Iraqi Revolt of 1920, as much a founding memory of the emerging state as the subsequent formation of the Iraqi armed forces and state institutions.

However, it was not until after the U.S.-led invasion and occupation of the country in 2003 that Iraq became the site of a full-scale armed resistance movement covering large tracts of the country. There were in fact several movements, some bitterly opposed to each other, but all determined to resist and to disrupt the U.S.-led occupation of the country and the political order that the United States and its allies were trying to bring into being. As in the case of other resistance movements, the decision to take up arms was shaped by the violence of invasion itself, by the opportunities it created, as well as by collective memories of earlier insurgencies against colonial rule. The behaviour of the United States and its allies and the prejudices they brought to the task of occupation tended to confirm the worst fears of many Iraqis about the true nature of the occupation. This laid the groundwork for resistance. Once initiated, the familiar cycle of reprisal and retaliation began to entrench itself, as shown by the U.S. assaults on the town of Falluja in Anbar province in the late autumn of 2004. These events fed the insurgency by convincing many in Iraq that the United States was determined to inflict collective punishment on the Sunni Arabs because of the role that they were imagined to have played collectively under the Ba'thist regime.[39]

In the summer and autumn of 2009, a series of massive suicide bombs were detonated in Baghdad, destroying the ministries of finance, of foreign affairs and of justice, killing nearly 200 people and injuring about 1,200. A statement posted on a website in October 2009 praised 'the martyrs [who] targeted the dens of infidelity' and claimed that the intention had been 'to punish the pillars of the Safawi and rejectionist state in the land of the caliphate', adding that 'the enemies only understand the language of force'.[40] A group calling itself The Islamic State of Iraq [*Dawlat al-`Iraq al-Islamiyya*] claimed that it had organized the attacks. An organization by that name had been active in the Sunni Islamist wing of the armed resistance movement during this period, but the authenticity of the claims could not be verified.

Nevertheless, it was part of a pattern of spectacular acts of violence that generally sought out two kinds of target. The first were the institutions and personnel of the new regime that had emerged following the establishment of the parliamentary republic in 2004–5. The second were religious and secular sites associated with the majority Shi`i population of Iraq, ensuring large numbers of Shi`i casualties. As the Christian minorities of Iraq discovered to their cost, this 'symbolic' targeting also included their communities, attacked by some wings of the *salafi* resistance for sharing the faith of the U.S. occupying forces. Thus police and army recruiting offices that were guaranteed to attract large numbers of unemployed Iraqis became particular targets of suicide bombers who could mingle with the crowd. The death toll in these incidents was unnerving, with some fifty killed and nearly 150 injured by a single suicide bomber at a police recruiting office in Takrit in January 2011. Similar attacks with similar casualty figures had occurred periodically throughout the preceding years. Equally, in

January 2011, Shiʻi pilgrims converging on Karbala to celebrate the Arbaʻin (the fortieth day after the day commemorating the death of Imam Hussein in 61 AH/680 CE) were targeted by suicide bombers who succeeded in killing more than eighty people in a series of coordinated attacks. This followed a pattern that had caused the deaths of more than 100 Shiʻi pilgrims at similar events during the preceding year.

The justifications given out in 2009 for the violence were common to many of the resistance movements in Iraq after 2003. The indictment was phrased in sectarian terms against the Shiʻi community and, by association, in ethnic terms against the Iranian interest that some believed stood behind all Shiʻi political figures and parties. It labels them as infidels and justifies the violence by claiming that Iraq's government had come to power by force and was imposing an alien, un-Islamic order on the country. As the name of the group – established in 2006 as an umbrella organization for a number of Sunni Islamist groupings – would suggest, the ultimate aim was the establishment of a state more in keeping with the group's ideas of Islamic legitimacy. The attacks were nevertheless precise acts of violence. They were targeted at carefully selected buildings and were timed for a particular moment in Iraq's unfolding political history. In this sense, the explosions and the killings had multiple messages. Some of these corresponded to the ideology of the group. Others, however, were connected to more immediate political goals, such as discrediting the prime minister, Nuri al-Maliki, prior to the 2010 elections, disrupting the planned U.S. withdrawal of forces from Iraq and exposing the Iraqi government as still dependent on U.S. power.

Opposition to the U.S.-led occupation of Iraq in 2003 had caused many Iraqis either to support or to participate in the armed resistance movements that had emerged as early as the summer of 2003. Across the country, there was resentment at the invasion and at the establishment of direct U.S. control through the Coalition Provisional Authority (CPA) in Baghdad. Few regretted the demise of Saddam Hussein and his clan, but the manner of his overthrow, the fact that it was carried out by U.S.-led forces and the shape of the new regime angered many. The exception was Kurdish Iraq, where the Kurdish Regional Government had been able to exist free of Baghdad's control since 1991, under the protection of U.S. and allied forces. For the rest of Iraq, however, these same years had witnessed the pauperization of most of the population, save those well connected to the ruling elite, at the hands of the very powers which invaded the state with such intentionally spectacular violence in 2003.[41]

The invaders brought with them a collection of exiled Iraqi parties and individuals who had, for reasons of self-preservation, fled the country during Saddam Hussein's long dictatorship, but had used their time in exile to cultivate ties with the United States and the UK, as well as with Iran and Syria. Having persuaded the U.S. administration of their value as intermediaries with Iraqi political society, they hoped to benefit from the patronage of American military power in Iraq. There was apprehension in Iraq therefore about the identity of those whom the U.S. forces favoured in setting up new state structures. In addition, there were those who were fearful and suspicious not simply of the individuals and organizations who seemed to be the new client base of American control of Iraq, but also of the very nature of the 'liberal imperialist' project so loudly proclaimed by some in the U.S. administration as the underlying rationale of the invasion. This exercise in social engineering planned to refound Iraq as a secular, liberal democratic state, based on a free enterprise economy and closely allied to the United States.

Ideological resentment, as well as hatred of those who seemed most likely to benefit from the American occupation, were supplemented by resistance to the very idea that foreigners should order Iraqis about. It touched a raw nerve for many Iraqis, reviving the historical memory of British colonialism and British rule, criticism of which had been a constant thread in Iraqi education. Dangerously for the occupiers, it also revived memories of the 1920 revolt that had convinced the British authorities that they could not afford to rule Iraq directly – a memory drawn upon by one of the resistance organizations in Anbar province that called itself *Kata'ib Thawrat al-`Ashrin* (Brigades of the Revolution of [19]20). In the recent past, foreign intervention recalled the punishing sanctions that had been imposed in 1990 by the UN Security Council, adamantly maintained by the United States and the UK in particular, effectively dictating the conditions of life of the bulk of the Iraqi people.

In the aftermath of the invasion, there were many reasons for different groups of Iraqis to try to resist the future that was being mapped out for them. However, resentment and resistance are not necessarily translated into violent action. Many Iraqis tried to communicate their opposition, criticism and suggestions to the U.S. administration, using the very networks that had made them relatively trusted interlocutors. Others, such as Grand Ayatollah Ali al-Sistani, could not be ignored by the United States, given his authority amongst the Shi`a of Iraq. His pronouncements on Iraqi governance, institutions and the constitution, in which he expressed strong opposition to some of the proposed measures, had a marked impact during the year of direct U.S. rule.

Nevertheless, it was the outbreak and development of *armed* resistance that profoundly affected the course of Iraqi politics and brought about radical changes in U.S. policy. In the process, it ignited a civil war in Iraq that cost tens of thousands of Iraqi lives, setting up new sectarian and ethnic geographies that will shape the country's politics for years to come. The arming of the resistance, or the translation of discontent into organized violence, was due to a number of factors. Many of these, in different combinations, have played their part in the emergence of similar movements in other countries, in the Middle East and beyond. It was the fate of the Iraqis that all of the most potent catalysts for armed struggle should have existed simultaneously in Iraq after 2003, making its eruption appear a surprise only to those in the United States and the UK who had engineered the military occupation in the first place.

Armed resistance reflects the nature of the power it faces, not simply in its tactical adjustments in combat, but also in its targets, its medium and short-term objectives and often in the methods it uses. It is also opportunistic, emerging from the field of possibilities that may have been opened up or may neglectfully have been allowed to develop by the dominant power. This was certainly true of the early appearance of the Iraqi resistance. The dissolution of the 350,000-strong Iraqi armed forces and security services in May 2003, soon after the establishment of the CPA, has rightly been cited as providing both the incentive and the opportunity to organize armed resistance against the occupying powers. It also provided the structure for such organization.

It was not simply that there were now 350,000 or so young men on the streets, trained in the use of firearms and explosives and angry that they had suddenly been made redundant, denied compensation or pension. In many areas of Iraq, particularly the rural north and west, the units of the Iraqi army that had seemingly dispersed in the brief war of March–April 2003 had in fact returned to their home villages and the towns where they had been recruited. When they were told that they had all lost their jobs and would receive no compensation, officers and men alike found themselves in a similar position, with no possibility of finding work, given the collapsed economy of Iraq. But they were linked in their misfortune by their shared background, their army experience and often by tribal and family ties that formed a framework of social solidarity in some of these areas. This was true, for instance, of the clans of the Dulaim from the area around Falluja. Furthermore, there was no mistaking the cause of their misfortune. It was not surprising, therefore, that some of them should have taken up arms, especially since open protest demonstrations in the streets of Baghdad, Ramadi and Tikrit had no effect, and it was soon clear that those who felt most aggrieved had no access to the CPA in the Green Zone in Baghdad.

For these early members of what was to become a widespread resistance network of localized groups, the motives were mixed. Some appear to have taken up arms in response to an immediate crisis in relations with the U.S. army units occupying their district. This was the case of the developing resistance in Falluja where, in late April 2003, the U.S. military unit occupying a school building fired live rounds at the crowd of demonstrators who were protesting about the arbitrary expropriation of the Al-Qaid school. Fifteen Iraqis were killed and more than sixty were wounded. In a promise of the repercussions to follow, one resident, whose son was wounded, stated flatly that 'We won't remain quiet over this. Either they leave Falluja or we will make them leave'.[42]

Other Iraqis seemed determined to make their mark on those who occupied Iraq, inviting retribution, but also asserting their presence and their right to be heard. This was particularly the case in the areas of Iraq now unhelpfully but characteristically labelled in the United States as 'the Sunni triangle'. Nationally, they were demanding the recognition that they felt they were being denied by American cultivation only of those sections of Iraqi society, such as the Kurds, the exiles and some of the majority Shi`a, who seemed to acquiesce in the U.S. political project. Locally, violence was a way of eliminating suspected collaborators with the United States and its allies.

There was a range of ideological motives at work, both amongst the foot soldiers and among the various councils and personalities directing the armed resistance. In the early months, some may have thought that mounting chaos and armed struggle would pave the way for a return of the Ba`th, even of Saddam Hussein himself. Apart from his sons and other members of his clan, who had found themselves suddenly ejected from supreme power and were now on the run, few were likely to have shared this dream. However, as the shadowy activities of *Al-`Awda* (the return) indicated, the resurrection of the Ba`th, purged of its discredited cliques, was something which some Iraqis did believe in, possibly even seeing the overthrow of Saddam Hussein as a means of renewing the party and the cause.

More common, however, were the Iraqi and Arab nationalists who vehemently rejected the presence of foreign forces on Iraqi soil, especially those of the United States and other Western powers that were additionally tainted in their eyes by their historical support for Israel. As some of their pamphlets made plain, identifying U.S. forces with those of Zionism lent to the Iraqi resistance the heroism of the defining and enduring struggle of the Arabs on behalf of Palestine. In Falluja in 2004, Shaikh Dhafer al-Ubaidi made this link clear in his speeches, accusing Zionists, imperialists and freemasons of conspiring to occupy Iraq and to foment sectarian conflict. Meanwhile, outside his mosque a large banner proclaimed, 'Sunnis and Shias are committed to defeating the Zionist plan'.[43] Adding to the charge and further exacerbating resentment at the course of events in Iraq was the belief that the very Iraqis favoured by the United States – often Shi'i or Kurdish – represented the controlling hand of Iran or wanted to see the fracturing of the Iraqi state. Fear about the future of Iraq under such circumstances was a powerful motive and drove many into the arms of the resistance.

One of the features of the resistance groups that identified themselves early in the occupation was the use of names that had markedly Islamic associations, such as the *al-Faruq* and *al-Abbas* brigades of *Mujahidin al-Iraq* (the Strugglers of Iraq), *Jaish Ansar al-Sunna* (the Army of the Supporters of the Sunna), *Jaish Muhammad* (the Army of Muhammad) and *Jaish al-Iraq al-Islami* (the Islamic Army of Iraq). Some were more nationalist and local in their orientation, whilst the others appear to have been constituted by Iraqis who saw themselves as *salafi*, opposing the invaders and their accomplices in the name of Islam and, specifically, in the name of an Iraq where Sunni rather than Shi'i Islam should rule. For these men, the invasion and occupation of Iraq was to be resisted, not simply because it meant non-Muslim Americans ruling over Muslim Iraqis, but because it seemed to open the door to the dominance of the Shi'a in the future governance of the country.

Quite apart from doctrinal concerns, those who were not from the Shi'i communities knew that such a dispensation would exclude them and their circles, given the ways in which power had always been mediated in Iraq through local and personal association. This sense of possible exclusion was reinforced by the attitude of the occupiers in their pronouncements on the tripartite division of Iraq. It sharpened resentments and made people more receptive to a specifically sectarian message. Sectarian and communal suspicions abounded in an atmosphere of insecurity where the known fixed points of the state were being dissolved and malign intentions were attributed to the occupiers. It was to become a lethal mix that exacted a terrible human cost as the insurgency gathered momentum, greatly magnifying its destructive power.

It was the arming of the resistance in Iraq that was to open up the wider possibilities of action, even against the formidable military power of the United States. The supply of freely available weapons ensured that it had the means to make an impact that was to reverberate for years to come. Few outsiders had recognized before 2003 how well armed Iraqi society was. The collection and display of weapons was part of an ethos of provincial life and had spectacularly come to the urban areas of Iraq as well. Even a regime as repressive as that of Saddam Hussein had made no effort to stop this process, and in some cases – privileged tribal groupings in different parts of the country, as well as Ba`th party members – had actually encouraged it.

The U.S. administration had not simply sent home angry young men armed with small arms when it dissolved the army. It had also failed to prevent the clearing out of the massive arsenals accumulated by the previous regime around the country. Some of these had in any case been looted immediately after the U.S. invasion. One notorious case was the April 2003 looting of the 36 km² site of al-Qa`qaa near Yusufiyya, southwest of Baghdad. Under the apparently unconcerned gaze of a U.S. army unit, extraordinary quantities of explosive were taken from this major Iraqi arms manufacturing site. By the time the Pentagon's Exploratory Task Force turned up in May, some thousands of tonnes of munitions had been removed, including nearly 350 tons of the most powerful high explosives. Yusufiyya became a boom town on the basis of the sale of these explosives, decanted, appropriately enough, into the sacks used by locals to store the potatoes for which the town is famous. The results were soon apparent. By November 2003, it was estimated that attacks on coalition troops were occurring at the rate of 1,000 a day.[44]

Even where the U.S. army had succeeded in collecting up some of this ordinance – enough to fill several football-field-sized areas near Baghdad – they failed to post enough guards to prevent Iraqis from helping themselves to the array of shells, mortars and other weapons conveniently stored there. As a memorable photo of this 'weapons park' taken in 2004 shows, the distinctive orange and white taxis of Baghdad were busy loading up anything that came to hand, with impunity and gratis. In addition to this, weapons flowed across Iraq's unguarded borders. Arms and explosives kept coming in very substantial quantities. They were sent by regional powers, such as Syria and Iran, which had no desire to see the United States succeed in Iraq, or were brought in by those who saw Iraq as a decisive battlefield against the United States, against the Shi`a or against Iran. Or they were simply part of the economies of supply and demand that flooded Iraq in those years with consumer goods. Given the relatively small number of U.S. troops in the country, the borders could not be sealed and the weapons continued to flow, more than making up for the occasional discovery of impressively large arms caches. In fact, the thin spread of U.S. forces was a further factor that made armed resistance seem particularly feasible for those Iraqis who resented the occupation. Although they tried to make their presence felt, the U.S. army could not counter the work of the insurgents or even act as a deterrent.

It was in this context that the other principal element of the Iraqi resistance began to develop. Based not amongst those who had enjoyed privileges under the old regime, but amongst some of the most under-privileged of urban Iraqis, the *Jaish al-Mahdi* [army of the Mahdi] emerged out of the Sadrist movement. This had been run by Muqtada al-Sadr following the murder of his father by agents of the Ba`thist regime in 1999. Its commitment to armed resistance in 2003 was due to many of the same circumstances that had led to the resistance movements of the north and northwest. In terms of motivation, there was equal resentment of the U.S. occupying forces. The United States represented for al-Sadr a power that had, by turns, supported Saddam Hussein in his war on Iran, overlooked the repression following the uprisings after the Iraqi defeat in Kuwait in 1991, as well as in 1999 when the poor eastern suburbs of Baghdad had erupted in protest at the killing of Ayatollah Muhammad Sadiq al-Sadr. Furthermore, the United States was seen as the leading advocate of the sanctions which the Shi`i poor – al-Sadr's main constituency – had felt most sharply for the previous thirteen years and the effects of which the Sadrist organization had tried to ameliorate.

This was more than could be said of the exiled Shi`i Islamist parties – the Supreme Council for the Islamic Revolution in Iraq (SCIRI) and *al-Da`wa* – which had moved back into Iraq under the protection of the United States and now claimed to speak for all Shi`a. They had been notoriously absent, except in the occasional symbolic attack on a police station or two, during the hard years of the 1990s, whereas the Sadrist organization had been active in the care of the poorest sections of the community. Yet when the uprising of 1999 took place, it had received no help from these exile groups, more concerned as they were with

safeguarding their own position, mistrustful of the Sadrists and dis-
dainful of the poor of the eastern Baghdad slums. However, these
were the very parties that seemed set to reap the benefits of the U.S.
occupation, elbowing out those who had stayed in the country and
using their own militias to extend their control across large swathes of
the country where they had no previous constituency.

As with the other resistance movements, the *Jaish al-Mahdi* developed out of the networks of the existing Sadrist organization in a
situation where violence was growing and arms were freely available.
Many of the conscripts who had found themselves unemployed when
the army was dissolved gravitated towards the organization, especially
where it dominated their neighbourhoods of origin. Equally, the collapse of the Iraqi economy and the startling rates of unemployment were
no respecters of community, but it was the poorer sections of the
country that suffered most. For many of them, the Sadrist militia
provided a kind of economic security. In 2004, in a bid to seize and
maintain control of Najaf, the *Jaish al-Mahdi* clashed directly with U.S.
forces. Some believed that the very future of Islam in Iraq was in danger
and all were fired up by Muqtada al-Sadr's call from the mosque in Kufa
where he had taken refuge: 'Make your enemies afraid, for it is impossible to remain quiet about their moral offences ... I beg you not to
resort to demonstrations, for they have become nothing but burned
paper. It is necessary to resort to other measures'.[45] Thenceforth, *Jaish
al-Mahdi* became a familiar part of the armed resistance, but occasional
ceasefires, behind the scenes deals, truces and political bargains meant
that it was only intermittently in direct confrontation with the forces of
the United States or of the Iraqi government.

One reason for this was due to the fact that, like all the other paramilitary organizations active in Iraq during these years, it became
increasingly involved in the sectarian civil war that began to take hold
after the elections of 2005. A parliament had been elected in which
the Shi'i parties and the Kurdish nationalists were overrepresented,
confirming the worst suspicions of many that the political order in
Iraq had changed forever, tilted now against those who found themselves without a voice. The growth of armed organizations on all sides
represented a broad spectrum of diverse and often bitterly hostile Iraqi
political forces, supplemented by fighters from across Iraq's borders.
This combined to produce a lethal combination of communal violence
in which not only the forces and institutions of the new Iraqi government and their American protectors came under attack, but so did the

members of Iraq's diverse religious communities and the symbols of their faith. Armed resistance movements on all sides had become instruments for a darker purpose in which the targets were selected for reasons of revenge.

As the years 2005–8 demonstrated, the paramilitary organizations became preoccupied by a violent political game in which resistance to the U.S. and allied forces, or to the slowly rebuilt security forces of the new Iraqi government, only formed part of their activities. For much of the rest of the time, their energies and their violence were aimed at other targets. They cleared neighbourhoods of people belonging to different religious sects or ethnic groups, and organized death squads that carried out the targeted killing of people who were on their blacklists. They set up roadblocks that murdered individuals from the 'wrong' sect with impunity, and detonated bombs at religious sites or neighbourhoods associated with people from another community. At the same time, they involved themselves in the protection rackets, kidnappings and smuggling activities that helped to finance their operations.

Terrible as the violence was during these years, it had a number of calculated purposes. Some used it to demonstrate their intransigent resistance to the new order emerging in Iraq. As the Islamic Army of Iraq stated, 'resistance must prevent the emergence and institutionalization of any state infrastructure from taking shape in Iraq that would facilitate the operations of the occupation forces or allow them to achieve their political goals of consolidation of their control over the country'.[46] For other organizations, violence was a means of communication, to ensure that they were heard and their own concerns and ambitions taken into account in the new order. This was certainly the case with much of the resistance based in the north and northwest of Iraq, as well as in western and southern Baghdad. Here, the change of U.S. strategy implemented by General Petraeus in 2007 brought many former members of the nationalist, tribal and Islamist resistance into the U.S. financed and armed 'Sons of Iraq' and used to protect their own neighbourhoods and districts.

Although these organizations were understandably mistrusted by the Iraqi government, they showed their worth to the U.S. occupation forces. By accepting American support and withdrawing key local assistance for the ideologically driven *salafi* wing of the resistance, they ceased their own attacks on U.S. forces and weakened some of the more intransigent Islamist groups.[47] One such umbrella organization, *Tanzim al-Qa`ida fi Bilad al-Rafidain* [the Organization of al-Qa`ida in the Land of the Two Rivers] had emerged in late 2004 and had associated itself with the pan-Islamic *jihad* of Usama bin Laden. Led by Abu Musab al-Zarqawi, it thrived in the years 2005–7 when sectarian violence and attacks on U.S. forces were at their height. Its leaders now resented what they saw as a betrayal by the tribal shaikhs and targeted them and other former allies relentlessly. Nevertheless, despite the deaths, those who supported the 'Sons of Iraq' scheme had calculated that armed resistance to the United States and the U.S.-backed government no longer served any useful purpose. On the contrary, it would isolate them still further from the emerging reward system of the new Iraqi regime. Violence had won them recognition and they were now seeking the benefits that political recognition could bring.

At the same time, the messages conveyed by the violence of the *Jaish al-Mahdi* were also having a political impact. They led to negotiations between the Iraqi government and Muqtada al-Sadr, in which the government made it clear that continued armed resistance would lead to his exclusion as a legitimate actor in Iraqi politics. Al-Sadr himself had become concerned about uncontrolled elements within the *Jaish al-Mahdi* and felt that much of it had outlived its usefulness for him as well – although he was certainly not about to disband it. Prime Minister al-Maliki drove home the government's own message with force. In 2008, he sent the Iraqi army into Basra and into the Sadrist stronghold of Sadr City in Baghdad to crush or at least intimidate them. Out of this came a Sadrist organization that lost many of the lucrative operations that it had established at the point of a gun in southern Iraq. But it was better placed to take part in the electoral process and emerged from the elections of 2010 as a key player in the months that followed. Eventually, with al-Sadr's help, al-Maliki was returned as prime minister and the Sadrists were rewarded with seven seats in the government of December 2010.

In their different ways, therefore, these two powerful branches of the armed resistance in Iraq had managed to find places in the emerging political order. They might not trust it or even like it, but they saw little point by this stage of using armed force against it. This did not mean, of course, that they disbanded their forces. Rather, they kept them in reserve should the need arise again. Muqtada al-Sadr returned to Iraq in January 2011 after four years of self-imposed exile in Iran. He summed up the stance of the movement when he urged resistance against all occupiers of Iraq, leading chants against the United States and Israel, claiming, 'We are still fighters. We are still resisting, we resist the occupation militarily, culturally and with all other kinds of resistance'. But he also stressed that the use of weapons should be confined to the security forces of the state – in the government of which his movement now participated.[48] At the same time, the foreign forces that had been so much a target of the resistance were indeed withdrawing from Iraq.

British forces had effectively withdrawn from Basra city some months before, but in the summer of 2009, they evacuated their last base, leaving behind only a few hundred men to help with the training of the Iraqi armed forces. The timetable for the withdrawal of the much larger contingent of U.S. forces was also mapped out, agreed upon by the Iraqi government and reinforced by the new administration in Washington. The end of foreign occupation was therefore in sight. Of course, this did not satisfy all those who believed that the use of violence could still give them a stake in the future of Iraq. The suicide bombings and other attacks of 2010–11 showed that armed resistance, although diminished, was still very much part of the repertoire of many. There were those who wanted to pursue their struggle against the Iraqi government, its security agencies and collaborators, seeing them by turns as agents of the United States or of Iran. There were also those who saw violence as the only way to confront the change in the sectarian balance of power that had taken place since 2003. In the year before the final evacuation of U.S. troops at the end of 2011, such attacks, as well as targeted assassinations, were killing some 300–400 Iraqis every month.[49]

In addition, there were many who hoped to undermine the government, to cast doubt on its competence, to disrupt the elections or to rekindle the sectarian civil war that had fitted in with their polarized image of Iraqi society. For its part, the government of Iraq, assisted by the United States and others, had built up a formidable security apparatus, ostensibly to crush the insurgency that had raged since 2003. Understandably, these measures gave rise to fears that the familiar outlines of the security state that had loomed so large in Iraq's recent history were beginning to re-emerge. Despite the existence of a parliament, it seemed to some that Iraq was now a land occupied by its own armed forces, with multiple checkpoints and a very visible presence of the security forces – as well as a less visible but ruthlessly effective network of hidden detention and interrogation centres.[50]

THE NATIONAL SECURITY STATE: VIOLENT DOMINATION AND RESISTANCE

By 2010–11, it was perhaps not surprising that armed resistance in Iraq was coming to resemble the forms that had emerged in a number of Middle Eastern states, including Iraq, in the preceding decades. In many cases, this mirrored the violence of the state apparatus itself. In some cases, resistance to the state had stemmed from a community's resentment of their subordination, ending the autonomy that they may have once enjoyed. At other times, resistance was grounded in ideological differences with the ruling regime or with the very rationale of the state itself, extending far beyond mere opposition to the government of the day. Sometimes resistance has had more to do with the provincial bases of the protagonists and anger at the seizure of the state by a particular faction. In short, throughout recent Middle Eastern political history, there has been an array of resistance movements that have taken up arms. Their purposes have been various. They have included self-defence, wringing concessions from central government, loathing of the political order, determination to shake people out of complacent acceptance of the injustices of an everyday authoritarian government, as well as attempts to capture the state for their own purposes.

The various forms of militant Islamist opposition to governments across the Middle East have conformed to these patterns of resistance, shaping both the targets and the tactics. Resistance in this respect has been driven by abhorrence of the secular and, in their view, un-Islamic preoccupations and alliances of the government. However, the violence of these groups and their assault on the personnel, institutions or symbols of power have not been due solely, or even primarily, to their beliefs about the need to bring in an Islamic order. These might explain their opposition to the ruling regime, but their responses have often been shaped by the methods used by those regimes to keep their hold on power. In effect, like their secular counterparts, they see themselves – not without reason – as fighting against the forces of military occupation.

Violent and coercive practices by regimes across the region have incensed, but also brutalized, those who oppose them. At the same time, regime strategies of entrapment and co-optation have created a political and social fabric of collusion and collaboration. This has driven some to think that violence may be the only way to break the seductive hold of an order that keeps the majority in subjection. Islamist organizations do not of course have a monopoly on the idea that violence will shake people out of their everyday complacency. But because they can draw on a powerful repertoire of religious beliefs, familiar to the mass of the population, they have had widespread success and support, despite unease about some of their methods.

Syria: Islamist Insurgency, 1978–1982

The Syrian Muslim Brotherhood's fateful decision in the 1970s to move from criticism of the Ba'thist government to the organization of armed attacks on its personnel and institutions was taken in circumstances such as these. Some in the movement argued that it would be folly to challenge the regime on the very terrain – armed combat – where it so ruthlessly excelled. Others claimed that it was precisely because it was a regime based upon force that this was the only way to deal with it. Prefiguring the bombers of Baghdad in 2009, sections of the Syrian Muslim Brotherhood, based chiefly in Homs, Hama and Aleppo, asserted that violence was the only language that such a blood-soaked regime could understand. They believed that a campaign of armed resistance would convince the ruling Ba'th party of the existence of underlying and ferocious opposition with which they would have to come to terms. For the more radical offshoot of the Brotherhood, *Al-Tali`a al-Muqatila* [the fighting vanguard], the destruction of the regime was the goal, and violence was to be the only way to achieve it. This was precisely why the Damascus branch of the Brotherhood was so uneasy about the idea. If violence were indeed the only language the regime could understand, then it would respond in the same idiom. Since its capacity was far greater than anything that the Muslim Brothers could muster, it would all end in disaster.[51]

The violence of the following years, culminating in the bombardment and massacre of thousands in the town of Hama after it had been seized by armed units of the Muslim Brotherhood in 1982, showed that the misgivings of the Damascus branch were all too well founded. But they had failed to win the argument in the 1970s and, as the Brotherhood's journal *Al-Nadhir* stated, once the struggle was under way, violence and revenge followed their own logic: 'We did not begin our *jihad* until the oppressors had begun to exterminate Islam and until after having received the broken bodies of our brothers who had died under torture'.[52] Some of the doubters may also have been influenced by the example of the Iranian revolution of 1978–9. This seemed to reinforce the idea that people fired up by their belief in Islam and Islamic leadership could overthrow even a well-entrenched and ruthless dictatorship. Many, not just in Syria, had seen in these events the possibility that open acts of defiance, even if they provoked the regime into brutal suppression, would help to open people's eyes to the reality of the regime. Equally importantly, they could break the myth of the all-powerful state, encouraging forms of resistance that might have been unimaginable a few months before.

This was an idea that had long been associated with political movements of all kinds both in the Middle East and elsewhere, when considering the arguments for and against armed defiance. In this respect, violence and armed resistance become the means of communicating not simply with the regime or the state agencies, but with the wider public. They are intended to convey messages of resolve, of the possibilities of defiance and of the loss of authority of a regime whose countermeasures might affect increasing numbers of people, alienating them and mobilizing them for the cause of resistance. These, at least, were some of the ideas that circulated in Syria at the time.

The outcome, as some had feared, was disturbing. On the one hand, violence was met by violence, and the Syrian government showed no hesitation in crushing any signs of resistance with maximum force. Units of the Muslim Brotherhood were hunted down with ruthless skill, and although they enjoyed considerable support and shelter in a number of cities, they felt the full weight of a state geared to rooting out and eradicating opposing voices, let alone organized armed groupings. The Muslim Brotherhood achieved some success in managing to sustain a campaign of bombings and assassinations for three to four years, which unsettled the ruling elite but scarcely dented the power of the Ba'thist state. Armed resistance was indeed the language it understood best and the idiom in which it was most practised.

On the other hand, as the propaganda and the targets of the Muslim Brotherhood showed, armed struggle took on an increasingly sectarian aspect. The regime of Hafiz al-Asad was characterized as an 'Alawi clique' (the religious community to which the president and many senior figures of the regime belonged in the clannish Syrian regime), identifying the government with a heterodox sect which few believed was Muslim at all, despite al-Asad's engineering of a *fatwa* declaring that it formed part of the Shi'i branch of Islam. This was, in any case, not much better as far as *salafi* members of the Muslim Brotherhood were concerned, since they did not regard the Shi'a as true Muslims either.[53]

Possibly hoping to capitalize on the riots that had broken out across Syria earlier in the 1970s in protest at al-Asad's apparent downplaying of the role of Islam in the new constitution, the Muslim Brotherhood repeatedly stressed the hostility of the regime to Islam itself. It tried to underline for all Muslim Syrians the desperate nature of the situation and to justify acts of violence against agents of the state, particularly those identified as Alawi. The killing of more than thirty Alawi officer cadets in the summer of 1979 was an example of this. They had been carefully separated out from their Sunni brother officers and then gunned down by the armed units that had stormed the military academy in Aleppo.[54]

Of course, this too was a language which the regime understood. This was not for doctrinal, sectarian reasons, but because of the importance of communal bonds of trust in a politics of conspiracy. Selection and promotion procedures for many in the Syrian security establishment were informed not simply by candidates' Alawi identity, but also by their affiliation with particular tribal groupings, clans and families close to that of the president. This was vividly illustrated in the siege and bombardment of the town of Hama in April 1982. The Muslim Brotherhood had staged an uprising in the town. They may have believed that this would be the catalyst to set the surrounding villages ablaze in a fury of revolt against the Ba'thist regime, or that it would spark sympathetic rebellions in other major towns. Neither development took place, and the Brotherhood's forces found themselves under siege in Hama itself. They were cornered in the old city where they had their base, but also where the narrow lanes and blind alleys made a formidable defensive position.

For Hafiz al-Asad, this was the kind of challenge with which he was well equipped to cope, mentally as well as materially. As the opening salvos of the artillery bombardment indicated, the Syrian security forces were not going to risk street fighting, choosing instead a blanket bombardment of the whole quarter, regardless of the thousands of civilians trapped there. Against this, the Muslim Brotherhood had no defence. Even in the area where it may have dented the resolve of the Syrian armed forces – the alleged reluctance of the regular Syrian army and air force to destroy a whole section of Hama and its population – al-Asad had a ready answer.

He deployed the Defence Brigades, commanded by his brother Rifaat, and recruited almost exclusively from the loyal clans and villages of the Jebel Alawi, al-Asad's home region. They had no compunction in executing the orders of the president to eradicate all opposition in Hama, whatever the cost, even if it meant killing large numbers of its inhabitants and razing a substantial section of the town itself. This was a dialogue in the language of violence. Here, the message of armed defiance by the Muslim Brotherhood was countered by the response of the Syrian regime in terms that conveyed their own ruthlessness and determination through the terrible fate of Hama and its inhabitants.

Syria: The National Uprising of 2011–2012

In the spring of 2011, when President Bashar al-Asad, the son of Hafiz al-Asad, faced a very different kind of challenge in the peaceful demonstrations that erupted in towns and cities across Syria, it was the regime itself that evoked the memories of this period of near civil war. The protests that had begun in the small border town of Dar`a in March and that spread rapidly throughout the country were said by the government to be the work of '*salafi* extremists', armed and financed from abroad and intent on bringing the kind of sectarian conflict to Syria that had been so bloody a feature of the politics of Syria's neighbours, Lebanon and Iraq. As the death toll mounted, with nearly 2,000 killed in the space of four months, the Syrian government made a great show of mourning the deaths of members of the security forces who had allegedly fallen victim to the 'armed gangs' that were now said to be roaming the streets of some provincial towns.[55]

In some places, it did seem that members of the security forces had been killed by protestors in running street battles when weapons became available. But they were also killed by the regime's largely Alawi plainclothes militia *al-Shabbiha* [the ghosts] that was used to sow confusion and to gun down regular soldiers who were reluctant to open fire on demonstrators. In some cases, there may have been more targeted killing, although nothing to compare with the violence used by the forces of the regime against demonstrations. In Dar`a itself, after weeks of protests and the torching of government offices, the security forces had effectively been denied access to the town. Indeed, the protestors felt bold enough to declare that the town was now a 'liberated zone'. As with Hama some thirty years before, this was too great a challenge to the authorities, and at the end of April, a military operation was put in motion with the aim of reasserting government control, whatever the cost in human life. However, again with an echo of events in Hama, of the two battalions sent to carry out this order, one, the

5th division, was reported to have refused to fire indiscriminately on the inhabitants. The 4th division, commanded by Maher al-Asad, the brother of the president, felt no such scruples, but then found themselves engaging in a shoot-out with soldiers of the 5th division. Only after some days and heavy fighting was the control of central government forcibly reasserted in the town. Dozens of inhabitants were killed and hundreds were arrested. Reverting to the language it had used with such success before, the Syrian official news agency announced that armed 'terrorist groups' in Dar`a had been confronted, that six had been killed and some 150 arrested.[56]

It then regrouped its forces to move in on other towns and villages that had dared to show collective defiance. By the summer of 2011, Syria was a country unmistakably under military occupation, making visible the violence of state power when that power was subject to widespread resistance. For the most part, this resistance took the form of peaceful marches and demonstrations as people congregated in the squares and streets of small towns as well as in larger cities to shout slogans against the government, against the family of the president and against the whole Ba`thist regime that had dominated Syria since 1963. As in the uprising of 2011 in Libya, the flag of the old regime was hoisted by the Syrian demonstrators, its black, white and green colours contrasting with the black, white and red of Ba`thist Syria. Symbolically, at least, it was as if the protestors wanted to erase the memory of fifty years of Ba`thist rule. However, as thousands of Syrians discovered, protest came with a terrible price in human lives, since there seemed to be no restraint on the violence of the security forces. In small towns, where there could hardly be safety in numbers, the risks were all too apparent and the death toll mounted.

In larger cities, such as Homs and Hama, as well as in Latakia and Dair al-Zor, there was more possibility of fighting back. Thus, again as in Libya, in some areas, faced by the violence of the regime, public protest and defiance became armed resistance. The more ruthless the government became in ordering the security forces to fire on unarmed demonstrators, the greater the number of defections by ordinary soldiers unwilling to carry out these orders. Their defection brought weapons and encouragement to those who were already organizing themselves to resist by force. During the summer of 2011 and into 2012, the toll of those killed in the uprising began to mount. By June 2012, more than 15,000 had died in the uprising, half of them civilians. This was due in part to the determination of tens of thousands of Syrians to continue to defy the authorities by coming out on the streets, whatever the cost, in a series of country-wide protests every Friday. But it was also due to the acquisition of weapons by resistance groups in the larger cities and by army defectors who had regrouped over the border in Lebanon. In some places, such as in Homs, city quarters were sealed off by the insurgents, no-go areas were created and attacks on government personnel and on government buildings became more frequent and more daring.[57] However, as the inhabitants of Homs, Hama and other towns found out, the government response was to hit back even harder, bringing tanks and artillery to bear on those areas that appeared to have escaped its control. Nevertheless, the resistance soon discovered that the government's forces could not be in all places at all times. Nor could the government rely wholly on the loyalties of all the members of the security forces.

The Syrian government came under increasing pressure from the EU, the United States and the Arab League, and was only too well aware of the precedent of Libya earlier in 2011. There rebels had succeeded in wresting nearly a third of the country's territory out of the control of the government, allowing the establishment of an opposition governing council on Libyan soil and facilitating foreign military intervention on behalf of the uprising. It was vital therefore for Bashar al-Asad to prevent any such development on the territory of Syria, however many lives it cost. In the summer of 2011, a disparate coalition of Syrian opposition forces formed themselves into the Syrian National Council [al-Majlis al-Watani al-Suri] (SNC) in exile in Turkey. Despite connections with groups and individuals inside the country, it was unclear that they had any effective say in what happened in Syria. Their authority to speak for the opposition was contested by other opposition forces and of greater significance for the organization of resistance within the country were the dispersed but connected Local Coordination Committees [*Lajan al-Tansiq al-Mahalliyya*].[58] Potentially more worrying for the regime in Damascus was the gradual coalescing of army defectors and armed insurgents into an admittedly shadowy outfit called the Free Syrian Army (FSA). Since it comprised individual soldiers rather than whole military formations, it was not a military threat as such. However, it did appear to be capable of carrying out guerrilla attacks that underlined the weaknesses of the government's attempt to hold down all of Syria by force.

However, its existence and its activities also posed a problem for the political resistance. For the exiled opposition, seeking to impress upon the international community the need to help protect Syrians against the violence of the Ba'thist regime, the existence of a Syrian military force leading an armed insurgency evidently complicated the picture. There was clearly concern in the SNC that the increasing number of attacks launched by the FSA would make it harder to portray the Syrian population as the helpless victims of government violence. Consequently, an agreement was reached in early December 2011 between Burhan Ghalioun (then chairman of the SNC) and Colonel Riyadh al-As'ad (nominally the commander of the FSA): in exchange for mutual recognition, the FSA would no longer launch 'offensive actions against the army', but would confine its use of force to the protection of civilians, even if that might mean battling the security forces responsible.[59] With the arrival of an Arab League observer mission in Syria later in the month, the FSA pledged to suspend its activities during the mission's visit. For the Syrians protesting against the government, it was imperative that the observers should clearly see the direction and source of the violence. Accordingly, hundreds of thousands of citizens took to the streets in defiance of the regime despite its visible deployment of artillery on the outskirts of the major towns, its rooftop snipers and its continued use of lethal force.

This resolution was to be severely tested. Only the day before the arrival of the first members of the Arab League mission, two massive bombs went off in Damascus, blowing up buildings belonging to the intelligence and security services. They caused nearly fifty deaths and wounded more than 150 people. The Syrian government claimed that these were suicide bombs set off by 'militants of al-Qa'ida'. However, the nature of the explosions, their location and, above all, the timing of the incident led to suspicions that agents of the regime itself had been responsible.[60] A similar pattern of events unfolded in 2012 with the arrival of a United Nations mission that tried unsuccessfully to broker a truce between the opposing sides, encountering the same obstacles as those facing the Arab League mission of the previous year. The increasingly violent episodes that marked the uprising underlined not only the dilemmas facing those who organize armed resistance, but also the concerns about the multiple messages that violence can transmit. For those in Syria thinking of extending and deepening the military struggle, it was important to ensure that armed protection of communities did not degenerate into communal hostilities, leading to the kinds of 'sectarian cleansing' that had taken place in Iraq in 2005–7. It was also necessary to weigh up the advantages and disadvantages of an extensive guerrilla campaign in terms of the morale of the regime, but more importantly of the Syrian security forces. Finally, there was the question of whether armed resistance in itself would undermine the powerful example of civil protest and nonviolent resistance that had been so marked a feature of the Syrian uprising for most of 2011.

Kurdish Rebellion in Iraq (1968–1991)

A similar logic shaped the fate that befell the Kurdish resistance in Iraq under the rule of Saddam Hussein in the 1980s. Drawing upon a long history of armed insurrection against the forces of central government in Iraq, the Kurdish nationalist parties – the Kurdish Democratic Party (KDP) and the Patriotic Union of Kurdistan (PUK) – could benefit both from the accepted idea of armed resistance against the forces of the state and from the networks, and weapons, which made it an operational possibility. However, their leaders were also well aware, having experienced it themselves in the 1970s, of the vulnerability of Kurdish resistance – the indefensibility of the major towns, the dependence upon cross-border connections and alliances, the divisions and differences amongst the Kurds themselves which could become acute when rivalries between armed paramilitary forces were added to the equation. Nevertheless, the precarious position of the Iraqi government three years into its disastrous war with Iran meant that, by 1983, it was possible to revive the idea of Kurdish resistance with some prospect of success by carving out an area of de facto autonomy, thereby defying, even helping to undermine, the regime in Baghdad.

Given the plight of the Iraqi government in 1983, facing imminent invasion by the forces of the Islamic Republic of Iran, powerless to seal its northern borders and unable to devote many military resources to the suppression of armed resistance in Kurdistan, the calculation of the Kurdish leadership seemed sound enough. For some five years, therefore, the armed *peshmerga* of the Kurdish parties set up alternative administrations in the large tracts of countryside controlled by the KDP and the PUK. They left the cities nominally under control of the Iraqi authorities, but, in terms of the sympathy of the population, these places were also dominated by the rebels. Baghdad continued to patronize, and to arm, Kurdish tribal irregulars – derisively labelled the *jahsh* – whose leaders were traditionally hostile to the main Kurdish parties and their leading families, or who simply had no confidence in their lasting success. But it could not use them in any effective way as an alternative focus of Kurdish aspirations.[61]

It seemed to some, therefore, that after all the false starts of the 1960s and the 1970s, the Kurdish parties might finally win, by force of arms, the space and the freedom of action that would make Kurdish autonomy a reality. However, all of this depended on the course of the war against Iran and on the durability of the regime of Saddam Hussein in Baghdad. By early 1988, the tide had turned in the war. Iran's dream of invasion had evaporated. Instead, the Iraqi armed forces, more professional and better equipped than ever, carried out a series of counter-offensives that put the Iranians on the defensive. It was then that Saddam Hussein and his advisers turned their attention to Kurdistan.

In March 1988, the opening salvoes of the al-Anfal operation were fired by the Iraqi forces in what was to become a systematic effort to destroy Kurdish resistance. This was to be achieved not simply by engaging and defeating the Kurdish guerrillas – the *peshmerga* – but also by laying waste hundreds of square kilometres of Kurdistan. Concentrating especially on the borderlands of Iran and Turkey, the Iraqi forces uprooted and resettled Kurdish communities. In many cases, they were simply annihilated if they were thought to be too supportive of the resistance organizations. Over a six-month period, the Iraqi armed forces used all means, including chemical weapons, to achieve their goal. By the end of 1988, this had left a swathe of devastation across Kurdistan, shattering and demoralizing Kurdish communities, causing the deaths of some 120,000 people and driving tens of thousands of refugees across the border into Turkey and Iran.[62]

Armed resistance could not be sustained in the face of the scale and the nature of the attack launched by Iraqi government forces against all Kurdish areas. As resistance collapsed, it took with it, so the Iraqi government believed, both the means and the imagination of future resistance against the authority of the central government. In fact, less than three years later, when the Iraqi forces were defeated in the war for Kuwait in the spring of 1991 and the Iraqi government faced a possible allied invasion, the Kurdish *peshmerga* reappeared, descending on demoralized Iraqi army outposts, capturing most of the major towns and driving the government forces from much of Kurdistan.

It was not to last. Once again, although diminished, the Iraqi army retaliated when it became clear that allied forces were not going to invade. This gave Baghdad the opportunity to crush the rebellions that had also broken out in the south of the country. Faced by this offensive and with memories of *al-Anfal* fresh in their minds, it was not surprising that more than a million Kurds fled across the borders into Turkey, rather than face the onslaught of the Iraqi army. More concerned with leading their people to safety, the *peshmerga* were obliged once again to abandon the military gains they had made and to disengage from the fighting. It was only the intervention of the Western powers that forced the Iraqi army to withdraw, leaving most of Kurdistan in the hands of the two major nationalist resistance organizations, the KDP and the PUK.[63]

These two examples show well the dilemmas facing those contemplating armed resistance against the national security state. On the one hand, the violence and brutality of the regime, as well as its lack of popular mandate, made violent resistance both imaginable and even necessary, enthusiastically supported by those who had suffered at its hands and often cheered on by a population which had had to live under its shadow. As a consequence, there were fewer scruples about taking up arms than there might have been in a state that more successfully disguised the true nature of its power. However, as these cases show, the regime's ability to retaliate and the terrible price it exacted for defiance underlined the high risks involved.

There is a report of a conversation between Masoud Barzani and a leader of the *jahsh* as they stood on a hillside in western Kurdistan looking out over the peaceful stone houses of the *jahsh* leader's village. As he gestured to the idyllic scene on the hillside opposite, the *jahsh* leader is said to have pointed out that although he had collaborated with the government in Baghdad, at least he could look with satisfaction upon his village and his people – and then added, 'And what does Barzan look like these days?' Allegedly, this made Barzani reflect with some sadness upon the price his own town had paid for resistance since it had been razed to the ground and its people dispersed during *al-Anfal*.

Despite these concerns, even where they confront a ruthless security state and the odds seem stacked against them, it is significant how appealing armed resistance to oppression can be. In these cases, one cannot discount the force of ideas and the imagination – as with the Muslim Brotherhood in Syria and the Kurdish resistance in Iraq. For adherents of the Muslim Brotherhood, this may have been linked to a sense of obligation to prevent gross injustice, to do everything in one's power to carry out a command that has divine sanction. The repertoire that can be drawn upon may include for some a sense of mission, for instance, by carrying out the injunction to 'command the good and forbid the wrong', by whatever means available.[64] This may not explain why an individual or a group of people do decide to act upon this injunction by taking up arms at a particular time and place, but it may well contribute to the ways in which they understand the situation and what may be at stake.

In the case of the Kurds of Iraq, strategic opportunity certainly played a part, but memory and the power of a narrative of resistance was also influential. To stand up to the dominant power of central government had been a thread within Kurdish society in Iraq for many generations. It had certainly formed a key constituent of the appeal of the main Kurdish nationalist parties. To defy Baghdad by force was woven into the very identity of many of those who found themselves confronting the military might of the Ba`thist regime in the 1980s. It was also a course of action that seemed natural and honourable among those who joined and supported the active resistance organizations. Although they had to bear the cost of resistance, as they did on a devastating scale in 1988, they were also produced by and makers of the same narrative, sharing many of the same memories. Armed resistance in this context was thus more than a mere calculation of advantage, a weighing up of the pros and cons of taking up arms against an oppressive occupying power. It was part of a moral universe that made sense of collective existence.

Libya: From Demonstration to Armed Uprising

In February 2011 in Libya, the resort to arms by those resisting the regime of Mu'amar Qadhafi was not the product of long reflection on the strategic advantages of armed insurrection. It appeared to have been the direct result of the violence used by the forces of government against those Libyans who had originally voiced their protests peacefully. It was this response that triggered a series of events that were to culminate in an armed uprising and in NATO's military intervention on behalf of the rebels, backed by the UN Security Council. Initially, however, the protests had been vocal but peaceful and had not involved large numbers of people. Libyans were well aware of recent developments in Tunisia and Egypt, and there had been some attempt to encourage a 'day of rage' against all the many failings of the Libyan government. In most respects, these were very similar to those that had mobilized protesters elsewhere in the Middle East: government indifference, the brutality of the security forces and youth unemployment.

However, the initial protest began modestly on 15 February as a very local affair in the eastern city of Benghazi. It was here that a lawyer,

Fathi Terbil, had been arrested for having had the temerity to question the government's account of what had occurred fifteen years before when some 1,200 prisoners had been killed at Abu Salim prison in Tripoli. He was acting for the families of those prisoners, and his attempt to get an answer out of the authorities led to his arrest. The families and some of his supporters then converged on the police head-quarters demanding his release. At this stage, the crowd, swollen by others as it marched towards its destination, probably numbered no more than 2,000. Inevitably, anti-government slogans were shouted, as were calls for Terbil's release. Although he was released, the crowd refused to disperse, and the authorities responded with water cannons, tear gas and rubber-coated steel bullets. They also organized a counter-demonstration by supporters of Qadhafi who attacked the protestors with iron bars, stones and broken bottles, driving them away from the public buildings and into the surrounding side streets of Benghazi where running battles continued into the night.

In the following few days, thousands more demonstrators came out onto the streets not only of Benghazi, but also of many towns in the eastern provinces of Libya, as well as in Zentan south of Tripoli. They were protesting against the government, but also specifically against the brutality of the security forces. Taking their protests to police stations and security headquarters, the marchers were faced by live rounds that killed dozens and wounded many more. This only angered the protes-tors further, and there were reports of police stations being attacked and burned down in cities such as Dernah and Tobruk. In Benghazi, units of special forces and, it was rumoured at the time, contingents of merce-naries brought in by the authorities to suppress demonstrations were entrenched in the formidable Katiba barracks. From here, they directed their operations and their fire against the demonstrators. The latter, enraged but also emboldened, tried to storm the barracks itself, armed with little more than bulldozers, Molotov cocktails and 'fish bombs' – the explosives used locally to stun fish in the seas around Benghazi. Thanks in part to a determined suicide bomber, Mahdi Ziu, who drove his car into the gates and blew them up, the barracks fell. This led not only to the deaths of nearly all of its defenders, but also to the seizure of the arsenal it contained – and the demoralization of the government authorities in the city.[65] The result was that Benghazi and other cities of the east fell rapidly under the control of the protestors turned rebels.

By this stage, after four or five days of escalating protests, the increased violence of the security forces had already caused rifts within

Libya's armed forces and within the state administration. Increasing numbers of police and army units stationed in the east were crossing over to the side of the rebels, bringing their arms and expertise with them and effectively removing central government control from the eastern half of the country. In the west, public demonstrations in Tripoli had been suppressed, with the security forces using live ammunition to drive people from the streets and from the symbolic spaces they had tried to occupy, such as Green Square in the centre of the capital. Demonstrations and protests in other towns in the west where government control was less complete succeeded in either persuading officials and local security to join their ranks or ejecting them from the towns concerned, making them outposts free from government control.

Thus, to the east of Tripoli, protestors in Libya's third largest city, Misrata, managed to bring most of the city under their control, as they did to the west of Tripoli at Zawiyya and in the mountains to the south in the largely Berber towns of Zentan, Garian and Jefren. Sounding increasingly beleaguered, Saif al-Islam Qadhafi, one of the sons of the Libyan leader, made a rambling television speech in which he promised unspecified 'reforms', but also threatened the country with civil war, stating that 'Libya is not Tunisia or Egypt'. In many ways, this was true. The same spirit of protest against similar failings by their government might have fired up thousands of Libyans, but the regime had shown that civil protest would be met by ruthless force. By that stage, nearly 250 protestors had been killed in the streets of Libya.[66] Although some army units had defected as a result of being called upon to fire on the demonstrators, others had shown their loyalty to the regime. In some cases, commanded by sons of Qadhafi – Khamis and Mu'tasim – they began a military campaign to reconquer those areas of the country that had slipped out of government control.

Within the governing elite, as well as on the ground, people began to identify with one side or the other. Thus, less than a week after the demonstrations had begun, the minister of the interior, Abd al-Fattah Yunis, a long-time associate of Qadhafi and a member of the Free Officers' Movement that had overthrown the monarchy in 1969, declared that he was joining the '17 February Revolution'. He was to claim that the breaking point for him came when he was ordered to shoot down the protestors in the streets of Benghazi. Initially he told the forces at his command not to shoot to kill, and then publicly announced his defection to the side of the rebels, bringing with him most of the security forces stationed in the east of the country. However, he recognized that there were other military units – the Presidential Guard Brigade, the 9th Armoured Regiment, the Deterrence forces and the Khamis Qadhafi battalion amongst others – that would fight to the death to defend the regime.[67]

This determination became apparent in the weeks that followed. Having crushed the rebels in Zawiyya, where much of the centre of the town had been devastated by two weeks of fighting, army units loyal to Qadhafi laid siege to the towns in the Jebel Nafusa and encircled Misrata. They then began to advance eastwards, with their principal objective being the city of Benghazi itself. With tanks, artillery and aircraft, these forces were much better equipped and trained than the rebels and, as they rolled eastwards along the coast, they appeared to be unstoppable. In a conflict where military prowess alone looked as if it would be decisive and in which every new military success for the Qadhafi loyalists made defections from his inner circle less likely, the Libyan rebels stood little chance. Their plight was underlined by Mustafa Abd al-Jalil, leader of the National Transitional Council [al-majlis al-watani al-intiqali] (NTC) and until then minister of justice in Qadhafi's government. The NTC had been formed in Benghazi on 27 February to coordinate and defend the uprising. In early March, aware of the emerging idea in the EU states particularly of imposing a no-fly zone over Libya to limit Qadhafi's military capabilities, he called for Western military assistance: 'Everybody should know that there is no balance between our capabilities and Muammar Gaddafi's. He is besieging cities to ban people from leaving them'.[68]

The rebels and Qadhafi were engaged in a conflict that appeared to each side to be a zero sum game. Each recognized that the survival of the one was only to be bought with the destruction of the other. As one of the enthusiastic rebels in Benghazi, Taher Salem, acknowledged, 'It's him or us. By supporting the revolution we have signed our own death warrants, so now we have no choice but to fight until this is over'.[69] For his part, Qadhafi made this plain in a speech on 22 February when he said, 'we will not forgive. For anyone who undermines the constitution ... by force, or other means, the punishment is death ... Anyone using force against the authority of the state or committing murder will be sentenced to death'. In answer to the major demand of the resistance movement – that he should step down and leave the country – he retorted, 'I will not leave the country and I will die as a martyr at the end'.[70] The battle lines were clear, as was the ultimate aim of each side – but in the armed struggle, it seemed that Qadhafi's forces were more likely to prevail.

By the middle of March, the pace of their advance accelerated. One town after another on the road to Benghazi was recaptured by forces loyal to Qadhafi's government. The speed of the advance and the likely fate of the rebels, as well as of the inhabitants of the towns that supported them, also accelerated international moves to check the advance. Some advocated the tightening of sanctions and called on Qadhafi to step down. But for those involved in a fight for survival, it was clear that nothing short of armed intervention would rescue them. This was the position of the rebels' National Transitional Council. It had been recognized some weeks before by France as the official government of Libya and was listened to sympathetically by the UK and the United States. Its position was also endorsed by the Arab League. Unusually, the League declared that Qadhafi could no longer be considered the legitimate leader of Libya and called for a no-fly zone to be established immediately.

Qadhafi did not help his case by delivering a defiant speech claiming that his forces were on the verge of recapturing Benghazi and promising to hunt down the rebels 'street by street, alley by alley, inch by inch'. This had speeded up the UN Security Council's passage of Resolution 1973 on 17 March. It was proposed by France, Lebanon and the UK, and, when it came to the vote, five members of the Security Council abstained but none opposed the resolution. This called for an immediate ceasefire and an end to violence against civilians. It authorized member states to take 'all necessary measures . . . to protect civilians and civilian populated areas under threat of attack in the Libyan Arab Jamahiriyya, including Benghazi' whilst specifically 'excluding a foreign occupation force of any form on any part of Libyan territory'.[71] Within hours, NATO, eventually assisted by planes from Qatar and the UAE, began to enforce the no-fly zone. Ostensibly aimed at preventing Qadhafi's forces from using air power against the rebels, it also involved the destruction of Libya's air defences and its air force. The NATO campaign soon developed into sustained attacks on the armoured units that were threatening Benghazi, as well as on all command and control facilities throughout the territories still controlled by Qadhafi's forces.

In this way, the immediate military threat to the seat of the rebel government in Benghazi was lifted, and in the weeks that followed, NATO provided close air support for the rebel forces. This was effective up to a point. It was generally better at blunting attacks organized by units of forces loyal to Qadhafi than at enabling the rebels themselves to advance westwards. The formidable arsenal controlled by Qadhafi loyalists, but also the rebels' lack of training, comprising as they did large numbers of armed civilians backed by a minority of trained Libyan rebel soldiers, led to a series of indecisive engagements as the towns along the coast changed hands repeatedly. NATO air power did not appear to make much difference here. Nor did it do much initially to relieve the sieges of Misrata and the towns of the Jebel Nafusa in the west of the country. Military training missions were despatched by France and the UK to help stiffen the military capabilities of the rebels. However, the repeated bombing of the Bab al-Aziziyya barracks in Tripoli suggested that NATO was trying to bring a rapid end to the struggle by killing Qadhafi himself – a charge strenuously denied by the governments of the NATO member states. They claimed that they were merely targeting 'command and control' centres that allowed Qadhafi to threaten civilians. They were in fact lending the formidable military support of NATO to the goal that the rebels had set themselves: the overthrow of Qadhafi's regime.

Eventually, during the summer of 2011, the military balance began to tilt against Qadhafi's forces. Their military assets were being gradually destroyed by the attrition of NATO air strikes, as well as by the determination and increased competence of the rebel forces. This produced a series of sudden and even unexpected breakthroughs by the rebels in August, moving out from their successfully defended positions in the Jebel Nafusa south of Tripoli and from Misrata. Within a matter of days, they converged on Tripoli where they met ferocious but sporadic opposition, allowing them to capture and loot Qadhafi's own compound at the Bab al-Aziziyya barracks by 23 August. With the capture of Tripoli by the rebels, the Qadhafi clan split up and fled – some to Algeria, others south and east towards his provincial base near Sirte and yet others across the Sahara and into Niger. Despite the occasional defiant broadcast by Qadhafi himself, whose whereabouts remained unknown for some time, the regime had collapsed. Within a matter of weeks, the provisional administration of the NTC had installed itself in Tripoli and had begun the task of reconstructing the state. Finally, after the death of Qadhafi, captured and killed on the spot by the rebels as he tried to flee Sirte, Mustafa Abd al-Jalil, the head of the NTC, proclaimed the final liberation of Libya on 23 October. Libyans across the country noisily celebrated their emancipation, while, symbolically enough, the corpse of Qadhafi, as well as those of his son Mu'tasim and of his minister of defence, were put on public display in the meat-chilling room of a battered shopping centre in Misrata.

Resistance to Qadhafi's regime had begun as peaceful protest, influenced by events in Tunisia and Egypt, but also sparked by local resentment of the repression to which all Libyans were subject. Within days, however, it was transformed into armed resistance and open rebellion, brought about largely in reaction to the violence of the security forces against the original demonstrators. The government had first deployed police, armed with the usual riot control equipment, but had then organized violent crowds of 'supporters' to attack the protesters. This only served to enrage the protesters further and, in the face of this, within a very short time, lethal force was being used by special troops loyal to the Qadhafi clan. Each of these stages provoked an ever more infuriated and increasingly violent response from the protestors.

The regime's countermeasures also led to a split in the administrative and security establishment. Police and army units, as well as mayors and local councils, recoiled from the violence that the regime was willing to use to end the protests. Some refused to fire on the demonstrators – and there was poignant testimony to this in the burnt-out shell of the Katiba barracks where the bodies of executed soldiers were discovered. It was presumed that they came from the regular army unit stationed there. Others who were in a position to do so simply threw in their lot with the rebels, denouncing Qadhafi and all he stood for and pledging their allegiance to the '17 February Revolution'. Armed resistance had therefore succeeded in ending the rule of Qadhafi in the eastern provinces of Libya. Given the balance of forces, the rebels found it harder to overthrow his rule in the western part of the country. Nor could they defend the gains made without calling in foreign military intervention. The logic of war had taken over. A military stalemate developed. It was finally broken by the combined power of NATO's air forces and the courage and organization of the increasingly well-armed Libyan rebels.

VIOLENCE AND ITS SHADOW

Armed resistance of all kinds has been a familiar feature of political struggles across the Middle East for much of the past century. Given the ways in which the region has been invaded, battered and reconfigured by the armed forces of states from outside the region, as well as from those within, this should not be surprising. Violence is integral to the idea and the organization of the state. It may be seen as a legitimate instrument of state power, or it may be disguised beneath the mundane surface of the everyday administration of the state. However, where it has become the main instrument of power, it can make violent resistance an option and even a necessity. Those who have captured the state by force place themselves in a position similar to those who have occupied it by military conquest. The distance between them and those they rule can make them seem as alien as the foreign invaders that have rolled across the Middle East in its recent history. This was remarked upon in late 2011 when the Egyptian prime minister, Kamal el-Ganzouri, appointed by the ruling military officers of the Supreme Council of the Armed Forces (SCAF) in the face of mass civilian protest, tellingly complained that he was being shunned by other civilian politicians who acted as if 'they're meeting the high commissioner of the occupation'.[72] Given the growing suspicion of the role that the armed forces were trying to carve out for themselves simply by virtue of their possession of the means of violence, the analogy was an apt one.

Whether or not resistance becomes violent will depend upon a range of other factors. Military occupation and coercive rule may be the necessary conditions, but they are not sufficient. As the cases above have shown, it will be a combination of circumstances that will determine whether or not people take up arms to resist a power that is seen as illegitimate and oppressive. The perceived moral bankruptcy of established power, the resonance of violent narratives and experiences among the population, the opportunities created by the existence of social networks, the availability of arms and the vulnerability of the targets – all of these can influence the fateful decision to fight against generally overwhelming odds. It can also be provoked almost as a reflex of anger or self-defence by the violent behaviour of those in power. None of these conditions will necessarily combine in the same way everywhere, but each have played a role in Algeria, Palestine, Iraq, Syria, Libya and elsewhere in the Middle East.

The circumstances that combine to make violent resistance seem both practical and desirable are broadly similar in very different settings. But so too are some of the consequences. These shape immediate outcomes through the success or otherwise of the use of force. But they can also have an influence on longer-term trends. For instance, the strategic secrecy and lack of accountability of a resistance organization can transform it into a regime as oppressive as anything it sought to displace. Armed struggle can lead to a style of politics where violence becomes part of political practice. No longer confined to challenging hegemonic power, it expands to become the main qualification for being taken seriously as a political player. The violent resolution of political disputes thus becomes a norm, the outcome decided by a balance of ruthlessness, guile and firepower. This in turn makes any material assistance pragmatically acceptable, whether it is a political movement resisting the forces ranged against it in armed insurrection, in a civil war or under a military occupation. As the examples of Palestine, Lebanon, Algeria, Iraq and Libya, amongst others, have shown, this in turn can open up a new chapter of external intervention and uncertain domination.

It is for these very reasons that some have been wary of taking up arms, however despised and oppressive the power confronting them may be. Power, after all, is multidimensional. By engaging with only one of its facets – that which involves the threat or use of force – the project of resistance itself will not simply be incomplete but could be fatally flawed. It may succumb to the forces outlined above and be taken over by those who command and organize the armed force itself, growing ever more distant from the original driving impulse to resist oppressive power. This is not a necessary development, as some political pessimists have suggested. However, if the logic of 'clubs are trumps' is to be avoided in the aftermath of successful armed rebellion, then a concerted effort would be needed both to enable public participation in the control of armed force and to guarantee a politics of pluralism and rights.

This will largely depend upon the imaginations of the resistance, the human capacities of its leaders and activists and the circumstances of that moment in a country's history that would let a truly alternative form of power emerge from the armed struggle. Power may indeed grow out of the barrel of a gun, but there is more than one form of power. The experiences of armed resistance in the Middle East would suggest that those who have used the gun in the struggle for power need to think differently about power itself if they want to avoid the same fate. This underlines the importance of exploring alternative ways of resisting power, the commitments they demand of people, as well as the spaces they may open up for autonomous political activity in the Middle East as elsewhere. These will be the themes of the chapters that follow.

2

Contesting Public Space

Resistance as the Denial of Authority

RESISTANCE THROUGH NONVIOLENCE

On Tuesday 25 January 2011, groups of people began to assemble in Tahrir Square in the centre of Cairo, dwarfed at first by the huge open space and by the towering buildings that surround it, and hooted at impatiently by the usual maelstrom of traffic that circulates in and around the square. Gradually the numbers grew, to such an extent that they succeeded in blocking the traffic and attracted the attention of the authorities. The riot police were sent in to disperse them with tear gas and baton charges. They intervened not simply because the thousands that had now assembled were taking part in an illegal public demonstration, banned under the 'emergency laws' in force since 1981. It was also because this was a demonstration that was calling for the immediate overthrow of Husni Mubarak, the eighty-two-year-old president who was now in his thirtieth year of office – and who seemed ready to stand, virtually unopposed, for a further six-year term in September of that year. Shouts of *'Irhal Mubarak!'* [Leave Mubarak!] and *'Yasqut al-Nizam!'* [Down with the regime!] made it clear where the sympathies of the demonstrators lay.

At the same time, other groups of demonstrators assembled in front of public buildings across Cairo, chased by the police, but reassembling in ways the police found increasingly baffling and difficult to control. Meanwhile, thousands came out on the streets of Alexandria, Suez and a number of Egypt's other major cities chanting slogans against the regime, waving placards that proclaimed their contempt for the president and defying police efforts to clear them off the streets. Hundreds of arrests were made and the riot police laid into the crowds, whilst other, more sinister security forces dragged demonstrators away in unmarked cars to unknown but grim destinations. Nevertheless, the demonstrators remained and returned in even greater numbers after prayers the following Friday, effectively occupying Tahrir Square and using it as the platform for continual denunciation of the regime of Husni Mubarak. Indeed, their one repeated demand was that Mubarak should leave office and, until that happened, they vowed not to leave the square. Astonishingly, within two weeks they had achieved their objective: on 11 February, the president stepped down, handing over power to the SCAF.

In its organization, staging and momentum, as well as in its uncertain outcomes, Egypt's 25 January–11 February popular uprising shares many of the features of other similar uprisings across the Middle East. It was in some measure inspired by the success of the 'Dignity Revolution' (*Thawrat al-Karama*) in Tunisia that had caused the autocratic president Zine El Abidine Ben Ali to flee the country in the night of 14 January after a month or so of public protests and street demonstrations. Popular uprisings had taken place in very different settings and at different moments of their countries' recent political histories, but these events shared a number of features that illuminate key aspects of nonviolent political resistance and thus the nature of the powers that confront them. In particular, two principal aspects of power emerge, thrown into relief by the demonstrations, public protests and confrontations of the *intifadat* [uprisings]. The first is the importance of public space and the contest between government and opposition over its occupation. The second is the centrality of the performances of the political authorities to project and reinforce their own credibility – and the consequences that follow when that fails to overawe the target audience.

By resisting the ways in which government demands conformity through defiant, sometimes disorderly public behaviour and by challenging its control over space, opposition can make its cause and its presence felt. It gives the lie to the picture that the authorities wish to project of an orderly society, respectful of power and of the public institutions of the state. Public defiance in turn mobilizes growing numbers of people, giving them a shared language in which to voice their grievances and providing a framework for action that can change the balance of power itself. It is for this very reason that, across the region, political authorities have responded with ferocious violence against open forms of public defiance and resistance. This has often been brutally successful in buying time for an embattled regime. However, when brute force fails to intimidate, or only inflames the situation, swelling the numbers of those who openly reject the authority of the government, a serious realignment of power has followed.

THE OCCUPATION OF PUBLIC SPACE: THE RESISTANCE OF PRESENCE

The importance of space in organizing power and projecting authority lies in the fact that it is where the state shows its public face. Here, the daunting state institutions form the built environment of power, presenting an edifice of seemingly solid material weight. They dominate the cityscape, sometimes by their outward show of opulence and power, sometimes by the frank brutality of their construction. In all cases, these buildings, which are such a key part of the urban setting in the Middle East as elsewhere, are designed as both the repositories and the projections of power. Their façades suggest and hide the locations where key decisions are made, excluding but also affecting the public. In some cases, as in the notorious detention centres, intelligence headquarters and 'ghost houses' that dot Middle Eastern cities and their suburbs, they are also the places where people disappear to suffer the full force of state violence, emerging, if at all, broken by torture and confinement.

Even without this sinister overtone, such buildings can also be seen as places that the public is obliged to enter, on terms set by the authorities, in order to comply with the many regulations that govern their lives. Thus the magnificent and disturbing relic of the Nasserist state in Egypt, the Mugama` building in Cairo's central Tahrir Square, sucks in countless thousands of Egyptian citizens every day in pursuit of the permissions, authorizations and other documents that the state requires for a truly bewildering range of activities. As they trail from one floor to another, to a variety of offices and counters in search of the right stamp and official authorization, citizens are brought into material contact with the state in a way that reinforces the hierarchy of power. This is reproduced in varying forms across the Middle East.

It is also clear where citizens are excluded. Not only are the palaces and the offices of the ruling elite closely guarded zones, but so too are many of the nominally public institutions of the state, be they ministries, party headquarters or parliaments. In this, of course, Middle Eastern states do not differ much from states everywhere. Except in the most face-to-face, local communities, access to the sites of political decision making and power is bound to be restricted, whether for reasons of security, of confidentiality, convenience or custom. However, as in these other countries, it does mean that there are large tracts of public space 'in between', as it were, the built environment of the state. The streets, bazaars, squares and parks of towns and cities form the spaces that, in their layout, organization and policing, act as further extensions of state power. These restrict citizens' freedom of action and bring them under surveillance of various agents of the state – police and security forces, uniformed and in plain clothes, informers, public health officials, traffic regulators and others.

By the same token, these become the very sites of confrontation with state authorities. Precisely because of their accessibility and their open character, streets, squares and parks become the assembly point for those wanting to contest state policy and authority. They provide an opportunity for mass protest, but they also provide two key features of resistance to the official narrative of the state: space and numbers. First, they are the physical dimensions of public space – sites where the public in all its sociability and diversity is to be found. In theory, they are open to all, encouraging negotiation and interaction among fellow citizens. In practice, they have often become places where the state displays and enforces its own monopoly of power and decision. It is precisely this that invites resistance. The public spaces form a shifting frontier between state forces and ordinary citizens – a frontier constantly challenged by those asserting their own claims to decide for themselves how to use these spaces.

Thus the very existence of an assembly that is unauthorized, even forbidden by the state authorities, asserts the citizens' right to be there and to act as they, not the government, see fit. It is both a statement of physical presence and a demand for recognition of rights. In some circumstances, it may also contrast the highly visible, open assembly of the people in the streets and the more covert occupation by the government of the spaces where the exercise of power is hidden from common sight. Contestation can therefore take place on a number of levels, enhanced often by the symbolic resonance of the spaces themselves. This was the case of the Place des Martyres in Lebanon in 2005, or the attempts to converge on Shohada (Martyrs, formerly Jaleh) Square in Tehran in 2009, or the occupation of Tahrir (Liberation) Square in Cairo in 2011.[1]

But there is a further feature of mass demonstrations in the public spaces that normally form part of the state's network of surveillance and control. This is the striking aspect of numbers – that is, the numbers of demonstrators, protestors or those who out of curiosity swell the crowds occupying the public space. On a practical level, this can offer protection against individual retribution by authorities keen to deter people from attending. Of course, if the authorities are ruthless and determined enough, numbers may not be much of a protection, even if they do confer a degree of anonymity.

Equally important, however, are the messages for the authorities of a vast crowd assembled in a public space. It can represent, in its capacity to organize, to assemble, to produce speakers and platforms, a form of representation of the interests of the public that is denied by the government. This can be representation of one section of the population or of a visible, symbolically powerful cross-section of the public at large. Whomever it claims to represent, such large assemblies suggest a degree of organizing ability that has gone unseen by a state that claims to be ever vigilant and all powerful. This has the twin effects of declaring publicly that the state is incompetent, since it can no longer read its subject people, and of shaking the confidence of the security establishment itself.

Both of these effects were visible in Cairo in January 2011. Those who helped to coordinate the protests made good use of electronic means of communication – Facebook sites on the Internet, twitter, e-mails and text messages from mobile phones – that were beyond the capacity of the state authorities to monitor. It also seems that the organizers of the protest demonstrations, before they coalesced in Tahrir Square, had gained access to the security forces' plans for breaking up and suppressing street protests. This allowed them to lay a trail throughout the electronic surveillance systems that ensured the riot police were always at the wrong place at the wrong time. Perplexed by the nature of the apparently 'leaderless' protests, the security forces spent a great deal of energy and used a good deal of violence trying to look for and arrest the small leadership cadre that they believed had to be at the heart of this, as of all other demonstrations.

On the other hand, the very scale of the numbers that congregate graphically argues against the government's claim to speak for the people as a whole. This challenge to authority is made all the more powerful if such numbers can be called out repeatedly, growing each time they assemble, affecting more and more districts of the city or spreading throughout the country. They give the lie to the official version of social harmony and sufficient representation through controlled and vetted national institutions. Even where, as in Sana`a in February and March 2011, huge counter-demonstrations were organized by President Ali Abdullah Salih to give the impression of a groundswell of support that would dwarf the protests calling for his downfall, the effort can backfire. In this case, it led to serious clashes between the different factions, resulting in deaths and injuries on both sides and invalidating the leader's claim to be presiding over social order. As became apparent a few weeks later, the passions roused and their repercussions were beyond his control.[2] In all aspects, therefore, there is a politics of resistance – resistance to the restrictions and confines placed upon public space by the authorities that equates to resistance to the restrictive and unequal forms of power that stand behind the public façades of the state.

Intifadat al-safar in Iraq (1977)

The struggle to assert common ownership of space, resisting state encroachment, by displaying the kinds of numbers that suggest a hinterland of potential resistance to government authority, has also been associated in the Middle East with the concerns of particular communities. Thus the marches, demonstrations and upheavals that came to be known as *intifadat al-safar* [the uprising of the month of Safar] in Iraq in 1977 bear witness to the determination of a section of the Shi`i population to exercise their right to perform the pilgrimage to Najaf and Karbala that they saw as integral to their religious identity. This was both in explicit defiance of an official order banning such demonstrations, and went against the Ba`thist government's determination that they alone should control all representations of religious or ethnic identity.

In February 1977, tens of thousands of Iraqis converged on Najaf to march to Karbala to commemorate the martyrdom of Imam Hussein – the twentieth day of the month of Safar, being forty days after the death of Hussein on `ashura in the month of Muharram. They were responding to a call for communal observance of a religious rite that could only alarm a government that was both secular, but also unrepresentative. Furthermore, they were making that observance highly public, occupying the roads that linked the Holy Cities, reclaiming in effect the public space of the highway to demonstrate both their devotion and their defiance of the government prohibitions. It had a galvanizing effect on the villages through which they passed, leading thousands more to join the processions.

The numbers grew not merely because of feelings of piety. The very public gesture of defiance gave different sections of the population the chance to express their grievances. Many of these were very down to earth. For instance, people were angry at the government's discouragement of the religious tourism that was the lifeblood of the Holy Cities. Furthermore, many of the villagers were outraged by the lack of government compensation in the face of the prolonged drought that accompanied falling water levels in the Euphrates. In addition, students resented the intrusive and oppressive Ba`thification measures that were trying to impose ideological uniformity in education. The banners and slogans of the marchers did not initially have any explicitly political character. However, this changed as the march proceeded, with shouts of '*Saddam shil idak! Sha`b al-`Iraq ma yiridak!*' ['Saddam remove your hand! The people of Iraq don't want you!'] becoming more common. The very numbers of the marchers carried a powerful message of defiance – especially since it was known that the religious leaders who had encouraged the march were already under house arrest. Thus the tens of thousands who marched embodied the popular authority of these religious leaders, countering that claimed by the Ba`thist government and displaying the loss of that authority, at least for a significant segment of the population.[3]

For that very reason, the government reacted with great violence. Police opened fire on the demonstrators, provoking them to lay siege to a police station in an attempt to get hold of weapons. The government then sent in army units, but found that soldiers who had been sent to deter and block the marchers sometimes threw in their lot with the demonstrators. This brought down an even harsher response, with armoured cars and helicopters used to intimidate and disperse the demonstrators. Faced by the scale of repression unleashed by the Ba`thist government, the marchers had no option but to flee. Hundreds were arrested and, after summary trials, a number of the leading organizers were executed. In order to drive home the image of a government re-establishing its power and control, not only were these executions given great publicity, but the Ba`thist leadership dismissed those members of the party tribunal thought to have been too lenient in the sentencing. It then reconstituted the tribunal and sentenced a number of the remaining detainees to death.

Iran: From Demonstration to Revolution (1978)

The mass protests, marches and occupations of public space that occurred in Iraq in 1977, admittedly on a limited scale, were reproduced on a much larger and sometimes decisive scale across the Middle East in the decades that followed. In Iran, the protests and demonstrations, which became both the symbol and the catalyst of the Iranian revolution, had begun modestly in Qom in January 1978 but accelerated and expanded until, by the end of 1978, they were regular occurrences in all of Iran's main cities. They precipitated government collapse, the flight of the Shah and the paralysis of the security forces. Furthermore, they provided the environment in which the new revolutionary leadership was able to plan strategically and mobilize effectively to replace the old order.

Although often portrayed as having its origins in the Qom demonstrations of January 1978, the contest over public space in Iran between sections of the public and the Shah's regime had begun long before. There was the memory of the demonstrations and riots of 1963 that had led to hundreds of deaths and the expulsion of Ayatollah Khomeini. There were also the demonstrations, public shutdowns and protests that had taken place in and around the bazaar and the universities from 1975 onwards, accelerating towards the end of 1977.[4] Most important for the signal they sent out about the widening of public space were the concessions made by the Iranian government that same year. Court proceedings were opened to public scrutiny through the presence not only of defence lawyers, but also of representatives of the media. The ban on demonstrations was lifted, as long as they were confined to the campuses of Iran's universities. The authorities thought that this would allow students to indulge in symbolic forms of protest without affecting the wider stage of Iranian national politics, since they would remain barred from taking their protests into the streets of the towns and cities of Iran.[5]

The significance of the demonstration by religious seminary students in Qom in 1978 therefore was twofold. In the first place, it showed that the strategy of containment adopted by the Iranian government in its effort to limit the public space of demonstration was unworkable. Second, the rallying of these students to protest against the alleged insult levelled by the government press at the exiled Ayatollah Ruhollah Khomeini gave the demonstration a powerful alternative focus of authority. Given Khomeini's role in the 1963 protests, their defence of him had both symbolic and historic resonance, and further presented the government with the challenge of their presence.

The students were signalling to the government but also to conservative clerics that there was a section of the Iranian public that would use its voice and its numbers to protest against the direction of the Shah's government. As the procession of the students on 8 January continued into the next day, it attracted other members of the public in Qom, constituting a crowd of some 10,000 in the streets of the city by the evening. When the police tried to block the street and to clear the demonstrators, violence erupted. The police pushed back protestors then baton charged the crowd and eventually used live ammunition to fire over their heads. When that had only a temporary effect, the police fired directly into the crowd. Many were wounded and it is estimated that five people died. The authorities believed roughly twice that number had been killed and rumours soon spread throughout the country that more than 100 had fallen. By their presence on the streets, the demonstrators had forced the government to take notice of them and to devise a strategy that would meet their claims. In the short term, the government's strategy was to beat and shoot the demonstrators, driving them from the streets and, apparently, restoring order to the city of Qom. These actions represented a violent counter-demonstration, intended to deter further public demonstration and to ensure that public space should not escape from government control.[6]

Disconcertingly for the government, these measures did not end the protests. On the contrary, by killing demonstrators, the authorities themselves had allowed a different and equally dangerous space to be opened up, now under the exclusive control of the mobilized public. This was the emotionally charged space of the religious calendar, which ordained the fortieth day after a person's death as the day of commemoration and also, therefore, recalling the manner of the death itself. This was a powerful imaginative space, understandable to all Iranians and beyond the power of the state to determine. Of course, it also had a very physical manifestation in March as displays of grief and commemoration took the form of demonstrations in the streets of Tabriz in particular.

Here, the authorities had thought to pre-empt powerful collective commemoration by barring access to the main mosque in the city. This merely enraged the crowds that had assembled to mourn the fallen of Qom. The government's attempt to interfere in the religious and social space represented by the forty days of mourning meant that the unrest rapidly spread into the streets of the city. A full-scale riot ensued, with battles between police and demonstrators for possession of the streets, the looting and burning of banks, liquor stores and government buildings – a clear symbolic demonstration of how the power of the status quo was perceived. In the end, the authorities called in the army. It brought lethal firepower to bear, killing some thirteen demonstrators (the opposition alleged at the time that 500 had died) and placing tanks strategically throughout the town to symbolize the government's reclaiming of public space.[7]

Worryingly for the state authorities, the commemorative assemblies were no longer confined to the city of Qom but appeared in other cities across the country simultaneously. This meant a significant change in the weight of the message conveyed by the protests. They had moved from a protest amongst Qom seminary students who might have been expected to complain about something that touched 'one of their own' to a series of events that suggested the involvement of a much larger political public. The killing of demonstrators by government forces threatened a more widespread and intense struggle for public space and voice. This is precisely what developed. It was accelerated by the continuing use of violence by a government that did not seem to have realized that the terms of reference of the protests had radically changed.

As the months of 1978 wore on, they witnessed widening participation in protest marches and demonstrations. What had begun as protest demonstrations began to take on the aspect of political resistance. The demonstrators tried and in some places succeeded in resisting government attempts to remove them from the squares and streets of Iran's cities or to deter them from reassembling to establish 'rights of occupancy'. Cumulatively, the battles against the security forces bore all the hallmarks of a campaign that had the state on the retreat, either physically and symbolically in the spaces vacated by the security forces or politically in the concessions made by the government throughout 1978. It was also a campaign that was increasingly coordinated by various sections of the public, as networks of university and seminary students, mosques, labour organizations and political associations began to mobilize their members and affiliates across the country.[8]

By the late summer/early autumn of 1978, the aspect of determined resistance became more marked. It was not simply that the demands of the protestors, emblazoned across banners held high by the marchers or voiced in revolutionary songs, became more radical, calling for the overthrow, indeed the death, of the Shah. It was also due to the very scale of the demonstrations. They created a spectacle visible both to those on the spot and to a wider television and newspaper audience in Iran and beyond. This greatly enhanced the power of the demonstrations and correspondingly sapped the authority and thus the morale of those who still surrounded the Shah, as well as his foreign backers. As tens of thousands (in September 1978, this rose to some hundreds of thousands) processed through the streets of Tehran or occupied the city's squares, the spectacle of numbers gave the impression of a citizenry on the move, united in purpose, even if the political agendas of the participants varied enormously. But at this stage, it was the seemingly unified mass that was so powerful an image and a performance. It was here that the public spaces of Iran's cities, seemingly free of state representatives and now occupied by the demonstrators, became a stage for the show of successful resistance.

The question that arises, however, is what it was that led to successful resistance through civil disobedience and demonstration in 1978–9, causing the overthrow of the Shah, the collapse of the Pahlavi monarchy and the installation of Ayatollah Khomeini as the leader of an Islamic Republic. Charles Kurzman has reflected on why the events of 1978, triggered by a very local event, spread out to become countrywide defiance of and resistance to the power of the Pahlavi state. Similar events in 1975 (even in 1963, although the circumstances were somewhat more removed in time) did not trigger a mass movement of civil resistance, even though the conditions appeared to be much the same. His conclusion depends on an understanding of the ways in which developments in the years preceding 1978 had led to what can be called 'revolutionary optimism' among the leading activists of the civil protest and resistance movements. They took heart from the concessions made by the government. These suggested that the authorities recognized the potential of collective action, despite simultaneous use of systematic brutality that was wholly in character.[9]

In fact, the use of violence by the authorities was sporadic and often uncertain. It bore no relation to the systematic and ruthless response of the Iraqi government to the *intifadat al-safar* in 1977. Although hundreds were killed and thousands wounded in the course of 1978 across Iran, there appeared to be inconsistency and even hesitancy in the use of armed force to win back the public spaces. In part, this may have been due to indecision at the top, as well as to differences of opinion among the Shah's advisers. But it may also have been due to the realization that the armed forces themselves, made up largely of conscript soldiers, were an unreliable instrument in the contest for public space. Even with the declaration of martial law in the autumn of 1978, it became clear that the government's possession of overwhelming firepower would not let it escape from its predicament.

Concessions in the face of open protest added to the authorities' uncertain handling of the armed forces and gave heart to the demonstrators. As one of the students involved in the demonstrations was to say, 'There were so many people. If it was just a small demonstration, I didn't go. But those huge demonstrations – fear had no meaning then'. More poetically, another participant said, 'I was in the middle of the crowd . . . wherever I looked I saw people in this great wave as drops in the sea, and I too was in the sea of this immeasurable gathering of the people of Iran. There was no "I" there, we were nothing but "we"'.[10] The members of the public became the chief weapons of resistance, demonstrating by their voices and their bodies both their right to be recognized and their defiance of the authorities' coercive power, as well as their rejection of the government's moral authority. Sustaining this momentum meant keeping up morale and giving people the impression that their reclamation of public space was yielding results. This was one of the chief tasks of those who had a clear idea of the major political goal – the overthrow of the Shah. He had come to represent the main obstacle to all the futures that had hitherto been denied. However, as many who witnessed these events and participated in them have testified, until very late in the day there was little idea that the Shah would fall, let alone that this would introduce revolutionary change of the kind that transformed Iran in the years that followed.

Iran: The Limits of Mass Protest (2009)

For that reason, but perhaps also because of wishful thinking, there were many who saw in the mass demonstrations of June 2009 against President Ahmadinejad the beginnings of radical, even revolutionary, change in Iran. The protests that erupted in Iran in 2009, following the contested outcome of the presidential election of June that year, were marked by familiar rhythms, but as the participants discovered to their cost, they were unable to prevent the installation of Ahmadinejad in his second term as president. The margin of victory claimed by Ahmadinejad over his nearest rival, Mir-Hussein Mousavi, was too great to be accepted at face value and, as more evidence emerged, it was clear that electoral fraud on a large scale had been committed.[11] It was this sense of outrage at the 'stolen election' that drove so many Iranians into the streets to protest against the subterfuge practiced by the incumbent and his supporters.

In terms of visibility and mobilization, they had the advantage that in the weeks prior to the election tens of thousands had gathered, untroubled by the security forces. The squares and streets of Tehran and other cities had been filled by people prominently displaying the green-coloured clothing, armbands, headscarves and even face paint that had become the symbol of Mousavi's election campaign. The 'human chain' of his supporters, organized a few days before the election, stretched some fifteen miles – the length of Tehran's main north–south road, Valiasr Avenue. Linked by green ribbons, carrying placards and chanting songs denouncing Ahmadinejad, the chain brought traffic to a standstill and gave the participants the crucial feeling of being part of something much bigger than themselves.[12] When their collective power was apparently denied on 12 June, it was not surprising that they should have had the resources and, crucially, a sense of their own potential to overturn the fraudulent election results.

Rallies, marches and demonstrations of what came to be called the 'Green Movement' rapidly filled Iran's public spaces, especially in Tehran. They brought together the hundreds of thousands who had voted for Mousavi, or perhaps more accurately against Ahmadinejad, identifying themselves through their use of the colour green, now associated with a broad coalition of forces that was calling for reforms of all kinds within the Islamic Republic. As Zahra Rahnavard, Mousavi's wife, put it, 'People are tired of dictatorship. People are tired of not having freedom of expression, of high inflation, and adventurism in foreign relations. That is why they wanted to change Ahmadinejad'.[13] Encouraged by Mousavi's example, the demonstrators made it clear at this stage that theirs was 'rightful resistance' within the full meaning of the term.[14] That is, they were exercising their rights within the terms of the Iranian constitution. This recognizes citizens' right to assemble and to march freely, as long as there is 'no violation of the foundation of Islam'. Furthermore, Mousavi had immediately lodged an appeal with Iran's Guardianship Council calling for the results of the election to be nullified, due to massive electoral fraud. He had called on his supporters to continue demonstrating 'in a peaceful and legal way', and said that he had 'asked officials to let us hold a nationwide rally to let people display their rejection of the election process and its results'.[15]

The demonstrations of Mousavi's supporters were largely peaceful in intent and were meant to show the state, in the person of the Supreme Leader, Ayatollah Ali Khamenei, not only the depth of feeling against what had happened, but also its extent. It was thus presenting him and those advising him with the powerful image of an alternative public, more authentic and representative in the eyes of those demonstrating than the bogus public of the fraudulent electoral returns. The importance of this was not only symbolic. It was also strategically geared to influencing Khamenei's decision about whether or not to call for a recount, an investigation or even a rerun of the presidential elections. Thus the numbers mobilized to march through central Tehran, Tabriz, Hamedan, Rasht and other cities was a statement of support for the defeated candidates. It was also an implicit threat that in the eyes of millions of Iranians the authority of the president had evaporated and was capable of seriously damaging the authority of those who tried to keep him in office. This is indeed what happened over the course of the following year. It had already been apparent in the demonstrators' chant on hearing the scarcely credible election results, announced with improbable speed a matter of hours after the polls closed: 'The president is committing a crime and the supreme leader is supporting him!'

Precisely because these were the stakes, there was a determined effort by the police and security services to clear the main demonstrations off the streets, leading to running battles, as the protestors fought back with stones and bottles. Ahmadinejad, who was well aware of the potential impact of the demonstrations by Mousavi's supporters, organized vast demonstrations in support of his own victory, seeking to bring out hundreds of thousands as a way of showing that public space did not belong exclusively to his opponents. Inevitably, when the rival groups of supporters met, there were violent clashes, adding to fears in the political establishment for the stability of the Islamic Republic itself.

Nevertheless, in the game of numbers, Mousavi and the other defeated candidates succeeded in rallying hundreds of thousands of supporters who flooded the streets of Tehran, converging symbolically on Azadi (Freedom) Square on 15 June, the day after Ahmadinejad's rally. Thundering slogans like 'Who stole the election!', 'Give us back our votes!' and 'We are the People of Iran!' rang out together with 'Allahu Akbar!', as the very scale of the demonstration overwhelmed the security forces.[16] The Ministry of the Interior had banned all such rallies, but there was apparent restraint on the part of the police and the *basij* militia, at least until the end of the day when shots were fired and violence took place on the fringes of the otherwise peaceful crowds. Possibly the very numbers of demonstrators stretched the capacity of the security forces and even the government militia.

It has also been argued that the continued presence of large numbers of international journalists, in Iran to cover the election, inhibited the government, since it did not want to be seen at this stage as only able to deal with the protests with violence. However, it may also have been connected with Ayatollah Khamenei's unexpected decision to order an investigation into the allegations of electoral fraud. This came two days after he had already endorsed Ahmadinejad's victory – but they were two days filled by demonstrations, protests and riots trying to get him to reconsider. The announcement may have been a way of buying time in order to defuse the protests. Many of the reformists were in any case sceptical about the ability or willingness of the ruling establishment to support charges of electoral fraud. Nevertheless, it was certainly encouraging for those who had taken the risk of demonstrating publicly against the outcome of the election.[17]

If Khamenei's intention was to calm the situation, his announcement had a far from calming effect. On the contrary, the demonstrations and protests continued in much the same way, gathering additional numbers. In his first Friday sermon since the election, Khamenei not only suggested that the election had been free and fair, but also issued an only partially veiled threat against those who continued to protest on the streets. Having suggested that terrorists and malign foreign powers were behind the demonstrations and were taking advantage of them, he said, 'the responsibility for the consequences should be shouldered by those who are not putting an end to it. Thinking that by turning out onto the streets you can pressure the officials with your demands is wrong ... If there are any consequences they will directly affect the leaders behind the scenes'.[18] The unmistakable threat in his words seemed to give a renewed licence to the *basij* and other security forces who were now determined to use violence and intimidation to deter people from demonstrating. Predictably, perhaps, at the end of June, the Guardian Council announced that there had been no fraud and that the results of the election should stand. Hashemi Rafsanjani, who, as head of the Expediency Council, had shown himself decidedly lukewarm about Ahmadinejad's victory, seemed to have been persuaded to get back in line and publicly supported the judgment.

This applied to others within the ruling bodies who may have felt uneasy about the blatant fraud of the elections and were concerned about the implications of this for the stability of the country and the authority of the offices of the Islamic Republic. However, they were also fearful about the possible loss of their grip on power if it seemed that they were making concessions under the pressure of mass popular protest. Quite apart from concerns about the immediate outcome, it would have gone against the very principles on which the main institutions of the Islamic Republic were founded. These enshrined the idea that their superior position within the clerical hierarchy and thus their more perfect understanding of Islamic law would always be a more authoritative guide for the Islamic Republic than the changeable currents of popular opinion. To have conceded this point would have made them and their offices redundant. It was not surprising therefore that, having peered over the edge of the abyss, they finally rallied behind Ayatollah Khamenei, lending their support to his endorsement of Ahmadinejad's presidency.

The demonstrations continued, but the violence used against the largely peaceful marchers became more pronounced – *basij* and other instruments of state power, often in plain clothes to disguise their official nature, were used against them. By August 2009, more than 200 people had been killed in the street protests, and an unknown number died in custody. Several thousand had by then been arrested as the authorities moved against demonstrators, writers, bloggers and those they believed were leading and inspiring the protests. President Ahmadinejad was sworn in against a background of continuing protest and demonstration and, as in Iraq in 1977 or in Iran in 1978, the government had to make up the deficit in authority by the use of coercive and deterrent violence. This was made explicit on the streets as crowds were dispersed with tear gas, riot police and by the use of plain-clothes security forces, some with firearms, others with iron bars. This was essentially the counter-demonstration of the government, reclaiming the public spaces that had until recently been occupied by the protestors and making explicit the fate that awaited those who tried to resist or challenge it. The security forces could attack the demonstrators with impunity, even killing some of them in public view, whilst inflicting on those arrested further violence and humiliation within the walls of Evin prison and other detention centres – the nature of which soon became public knowledge.

Many who had joined these protests were not simply objecting to the fraudulent elections or showing their support for the main opposition candidate, Hussein Mousavi. The age, the social and demographic profile of many of the marchers and their own testimonies suggest that they were driven by a broad anger and frustration against the system of government under which they lived. Theirs was a form of resistance against a political order that they regarded as oppressive, interventionist and unaccountable. This became more evident in the demonstrations that took place in the latter part of 2009 and into 2010. Subverting the official rallies that were convened, for instance in September, to celebrate Quds [Jerusalem] Day, the protestors could assemble in large numbers legitimately. However, they would suddenly produce green flags and symbols, turning the gathering into a sea of green, holding up placards, signalling the opposite of the solidarity called for by the authorities. This was reinforced by slogans such as 'Neither Gaza nor Lebanon – my life belongs to Iran!', 'Whether in Gaza or Iran – death to tyrants!' or 'Idol-breaker Karrubi! Break the Great Idol!' (turning a slogan of the 1978–9 revolution that had urged Khomeini to break the power of the Shah to mean that Khamenei should be overthrown).[19]

Similar efforts to subvert the `ashura ceremonies and parades were met with open violence by the authorities and their armed auxiliaries, leaving nearly forty dead in days of rioting in December 2009. Once again, the continued resilience of the Green Movement caused the government to organize massive counter-demonstrations across the country, proclaiming an *intifada* for (Imam) Husain, and enlisting the support of some of the most popular chanters of religio-political stories to draw the crowds.[20] By February 2010, the government had perfected these techniques, and when it appeared that the protesters might try to make use of the anniversary of the 1979 revolution to come out on the streets in force, tens of thousands of government supporters were bussed in to flood Azadi Square and the surrounding streets. Meanwhile force was used to break up any gathering of Green Movement protesters, dozens were arrested and show trials were instituted for those accused of masterminding the demonstrations, often resulting in heavy prison sentences. At the same time, dissidents and would-be protestors were continually reminded of the price they might have to pay for open dissent. This was driven home to them by the assassination of figures associated with the opposition, by the hidden deaths and publicly announced executions of dissidents in Iran's prisons and by sermons like that of Ayatollah Ahmad Jannati, chairman of the Guardian Council, when he thanked the head of the judiciary for executing protestors and urged him to 'execute others if they do not give up such protests'.[21]

For many of the protestors, the very act of demonstration and de-fiance was an act of meaningful resistance, whatever the outcome. By transforming public space into a site of protest, and by subverting official ceremonies, they were showing the failure of the regime to intimidate them, let alone to win their allegiance. Both in terms of self-expression and in terms of communicating with their fellow citizens, they were laying the groundwork for an alternative vision for Iran, one that was a direct challenge not only to the power elite, but also to the practice and the legitimation of power in the Islamic Republic. However, this was no longer the representation of an alternative public, a suppressed majority that was finding its voice, as had been the case in the mass demonstrations of June 2009. Nor would this have an effect of equal power on the ruling elites whom the demonstrations were intended to impress. On the contrary, as the intentions of some became more radical, they found that they parted company from many of their fellow marchers, as well as from the more senior political figures who were seeking to use these events to their own political advantage.

These senior figures had no compunction about manoeuvring to limit the power of some of their rivals within the state apparatus, but they were not willing to see that apparatus overthrown. From this perspective, mass resistance through civic protest and demonstration was meant to be part of a game that would lead to realignments within the major institutions of the state. It was not meant to bring down those institutions. This makes the events of 2009 in Iran closer to the 'Cedar Revolution' of 2005 in Lebanon than to the events of 1978 in Iran itself. Some of the parallels with Iran's recent revolutionary past seemed to be strong in 2009, particularly during June and July, but the Green Movement possessed neither the momentum nor the growing sense of collective possibility that had been so powerful in 1978. Rather than collecting an ever larger coalition of forces, it had begun as a broad-based movement of protest concentrated against the presidential election but gradually shed numbers. The diversity of those involved became more pronounced, and the resilience and ruthlessness of the incumbent regime became clearer, limiting its effectiveness. The intent may have been to resist, but the nature of the object of resistance – the protean and divided state – had both encouraged the forms of direct protest and proved to be an elusive target, as well as one in which some elements of the resistance were themselves implicated.

Egypt: The Acceleration of Civil Resistance (2011)

The protestors and demonstrators who brought down President Mubarak in February 2011 had a more clear-cut objective, daunting as it was and improbable as such an outcome might have seemed only a few weeks before. During the remarkably short period between the initiation of mass protests on 25 January and the resignation of President Mubarak on 11 February, it became clear that two apparent strengths of the system were also its two major weaknesses when confronted by mass protest, civil disobedience and nonviolent resistance. The first was the security state's ability to dominate public space, reinforcing that dominance and the message behind it through public displays of power. The second was the focus of all eyes on the person of the president, again driving home the message that he was the fulcrum of the system, unrivalled and in command. In Mubarak's case, this was underlined by the fact that, in his twenty-nine years in office, he had not even appointed a vice-president, allowing only his son Gamal Mubarak to share some of the limelight as Secretary General of the ruling National Democratic Party (NDP) and potentially as his designated successor to the presidency.

The skill of those who started and organized the mass resistance to Mubarak's rule and the intimate familiarity with these aspects of state power by the millions of Egyptians who joined in these events meant that these strengths were turned into weaknesses. Both aspects had had such an impact on their lives, giving cause and focus to their protests, that they knew immediately how powerful it would be to reverse the process, physically capturing the streets and symbolically (as well as actually in some cases) turning the image of presidential authority on its head. Wael Ghonim, one of the many contributors to the movement that grew into and out of the campaign of nonviolent resistance, had started a page on Facebook entitled 'We are all Khaled Said' in 2010. This became one of the sites of mobilization and communication that fed into the protests in early 2011.

The site was named in memory of a young victim of the kind of public display of brute power that had been so characteristic of the Egyptian security apparatus. In June 2010, Khaled Said was seized in an Internet café in Alexandria by members of the security forces, brutalized in public and then dragged off to be beaten to death, his body dumped in a street shortly thereafter. It turned out that he had been investigating corruption in the police and was targeted as an example, the officers involved thinking that they could act with impunity to show who were the masters of the streets. In fact, the public outcry at this most blatant case of police brutality was such that an investigation was ordered, although, as always, it failed even to approach those who were really responsible.[22] Nevertheless, the case was all too familiar to Egyptians. Many of them had experienced the casual brutality of security forces who were only answerable to superiors for whom order was more important than the rights of the citizen.

Ironically, it was this very act that was turned into a symbol of an unbearable system. It also became a mobilizing technique, bringing together all those who had been on the receiving end of power of this kind. Although compiled after the fall of President Mubarak, a filmed representation of the key moments of the '25 January Revolution' – set to stirring music – significantly devoted its first few minutes to a succession of clips taken at different times and places of casual police brutality as anonymous Egyptians were slapped, punched, kicked and humiliated in public.[23] The potent symbolism of this was evident when, within the first few days of its launch in mid-January 2011, Ghonim's Facebook site had some 80,000 subscribers. It was calling for mass demonstrations to protest against the kind of regime that allowed this and other abuses of power to take place and selected the doubly symbolic date of 25 January as the day of protest. In this, it was not alone. Other individuals, groups and associations that had joined together to call for public demonstrations were also playing upon the significance of that date.

It was a national public holiday instituted by President Mubarak in 2009, ironically enough, to mark 'Police Day'. This had been intended to celebrate the heroism and self-sacrifice of the Egyptian police on the day in 1952 when some fifty Egyptian policemen had been killed in Ismailiyya by the British forces occupying the Canal Zone. For those contemplating protest, it was equally significant that on the day following the attack in Ismailiyya in 1952, there had been mass protests in Cairo against symbols of British domination – a day known as the 'burning of Cairo' that had in turn contributed to the collapse of the Egyptian monarchy a few months later.[24]

Whether those who hoped to encourage mass demonstrations in January in Egypt believed that their protests would bring about a result as dramatic as this is uncertain. What is certain, however, is the empowering belief that this might indeed be possible. On 14 January 2011, the Tunisian president, Zine El Abdine ben Ali, had been forced to flee the country with much of his family, after twenty-three years in office and only a few weeks of demonstrations and riots. These had begun in the poor south of the country, sparked by the desperation of Mohamed Bouazizi who had set himself alight in protest against his casual and callous harassment by the local authorities in Sidi Bouzid. This act had touched a chord amongst many Tunisians and had drawn increasing numbers into the protests, motivated not simply by their contempt for the police and the authorities in general, but also by their dire economic situation, the spectre of unemployment and the gross disparities of wealth between themselves and the ruling elite. At the pinnacle of economic wealth and political power stood the unmistakable figure of President Ben Ali who rapidly, therefore, became the focus of the protests.

Initially he ordered the state security forces to drive the demonstrators off the streets by any means necessary, but their violence only exacerbated the situation. Rather than deter and intimidate the protesters, it had caused riots to spread until they engulfed the streets of the capital Tunis, bringing with them the clarion call for the president to go. The riot police appeared unable to cope and even the more sinister and violent units of the Tunisian security apparatus could not make an impact, despite the numbers they killed. When the armed forces command told the president that the army would not use force against the protestors, it was plain that nothing now stood between him and the hundreds of thousands of Tunisians who had poured into the streets. It was then that he fled the country.

The images of this dramatic sequence of events were freely available in Egypt and the parallels were all too clear. There was a common range of very familiar grievances, and the events in Tunisia showed how the apparent strengths of an autocratic regime could be exploited to become its vulnerabilities. The peaceful occupation of public space, standing up to the violent response of the regime, the paralysis of the economy through strikes and walkouts, the relentless focus on the departure of the autocrat and the need to shake the confidence of the armed forces in his ability to manage escalating unrest – all of these elements had been brought together successfully in Tunisia and appeared to set an example for Egyptians.

One further aspect of the uprising in Tunisia was the absence of a single party or organization to direct and manage the resistance, or to tie it to a particular vision of the country's future. There had been co-ordination, but it was co-ordination that came out of local organizations and neighbourhoods, as well as from groups linked through electronic communications that eluded the authorities. Thus local branches of the Union Générale Tunisienne du Travail (UGTT), rather than the national leadership, had initially taken the lead in a number of provincial towns. Equally, neighbourhood organizations, both in poorer towns and quarters, had mobilized and emerged out of local associations. They in turn had linked up with students' groups and with lawyers' syndicates and other professional groupings in Tunis in particular. These many tributaries of a genuinely popular movement had known instinctively, like the ordinary Tunisians who poured into the streets, what sites to occupy and where and how to face down the kind of power represented by Ben Ali. They had after all experienced it in some form for most of their lives and knew intimately the techniques it had used to keep people in their place. A very similar process got underway in Egypt, where the apparent absence of an identifiable leadership cadre of the popular resistance movement was one of its strengths. The security state could only 'read' opposition activity in terms of leadership committees, secretariats and party organization. It was therefore blind when faced with the seemingly leaderless protests.[25]

In the days before the demonstrations of 25 January, at least three people set themselves on fire in Egypt, one near the Egyptian parliament and another on the roof of his house in Alexandria. There were reports of a further four such cases in other parts of Egypt, and although the motives of all cannot be verified, they seemed to convey the desperation that had marked the beginning of the Tunisian uprising.[26] The protests that erupted on 25 January did not spring from these acts of self-immolation, but they added to the atmosphere of exasperation and dissent. Rallies, demonstrations and protests were planned across the country, with particular emphasis on the major cities of Cairo, Alexandria and Suez, but with others planned for towns in Upper Egypt and the Delta.

In each city, the protests homed in on a range of different buildings and public sites associated with the regime, but also with aspects of Egyptian public life that had been curbed and repressed by the years of dictatorship. Thus, in Suez the ruling NDP building was surrounded and then set alight, police stations were besieged and the public spaces around government offices occupied. In Cairo, thousands converged on Tahrir Square, the central site of public demonstration in the shadow of the Mugamma` and with the NDP headquarters looming in another corner. But there were also protests and demonstrations outside the main court buildings and the journalists' union – public institutions central to the rights of Egyptians, but dominated and cowed by the regime over the years. In a tactic designed to baffle, outmanoeuvre and overstretch the security forces, many of the protestors kept up a mobile form of demonstration, dissolving and reassembling to create 'flash-mobs' across the city that the riot police found difficult to track, let alone to prevent or to suppress.[27]

Contributing to all this activity and providing much of the mobilizing power by word of mouth and electronic communication was a range of loosely linked but like-minded groups. They included student and professional groupings, football supporters' clubs who combined with political activists associated with organizations such as Kifaya (The Egyptian Movement for Change), the Ghad Party, the much more extensive youth wing of the Muslim Brotherhood, the communists, as well as with groups that had emerged out of earlier protests, such as the April 6 Movement – more of a network than an organization. They were joined by unofficial labour unions and by activists working independently of the state-sponsored official Egyptian Trade Union Federation. There was some co-ordination, but the nature of the protests and demonstrations was such that they were all acting more or less in unison. They were pursuing similar objectives by similar methods and were aware, through years of encounters with the power that confronted them, of the nature of that power, where it could be most dangerous but also where it was vulnerable. As in Tunisia, thousands of Egyptians who were drawn into the protests shared these same experiences and thus were receptive to the calls to assemble and to vent their anger at the regime.

As the novelist Alaa al-Aswany noted when he went to address some 30,000 assembled in Tahrir Square on 25 January, it was the youth of the crowd that impressed him, seeing young people from a variety of backgrounds, but all sharing the same dismal prospects of unemployment and marginalization whether they were university graduates or not. The slogans 'Down with Husni Mubarak!' and 'The People Say Out with the Regime!' rang out across the square, encapsulating for many what needed to change before anything else could be expected to improve people's lives in Egypt.[28] In the words of organizers and participants alike, Mubarak and his circle, having ensured their exclusive control of Egypt for the previous thirty years could not now escape the responsibility for the 'torture, poverty, corruption and unemployment'. These were the visceral words used to focus the demonstrations of 25 January, announced on a Facebook site and in thousands of pamphlets. It was the message that was proclaimed with increasing vehemence as the protests intensified, making the departure of Mubarak the single, unshakable demand of the civil resistance movement, around which it could coalesce. It had immense symbolic power as well as potential repercussions for a political order that had been constructed around his person.

For that very reason, the authorities hit back ferociously, sending in riot police armed with tear gas, rubber-coated steel bullets and water cannons, as well as plain-clothes security officers who used iron bars and clubs in an effort to beat the demonstrators into submission and disperse them. In the first day, more than 800 were arrested and some four people were killed, three of them in Suez where the fight for the streets and the torching of the NDP headquarters was met by ferocious violence. However, worryingly for the authorities, the demonstrators held their ground, or melted away and reformed in other places, leading to running battles during the next few days that paralysed the centres of the major cities. Huge quantities of tear gas were used and serious violence inflicted on the protestors who had assembled outside court buildings, hotels housing foreign journalists and party headquarters. It made little impression, since the protests were gathering pace and affecting large parts of the country. Practical advice on how to organize civil resistance and stand up to the riot police was meanwhile being spread by photocopied pamphlets, through the Internet and by e-mail. It advised people on what to wear, how to counteract the effects of tear gas, how to push back against the containment tactics of the police, as well as how to assemble for demonstrations, how to occupy buildings and how best to focus slogans for maximum effect.[29]

All of this came into play on Friday 28 January, declared to be 'The Day of Fury and Freedom'. Across Egypt, hundreds of thousands of protestors turned out, met by baton charges, tear gas, rubber-coated steel bullets, water cannons and birdshot in Cairo, Alexandria, Suez and other major cities. The security forces, both uniformed riot police and plain-clothes officers, flooded the streets, squares and bridges in a graphic and unmistakable struggle with huge numbers of demonstrators for the occupation of public space. The deterrence of everyday power had failed and open violence was now used instead. Across the country, possibly hundreds were killed, thousands wounded – many of them blinded by the birdshot used by the police – and hundreds arrested. Nevertheless, in Mansoura, Damietta and in Cairo itself, the headquarters buildings of the ruling NDP were looted and set ablaze, as were countless police vehicles. By the afternoon, it was clear that the police were unable to contain or control the hundreds of thousands who were out on the streets, let alone to prevent more from joining them in the centres of the cities. In Cairo, for instance, the relentless press of numbers, despite the violence of the security forces, won the battle for Qasr al-Nil Bridge, enabling hundreds of thousands to cross from the west bank of the Nile to the east and opening the way to Tahrir Square. Towards the end of the day, the police and security units were exhausted, losing heart and energy, and their numbers seemed to dwindle.

It was then that two significant developments took place that were to have a bearing on the developments that followed: the Egyptian army appeared on the streets and Mubarak made a brief announcement on TV that he was sacking his government. The army's show of force as military vehicles took up position across Cairo provoked an ambivalent response among the protesters. Some feared it was a prelude to a violent and bloody struggle for the streets, and a tank and two scout cars that rolled into Tahrir Square were promptly attacked and set on fire by the protesters, although their crews were rescued. Others, however, saw the army's arrival as a hopeful move, recalling the part played by the armed forces in Tunisia when their commanders made it clear that they were not going to fire on their fellow citizens. This had tipped the balance and caused President Ben Ali to relinquish power and flee the country.

Similarly, there were those in Egypt who saw military intervention as a signal that the normal apparatus of repression had failed and that another game was afoot. Already the slogan 'The People and the Army – One Hand!' was being heard and seen on placards. This was voiced with redoubled strength after Mubarak's brief television appearance that evening in which he announced that he was dismissing his government, pledging improbably that the new government would 'tackle unemployment and promote democracy'.[30] In response, tens of thousands surged onto the streets, in defiance of the curfew proclaimed by the authorities. They called en masse for the resignation of Mubarak himself.

By now, some eleven of Egypt's twenty-eight provinces were gripped by mass protests, and the army moved into both Alexandria and Suez where the police force had more or less given up trying to preserve order. In fact, during the next twenty-four hours the police – even the ordinary police officers responsible for traffic and neighbourhood patrols – more or less disappeared from the streets of Egypt's major towns. This bizarre move left Egyptians apprehensive about the security of their homes and premises. However, it also compelled them to organize themselves and to form neighbourhood watch committees to ensure public security. It was thought to have been an attempt by the Ministry of Interior to impress on Egyptians what things would be like in the absence of the reviled police forces. It might also have been intended to cause the thousands of demonstrators to rush back home to guard their own interests against unspecified looters. If so, the move backfired spectacularly.

As the curfew continued to be disregarded by the thousands on the streets, Mubarak made a series of moves that more or less acknowledged that he was now wholly dependent on the armed forces for his survival in office. The police and security establishment that had been so much part of the edifice of his regime had apparently disintegrated in the face of the power of sustained civil resistance. The kind of power that they represented was now inadequate to the task of recapturing the streets, squares and public spaces of Egypt. Marking this transition, Mubarak finally appointed a vice-president, Omar Suleiman. A military officer who had been one of the most powerful men in the country as head of the Egyptian General Intelligence Service since 1995, he was not a reassuring figure if the hope was for reform. The slogans of the protestors soon linked the names of Mubarak and Suleiman in unflattering ways.

Nevertheless, his appointment, together with the appointment of another general, Ahmad Shafiq, as prime minister and the dismissal of the hated minister of the interior, Habib al-Adly, showed the public that a serious shift in power had taken place at the top – a shift caused by their own efforts and by their ability to resist the intimidation and violence that had been so much part of the authorities' usual reaction to any kind of protest or opposition. Some argued that nothing less than a military coup d'état had taken place and that Mubarak, from this point on, was to see authority draining from him, even in his inner circle. This meant that, although the focus of the demands of the protestors was still the president himself and the need for him to go, the real contest was now between them and the armed forces. His dismissal was to be the test of whether the people and the army really were working in harmony as the slogans rather hopefully suggested. Continued mass demonstrations faced the armed forces with a direct challenge for the repossession of public space in Egypt.

Initially it seemed that the armed forces were going to take up that challenge in earnest when, the very next day, tanks rolled into the centre of Cairo and other cities, and, incongruously, F-16 fighters flew low along the Nile and buzzed the assembled thousands in Tahrir Square.

Despite this impressive show of firepower, it was evident that, on the ground, it was numbers that counted. The tanks were blocked by a press of bodies that they could not clear and did not choose to kill. The buzzing of the square was treated with derision as an empty gesture and, encouraged by the dismissal of the minister of the interior, hundreds converged on the nearby building of the ministry of the interior where police and intelligence officers opened fire, provoking the firebombing and the eventual evacuation of the building.

In the days that followed, the army, although circling the square and guarding other public buildings across Egypt, showed no inclination to shoot down the protestors. On the contrary, as tens of thousands converged on Tahrir Square, the soldiers were visibly relaxed both there and when faced by huge demonstrations in Alexandria, Suez, Mansoura and Damanhour. When the armed forces high command then announced in the evening of 31 January that it would not use force to silence the 'legitimate' demands of the people, it gave heart to all those who had taken the still risky step of defying police and military authorities to make their point. As one of the protesters said at the time, 'People have lost their fear' and the morale boosting effect of this could hardly be overestimated.[31]

On 1 February, a week after the original demonstrations, some two to three million people came out on the streets across Egypt, reclaiming public space and showing their defiance with their bodies and with their voices – chief among the slogans, blazoned also on banners, was the one word '*Irhal!*' [Go!], repeated endlessly. It was estimated that nearly a million crowded into Tahrir Square, the site that had become the symbolic epicentre of the uprising. The international media relayed the images of this vast sea of people across Egypt and throughout the world, while countless mobile phones captured this spirit of defiance and solidarity and communicated it to other towns. The Square itself had become a focus not simply of protest and demonstration, but also of debate, entertainment and sociability. Foodstalls had sprung up, as had medical stations, debating circles, tents and shelters for those who stayed there the night – one labelled 'Freedom Motel' in Arabic and English – walls of newspapers and freely distributed pamphlets. In the words of the novelist Ahdaf Soueif, who wrote regularly about her participation in the Tahrir Square demonstrations, 'We have come together, as individuals, in a great co-operative project'.[32] For the protestors, the key was not to lose momentum, even as shifts began to take place at the summit of the state. As a member of the April 6

Movement, Israa Abdel-Fattah said at the time, 'We don't want life to go back to normal until Mubarak leaves'.[33]

This was all the more necessary since Mubarak had announced that he would be retiring in September 2011. Furthermore, the new prime minister was quoted as saying, 'Everything is subject to amendment, without limits', and the vice-president had initiated a dialogue with some representatives of the protest movements.[34] The danger was that the momentum of protest and resistance would be lost, since concessions such as these might be enough to persuade some that the principal goals had been achieved. In these circumstances, it could prove harder to repeat the massive turnouts that had been achieved so far. Ironically, the next move by elements within the regime to end these protests by using extreme violence had exactly the opposite effect and re-energized the demonstrations.

On 2 February, thousands of alleged 'Mubarak supporters' converged on Tahrir Square armed with iron bars, clubs and stones, and launched a violent assault against the thousands camped in the square. The soldiers surrounding the area evidently had orders to let them through, and this allegedly spontaneous demonstration of loyalty to the president fell upon the protesters, using horses, even camels in a disorderly charge aimed at driving people from the Square. The demonstrators fought back, however, and running battles raged in and around the Square for some hours, costing the lives of at least five people and inflicting injuries on hundreds more. Eventually, the occupiers of the Square fought off their attackers and set up defensive barricades. They also captured a number of their assailants and found that many of them were members of the security police in plain clothes or else were civil servants, bussed in to put on a display of loyalty to a faltering regime. It was a tactic that misfired and obliged the prime minister to apologize the next day for the violence, declaring that it was a 'fatal error' that would now be fully investigated.[35] As if to make the intentions of the new military masters plain, army vehicles formed a protective barricade between the two sides and then moved against the pro-Mubarak demonstrators, clearing them from the overpass from which they were threatening the occupants of the square.

This turn of events re-energized the protests. People demonstrated their outrage at the methods used by the regime, showing that they were determined to maintain their protests on a scale as great as or even greater than before. The Friday following was designated as 'the Day of Departure', and vast numbers crowded into Tahrir Square but also came out in their hundreds of thousands onto the streets of Alexandria, Suez, Port Said, Rafah, Ismailiyya, Zagazig, al-Mahalla al-Kubra, Aswan and Asyut. The length and breadth of Egypt, possibly millions of people reclaimed public space in Egypt's cities, showing both their contempt for Mubarak's regime and the scale of the problem facing any authority that might try to stand against this tide of popular feeling.

In this, they were directly addressing the military high command. Its main representative, Field Marshal Muhammad Hussein Tantawi, the long-serving minister of defence, made a point of visiting Tahrir Square, ostensibly to speak with the soldiers, but also to be seen to talk to some of the demonstrators. The prime minister then told the BBC Arabic Service, 'In effect, the president has stepped down already. We need him during these next nine months'.[36] However, it was the intention of the protest movement to ensure that Mubarak was precisely the person that the military authorities did not need, and that he would come to be seen as a liability. In doing so, they were aware not only of the differences within the military establishment, but also of the increasing nervousness of the military's main backer, the United States. The mass demonstrations, the international press coverage and the increasing numbers of signs that appeared in English – such as the ubiquitous 'Game Over' posters – were aimed at the security establishment of the state, but also at their American backers. President Obama had begun to talk openly of the need for an 'orderly transition' amidst rumours of American efforts to secure an immediate transfer of power from Mubarak to a military triumvirate.

For this very reason, as well as for his long association with President Mubarak and the key role he had played in the national security state in Egypt, Omar Suleiman was deeply mistrusted. It was not surprising that his efforts to negotiate with some representatives of the protest movement eventually stalled. He was unwilling to grant most of their main demands, chief amongst these being the immediate resignation of his mentor, Mubarak. However, the demonstrators showed their skill in maintaining not only the spirit of resistance, but also the spirit of organized cooperation in Tahrir Square and across Egypt. Local organizations had come into their own and were beginning to show that the problem could no longer be seen as a 'security problem' to be dealt with accordingly.

On the contrary, Tahrir Square became a symbolic and powerful image, but also a mechanism of popular protest. It was something akin to a popular assembly in constant session. During the day, the numbers swelled to hundreds of thousands, falling away during the night to a few thousand – sufficient to occupy the key centre and approaches to the square and sleeping within the treads of the army vehicles to ensure no sudden moves by the military to clear the square in the middle of the night. A stage had been erected at one end of the square, allowing a variety of people to address that part of the crowd that was interested, and a large white sheet at the back provided the screen on which important televised broadcasts could be projected. It was also clear that it would be here that any deal hammered out with the vice-president would have to gain approval by acclamation. Unless it satisfied the main demands common to most of those present – the immediate departure of Mubarak, the dissolution of parliament, the release of all political prisoners and the repeal of the emergency laws that had been in force since 1981 – it would not stand a chance of acceptance.

Maintaining this mechanism was a large cross-section of Egyptians. Factory workers, shopkeepers, members of all sections of the middle class, graduates and the unemployed assembled regularly in the square. They were buoyed up by the knowledge of what they had achieved simply by standing up and occupying public spaces, forcing the authorities to take them into account. They took strength from the entertainments, discussions, performances and chants that found their own rhythm and gave the impression that the whole of Egyptian public life was represented in the square. Symbolically and powerfully, Christians and Muslims linked arms to signal their solidarity as Egyptians, taking turns to guard the others while they prayed. Under a banner proclaiming '*Shaikh wa-qasis li-yarhal al-ra'is*' ['shaikh and priest [together] for the departure of the president'], Muslim and Christian Egyptians called for the fall of Mubarak. One group of young men, carrying a box to represent Mubarak's coffin, jogged back and forth across the square amidst the press of people, chanting slogans against the regime. Meanwhile, hanging from lampposts in the square were large effigies of the president and others associated with his rule. Graffiti calling for the downfall of the regime were sprayed not only on walls, but also on some of the military vehicles where no effort was made to scrub them off. As one of the participants, Ahmad Mahmoud, told a foreign correspondent, 'I will come every day until he leaves because now I know we have won ... When we stopped being afraid, we knew we would win'.[37]

Despite the relatively relaxed attitude of the armed forces, the vulnerability of so many people gathered in one place meant that there was a need to maintain the momentum beyond Tahrir Square. Thus, at the time of the largest demonstration yet in the square, on 8 February, there were similarly large demonstrations at some twenty-five other sites across Egypt, as well as the increasingly visible participation by the labour unions at key strategic sites, in transport, the canal cities, the cotton mills and the steel industry. The vice-president vainly urged everyone to return to work and to bring the crisis to an end. Unwisely, he accompanied this with a veiled threat to impose martial law and stated, 'We don't want to deal with Egyptian society with police tools'. In fact, this was already happening. Increasing numbers of people identified in some way by the authorities as activists were being arrested and interrogated by the army.[38] However, this only widened the scope of the activities. The crowd moved on the Egyptian parliament made it clear that this was to be another target. More importantly, increasing numbers of workers came out on strike in sympathy with the demands of the protestors, paralysing the Egyptian economy. The stock market remained closed, and soon bus drivers, lawyers, textile workers and other unions were joining in.

Faced by this solid wall of protest, the military acted. In a move reminiscent of coups d'état across the Arab world in the twentieth century, the SCAF (meeting under the chairmanship of Field Marshal Tantawi but conspicuously in the absence of President Mubarak) issued 'Communiqué Number One' [*bayan ruqm wahid*] on 10 February. However, instead of declaring martial law, it asserted the legitimate rights of the people and stated that it would remain in continuous session 'to protect the nation and the achievements and aspirations of the great people of Egypt'.[39] It was then announced that President Mubarak would make a statement that evening. This created a fever of anticipation as hundreds of thousands gathered across Egypt, believing that this was going to be the moment when Mubarak finally capitulated and relinquished the presidency. They were to be disappointed. When he appeared on television, Mubarak reiterated that he had no intention of standing down, but would instead be handing certain powers to his vice-president. The vice-president then appeared and told everyone to go home and go back to work – and not to listen to foreigners, echoing Mubarak's suggestion that the demand for his resignation was instigated from abroad. These performances sealed Mubarak's fate, as well as that of the vice-president.

Across Egypt, there were calls for the largest ever demonstrations on the following day, Friday 11 February. People were outraged by what they had just heard. Powerless to prevent this, the army units on duty at public buildings found themselves surrounded and outnumbered by hundreds of thousands of their fellow citizens. The protestors isolated the Egyptian Radio and Television Union (ERTU) building in Cairo, staged a sit-in outside the presidential palace and converged in their thousands not only on Tahrir Square but, across the country, on all the public spaces that had formed so much a part of the previous weeks' protests. The military council saw that it was powerless to counter this mass movement and met in emergency session. Within a couple of hours, Mubarak had flown with his family to his villa in Sharm al-Shaikh, and in the afternoon the vice-president appeared on television to announce in the briefest of possible statements that President Mubarak had relinquished the presidency and had handed over power to the SCAF, headed by Field Marshal Tantawi. This was now the supreme executive authority in Egypt. Celebrations broke out across the country and a great shout went up in Tahrir and elsewhere. It summed up the sense of achievement of those who had taken part in this massive demonstration of popular civil resistance, unparalleled in Egypt's history: 'We held our ground. We did it'.[40]

It was indeed an extraordinary outcome. However, as many of those who took part realized, the resignation of the president, dramatic as it appeared, was just the beginning. The real challenge lay in trying to translate the kind of popular power seen across the cities of Egypt during these few brief weeks into the more fundamental change that so many desired. They were aware that Tantawi and others on the SCAF were themselves clients and long-time associates of the departed president and strongly suspected therefore that they would not willingly oversee radical changes in the dispensation of power. Throughout 2011, therefore, there were repeated re-occupations of Tahrir Square and public demonstrations in other Egyptian cities. These were never to be on the scale of the demonstrations of January and February, but they often brought large numbers of people out into the streets to make it clear to the SCAF the scale of public displeasure at delays and apparent reluctance to put on trial many of the leading figures of Mubarak's government, including the president himself and his son. In the absence of a parliament, the elections for which were repeatedly postponed, taking place finally in the period November–January, it was almost as if these crowds symbolically represented the people of Egypt as a whole.

Naturally, the momentum could not be sustained on a continuous basis, not least because of the inevitable difficulties faced by ordinary people in trying to combine this with their everyday lives. It also became clear that different political agendas and causes were enthusing different sections of the Egyptian public. The original focus on the removal of the president became more blurred once he had resigned, and other issues relevant to Egypt's future began to create differences of opinion. This could still be mobilized, as in April 2011, when the original coalition of forces returned to Tahrir Square to demand the immediate trial of the fallen president and his associates. However, it was harder to sustain, for instance, in late June 2011, when tens of thousands, rather than hundreds of thousands, came out to protest about the failure to prosecute security officers responsible for the deaths of nearly 800 Egyptians in the uprising of January–February. The fact that nearly 1,000 were injured in the two days of protest that followed indicated that the SCAF felt more confident about its ability to use force when the target was the security state itself. This was even more vividly illustrated at the end of July when thousands of demonstrators again assembled in Tahrir Square for a protest march to the ministry of defence. They were not simply confronted by solid ranks of soldiers who blocked their way, but were attacked with great violence by *baltagiyya* [thugs] who came at them from all sides, armed with rocks, iron bars and knives.[41]

The attempt to protest at the methods and the intentions of the SCAF provoked mixed feelings in Egypt. Although it was mistrusted by many as an authoritarian hangover from the old regime, others saw it as the guarantor of order and the body that would ensure and oversee the forthcoming general elections. This was certainly the message being relayed by Egypt's state media. They had flirted with the new liberties in the immediate aftermath of the fall of Mubarak, but reverted to being the mouthpiece of the supreme executive power in the state within a matter of weeks. It was partly in response to this that Coptic Egyptians assembled in their thousands, joined by hundreds of their fellow citizens, to demonstrate outside the Egyptian state broadcasting authority building in Cairo in early October. They were protesting at both the SCAF's failure to secure Coptic churches from attack (several had been burned down in the previous weeks) and at the biased coverage by the state media. The security forces, including the military, reacted with extreme violence, enlisting the support of dozens of armed thugs, portrayed by the state media as 'concerned citizens'. The demonstrators were attacked and dispersed, leaving some twenty-seven people dead and hundreds wounded.[42]

These events only redoubled the mistrust and resentment of many in Egypt at the way in which the SCAF was behaving – resentments that increased in the run-up to the first round of the Egyptian general elections in November 2011. However, it was then that the SCAF overstepped the mark. It tried to pre-empt the constitutional debate by proposing a measure that would limit democratic oversight of the armed forces and possibly give them a veto on the forthcoming constitution. When combined with the realization that SCAF's timetable for its hand over of power to civilian authorities would not take place until as late as 2013, after the scheduled presidential elections, this brought hundreds of thousands of Egyptians back into Tahrir Square and into the main squares of Alexandria and other cities on 18 November.

Possibly hoping to prevent the mass assemblies that had been so powerful earlier in the year, the security forces – riot police backed by military units – moved rapidly into position and used extreme violence against the protestors. This caused dozens of casualties in the first few days, but only served to bring more people out into the streets. In Cairo, the protestors tried to storm the building of the ministry of the interior, still the seat of the most repressive elements of the regime. The slogans now called for the resignation of Field Marshal Tantawi and of the SCAF. Running battles developed, with the rocks and Molotov cocktails of the demonstrators being met by rubber-coated steel bullets and birdshot fired into their faces by the security forces, as well as clouds of CS gas – a stronger version of the tear gas used earlier in the year. Meanwhile snipers took up position near the ministry of the interior, firing at those who tried to approach. Within three days, nearly fifty people had been killed. The civilian government resigned, and it seemed to many in the square that, dangerous as the situation was, they were finally coming close to completing the job that they had begun in January. In the words of one of the demonstrators, Mai Adly, who was reporting on events, 'People have come down from their homes to join us; they removed the head once and now they are back again to strike down the body'.[43]

However, SCAF remained in power and eventually the demonstrators dispersed, even if a small number retained a token presence in Tahrir Square. Although the demonstrations had brought hundreds of thousands out in sympathy, they had also failed to ignite the kind of countrywide uprising that had been seen earlier in 2011. In part, this may have been because the image of the armed forces, enhanced by the state media, was still relatively positive for many Egyptians, despite the fears of others. But it was also due to the fact that one of the main demands of the protestors – the postponement of the imminent general elections – found little sympathy around the country. On the contrary, many who might have shared the mistrust of the authoritarian state nevertheless believed that it was imperative to set the electoral timetable in motion, especially when SCAF made a concession by agreeing that presidential elections would take place in June 2012. This appeared to many, especially to the Muslim Brotherhood and other Islamist parties that hoped to make substantial gains in the forthcoming elections, the best way of ensuring an early hand over to civilian authority.

In this way, the demonstrators of Tahrir and elsewhere in November, as well as in December 2011, discovered the limitations of mass protest. It was not simply that their numbers were never as great as they had hoped or that the military authorities were able and willing to use ferocious violence against them, seemingly with impunity. It was also that the public setting had changed in two important ways. On the one hand, 'the public' had changed. Earlier in the year, it had reasserted itself symbolically but also in physically powerful ways to unseat President Mubarak, dividing the regime and giving the lie to his claim to overall authority. However, it was now divided in itself. In the course of the year, the component parts of the bloc that had used mass demonstration so effectively had split. Each was pursuing its own goals and developing its own strategies to take advantage of the new setting of Egyptian politics. On the other hand, equally important was the fact that the prospect of elections and of representative institutions now promised to open up new kinds of public spaces for the citizens of Egypt.

Those who had made gains in the first rounds of the elections – principally the Islamist parties Freedom and Justice (FJP) and al-Nour – had little interest in disrupting, let alone suspending, a process that seemed set to deliver them an overwhelming majority in the new parliament, with all this could mean for the drafting of a new constitution. They too were wary of the entrenched power of the officer corps and of the intentions of SCAF, but refused to lend their mass support to the continuing public protests of the year's end. Even when the open violence of the armed forces against the remaining demonstrators provoked new surges of protest – as in the mass demonstration of 22 December against the killings of the preceding few days and against the public humiliation by soldiers of female demonstrators – the Islamist parties refused to endorse the protests.

However, there was an attempt to recapture the power of mass demonstration in June 2012. It was then that a combination of rulings from the Egyptian judiciary and SCAF dissolved the recently elected parliament, asserted the primacy of the military in any future constitutional settlement and threw doubt on the victory in the presidential election of the Muslim Brotherhood candidate. Faced by the possibility that the old regime of military-backed authoritarian power had reasserted itself, tens of thousands of Egyptian citizens gathered in Tahrir Square to embody once again a mobilized public, reclaiming public space. In the absence of representative institutions, this appeared to be the only way in which power could be made accountable. Yet, as the events since the downfall of President Mubarak had shown, it was a precarious undertaking, inviting both violent repression and possibly fragmenting the Egyptian public itself. In fact, Muhammad Morsi of the Muslim Brotherhood was declared the winner and became the first democratically elected president of Egypt. Nevertheless, the mass occupation of public space, reinforced by the memories of early 2011, had been a vivid reminder to those at the summit of the state of the conditional nature of their power.

Bahrain: Family, Sect and Power

Just as the success of the uprising of popular resistance in Tunisia in January 2011 gave hope as well as inspiration to Egyptians, so the latter's success in February inspired discontented Bahrainis to mobilize in a similar way. A familiar combination of factors had been at the heart of the periodic demonstrations, riots and civil disturbances that had marked the politics of Bahrain during the previous decade and a half. The protest movements had gone through various stages during those years, as Bahrainis tried to resist government encroachment on, indeed removal of, their rights as Bahraini citizens, as well as to voice concerns about unemployment and economic inequality. The combination of state repression, denial of voice, economic discrimination and elite privilege that confronted the dissenters provoked various kinds of resistance. These were expressed in a familiar repertoire of symbolic protests. Sometimes, as in the 1990s, this had led to violent attacks against targets associated with the government or security personnel. More often, and more frequently in the twenty-first century, it involved mass demonstrations, strikes and public confrontations with the security forces.

The communal imbalance of Muslim sects in Bahrain between a Shi`i majority and a Sunni minority (to which the ruling house of the Al Khalifa and most of the elite families of Bahrain belong) has added a certain sharpness to the conflict on both sides.[44] Although by no means the only reason for the mobilization of Bahrainis at various times against the dominance of the Al Khalifa, sectarian difference has been a powerful mobilizing factor, used by both the protestors and the government and their allies. Thus the denial of voice to the majority can be portrayed as civic discrimination against the Shi`a as a community. Equally, the uneven distribution of wealth that privileges the ruling family and its associates, at the expense of the bulk of the population, can be represented as the deliberate impoverishment of the Shi`a. They are also the ones whose precarious economic position makes them most vulnerable to unemployment. In addition, large sections of the capital Manama, as well as most of the villages that surround the capital in the north of the island of Bahrain, are exclusively inhabited by Shi`i Bahrainis, sharing a similar economic predicament.

For its part, the government of Bahrain has played upon a familiar theme common to authoritarian regimes, claiming that all movements for change, especially those that advocate direct action, must be working on behalf of malign foreign powers. In this case, the protestors from the Shi`i population have been accused of being inspired by their co-sectarians in Iran, a state accused of having predatory designs on the island of Bahrain. The Bahraini government has found enthusiastic endorsement of this charge from the Sunni Muslim ruling houses of Saudi Arabia and its other Gulf allies, as well as by Western powers with strategic interests in the Gulf. All are equally nervous about the expansion of Iranian power, fearful of calls for accountability and, in the case of Saudi Arabia, equally mistrustful of its own Shi`i citizens in the Eastern Province.[45] It is thus possible to see how resistance and protest, as well as government responses, can take on a distinctly sectarian flavour.

The accession of a new ruler, Shaikh (later King) Hamad bin Isa in 1999, allowed the government to make the kinds of concessions that had been impossible for its predecessor. The security forces continued their campaign to uproot organizations responsible for the sporadic bombings and violence of the previous years, but the new ruler did detach the political opposition from the hardcore of violent resistance. He abolished some of the intrusive and repressive security laws, released political prisoners and invited exiles to return and to set up legitimate opposition parties and newspapers. He also promised the establishment of a constitutional monarchy, with the introduction of a new constitution, followed by parliamentary elections in which the franchise would be extended to give women the vote. Many of these promises were followed up, and the National Action Charter, approving the introduction of a new constitution, gained some ninety-eight per cent of the votes in a referendum in 2001. Even if many of the opposition parties felt that the constitution that was finally promulgated in 2002 fell short of their expectations – and of the pledges that King Hamad had publicly made – it appeared to set Bahraini political life on a new footing, although the major opposition parties, Shi`i Islamist, socialist and Arab nationalist, boycotted the parliamentary elections of 2002.

However, the structural inequalities remained, as did the legacy of bitterness and incomprehension that had been left by the events of the 1990s. Within the state security forces, the use of violence against demonstrators, village communities and detainees continued. This in itself not only provoked resistance and confrontation, but also provided fresh grounds for protest and demonstration even at times when the general political situation was relatively calm. Localized protests and the often violent police response added a communal flavour to the events. The demographics of Bahrain and its villages pitted mostly Shi`i demonstrators against security forces that were almost exclusively Sunni Muslim, many not even of Bahraini origin. This, in turn, ensured a wider resonance and more extensive forms of protest and resistance across the island.

As in other countries, one of the features of the organization of protest was the determination to claim a space free from government or security force intrusion, building barricades and deploying young men armed with stones to deny government forces access. Because of the layout of the sites of confrontation – generally villages, but sometimes specific quarters of the towns – such resistance was often a concentrated, community-based affair, drawing in the security forces and challenging them to recapture public space to end this open defiance. But such encounters, filmed and broadcast independently where the protesters could manage this, were also meant to symbolize a larger confrontation: the resistance of ordinary Bahrainis to the kind of state that would prevent them exercising their civic rights.

In some places, the dispute was mainly about place. Thus the residents of the fishing village of Malkiyya found themselves battling the authorities through direct action in 2007. It was then that a cousin of the king expropriated seafront land that would have cut them off from their livelihoods. Protests and demonstrations followed, leading to clashes with the police, arrests, allegations of torture and abuse and further protests which developed into running battles between the young men of the village and the riot police. Eventually, it brought about intervention by the king to restore order – he commanded his cousin to relinquish the land in question.[46] Similarly, in 2009, when the residents of the coastal town of Sitra tried to protest peacefully against a planned land reclamation scheme ordered by the ministry of defence, they were attacked by security forces.[47] As Salman Hassan, a resident of Malkiyya, said at the time, 'When we demonstrate peacefully, when we just hold banners, they don't like it. They want us to burn things so that they can say, "See, you are destructive"'.[48]

However, the protests and demonstrations were also about another kind of space – the political space in which Bahrainis would exercise their civic rights to act and to communicate, free of government interference or of the threat of violence by government agencies, especially the police and the Special Security Force. The authorities periodically arrested the leaders not only of some of the opposition political parties such as the Haq Movement, but also of activists in Bahraini human rights organizations. They were charged with 'links to terrorist networks' and 'endangering state security'. These and other charges were made possible by the extremely restrictive clauses of the State Security Measures Law of 1974 and the Penal Code of 1976 and its subsequent amendments. Even in relatively peaceful years, this gave a clear indication of how the government viewed any challenge to its monopoly of power.[49] This was a battle over the space in which it might be possible to organize 'rightful resistance'.

In the run-up to the 2010 elections to the Lower House of parliament, there were further encroachments on citizens' rights. Although the Lower House has limited powers and its legislation can be vetoed by the unelected Upper House, the government tried to engineer an outcome that would suit its own purposes. It arrested some 300 people in the summer of 2010 on charges of threatening state security. These included members of some of the parties that were boycotting the elections, as well as bloggers and human rights activists. When human rights organizations protested, the government moved to dismiss their leaders.[50] When the elections finally took place, they produced a parliament in which the Shi'i-based Al-Wifaq party won nearly half of the seats in the forty-seat chamber, leaving most of the others to be won by independent candidates.

This was an encouraging result for the opposition, despite allegations
of electoral irregularities aimed at preventing Al-Wifaq from winning a
majority. Shaikh Ali Salman, the leader of Al-Wifaq, could thus at least
claim that his strategy of pursuing 'rightful resistance' through the
electoral process had paid off. Of course, it had also raised hopes and
expectations. Yet the very structure of the system suggested that the
status quo would not change and these expectations would remain
disappointed. The uncle of the king, Shaikh Khalifa bin Salman Al
Khalifa retained the post of prime minister, as he had for forty years.
A focus of general dislike and suspicion, he had long been associated
with the most brutal aspects of the authorities' repression. Despite the
talk of a constitutional monarchy, the king retained supreme executive
power.[51]

With this background, and set against the long history of popular
mobilization and resistance, it was not surprising that the events in
Egypt in February 2011 should have inspired people in Bahrain, just
as the Egyptians had been inspired by events in Tunisia in January.
Already in the first week of February, there were calls for a 'Day of
Rage' on Monday 14 February – the tenth anniversary of the publication of the National Action Charter in 2001 – to underline the unful-
filled promises of that document. As in Egypt, the call went out by
various means and from a variety of sources, both through existing
networks of parties, activists and human rights organizations, and by
electronic means. A Facebook page was created that outlined the main
demands, including the repeal of the 2002 constitution, the dissolution
of parliament, the need for a prime minister directly elected by the
people and a government answerable to the people's representatives.
It also asserted that the Al Khalifa should reign but not rule and thus
should have no executive powers. In addition, it demanded an end to the
policy of *tajnis* [naturalization] that was believed to be altering the
demographic balance between Sunni and Shi`a in the islands.[52] Within
days, thousands had signed up.

On 14 February itself, thousands assembled in the public squares and
streets of many of the predominantly Shi`i villages south and west of
Manama, as well as in some parts of the capital. The numbers involved
were large, but they were spread out in different locations. Nevertheless,
they gave the impression of general popular resistance, since people
appeared to have coordinated their actions, rather than, as had been
the case in previous years, demonstrating separately because of local
grievances. Thus demonstrations took place in villages as far apart as

Nuwaidrat in the east of the island, Karzakan to the west, as well as in the 'steadfastness triangle' comprising the three villages of Daih, Sanabis and Barhama on the outskirts of Manama. The overstretched riot police and other security forces responded violently, firing tear gas, rubber-coated steel bullets, baton rounds and buckshot to disperse the thousands of demonstrators and to reclaim public space. In doing so, they not only injured and arrested hundreds, they also killed one of the demonstrators, Ali Abd al-Hadi Mushaima.

This provoked tens of thousands to turn out the next day for the funeral of Mushaima, forming an angry cortege that followed his coffin to the cemetery, waving Bahraini flags, as well as Shi`i banners, and shouting slogans against the regime. The security forces again attacked the crowd, firing tear gas and the pellet guns that cost another Bahraini, Fadhil Matrouk, his life. The violence of the security forces, far from causing the marchers to disperse, led them to descend upon the large open space of the Pearl Roundabout – an extensive circle of grass surrounding a distinctive white concrete monument on the western edge of Manama, close to the villages of the 'steadfastness triangle'. Thousands soon assembled there in a conscious imitation of the encampment in Cairo's Tahrir Square. Meanwhile, the Al-Wifaq party announced that it was withdrawing all its members from parliament in protest against the killings, indicating that the route of 'rightful resistance' had given way to more direct forms of resistance. Faced by the violence of the state authorities, mass action seemed to be called for. The contest was now not simply for public space in a physical sense, but for the political space that the demands of the protesters for their rights as citizens were seeking to open up.[53]

As in Tahrir Square, the demonstrators at Pearl Roundabout declared they would not move until they had achieved their main demands, chiefly the dismissal of the prime minister, the dissolution of parliament and the redrafting of the constitution to produce a government answerable to the people's representatives. They began to organize themselves, bringing food and blankets and setting up tents and shelters, indicating a prolonged stay. The security forces melted away, avoiding confrontation, and it was for the citizens now to show that they could maintain an orderly and peaceful presence that was nevertheless a direct challenge to the authorities. As one of them stated at the time, 'This is our moment. This is our time. And we will take it'.[54] As if acknowledging at least the immediate cause of their grievances, King Hamad appeared on television to offer his condolences to the families of the two victims of police violence and promised to start an enquiry into their deaths.

However, another kind of response came only a day later. In the early hours, the security forces carried out a raid on the encampment, using extreme force to clear the circle, destroying the tents and beating up those they found. By the end of the attack, three men had been killed and one later died in hospital. With the roundabout now cleared of demonstrators and the roads to it sealed off by the military units, the protestors regrouped around the Salmaniyya Hospital where the dead and wounded had been taken. Thousands showed their anger, rallying around the hospital, joined by the doctors who were equally outraged by this evidence of the violence used by the security forces against peaceful demonstrators. To chants and shouts of 'Down with the king! Down with the government!', one doctor addressed the crowd, making plain his feelings: 'For generations they have treated us as spoils of war, almost like a ransom to be used for their pleasure ... The regime's stranglehold must be broken!' Although Pearl Roundabout was now closed off, the demonstrations would continue, as Ali Abbas, one of their number said, 'We will keep hitting the streets until we get freedom and rights ... The people are raging and they know we can get things done. Egypt has taught us that. It is not a lesson we can forget'.[55]

The security forces attacked the funeral procession of those killed at the Pearl Roundabout, causing further outrage. But the same day, Crown Prince Salman bin Hamad ordered the armed forces back into barracks and off the streets. Thousands of people converged once more on the now vacated Pearl Roundabout and showed their continued defiance. One large banner blazoned the words of the chant that had been so characteristic of the protests in Cairo: '*Al-sha`b yurid isqat al-nizam*' [the people want the fall of the regime], the stresses on the final syllable of each word forming a powerful, even mesmeric rhythm.[56] By making this concession to the rights of the people to protest peacefully, the Crown prince signalled the opening of a dialogue that promised further concessions. The problem was that so much blood had flowed, and so much suspicion had been generated, that the demonstrators were now demanding a series of preconditions before meaningful talks could begin. These included the release of all political prisoners, the resignation of the prime minister and of the appointed government, half of which comprised members of the Al Khalifa family.

To reinforce the power behind their demands, the protestors organized a massive demonstration of tens of thousands of Bahrainis on 22

February that stretched some two miles from the Bahrain Mall to the Pearl Roundabout – now renamed Martyrs' Square. Demonstrating their patriotism as Bahraini citizens with the sea of Bahraini flags on display, the thousands marching peacefully along the route nevertheless made their demands clear: 'The People Want the Fall of the Regime!' 'We Want a New Government!' 'The People Want to Rule the Country!' Youth activists, trades unionists, teachers, lawyers and other professionals, as well as members of the political parties across the spectrum of dissent, Al-Wifaq, Wa'ad and the Haq Movement, came out in support. The state television channel studiously ignored this massive presence of dissent, and concentrated instead on filming a much smaller counter-demonstration in support of the king, organized significantly outside one of the main Sunni mosques in Manama.[57]

Once lodged securely at the Pearl Roundabout, the demonstrators went about organizing themselves on a more permanent footing. As in Egypt's Tahrir Square, the social presence of citizens transformed the area into a truly public space. This was to be an important part of the message of nonviolent resistance to those forces that wanted to close it down. Committees were set up to take charge of communal cooking, medical needs and childcare. Others engaged with the media, careful to ensure that the various messages of the protests received the widest possible audience. Tents were erected for professional groups, as well as for discussions and lectures, and some acted as focal points for particular villages. A central stage was built and this provided a platform for a wide range of views, as well as for announcements and entertainment. It was also the place where a succession of political figures came to report on progress in their talks with the government and to gain public backing for different approaches, giving it the air of an assembly in constant session.[58]

In fact, apart from an agreement to release political prisoners, the dialogue with the Crown prince produced little. It seemed to some that the occupation of Pearl Roundabout, although much filmed by foreign television crews and generating a sense of solidarity and determination, had almost come to be accepted by the authorities. As long as the occupation of public space was confined to this area, it did not appear unduly to inconvenience the government. The demonstration was in danger therefore of losing much of its force. It was becoming almost routine, an accepted part of the landscape, however much it may have allowed the participants to feel that they were taking part in meaningful political action.

However, the attitude of the authorities changed markedly when the demonstrators moved out of the confines of the square and marched on targets that were central to the case they were trying to make. On 8 March, thousands turned out for a demonstration that targeted the Immigration Office in Manama, shouting the slogan of 'The naturalized must get out!', drawing attention to the government's sectarian naturalization of Sunni Arabs and even non-Arabs to change the demographic balance of the island. This was followed on the Friday by an attempt to march on West Rifaa, the residential quarter of the ruling Al Khalifa. Thousands of protesters were met by lines of apparently civilian supporters of the ruling family who blocked their way, using rocks, sticks and iron bars to attack the marchers. The riot police initially looked on and then joined in, trying to break up the demonstration and to prevent it from reaching its target. At the same time, a concerted effort was made to intimidate those who were seen as leaders of the protests, as well as civil rights activists – an attempt that was officially represented as the result of the growing anger of 'concerned citizens'. In order to reinforce this, more pro-regime demonstrations were organized, and clashes erupted at the campus of the university. This was all occurring against the background of widespread charges in the government media that the protests were largely orchestrated by 'foreign powers', meaning Iran.[59]

These developments provoked an about face by the Crown prince, although some have interpreted this as more a rift within the ruling house between those advocating the violent suppression of the demonstrations and those holding out for dialogue. On 13 March, the mass demonstrations moved in on Manama and surrounded the financial district. They also succeeded in driving back police who appeared to be moving once again against the occupiers of Pearl Roundabout. The Crown prince appeared on television warning that 'any legitimate claims must not be made at the expense of security and stability', and although he continued to promise national dialogue, there were rumours that the Saudi National Guard was getting ready to intervene.[60]

The rumour became a reality the following day when a 1,000-strong contingent of Saudi troops, accompanied by some 500 police from the UAE, crossed the causeway to Bahrain in a move that Al-Wifaq described as a 'declaration of war'. In fact, the numbers of Saudi forces in the island may have been three times as many as was officially acknowledged at the time.[61] The reinforcement and powerful political support of the Gulf Cooperation Council (GCC) states – and in the background that of the United States – gave the Bahraini authorities the capability and the licence they had sought for the violent suppression of the month-long mass demonstrations. Martial law was declared, leaving the security forces free to use violence on a scale that was more than a match for the numbers the opposition could bring out in peaceful protest.

During the weeks that followed, the Bahraini authorities used force freely to recapture public spaces, to close down all political space and to pursue and often kill those whom it regarded as organizers of the waves of protest. Within a couple of days, the security forces, with Saudi assistance, had cleared Pearl Roundabout and suppressed further protests in the neighbouring villages, bringing in bulldozers to demolish the distinctive monument at the heart of the square that had become an icon of popular resistance. In the days and weeks that followed, some twenty members of the public were killed and hundreds wounded, accompanied by systematic arrests, detentions, torture and disappearances of opposition figures, of people associated with human rights organizations, of critical journalists and of bloggers accused of maintaining the electronic networks of resistance.[62]

In the months that followed, the repression intensified, leading to the closing down of opposition organizations, the hasty and rigged trials of individuals accused of sedition and other charges that carried the death sentence or long terms of imprisonment. Bahraini students and academics were dismissed for having taken part in demonstrations or even for having voiced dissent. Others were forced to sign oaths of allegiance to the regime to avoid a similar fate. Meanwhile, thousands of mainly Shi`i public employees lost their jobs in purges that seemed driven more by sectarian prejudice and revenge than by any concern about weeding out dissidents.[63] Public space was rigorously policed, preventing any significant mass protest from gathering, even if riots and demonstrations continued to erupt in various localities as youths engaged in hit-and-run raids with the riot police in places like Sanabis, Budaiya, Janusan and Malkiyya during the summer and into the autumn.[64]

Curiously, the continued unrest formed the backdrop to the sessions of the Bahrain Independent Commission of Inquiry set up by King Hamad in June under the chairmanship of the Egyptian jurist, Cherif Bassiouni. It was charged with examining the circumstances of the uprising of spring 2011, the behaviour of the security forces, as much as the actions of the demonstrators. The king had felt obliged to launch the commission in order to prevent an international commission of inquiry from being set up by the United Nations. Disturbingly for the Bahraini authorities, its principal ally and protector, the United States, had appeared to endorse such a move in June 2011 by calling at the UN for the scrutiny of the human rights record of the Bahrain government. The commission eventually produced its report in November 2011.[65]

The report confirmed the scale of the human rights abuses that had taken place in Bahrain during the preceding months and found no evidence for the Bahrain authorities' repeated claim that Iran had played a part in stirring up unrest. However, to the anger of the victims of the sustained abuse and to the exasperation and incredulity of the opposition parties and others, it would not state that these systematic abuses were part of Bahraini official policy. Nor did it name the individuals responsible for the deaths, torture and intimidation of so many Bahraini citizens. For the latter, it was clear that the report had served its purpose for the king and members of his family. However, it was unlikely to have any lasting effect on the balance of power in the country unless the citizens themselves were empowered to act to ensure such abuses did not happen again. This was only likely to happen if the original goals of the protest movement could be realized. In the absence of such radical change, resistance and its suppression would continue to be marked by violence – as was poignantly testified by the death of Abdulnabi Kadhem at the hands of the police in the village of A`ali just before the ceremony launching the BICI report.[66]

PUBLIC DEFIANCE OF FOREIGN OCCUPATION: SIGNALLING RESISTANCE

Where a clear line of separation can be drawn between the state and those subjected to it on the basis of their identity – ethnic, sectarian or class, or a reinforcing combination of all three – mass demonstrations and the denial of spaces to the authorities and their security forces can cause a sense of beleaguered solidarity among those in power. To some extent, this has been visible in Bahrain. It has therefore been part of the government's strategy to suggest that the motives of the protestors are largely sectarian and that they have been duped by a foreign power. However, drawing attention to the collective nature and common plight of the protestors, underlining their differences to those they challenge, can also mobilize people.

It becomes a means of rallying support amongst fellow citizens, the 'propaganda by deed' that is intended to show up the nature of the divide between them and the state authorities. It can be a way of voicing the concerns of the voiceless, not simply in terms of detailed demands but more fundamentally in terms of the right to voice these demands in the first place. The sites of protest become precisely those places 'in between' the institutions of state power to which the citizens are routinely denied access. Resistance of this kind can also be expressive. It is a loud proclamation of the refusal to submit meekly to domination or to accept the rationale of the power that is exercised over them. Manifestations of this kind are a way of signalling the presence of a distinct public actor that cannot be ignored, whether that actor is characterized as a distinct community or a class. They are a means of winning recognition, possibly opening the way towards concessions.

Palestine: The First Intifada (1987–1991) and Resistance to the Wall (2003–2011)

All of these elements were visible in the first *intifada* [uprising] in the occupied Palestinian territories in the late 1980s. Hitherto the most visible forms of Palestinian resistance had largely been armed resistance, almost exclusively conducted by Palestinian organizations outside the territories occupied by Israel. The defeat of the PLO forces in Lebanon and their expulsion from that country in 1982–3 left the 1.5 million Palestinians living under Israeli military occupation with little hope of liberation and fearful of expulsion or of permanent subjugation to the Israeli state. Israeli settlements across the occupied territories had rapidly increased, East Jerusalem had long been annexed to the state of Israel and a growing trend in the religious wing of Zionism was staking a permanent claim to much of the West Bank. At the same time, despite employment opportunities in Israel, the daily humiliations of checkpoints, identity checks and everyday encounters with Israeli security forces, as well as the underdeveloped and depressed condition of the Palestinian economy under occupation, meant the existence of a groundswell of resentment, based on nationalist, religious and economic concerns.

It could fairly be said of the Palestinian condition in 1987 that it was a combustible mixture of grievances awaiting a spark. When that spark came, in the form of a traffic accident that cost the lives of four Palestinians from Jabalya refugee camp in December 1987, there was little doubt about the spontaneity and widespread nature of the outrage that it provoked. The truck that had crashed into the van carrying the Palestinians at the Erez border crossing was Israeli, and the following day a young Palestinian was shot dead by Israeli forces in the protests that broke out in Jabalya camp. These aspects of the case only redoubled the anger of locals and the wider Palestinian community. As in the Iranian city of Qom in January 1978, or in the self-immolation of Mohamed Bouazizi in the Tunisian town of Sidi Bouzid in December 2010, an event that began as a local incident rapidly became the start of something much larger. In the relatively compact society of the occupied territories where communications were good, initial protests rapidly developed into widespread demonstrations. These seemed to give vent to the grievances of twenty years of military occupation.

Here, too, there was a contest over space. In the setting of the occupied Palestinian territories, the struggle was to assert the right of Palestinians to control their own space, as Palestinians, free from the demands of the Israeli security forces. This formed the basis of their recognition as Palestinians, with their own rights and claims to self-determination. In this respect, the struggle resembled the anti-colonial uprisings and demonstrations that had been a feature of Middle East politics in the first half of the twentieth century when so much of the region had been under British and French control. The determination to find a voice in which to express the political aspirations of the inhabitants of the occupied territories also shaped the tactics of the uprising. Ways were found to resist their classification as subject people under military occupation and to restate their identity as agents capable of shaping their own future. This was a reaction to the fact that they had been historically overlooked and taken for granted not only by the forces of occupation, but also, many felt, by the leadership of the Palestinian nationalist movement in exile.

Symbolic defiance of the Israeli occupation forces was one way of realizing these objectives. At a time when to raise the Palestinian flag – or even the colours of that flag – in the occupied territories was prohibited by Israeli military regulations, it made it perversely easy to commit multiple small acts of resistance. Flags, stickers and graffiti appeared everywhere on a scale that the Israeli forces were unable to prevent – and in failing to do so, seemed weaker and less in control than they liked to appear. As other anti-colonial resistance movements had discovered in the twentieth century, these small gestures of defiance became a way of involving large numbers of people, many of whom would normally have shied away from overt acts of resistance. In doing so, greater numbers of the public became engaged. Sometimes this was because of the confrontations with the Israeli forces that even such small acts could provoke. Sometimes it was because the very act itself opened up people's eyes to the possibility of creating an impact through their own actions. As in other cases of civil resistance, this was a crucial step in preparing the ground for collective action. In a situation where the official representatives of the Palestinian people were scattered across the Middle East, unable to advance their cause, it was they, rather than the Palestinians living under occupation, who seemed to be denied agency and purpose. By contrast, Palestinians in the West Bank and Gaza were discovering the empowering force of resistance.

Confrontations with the Israeli security forces redoubled in the streets of the West Bank and Gaza. Temporary barricades and burning tyres were set up as markers of place, signalling that this would be a zone from which Israel would be excluded. It was also a provocation that drew Israeli security forces into range of the stones and catapults of the young Palestinians waiting to show how they could stand up to the overwhelming power of the Israeli army. At the cost of widespread injuries and deaths (more than 1,000 Palestinians were killed and roughly 18,000 wounded by Israeli forces during the course of the four-year uprising) this became for many inside the Palestinian territories and beyond the overriding image of the *intifida*: children and teenagers throwing stones at heavily armed Israeli soldiers and armoured vehicles.[67] As potent in its way as the famous image of the confrontation between the line of tanks and the man holding a plastic bag in Tiananmen Square in the summer of 1989, the 'children of the *intifada*' became a theme of immense power in images and words.[68]

As a statement of the determination to re-appropriate a place that was rightfully Palestinian, the barricades and the stone throwing extended beyond the urban patrol routes of the Israeli army into the network of roads that connected the many Israeli settlements dotting the occupied territories, on the West Bank in particular. Just as the Israeli armed forces and settler movement had used overwhelming force to occupy and to expropriate Palestinian land, so the young men of the *intifada* used their own forms of direct action to signal that this was not unopposed and to disrupt the generally untroubled tenor of settler life. The deliberate and sustained acts of defiance and confrontation became a way of symbolically asserting the Palestinian identity of the place and, in doing so, of the political existence of the Palestinians themselves as a people rooted in the territory, resisting subordination, expulsion or marginalization.

One intended audience of this message was the exiled Palestinian leadership. It was felt to be remote from the everyday concerns of the Palestinian people living under occupation. Thus mobilizing for resistance became a way of announcing the presence of ordinary Palestinians as political actors – just as the Palestinian armed resistance had done some decades previously. Mobilization was accelerated by the rapid emergence of Palestinian political structures internal to the occupied territories. The Unified Leadership of the Uprising, although soon adopted by the PLO and others outside the borders of Palestine, was nevertheless an organization that had sprung from the determination of the young 'insiders' to make their own mark on history. They were demonstrating that they could also coordinate and shape a campaign of resistance to Israeli military occupation that might in the end be more likely to produce Israeli concessions and boost Palestinian self-confidence than the armed struggle that had been organized from outside the territories of Palestine itself.

The Unified National Leadership of the Uprising was not the only form of Palestinian organization, but it helped to crystallize the demands and grievances of the Palestinians through such publications as the '14 Points' of January 1988. It also articulated larger political aims, such as the right to self-determination and an independent state, making a series of specific demands at the same time. These gave a clear idea of the long-running complaints that had triggered the uprising. They called for an end to all settlement building, an end to land seizures, the elimination of roadblocks, the granting of building permits, as well as the freeing of prisoners and the lifting of a string of restrictive measures that were such an intrusive and resented part of people's lives.[69]

Part of the strategy was to organize street demonstrations to reclaim public space and draw international attention to the plight of the Palestinians. But another part involved the tactics of nonviolent resistance such as boycotts, shutdowns and strikes. The Israelis were powerless to prevent such actions, and they helped to deepen feelings of solidarity amongst the Palestinians. The latter, now mobilized across the occupied territories in an unprecedented way, began to take actions that only made sense, or became effective, when sufficiently large numbers of individuals participated. Aimed directly at the occupying authorities, campaigns were begun for the non-payment of taxes, for the burning of ID cards and for resignations from posts in the administration. Within the Palestinian communities themselves, new self-help groups emerged, along with alternative economies of barter and new forms of administration. Where possible, forms of self-sufficiency were encouraged and a boycott of Israeli goods implemented.[70]

However, over time, the overwhelming coercive force and the resources at the disposal of the Israeli security forces, combined with the frustrations, internal bloodletting and natural slowing down of the momentum of symbolic protest began to tell against those trying to extend the resistance potential of the *intifada*. Mass arrests, targeted killings and the casualties inflicted by rubber-coated steel bullets, tear gas and even live rounds took their toll of the leadership and of the mobilized followers. They had kept the *intifada* going for some years but became disheartened by the apparent failure to produce immediate results. In fact, the consequences were profound, although they were not to be visible until the 1990s. Most importantly, Palestinian civil disobedience and mass resistance to Israeli military occupation convinced many in Israel that the status quo could not continue. Whilst the security forces might have been able to suppress the more obvious public manifestations of defiant resistance, they could not disrupt the politicization and mobilization of the Palestinian public in the territories that they occupied.

This did not produce a uniform Palestinian politics – far from it – but it did force upon Israel and others the need to recognize the distinct politics and political identity that was Palestinian, rather than the by-product of the regional political ambitions of other states. In this sense, it re-established the Palestinians as political actors with whom Israel would have to negotiate. They could not merely be classified as a security problem that could be dealt with by security countermeasures. The barricades, the flags, the slogans and the stone throwing had been the spectacular outward show of the resistance of the *intifada*. Less spectacular, but more lasting in their effects, were the patterns of resistance that had extended and deepened Palestinian civil organization. Building upon the many forms of local self-help that had emerged as survival strategies under occupation prior to 1987, the *intifada* had provided the opportunity and the need to bring these efforts together and to expand them into a sustained resistance movement.[71] In doing so, they had given solidity and meaning to the PFLP poster slogan which proclaimed, 'I Resist therefore I Exist', and had reconfigured the Palestinian people as a political actor that demanded recognition.

As with any emerging political field, Palestinian politics in the occupied territories was also a contested space not simply by the Israeli forces, but also by different Palestinian organizations. Sometimes this was connected. Twenty years of occupation and Israeli intelligence infiltration of Palestinian communities had left a legacy of collaboration and mutual suspicion. This took its toll as the early idealism of the *intifada* began to give way to feelings of despair and bitterness at mounting casualty rates. Notoriously, Palestinians turned on each other with nearly as many dying at the hands of fellow Palestinians as had succumbed to Israeli violence. Informers and collaborators were hunted down in a dangerous atmosphere where even an accusation or a suspicion could be fatal. In some respects, it was the reassertion of the logic of armed resistance, as violence came to be seen as a way of proving oneself amongst the *shabab*. What had begun as a rite of passage to manhood, such as throwing stones at Israeli forces or painting graffiti on walls or indeed being arrested and beaten by Israeli soldiers, gradually became a proven willingness to use lethal force. This was to be a token of loyalty to the cause.[72]

The turning towards violence and disillusionment with what had been achieved through civil disobedience, riot and nonviolent resistance weakened the power of the *intifada* and contributed to its loss of momentum by 1991. It was for another generation of Palestinians to rediscover the power of nonviolent protest some fifteen years later in the wake of the violence and paralysis brought about by the *intifadat al-aqsa*. During the intervening years, many ordinary Palestinians had used strategies of everyday resistance to cope with the difficulties of life under occupation, sustaining solidarity and maintaining social networks throughout an increasingly fragmented territory. The outbreak of the uprising known as *intifadat al-aqsa* in 2000 led to frequent Israeli armed incursions into those areas nominally under Palestinian control. It also led to increased restrictions on movement between Palestinian towns and villages. Most obvious in this regard was the building of a wall and fence along some 700 km, nominally following the 'green line' that had marked the border between the West Bank and Israel up to 1967. In fact, it took a meandering course that sometimes intruded deep into Palestinian territory, cutting off villages from their fields and effectively expropriating hundreds of hectares of Palestinian land.[73]

It was in this context that there was a revival of interest in the possibilities of nonviolent protest and demonstration. At a number of points along the course of the projected separation barrier, Palestinian village communities organized local protests to try to prevent their lands from being expropriated or cordoned off on the pretext of Israeli security. In 2003–4 at the village of Budrus, some 30 km northwest of Ramallah, the inhabitants, led by one of their number, Ayad Murrar, organized themselves to take direct nonviolent action. The local protest was aimed at preventing the uprooting of a large section of the villagers' olive groves to make way for the barrier, as well as at blocking the Israeli authorities from cutting off some 300 acres of their land from the village. The villagers organized sit-ins, marches and protests in defiance of the Israeli curfew, signalling their willingness peacefully to resist violence in order to achieve their objectives. The men, women and children of the village were joined by other Palestinians in a prolonged and sustained protest. It was initially met by baton charges, rubber-coated steel bullets and arrests. However, faced by the growing attention of the international media and by the determination of a whole community, the Israeli military authorities concluded that it would be better simply to re-route the barrier. In this way, local nonviolent resistance succeeded in winning a small but, for the village whose lands had been restored, significant victory.[74]

Similar protests and demonstrations were organized at other villages that were in danger of losing much of their land to the barrier. At Ni῾lin and Bil῾in, both situated west of Ramallah, villagers and Israeli, European and American activists tried to resist the course of the barrier. They took direct action that sometimes involved stone throwing or efforts to push down the parts of the barrier that had already been built. In both places, the Israeli security forces responded with more sustained violence than they had at Budrus a couple of years previously, firing rubber-coated steel bullets and live rounds, as well as tear gas grenades that caused numerous injuries and cost the lives of some five Palestinians at Ni῾lin in the course of 2008–9.[75] In an attempt to avoid international attention being paid to these sites of resistance, the Israeli military authorities declared in early 2010 that the territory between the barrier and the villages themselves would be designated as 'closed military areas' every Friday for the following six months. This did not have much effect, and the demonstrations not only at Bil῾in and Ni῾lin but also at al-Ma῾asara and Nabi Saleh became regular events, scenes of symbolic defiance and public performances that were visited by local and by international politicians to witness these events, but also to show solidarity. They remained, however, sites of danger and violence. This was clear from the casualty toll of those hit by rubber-coated steel bullets or tear gas canisters. Some were seriously injured, even killed by the inhalation of the copious amounts of tear gas fired by the Israeli security forces.[76]

There were, however, other possibilities of nonviolent resistance. One of these was to take objections to the route of the barrier to the Israeli courts, following a path of 'rightful resistance'. This had in fact been pursued with some success by the Bil'in popular committee. In 2007, it succeeded in winning a judgment from the Israeli Supreme Court that instructed the Israeli authorities to redraw the line of the barrier near Bil'in, since its current route was '"highly prejudicial" to the villagers and not justifiable on security grounds'. This was seen as a great victory in the village, since the judgment meant that they stood to regain some 140 hectares of the 200 that had been seized.[77] However, they had to go to the courts again to contest the authorities' redrawing of the line of the barrier, and although they won a further judgment in their favour in 2008, they were cautious about the eventual outcome – understandably so, since it took some four years for the Israeli army finally to move the barrier in 2011, as ordered by the Court.[78]

Developments such as these, together with the split between the PA administration in the West Bank and the *Hamas*-led administration of Gaza, encouraged a renewed interest in the idea of *masira silmiyya* [peaceful protest] and *intifadat al-sha`b* [the people's uprising], particularly in the West Bank. Seeking to recall the solidarities and initiatives of the 1980s, boycotts of Israeli goods were organized, especially those manufactured in the Israeli settlements that now dotted the West Bank. These were sometimes marked by the symbolic burning of such goods or by poster campaigns reminding Palestinians of the need to re-examine their patterns of consumption, with campaigns such as 'Your conscience, your choice' targeting these items. Most striking was a giant poster near Ramallah that resembled a regular commercial billboard for ice cream (made in Israel or in one of the Israeli settlements) with the picture of a man delightedly eating ice cream – but underneath was the slogan which read, 'Mmmm . . . ice cream with the taste of occupation'. Even the leaders of the Palestinian Authority endorsed these moves. President Mahmoud Abbas extolled nonviolence as a strategic choice for the Palestinians, and the prime minister, Salam Fayyad, took part in protest marches or in the symbolic planting of olive trees on land that the Israeli military authorities had declared as off-limits.[79]

The Bil'in popular committee even went to court in Quebec in Canada in 2008 to sue two Canadian firms that were involved in the construction and marketing of the Israeli settlements that the villagers saw as the main reason for the seizure of their lands. Under Canada's Crimes against Humanity and War Crimes Act (2000), it was stipulated that the transfer of civilians from the occupying power into the territories it occupies is a war crime. Bil'in was seeking to get a judgment that would rule that the construction of the settlements was indeed illegal, that the Canadian companies should cease all activity that affected the lands of the village and should also pay punitive damages.[80] In the event, the case was dismissed by the Montreal court in 2009 on the grounds that it was out of its jurisdiction, since Israel was the more appropriate place for bringing such a case. This judgment was upheld by the Appeal Court in 2010, although the way was left open for a possible civil suit in the future.[81]

The international dimension was particularly in evidence in the growing campaign aimed at mobilizing not only the Palestinian public, but also North American and European publics, in an economic boycott of Israeli goods. The 'Boycott, Divestment and Sanctions' (BDS) campaign was launched in 2005 by a coalition of more than twenty-five Palestinian civil society organizations. It called not only for the boycott of Israeli goods, but also for the withdrawal of investment in Israel and in companies with major economic interests in Israel, as well as for the imposition of sanctions aimed at excluding Israel from representation in a number of international bodies. Consciously recalling the anti-apartheid campaigns against white minority rule in South Africa, and referring to the body of UN resolutions, the BDS organizers urged 'various forms of boycott against Israel until it meets its obligations under international law'. These were defined as the withdrawal of Israel from all lands occupied in 1967, the dismantling of the separation barrier, full and effective equality for all Arab citizens of Israel and 'respecting, protecting and promoting the rights of Palestinian refugees to return to their homes and properties'.[82]

Targeting particularly agricultural and other produce of the extensive network of Israeli settlements in the occupied Palestinian territories, the BDS campaign gathered momentum during the years that followed, creating a network of support through civil society associations in Europe and North America. This led to a number of symbolic actions that drew the attention of consumers to the origins of everyday products available in supermarkets, and caused some institutions to reconsider their investments. However, the main focus was in the occupied Palestinian territories, where the entanglement of the Israeli economy with that of the West Bank was long standing and extensive. This made the task of the BDS organizers all the more difficult, even if the Israeli Knesset unwittingly boosted the morale of the campaign in July 2011. It was then that it passed the Boycott Prohibition Bill allowing civil prosecutions to be brought against any individual who advocates 'a boycott against the State of Israel', defined as 'deliberately avoiding economic, cultural or academic ties with another person or another factor only because of his ties with the State of Israel, one of its institutions or an area under its control, in such a way that may cause economic, cultural or academic damage'.[83] This suggested that, modest as the effects of the campaign had been, it was touching a raw nerve in the occupying power.

Nevertheless, nonviolent resistance appeared to be most visibly successful at the local level, combating encroachments on Palestinian land in the West Bank caused by the growth of the Israeli settlements, as well as the frequently connected expropriation of land along the length of the separation barrier.[84] Successful as some of the actions had been in limited places, in the wider context, resistance through voluntary boycotts of Israeli settlements and their produce faced an uphill struggle against the facts of economic life under occupation: the Palestinians annually purchased some $200 million worth of the goods made in the settlements and about 30,000 Palestinians worked in them. Furthermore, by 2010, as the Palestinian academic Khalil Shikaki said, there was a larger dilemma facing the Palestinians that threw into question all forms of resistance: 'The society is split. The public believes that Israel responds to suffering, not to nonviolent resistance. But there is also not much interest in violence right now ... in essence the public feels trapped between failed diplomacy and failed armed struggle'.[85]

Resisting Syria in Lebanon

On 14 February 2005, a massive explosion detonated on Mina al-Husn on the Beirut seafront, killing the former prime minister of Lebanon, Rafiq al-Hariri, as well as twenty other people and wounding a further 100. No one claimed responsibility for the blast, but initially the Syrian security services were widely regarded as having engineered it. Their frequent use of assassination as a way of silencing their Lebanese critics, and the falling out between the Syrian government and al-Hariri that had forced him out of the premiership only a few months previously, made them the chief suspects. Convinced of this connection, thousands of Lebanese soon began to assemble at the site, staging a massive demonstration of protest against the Syrian military presence in the country and against its allies in the Lebanese government and security apparatus.

Within a few days, the demonstrations had grown in size and in drama, taking on a shape and a permanence that indicated a radical departure from previous more modest, rapidly dispersed protests against the Syrian military presence. As well as organizing processions that wound their way through the main streets of Beirut, the demonstrators also congregated in the open space of the Place des Martyres in the centre of the city. Symbolically charged with the echoes of national self-sacrifice evoked by its very name, the space acted as a magnet for a wide spectrum of Lebanese citizens determined to make a stand against what they felt was an oppressive and complacent status quo in Lebanon. In early March, giant screens were set up in the square to show the tens of thousands assembled there the drama that was playing out in the chamber of the nearby parliament. It was then that they saw the prime minister tender his resignation, to cheers in the square and shouts for 'Freedom!' and 'Sovereignty!'. Although the Lebanese security forces had half-heartedly tried to restrict the numbers of people gathering in the square, the flimsy barriers were overturned and people flooded in, showing the security forces how powerless they were in the face of such numbers, whilst paradoxically chanting, 'We want no other army in Lebanon but the Lebanese army!'.[86]

Given the violence of the event that had precipitated it, as well as the harsh treatment that had been meted out to those who had previously tried to use this space as a site of public protest, these acts of defiant nonviolent resistance took a great deal of courage. However, it was soon apparent that the Lebanese authorities were not going to intervene. On the contrary, the numbers of the demonstrators grew, their presence became more permanent and their demands more focused, deterring the government from sweeping them off the streets by strong-arm tactics. Within a few days, they had become the vehicle for a broad coalition of Lebanese political parties and organizations. They united to demand the withdrawal of Syrian forces from Lebanon, the resignation of the government and of the president, the dismissal of senior security officials and the calling of new parliamentary elections, free of Syrian interference. Within a matter of weeks, most of these aims had been achieved, and the labels of *intifadat al-istiqlal* [independence uprising] and the 'Cedar Revolution' had been applied to these events, indicating their dramatic effect on the balance of power in the country.

Although labelled a 'revolution', the events in Lebanon in 2005 that followed the assassination of the former prime minister, Rafiq al-Hariri, did not achieve as dramatic and radical a change in the Lebanese state as had those in Iran in 1978–9. It is true that the government of Omar Karami resigned, the parliament was dissolved and new elections were called. Furthermore, the 14,000 Syrian forces stationed in Lebanon withdrew from the country, weakening, if not neutralizing, Syria's capacity to play a key role in Lebanese politics.[87] Despite these successes, some of which can be attributed to the momentum initiated by the popular demonstrations, marches and occupations of the spring of 2005, the political outcomes were more ambiguous, as far as the lasting structures of power in Lebanon were concerned. Thus the initial demonstrations could be interpreted as resistance to what many saw as a Syrian military occupation of the country. This was indeed the theme of many of the posters, placards, banners and chants in evidence in the first few weeks.

By the same token, however, they provoked some very large demonstrations in favour of the continued relationship with Syria. Reflecting the divided nature of Lebanese politics, and indeed of Lebanese society more generally, Hizbullah countered these moves. On 8 March, coinciding with a Syrian national holiday that commemorated the Ba`thist revolution of 1963, Hizbullah organized a massive rally of some hundreds of thousands in the downtown section of Beirut, close to the Place des Martyres on Riyadh el Solh Square. The message was clear: surrounded by a sea of Lebanese flags, Hassan Nasrallah, the leader of Hizbullah declared, 'We are here to thank Syria which has stayed by our side for many years', rejecting what he claimed was U.S. interference to engineer Syrian withdrawal. The vast crowds easily outnumbered the anti-Syrian demonstrations of the previous days and tried to project the image, through their public presence, of a more representative citizenry supportive of Syria.[88]

Not to be outdone, the organizers of the calls for Syrian withdrawal and for the reassertion of Lebanese sovereignty mobilized in an effort to represent through the presence of sheer numbers a demonstration in the Place des Martyres that would dwarf the event of 8 March. In the symbolic arithmetic of this politics of dramatic representation, the scale of the demonstration was intended to impress upon the Syrian leadership, as well as on President Lahoud of Lebanon and the Lebanese security apparatus – both seen as complicit with the Syrian authorities – the depth and extent of Lebanese rejection of Syria's military presence. In a demonstration called for 14 March – a month since the assassination of Hariri – a crowd estimated at nearly one million people converged on the square. In the sea of Lebanese flags, slogans and placards asserting the sovereignty and independence of Lebanon were prominent, as were those that told the Syrians to go, disparaged the Lebanese president and asserted the control of the Lebanese people over their own future: 'Down with the security and intelligence state!', 'This crowd made in Lebanon!' and 'You're leaving, right?', 'We surprised you, right?' (using a characteristic Syrian dialect expression).[89]

Building on the momentum of this demonstration, a more permanent presence was organized in the Place des Martyres by those who felt that the transitory nature of marches, demonstrations and counter-demonstrations should give way to lasting assertion of defiance and resistance. With the occupation of the Place des Martyres and its tented encampments, young Lebanese made a point of joining each other in a mass protest, regardless of sect and community, the usual dividing lines of Lebanese politics. As many of them testified at the time, this was more than just a protest against the Syrian armed forces. They meant to signal, by their presence, resistance to the fragmentation of Lebanon, to the grip of the warlords and leaders who had divided the spoils for so long. It was thus also against the compartmentalization caused by the long-established confessional system of representation in Lebanese politics that placed emphasis on an individual's religious identity. Mohammed Ghadieh, one of those who had been present in the square from the beginning, made it plain when he said, 'People are sick of sectarianism. Before, our leaders played politics on us … They made us fight. Now, we're not following our leaders. Our leaders are following us'. And, optimistically, he added, 'This is not a camp, it's a revolution'.[90]

In this more fundamental resistance project, however, they were less successful. The problem was that the Lebanese state itself was so fragmented, parcelled up between various factional leaders who had worked out a *modus vivendi* with each other, that the occupation of public space did not have the same resonance as it had once had in Iran in 1978 or was to have in Egypt in 2011. It was certainly eye-catching that so many young Lebanese believed that there was a Lebanon on behalf of which they could demonstrate. However, the idea of a Lebanese political public was much more ambivalent, composed as it was of communities each of which had rather different notions of what comprised *their* Lebanon.[91]

This became rapidly apparent in the counter-demonstrations organized by Hizbullah and others who had benefited from the long-term presence of the Syrian army or who mistrusted the political forces that seemed to be lining up behind the demonstrators. These demonstrations and marches used very similar techniques and a repertoire almost identical in its symbolism to that used by the 14 March movement, as the anti-Syrian demonstrators came to be called. They drove home the message that they too were dedicated to a vision of Lebanon and Lebanon's independence – but a vision that had radically different consequences for the country's alignment and constitution.

Moreover, these were demonstrations that embodied a very different notion of resistance. This was resistance to imperialism, to Israel and to the growing influence of the United States and its allies in the shaping of Lebanese governments. For Hizbullah, which had begun as an armed resistance movement against the Israeli military presence in the south of Lebanon in the 1980s, this was an extension of that same message. This time, however, it was using the very means of mass demonstration, occupation and presence that had been employed by their opponents. They too were signalling determination, numbers and presence on a scale that could not be ignored by those trying to bring some order to Lebanese politics. This was most obvious in the aftermath of the 2005 elections that produced a government not at all to Hizbullah's liking. In December 2006, Hizbullah organized a mass demonstration in downtown Beirut, congregating also outside the office of Prime Minister Hanna Siniora. They demanded his resignation, claiming that he was too pro-American, anti-Syrian and did not have Lebanon's interests at heart. As with the demonstrators of 2005 who had helped bring Siniora to power, Hizbullah set up an encampment in the same public space and declared that they would not leave until the prime minister resigned. Essentially the party was demanding a larger number of seats in the government in order to wield veto power over any measures with which it disagreed. However, it portrayed its demonstration, in the words of a Hizbullah member of parliament, Ali Ammar, as 'the will of the majority of the people – most of whom want to escape this crisis and form a unity government'.[92]

The Lebanese case illustrates well the limitations of the strategy of marches and demonstrations to occupy public space where the idea of the public, and thus of public space itself, is so fragmented and contentious.

Given the amorphous and mediated nature of the Lebanese state, it was difficult to conjure into being a Lebanese public that opposed the state as such or tried to resist its encroachments. On the contrary, the state itself was a reflection of the communal and political alignments of Lebanese society and of the wider region. The shifting frontiers between state power and social forces were located elsewhere, amongst the communal and militia leaders whose bargains and pacts determined precisely how much authority and power the state should be allowed to wield.

In working out these formulae, the leaders were generally more preoccupied with the manoeuvres of their rivals and with the alignments of regional states than they were with their constituents who, in total, comprised the fractured public of Lebanon. The irony, therefore, was that public demonstrations and asserting presence in public space were tangential to the actual dispensation of power. As some of those involved in the Place des Martyres occupation were to admit somewhat wryly later on, the coming together by thousands of young Lebanese regardless of communal background was an inspiring sight, but the most substantial outcome – the dissolution of parliament and the calling of new elections – landed them each individually back in the same place from which they had set out. When they left the encampment and returned to their constituencies to vote, they found themselves entangled in the old structures of communal and divided power.

In this sense, therefore, the problem for those Lebanese who mobilized to protest the murder of al-Hariri was that they were too much part of the very thing they were trying to resist. Only in the case of resistance to Syrian domination of Lebanese politics could enough momentum be mobilized to make such tactics effective. Even here, as the massive Hizbullah counter-demonstrations showed, the population was divided about the value of the Syrian military presence. Some of the demonstrators held to a wider and more radical agenda that implied resistance to the long-established political set-up in Lebanon, but they made little headway. They could not extricate themselves from the very networks that sustained the system itself. Indeed, their political patrons did all they could to ensure that this was not on the agenda, seeking to prevent the coming together of a genuine Lebanese public around such a project.

NONVIOLENCE AND THE MOBILIZED PUBLIC

There are many strategies of nonviolent resistance to overwhelming power. Some, such as mass demonstration and the occupation of public space, are aimed at re-establishing the presence and the voice of a political public in the true sense – that is, as citizens. This may be against foreign occupation and the subjection that goes with it. Collective action to contest this subjection asserts the political existence of the community, be it ethnic, regional or national, demanding recognition as a political actor. The same applies to those resisting local and exclusive forms of power that demand obedience to and the unquestioning acceptance of the authority of a self-appointed elite. Here, the struggle is to reassert the existence of a political public, a body of citizens with differing views perhaps, but with equal rights to air those views and to act upon them.

In both cases, as developments in recent decades across the Middle East have shown, those who take direct action through nonviolent mass demonstration challenge those whose rule depends ultimately on their command of armed force. There is the obvious challenge to the capacity or to the will of those in power to use that armed force extensively and ruthlessly. The fate of the Shah of Iran, of Ben Ali in Tunisia and of Mubarak in Egypt showed that in the final analysis this was lacking and they fell. However, the behaviour of the Israeli military authorities, of Bashar al-Asad's government in Syria, of the Al Khalifa dynasty in Bahrain or of the government of the Islamic Republic of Iran have also shown that this is a challenge which others have been willing to meet. They have used not simply overwhelming firepower, but also the assets of regime cohesion and loyal security services, as well as timely external support, or simply lack of intervention, to suppress mass protests and nonviolent resistance, at least in the short term.

However, even in defeat, and at the cost sometimes of thousands of lives, resistance of this kind has demonstrated the existence of a mobilized, hostile and possibly unforgiving mass public. As the Palestinian and Iranian cases have shown, this has provided the basis for future action, both in terms of the repertoires of performance and through the memory of resistance and the kinds of organization that may come out of it. Indeed, this is the other facet of nonviolent mass mobilization. Through internal communication, now made that much easier through the new electronic media, the atomized subjects can transform themselves into collective actors. When this is supplemented and enhanced by creative productions of defiance, through songs, poems, plays and visual arts, it can cement identities that become inaccessible and resistant to those who rule through the gun.

The transformation of urban space into truly public space has been a key part not simply of the strategy of this kind of resistance but also of its intent. It is for that reason that there have been such ferocious battles to control it. One side uses it to demonstrate their existence as a mass public deserving of respect and recognition. Against them stand those who want to preserve it as the parade ground of social control, a fitting adjunct to the security forces' barracks that the buildings of the state institutions have effectively become. In 2011, both in Tunisia and in Egypt, the authorities lost that battle. The courage and persistence of the demonstrators and their capacity to withstand the violence used against them made their existence as a mobilized, cohesive political public a reality. The realization of the implications of this created the cracks that brought down the presidents of both countries. Neither in Tunisia nor in Egypt were the military establishments willing to contemplate the kind of violence that would have been necessary to reassert control over public space when the public itself, numbering millions of active citizens, was occupying that space. In both countries, those who used these methods successfully to resist the power of the regime now face the equally daunting task of transforming victory over public space in the streets into public control of the institutions of the state itself.

3

Imposition and Resistance in Economic Life

Burning buses, smashed storefronts, the whiff of tear gas and the crack of rubber-coated steel bullets became familiar features of city life across many parts of the Middle East in the first half of 2011. But they had also been regular in episodic occurrences from Morocco in the west to Jordan in the east towards the end of the twentieth and the beginning of the twenty-first centuries. In January 1977, the 'bread riots' shook Cairo, Alexandria and other Egyptian cities. The protestors mocked the then president Anwar Sadat with slogans like '*Wain al-futur, ya batal al-'ubur?*' [Hero of the crossing, where's our breakfast?], putting his military prowess of 1973 into the balance against the sudden price rises he had caused by abruptly removing food subsidies. A similar picture had developed, for very similar reasons, in Casablanca in June 1981. Rioters took hold of the commercial city centre, attacking banks, shops and symbols of government authority. They were expressing their outrage both at the government's removal of subsidies on basic foodstuffs and at its inability to provide jobs. Likewise, in Algeria in October 1988, widespread rioting paralysed the cities. Young Algerians – labelled '*hittistes*', since they seemed to have nothing better to do than to prop up the walls [*ha'it* in Arabic] – protested vehemently at their dismal employment prospects and at the impoverishment of the population in this oil-rich state. Symbolically they tore down the national flag of the revolution and hoisted an empty couscous sack in its place.[1] In 1989, riots of a similar kind in Ma`an, Jordan, brought down the government and forced the king to reinstate the Jordanian parliament.

In the following decades, riots and protests erupted periodically across the region. They expressed the anger of a largely young population at a broadly similar set of complaints: unemployment, rising prices and blatant economic inequalities that favoured the few over the many. It was not until December 2010, however, that these factors came together in Tunisia to produce a mass popular uprising that succeeded in overthrowing the president, Zine El Abidine ben Ali. When the 26-year-old Mohamed Bouazizi from Sidi Bouzid set himself alight in protest at the authorities' refusal to let him earn a living by closing down his roadside fruit stall, he ignited a spark that ended with the flight of Ben Ali less than a month later. The power of his act of self-sacrifice was that it could be recognized by all Tunisians as standing for everything that had gone wrong in their country in the preceding decades – economic development that ignored the poor and unemployed, as well as the everyday, almost casual abuses of power by the authorities throughout the country.

These protests were the latest signs of popular anger and exasperation. But they have been recurrent events in modern Middle Eastern political history as the region was increasingly drawn into a global economic system that obliged its inhabitants to march to its tune, regardless of the impact on their interests and their welfare.[2] The 'great transformation' of industrial capitalism transformed economic institutions and dramatically affected the lives of millions across the region, as it had in Europe. In the Middle East, this had taken place as a result of Europe's imperial expansion and capitalist power. Sometimes this was in cooperation with the governments of existing states in the region; sometimes it was achieved through direct imposition. It introduced new institutions, such as private property on a massive scale. This brought with it new relations of production in which human labour was counted merely as one factor among many. To facilitate these processes, new financial instruments were developed that fundamentally changed the ways in which people did business. Furthermore, new technologies marginalized and made redundant traditional skills and the communities that depended upon them. It was also clear that power followed the ownership of capital. This caused a shift in the forces that determined fates of the peoples of the Middle East. These were now outside the region entirely, or were commanded by the new social classes that had managed to profit from these opportunities.

Given the nature of the changes brought about in people's lives and the lack of control they had over these developments, it is not surprising that their fear and resentment of economic conditions – and of those whom they held responsible – should have periodically burst out into violent protest. As in the case of armed resistance, although generally less organized and more sporadic, violent demonstrations of anger, either by urban crowds or by peasant communities, were ways of communicating with those in power. They were meant to drive home the message that people had reached the limit of their endurance and that the everyday economic order could not continue without risking a greater escalation of protest. In that sense, therefore, like the armed resistance of the colonial and post-colonial periods, they were demanding a change of direction, even a fundamental change of regime.

State authorities across the region generally responded with a mixture of repression and concessions. Occasionally such protests, when linked to larger shifts in the balance of power within a country, set in motion more radical changes. However, this was usually indirect and often ambiguous in its outcome. Thus, in Egypt, the mounting wave of strikes and industrial action, as well as the demonstrations and riots of the 1940s, contributed to the overthrow of the old regime in July 1952. The new rulers did redraft the social compact, but at the cost of decades of military dictatorship. In Algeria, the 1991 elections were called in part as a consequence of the unrest of 1988. However, when the results were annulled by *Le Pouvoir* [the military clique at the head of the ruling FLN], it ushered in nearly a decade of bloody civil war. In 2011, it was one of the preoccupations of those involved in the uprisings in Tunisia and in Egypt that their efforts should not only produce more accountable government, but also a more equitable economic order.

When confronting the seemingly overwhelming power of global capitalism – seen most recently in the entrenchment of globalization and the dominance of neoliberal orthodoxy in economic affairs – various strategies of resistance have been used. Initially, this resistance was entwined with the politics of nationalism, since European imperial powers directly controlled the major economic assets of the region, in banking, industry, communications and oil. Further signs of resistance appeared during decolonization. It was then that nationalist elites in the Middle East had won control of the assets previously owned by Europeans. They were allegedly managed 'in the name of the people', but in reality the new elites used them in their own interests. In the 1970s and 1980s, they were well positioned to seize the opportunities offered by the reinvigoration of neoliberal capitalism and the dramatic rise in energy prices. It was this that provoked the riots of the 1980s onwards.

Former champions of national resistance and economic self-sufficiency now became complicit in the new forms of wealth creation. Internationally, through global finance capital and domestically, through the hold they and their associates had on the levers of state power, they created the basis for 'crony capitalism'. This has been the outcome of the waves of *infitah* [economic opening] – misleadingly labelled 'economic liberalization' – that have reshaped the economies of most Middle Eastern states in the past decades.

Resistance to these trends did not simply take the form of riots and demonstrations. New forms of collective organization began to emerge, sometimes within the framework of the old workers and professional associations, sometimes outside them. Trades unions and professional syndicates had long existed in the region and were seen as useful by the regimes of the newly independent states. However, in this setting they were meant to underpin a corporatist vision of the nation where different sections of the labour force would work in close cooperation with the new state-appointed managers of the national wealth. From one perspective, this could be seen as a way of involving labour in the new planned economies, helping to channel their concerns and grievances upward to those who controlled state-owned industry and land.

However, the system was also a means of exercising social control and of preventing the disruptive effects of class conflict. Official unions and syndicates across the Middle East thus played two roles: they were both agents of government and representatives of their members. In the eyes of the state authorities and increasingly of the members themselves, it was their role as enforcers, rather than as tribunes, that determined the behaviour of their ruling councils. As the rationale for corporatism decayed with the embrace of neoliberalism and the privatization of state banks and industry, so the distance between union leaders and the members became ever wider. This was a major factor in the revival of collective protest through strikes, demonstrations and factory occupations in the late twentieth and early twenty-first centuries. Workers were resisting the encroachment on their rights, as well as the deterioration of their conditions of employment. Under the old, corporate arrangements, these had been protected, so they had thought, by the original social compact with the state. However, in the changed conditions of the time, the complicit union leadership became themselves the target of organized collective protest.

In addition to this very obvious aspect of labour resistance, another thread of resistance has appeared in different forms and in different places across the Middle East during the same period. It too has stemmed from concern for a moral economy breached by the relentless power of industrial capitalism. It has given rise to attempts to resist the morally compromising and often demeaning entanglement with global capitalism, through the creation of alternative economies, or, more modestly, the creation of spaces in which the rules of the dominant capitalist economy could be suspended. Seen as morally repugnant by some and theologically suspect by others, capitalism could be resisted by everyday strategies, as well as by the imagination of an alternative order. The aspiration was freedom from the dictatorship of the market, the tyranny of the commodity and the heartless inequalities of capitalist wealth creation. The hope of many was that this would allow productive economic activity but without succumbing either to the norms of global finance capital or to the powers that stand at its back.

Aspects of imagined and organized resistance can be seen in the traditional practice of *hawala*, religiously sanctioned under Islamic rulings, but also supremely useful. In a related sphere, this can also help to explain in part the emergence of a substantially resourced Islamic banking sector towards the end of the twentieth century. In more site-specific fields of activity, economic measures involving boycotts and attempts at self-sufficiency have also been part of Palestinians' efforts to resist entanglement with and domination by Israeli power. Across the Islamic Middle East more generally, practices that have been grounded in an understanding of Islamic prescriptions for a fairer economic order have appealed to all classes. They have held out the promise of a defensive bulwark for a sphere of moral yet effective economic purpose, autonomous and free of outside intervention, in a spirit of resistance to a system of power driven by global capital.

IMPERIALISM AND THE COLONIAL ECONOMY

The nineteenth and early twentieth centuries saw the incorporation of the Middle East into the global economy on very unequal terms. The imperial European states and their financial institutions enjoyed an unmatchable advantage in terms of economic and financial power. The capital at their disposal, the markets they represented, their technologies, as well as new systems of administration, gave them direct or indirect control over resources across the region. Long before European military forces planted themselves as occupying powers in much of the

Middle East, European economic power had begun to shape the lives of people in the region. The encouragement of the cultivation of crops such as cotton in Egypt, the dismantling of domestic silk production in the Levant, the opening up of coal mines in Anatolia, the displacing of traditional crafts and skills in small workshops across the region – all of this bore testimony to the gradual encroachment and transformative power of European capital. It affected people's livelihoods and introduced new procedures at state and local levels, requiring conformity to unfamiliar institutions and to often irksome rules.

Strikes and Protests in Ottoman Turkey, Egypt and Qajar Iran

Across the Middle East, people tried to resist this encroachment and to fend off, as best they could, the immediate effects on their own livelihoods, districts and local economies. Sometimes this led to violence and protests directed against the new technologies, such as the strike which paralysed the Eregli Coal Company at Zonguldak on the Black Sea coast of Anatolia in 1908.[3] Sometimes it involved violence against the institutions and the personnel who were held responsible for the changed conditions. Often it took less obvious forms of resistance, more akin to those described in other settings where a show of outward compliance disguises an attempt to turn the situation to the advantage of the subaltern. Accounts of the decades-long effort of the 'Tobacco Régie' in the Ottoman Empire to regulate tobacco cultivation show how successful such resistance could be.

The Régie had been set up to control tobacco cultivation and sale throughout the Empire, holding out huge profits to the European banks that ran it. Potentially, therefore, it could help the Ottoman government in its negotiations with the Debt Administration instituted in 1875 by major European powers to handle the bankruptcy of the imperial government. However, farmers' and traders' rejection of this unwarranted foreign, centralized control of their livelihoods was expressed initially in direct action. For instance, it was this that caused the May 1887 riots in the port of Samsun and the burning down of the Régie's buildings. The problem was that open defiance and violent disorder brought down on the protestors' heads retribution by government security forces. Much more successful was the strategy of simply evading the Régie's control by appearing to comply but in fact smuggling tobacco across the Empire. Such was the scale – and the profitability – of these operations that even after a decade of trying to police this practice, in 1896 some ten million kilos of tobacco were being sold as contra-band, as against the eight million kilos sold by the Régie.[4]

At other times, where the strategy of resistance was neither practical nor prudent, flight and exile were the only options. This could either be abroad, such as the emigration of Lebanese villagers at the turn of the nineteenth century, hit by the crisis in silk cultivation,[5] or it could be internal migration within the country itself, as in the migration of Iraqi peasants from the heartless conditions of landlessness and debt in the southeastern provinces of the country. So severe did this become that the ruling landed interest in Iraqi politics under the monarchy tried to force the peasants to stay on the land, condemned to suffer their fate through the notorious law governing the 'rights and duties of the cultivators' of 1933. It proved to be virtually unenforceable, such was the peasants' resistance to economic conditions that were little better than slavery, and led to the rapid growth of the shanty town *sarifas* around Baghdad in the 1930s and 1940s.

Ironically, although these peasants had avoided direct resistance by taking flight, the political consequences of their actions both in Lebanon and in Iraq were to be felt generations later. It was then that some of the descendants of these same rural exiles became key players in the new forms of resistance that marked late twentieth and early twenty-first-century politics in both countries. In Lebanon, this could be seen in the emergence of Amal in the 1970s, and in Iraq the Sadrist movement from the 1990s onwards bore witness to the decades-long impoverishment of the Shi`a of eastern Baghdad. At the time, however, the initial flight had been a symptom of the disruption of a rural economy. However restricted and unequal the original rural economy might have been, it had been grounded in social relations that made sense to those involved, operating its own moral economy free of the commodification of land and of labour inherent in the new capitalist order.

The new forms of property ownership, of industrial production and of communication and trade, as well as the new divisions of labour, opened society up to the transformative power of global capitalism. Nevertheless, they also called into being forms of resistance that were geared directly to challenging the absolute control of capital. In this respect, people began to organize and to take new forms of collective action. In Egypt, workers in a wide variety of crafts and trades found new ways of organizing to defend the erosion of their customary rights or to defend themselves against an increasingly regulated state and an unequal balance of forces in the economy. Sometimes they fell back on the older subterfuges of tax evasion, of resistance disguised as compliance. But increasingly, they organized themselves to use the courts and to withdraw their labour to reinforce their cause.

As the 1907 strike of the cabbies of Cairo demonstrated, these strategies won concessions. Their success also gave heart to other workers, leading to a wave of strikes across the country, encouraged by the emerging Egyptian nationalist movement. This resulted in the founding of the first trade union in Egypt for Egyptians, the Manual Trades Workers Union [*niqaba `ummal al-sana`i al-yadawiyya*] in 1909.[6] The new world order of global capitalism had begun to dominate much of the Middle East, but in doing so, it had created the conditions and the terms of resistance to its progress. The measures by which capital tried to increase its hold provoked new forms of resistance in the Middle East as in other parts of the world. People were not necessarily resisting the intrusion of new industries, but rather trying to ensure that the methods and the conditions of labour that they brought with them were sufficiently humane for them to operate to the mutual benefit of both owners and workers.

Of course, under such conditions, property ownership was itself contentious. On the one hand, there were many in the Middle East who benefited greatly from the new economies of the region and from the link with European capital. In different countries, an emerging entrepreneurial class appeared. Sometimes its members were linked through family ties to the rising political elites of the new states. Sometimes middlemen and entrepreneurs were associated with particular communities that enjoyed privileged access to the educational and other institutions established by the European powers. This was the case of the Christians of Syria and Lebanon, or the Jews of Algeria and Iraq. At times, this led people to identify the unequal wealth of capitalist accumulation with religious or ethnic difference. This could obscure the inequality of the system itself, turning social animosity against a whole community, now mistrusted for their links with foreign powers. At other times, as in the strikes on the Anatolian Railway Company in 1908, similar suspicions led to a split within the trade union itself. This divided the largely Christian leadership and the predominantly Muslim membership when it came to clinching a deal with the mainly European Christian employers and managers. Aptly enough, this has been interpreted as a sign of 'the already faltering brotherhood of Ottomans', as the moral economy that had bound them together was subjected to the conflicting interests of capital and labour.[7]

On the other hand, foreign ownership was a reality. European capital had been used to build up new forms of industrial and agricultural production, either through loans or through direct investment. It ended up by owning great swathes of the economies of Middle Eastern states, or by controlling these same economies through various debt repayment schemes. In Egypt, joint ventures between local families, often Jewish, such as the Mosseris, the Cattaouis or the Rolos, or Alexandrine Greek, such as the Salvagos, Zervoudakis or the Benakis, and British and French companies became one of the marked features of the growing Egyptian economy.[8] In negotiating concessions for trade monopolies or for the exploitation of natural resources, European companies, often with the direct backing of their governments, could ensure that they won advantageous terms from local political authorities that were often weak, divided and always short of cash.

It was inevitable, therefore, that the question of ownership should have become deeply implicated in political struggles for national self-determination. One of the most famous and successful of these was the tobacco boycott in late-nineteenth-century Iran. This was organized to protest the autocratic Qajar Shah Nasir al-Din's grant of a monopoly to produce and to sell tobacco to the British Imperial Tobacco Company. The concession of 1890 provoked furious and coordinated protests across the country. These were backed by the religious leadership and by the most illustrious Shi'i Marja' of the day, Ayatollah Mirza Shirazi. The protests were also supported by the merchant class. It united to close the bazaars in most of Iran's major cities. Equally dramatic, the cause was taken up by hundreds of thousands of Iranians who obeyed Shirazi's *fatwa* banning all use of tobacco products. Such was the effect of this sustained and popular protest and the mobilizing capacity of such a symbolically charged issue that the Shah was forced to rescind the concession in early 1892. In this, he was influenced probably more by the array of religious and political forces standing against him than by the rumoured refusal of his own household either to consume or to provide him with tobacco whilst the *fatwa* remained in place (it was repealed by Shirazi once the concession had been terminated).[9]

The Iranian tobacco protest demonstrated an unparalleled scale of mobilization against a measure that had promised to damage the material interests of sections of the Iranian population, as well as to extend the already substantial control of foreigners over yet one more aspect of life in the country. It was also linked to a growing feeling of resentment at the autocratic style of the Shah and can therefore be seen as a prelude to the accelerating moves for political reform that were to challenge his successor in 1906. However, this was not the only way in which foreign economic monopolies were resisted. Soon afterwards, in Egypt, Talaat Harb, an Egyptian entrepreneur sympathetic to the growing call for Egyptian self-government, began to put into place his plans for the development of an indigenous Egyptian capitalism. This was intended to rival and to displace the dominance of the European financial interests that so marked Egypt's commercial and industrial life at the turn of the century.

Although scarcely cast in the heroic mould of the earlier political and military resistance of Colonel Ahmad 'Orabi Pasha, or of the later champions of the Egyptian nationalist parties, Harb neverthe-less represented a growing trend. This included people, not simply in Egypt, who believed that the productive power of capitalism could be more successfully harnessed to the service of their countries, if control lay within those countries, rather than in the major financial centres of Europe. In Harb's case, this was by no means a bid to create financial institutions independent of foreign capital. On the contrary, he and others who thought like him, such as the members of the commission under Ismail Sidqi that looked into commerce and industry in Egypt during the period of the British protectorate, were to stress the importance of cooperation with external capital.[10] It was more that they believed in building up an indigenous cap-ital base in order to alter the terms of trade that had made Egypt and European firms or governments such unequal partners in any enterprise.

This idea impelled Harb to build up the Misr Bank and its chain of companies, achieving considerable success and making the group a significant player in the Egyptian economy. Nor was he the only one to be pursuing such a strategy. Indeed, the enterprise can be seen as a way of providing a newly assertive Egyptian bourgeoisie with avenues of expansion and profit, disguised as national self-determination. This strengthened the link with the emerging nationalist parties and gave the whole endeavour a populist aura that lingers still in the memory of many.[11] It was reinforced by the republican regime that followed the 1952 revolution. President Gamal Abd al-Nasser, despite eventually nationalizing Misr Bank and all its enterprises, honoured the memory of Talaat Harb by naming one of Cairo's main squares after him and erecting a large bronze statue of him in the middle of it. Nasser's successor, President Anwar Sadat, carried on the tradition, going so far in 1980 as to award Harb posthumously Egypt's highest honour, the Order of the Nile.

However, as a strategy of resistance to the encroachment of European capital, it was always going to suffer from a major flaw. Harb, no less than any other entrepreneur in Egypt at the time, was heavily involved in the financial world, as it was then constituted. If this meant raising capital abroad, as it surely did, or entering into joint ventures with European companies, then he would seize the opportunity. The raison d'être of his companies, after all, was to compete successfully and to make the kinds of returns which only successful capital expansion would allow. The drive to increase productivity and to enhance his group's profitability was the logic that governed his economic strategy. This would inevitably limit the degree to which the Misr Group could ever work only in the interests of distinctively Egyptian capital, even if such a concept were practical. The conditions of global capitalist expansion and the financial markets of the day made this unlikely.

For those seeking to organize in defence of the labour force that worked in locally owned enterprises, this was self-evident. However, some nationalist groups linked to local entrepreneurs in Egypt, Syria and elsewhere were reluctant to encourage confrontations between labour and national capital. Similar inhibitions affected the Islamist organizations, specifically the Muslim Brotherhood, when it became involved in organizing labour during the 1940s in Egypt. It was noticeable, for instance, that during this period, at the height of labour and nationalist activism, the Brotherhood was keen to encourage strikes in foreign-owned factories, but discouraged strike activity in factories owned by Egyptians in the same sector.[12]

However, these views were not shared by secular socialist and communist unionists, since, from their perspective, the interests of capital knew no national boundaries and manifested themselves everywhere in similar ways. Whether the company concerned was technically owned by an Egyptian, an Iraqi or a Syrian, the logic of its position as a profit-seeking outfit would lead it to exploit labour in order to enhance its profit. For the organizers of labour, this was the overriding consideration, and it was this that underpinned an increasing level of labour activism during the dying days of colonialism and the early years of post-colonial independence.[13]

In Egypt, the textile industry in particular became the site of effective trade union activity, with the founding in 1945 of the Workers' Committee for National Liberation – its name indicating that this was not simply about the battle for workers' rights. This trend was to become even more noticeable with the committee's adherence, along with a number of other political organizations, to the National Committee of Workers and Students that organized a general strike in February 1946 to mark 'evacuation day'. It brought tens of thousands of workers and demonstrators out onto the streets to demand that the British withdraw their forces from the Nile Valley.[14] The mingling of nationalist demands with those concerned with the conditions of labour, such as pay levels, lay-offs and workers' rights, became a marked feature of labour activism in Egypt and elsewhere during this transitional period.

However, the workers in Egypt discovered, as did their counterparts across the Middle East, that nationalist regimes did not look kindly on independent workers' representation or champion their demands against those of capital. On the contrary, the newly established regimes were more interested in imposing order. They were therefore intolerant of any union activity that did not come directly under their control. This was demonstrated soon after the July 1952 coup in Egypt that overthrew the monarchy and brought the Free Officers to power. In mid-August, workers went on strike and staged a sit-in at the textile mills of Kafr al-Dawwar. They demanded the right to organize an independent trade union, the dismissal of oppressive managers at the factory and the granting of economic benefits. The new government chose to see this as part of a larger plot by communist forces to sow discord and over-reacted by sending army units to surround the factory. The soldiers fired on the workers' demonstration, and in the ensuing clashes, three members of the security forces and four workers were killed. Hundreds of workers were then arrested and some thirty were charged with various offences by a military tribunal that sentenced to death two of their number, Mustafa Khamis and Muhammad al-Baqri. They were executed in early September and a dozen of their co-workers were sent to prison.[15]

The same desire by new nationalist regimes to control all aspects of economic life also undermined the position of indigenous capitalists in the wake of independence. They were seen, with some exceptions, such as Talaat Harb, as potential fifth columnists, linked umbilically to European interests through their commercial and financial ties to the capital markets. When their connections to the overthrown parliamentary regimes were added to the charge, it was made to appear that such a class could only serve its own interests, even if it meant working against the interests of the nation. This was the message that came from the government of Egypt under Nasser in the 1960s, from Salah Jadid's Ba`thist government in Syria, as well as from the Iraqi Communist Party in Iraq during Abd al-Karim Qasim's rule and from its Ba`thist successor government under Ali Salih al-Sa`di. Resistance to economic domination, whether by Western capital or by its domestic allies, needed therefore to come from a different source.

This source was to be the apparatus of the newly independent state itself – at least in the eyes of the young army officers who emerged to take over states from Algeria to Yemen, including Libya, Egypt, Syria and Iraq. Consequently, the nationalizations that followed many of the coups d'état of the 1950s and the 1960s were aimed not simply at the foreign-owned interests in these countries, but increasingly at the enterprises owned by the local bourgeoisie. Creating a centrally planned economy, regulated by state-appointed agencies, working towards a development plan that was intended to make a rational calculation of the country's needs – these were the elements that were thought to constitute the formula for successfully resisting entanglement in and subordination to the global capitalist system in which the former imperial powers still played such a leading role.

This was not, of course, a vision of economic sovereignty confined to Middle Eastern states. On the contrary, it was very much part of the economic plans unveiled in the wake of the Russian and Chinese revolutions. Nationalization of banking and industry, central planning and economic autarky were proposed not simply as powerful engines for the development of their national economies, but also as alternative economic systems. Ambitiously, these were meant to provide the basis for a fairer and a more efficient global economic order than that which had arisen under capitalism. For those in the Middle East who had long resented and had tried to resist domination by Western powers, this was a seductive vision, whatever doubts they may have had about the driving Marxist rationale at work in Russia and China. Before the contradictions and weaknesses of this system became apparent, the promise it held out exerted a powerful appeal. It seemed to many to be the way to realize a vision of indigenous capital development, combined with a concern for social justice and local norms that had been absent in the European economic exploitation of the region.

NATIONALIZATION, PRIVATIZATION AND
THEIR DISCONTENTS

Labour Unrest in Egypt and North Africa: From Corporatism to the *Infitah*

For some years, the impetus of nationalization carried forward the governments of Syria, Egypt, Algeria, Tunisia, Iraq and Yemen, both North and South. They benefited from the popularity of the measures that uprooted decades of foreign control, as well as from the surpluses available to finance the ambitious welfare states promised by the revolutionary regimes to their peoples. It was during these years – roughly spanning the 1950s to the 1970s – that the social compact, later known rather derisively as *dimuqratiyyat al-khubz* [the democracy of bread], was being established.[16] Essentially, this comprised an unwritten understanding that the government would carry through social and economic reforms and the development of the national economy, largely untrammelled by systematic accountability. It was thus no democracy at all, but a compact whereby the government committed itself to the ideals of social justice, as well as to economic and educational provision for all, in return for popular acquiescence.

The main components that were to keep it in place, other than the coercive monopoly of the state itself, were the institutions of the welfare state – health, education, subsidized housing, agricultural cooperatives – as well as government subsidies not only of public services, but also of a large range of basic consumer goods, such as flour, sugar, cooking oil and fuel. In addition, government-sponsored organizations reflected the corporatist ethos shared by most of these nationalist, republican regimes. They were intended to bring different sections of the working public into line, through professional associations, peasant leagues, youth and women's organizations and trades unions. In Egypt, the government of the Free Officers, having suppressed the spontaneous workers' action at Kafr al-Dawwar, went on to draft new labour legislation. This granted some of the workers' demands regarding security of employment and fringe benefits, but it also prohibited strike action and made arbitration in any dispute compulsory.[17] Thus recognition for workers' rights, including the right to organize and to bargain collectively, depended on the government's complete control of the process.

The unions that were set up were intended primarily to discipline and to channel the potentially contentious politics of class into a more harmonious and supportive system. They had a key role to play in ensuring conformity and in communicating government messages on welfare, on consumption and on rights to their members. In Egypt, all unions were obliged to belong to the Egyptian Workers Federation, formed in 1957. In 1961, this became the Egyptian Trade Union Federation (ETUF), but the system of control remained in place, with the government appointing most of the executive board and introducing the practice whereby the president of the Federation was also the minister of labour. Informally, depending on the personalities involved, the condition of the state and sometimes the sector of the economy, this machinery could pass concerns upwards. But this was always on the government's own terms. In many respects, therefore, it was a system of broad-based co-optation and surveillance in which any form of resistance could be detected in good time and dealt with appropriately.

As long as the benefits of the system were apparent to those involved, there was limited incentive for resistance. On the contrary, in many countries, real wages increased substantially, along with benefits like job security, health care, subsidized housing and food, as well as pensions. This is not to say that outbreaks did not occur, sometimes spontaneous, sometimes well organized, sometimes sublimated or assumed into other causes of unrest. For instance, in 1964, as a result of an acrimonious mass meeting of the newly formed, government-controlled General Union of Agricultural and Manual Workers at Aja in Daqahliyya province in Egypt, a group of workers broke away to form their own, independent worker-led organization.[18]

However, the problems for the system as a whole began when the state could no longer deliver its part of the bargain. Economic stagnation, loss of investment and productivity, as well as war and the expense of maintaining the national security state, added to the crisis of the socialist economies by the early 1970s. This posed a crisis of social control that by its nature could not easily be compensated for by intensified repression. It also suggested to some within the bureaucratic elite that other economic strategies were needed. The vision of autarky and self-sufficient development was fast evaporating. It began to appear that access to development capital could only be gained through political realignment with the very forces that had once been denounced as parasitic allies of neo-colonialism. It was a message that many within the elite were already predisposed to hear. The dividing lines between public and private had become increasingly blurred in the decades during which holding public office could also be a path to self-enrichment.

It was in these circumstances that the idea of the *infitah* – or economic opening – began to inform policies across the region. It took some decades to materialize, but it implied a basic reorientation of central, state-planned economies of the Middle East. In theory, they were to be transformed into economies where private enterprise would play an increasing role and where foreign investment would once again be welcomed, with all that implied in terms of joint ventures, foreign ownership and frameworks for free exchange rates. It was accompanied by a political change of direction internationally and domestically that involved the abandonment of the rhetoric of socialism and the alliances it had implied. It also signalled a willingness to accept the conditions imposed by outside investors – international financial institutions, such as the World Bank and IMF, as well as aid-giving governments and the private financial interests seeking a return on their investment. For many, this raised the spectre of the very system of external control that had been resisted so determinedly in the struggle for true independence.

The measures carried out by Middle Eastern governments at the behest of external donors or creditors compounded these fears, sparking some of the riots that were experienced in countries where *infitah* of one sort or another was being implemented. Thus, in 1977, the decision by the Egyptian government to introduce some of the required price reforms by cutting subsidies on flour, sugar, cooking oil, petrol and butagas provoked an immediate and outraged response by hundreds of thousands of Egyptians. On 18 January, workers at the Helwan steelworks went on strike and gathered in Tahrir Square and elsewhere in Cairo where they were joined by thousands of others. Similar demonstrations erupted in the major cities the length and breadth of Egypt. Symbols of government authority, such as the Arab Socialist Union building in Alexandria and a police station in Saidna Zaynab in Cairo, were set on fire. At the same time, banks were attacked, as were luxury shops and casinos on Cairo's Pyramids Road, long associated with the inaccessible wealth enjoyed by the few. The slogans of the protestors matched this twin indictment of government repression and inequality: 'We want a free government, life has become bitter', 'They eat chicken and drink whisky and we eat *ful* [beans]'. The following day the armed forces intervened and imposed a curfew, leaving nearly fifty people dead and more than 600 injured. Despite the arrests of some hundreds of Egyptians and the subsequent trials that tried to blame a small number of 'agitators' (all of whom were eventually acquitted), the government rescinded the price rises and effectively acknowledged the power of the protests.[19]

Not long afterwards, a series of strikes organized by the UGTT in Tunisia began. Starting in 1977, these were protests against the erosion of living standards and of workers' rights experienced since the enthusiastic embrace by the Tunisian government of the economic 'restructuring' proposals of the IMF and World Bank. They grew increasingly vehement, culminating in a general strike in January 1978 that precipitated armed intervention by the security forces. This led to violence and heavy casualties, some putting the estimates of those killed as high as 200. Morocco, undergoing its own version of the austerity plan introduced by the IMF and the World Bank, experienced similar riots and protests a couple of years later in 1981.

In May of that year, the Moroccan government suddenly announced dramatic price rises for a range of basic foodstuffs, as well as cuts in the education budget. These measures were met within days by protest demonstrations across Morocco. The government responded in a muddled way, arresting hundreds but also rescinding some of the price rises. This seemed to provoke people still further, especially the high school students, since the government chose this moment to inform them that roughly eighty-five per cent had failed their school leaving exams. The Moroccan trade union congress, the UMT, called for a general strike in Casablanca, the country's commercial capital, on 18 June. It succeeded in closing down the city entirely. But it was then that the riots in Casablanca began in earnest, with thousands of demonstrators smashing shop windows in the most affluent parts of town, burning buses and cars and breaking into banks across the city. The police were overwhelmed and the army was called in to suppress the riots. It proceeded to do so as if it were fighting an urban guerrilla enemy, relentlessly moving tanks and armoured personnel carriers into the town and reoccupying it block by block. Within two days, Casablanca had been reoccupied, but at the cost of about 200 dead (some alleged 600 were killed throughout the country), the arrest of hundreds and the virtual closing down of the trades union organizations in the city. Meanwhile rioting spread to towns across the country.[20] As in other cases, the government annulled much of the austerity package and used a combination of overt repression and the reinstatement of subsidies to restore order.

The enforced calm was not to last. In 1984, in both Morocco and Tunisia, rioting and demonstrations broke out once more. In Tunisia, the protests had begun in the poorest, southern region of the country at the end of 1983 and followed yet another attempt by the government to comply with IMF and World Bank recommendations to 'stabilize' the economy by removing subsidies. It led to massive price increases for which the population was ill prepared. The rapid spread of demonstrations to other cities, including the capital Tunis, suggests that people were mobilized by measures that affected them all. But in Tunis in particular, the core of the protestors were high school and university students who were angered more by cuts in the education budget and by the prospect of graduate unemployment. President Bourguiba sent in the security forces, both police and army. These launched a violent attack on the protestors, causing perhaps as many as 150 deaths. But in a now-familiar pattern, after some days of demonstrations, repression and protest, the president announced the repeal of all price rises, and within a week or so, the protests had ended.[21]

These were initial, often disorganized or uncoordinated, forms of resistance to the cracks that were appearing in the social compact. They expressed a combination of fears and frustrations about what the future might hold. However, they were all sparked off by the introduction of measures, such as the removal or reduction of subsidies, that had an immediate impact on people's well-being, in a way that the longer-term, structural changes would have yet to show. In many respects, the manner of the government's introduction of these measures – suddenly, peremptorily and with no prior discussion, let alone consultation – ensured that the protests were not simply targeted at the economic measures themselves. They were also an indictment of the form of authoritarian government itself. The violent response of the security forces ensured an escalation in the conflict. It also meant, given the coercive power in the hands of the authorities, that the protestors could be manoeuvred onto the very field where the government could 'make an example' of them. The image shifted away from scrutiny of the government's economic policies or its ineptitude to the 'maintenance of law, order and stability'. This was spiced up by government spokesmen from Rabat to Cairo alleging that dark forces were at work behind the protests, blaming Islamists, communists or, bizarrely, in the case of the Moroccan authorities at one point, Zionists.

Organized Labour and Workers' Protests in Egypt (1995–2011)

Resistance in the form of open protests became more frequent with the growing severity of the austerity demanded by the dominant model of economic reform. At the same time, the promised benefits of these reforms failed to materialize as far as the mass of the population was concerned. Fears about economic prospects and about conditions of employment led people to resist the control of the authoritarian, corporatist state. In Egypt, for instance, in the 1980s and the 1990s, there was a struggle for control of the existing professional associations. These decades witnessed fierce battles between the membership and the authorities to secure control of the Lawyers Syndicate and the Engineers Syndicate. There were charges and countercharges of rigged elections, leading sometimes to direct government intervention.

The Egyptian authorities became increasingly anxious about the syndicates' direction and impact. This was largely because they threatened to become spaces for the voicing of dissent, not simply against government economic policy but against the government itself. Various means were tried to regain control of them and to use them once again as top-down disciplinary organs of the state, pre-empting their transformation into vehicles for bottom-up demands, let alone for sustained lobbying or protest. Given the power of the state, this was always an unequal struggle. Nevertheless, in some cases, victories could be won by those who were determined and organized enough to resist government encroachment.

Thus, with the introduction of Law 100 in 1993, nominally 'guaranteeing democracy in professional union elections', the government gave itself greater scope to interfere in those elections. However, the Muslim Brotherhood and other critics of the government managed to gain representation in a number of syndicates, especially the Lawyers' Syndicate. The government responded by sequestrating its assets, but after some years, in 1999, the Egyptian Supreme Court ordered that this be lifted, paving the way for new elections. In order to prevent a resurgence of Muslim Brotherhood candidates, the authorities promptly arrested a large number of its leaders, hoping to intimidate them prior to the elections. The move was not wholly successful. A continuing game of cat and mouse ensued between the government and its opponents through the maze of syndicate legislation and procedures.[22]

The complaints of these organizations were only partly related to the deteriorating economic situation. Their protests were also due to the restrictions imposed on them by the government. These measures affected both the discharge of the professional duties of their members and their autonomy as organizations representing those members. It was not so much the specific measures associated with the *infitah* that were provoking them, therefore, but rather the general conditions in which the original compact of the corporate state seemed to be breaking down.

The opportunities created by the openings of the *infitah*, particularly for those connected with the ruling regime through family or other long-standing ties, had certainly underlined the inequalities in the system and the redundancy of the old corporate ethos. For the professional syndicates that had been part of that system, the old rationale had therefore begun to decay. In its place, a tougher bargaining spirit was emerging, in which the associations would increasingly reflect the interests of their members rather than those of the state, since the state itself was viewed as having been captured by a self-interested, unrepresentative clique. It was not surprising, therefore, that they should have become increasingly resistant to the state's efforts to impose the old forms of control.

If this was the case with the professional syndicates, it was to be even more marked in the trade union movement across the region. Again, Egypt had a long history of unionism and a trade union structure intimately bound up with the institutional power of the corporate state. It provides, therefore, a vivid example of the gradual emergence of resistance to the new forms of economic power shaping the lives of Egyptians in the early twenty-first century. It was then that the full impact of the restructuring of the Egyptian economy was felt as redundancies, deteriorating conditions of work, depressed wage rates and diminishing pension benefits affected ever larger numbers of people.

In Egypt, the overarching ETUF of the Nasserist era faced two ways. It was meant to represent the interests of its members upwards to the government. At the same time, it was intended to relay the government's edicts downwards to the workers. The relationship was memorably summed up in Nasser's own assertion that 'The workers don't demand. We give'.[23] Inevitably, within such a framework, ETUF, the only permitted stage for union activity, became deeply implicated in the operations of the one-party state. It was drawn into the implementation of the national economic plans and was obliged to persuade or simply to tell their members what role they must play in this process. They did relay concerns from below, but since it was not from here that they derived their power, the leadership rarely stood up to the government and, in any clash of interests, would almost always side with the authorities. Even if the senior leadership of ETUF rarely defied the government, the same could not be said for their members, or indeed for some of the local branch leaders of particular unions. Some of these found themselves taking on both the government and their own union leadership.

While the corporate state and the implicit bargain on which it was founded were operating without severe problems, there were few signs of defiance and the existing arrangements for the settlement of disputes seemed to work. The guarantee of employment rights, wage rates, health insurance and pensions, together with initiatives to encourage worker participation, ensured a relatively acquiescent labour force. The system of unions and syndicates thus formed a recognizable part of the limited system of interest representation in Nasserist Egypt. The economic and political crises characteristic of the ending of Nasser's presidency and the change of direction that began soon after Anwar Sadat succeeded to the presidency in 1970 altered these terms of reference. The *infitah* declared by Sadat in the mid-1970s promised much more than it delivered. It did little to lift state control of the economy or to encourage private enterprise, but it did signal a transformation of the ways in which the political elite had begun to think about the future of Egypt and its economy. It was also in large measure a response to the desperate shortage of capital that had already become apparent in the late 1960s, putting great financial strain on the maintenance of the welfare state and the social compact that had underpinned it.

The effects of this on relations between labour and capital, and thus on the organizations representing labour, began to be felt in the 1970s. Soon after the war of 1973, labour, unrest over pay and conditions erupted in the shipyards of Alexandria, among the public transport workers in Cairo and in the textile factories of al-Mahalla al-Kubra. The 1976 strike and violent protests at the Misr Spinning and Weaving factory at al-Mahalla brought government reprisals. The security forces intervened, causing the deaths of some fifty workers, arresting 2,000 in all following the violent ending of the occupation of the factory. These events had largely taken place despite the national union leadership in ETUF. However, the riots and demonstrations of 1977, initiated by workers from Helwan and Alexandria, put such pressure on the reluctant ETUF leadership from below that they finally had to endorse the strikes and demonstrations calling for a restoration of basic subsidies.[24]

In the 1980s, following the death of President Sadat and the succession of President Husni Mubarak, labour unrest and workers' activism, often outside the recognized union framework, became even more marked, echoing simultaneous developments in Morocco and Tunisia. In 1983, a wave of strikes, stoppages and sit-ins hit industries as diverse as textiles, engineering, chemicals and pipe manufacturing. Management – and behind it, the government – responded sometimes with concessions,

sometimes with the full force of the state security apparatus and sometimes with both. This was the case in the spectacularly violent ending
to a workers' occupation of the Helwan Light Transport factory. The
government sent in riot police armed with tear gas and electric cattle
prods to evict the workers. But, having cleared the plant in this way, the
management ceded to the workers' original demands for place of work
compensation.[25]

In 1984, the Egyptian government doubled workers' contributions
to health insurance and pensions and simultaneously raised the prices of
basic foods. This brought out sharply the differences between the workers and the union representatives, since the ETUF leadership supported
a law that outraged thousands of workers across the country. This was
soon evident in September at Kafr al-Dawwar where workers refused
their pay cheques and began a sit-in. They were joined by thousands of
others, all calling for the rescinding of the law and of the price increases,
but also for the dismissal of both the head of ETUF and of the prime
minister. The security forces surrounded the factory, but some of the
workers broke through the cordon to encourage others to join them. It
was not long before the demonstrations in the town turned into a riot.
The Central Security Forces used tear gas and automatic fire while the
demonstrators torched police vehicles and attacked symbols of state
authority, including the offices of the ruling NDP. The riots continued
for three days during which three workers lost their lives, dozens were
injured and thousands were arrested. However, the demonstrations did
succeed in forcing the government to cancel the price rises and to withdraw the insurance contribution law 'for further study'.[26]

Marsha Pripstein Posusney has persuasively argued that much of the
workers' protest of the 1980s was characterized by two factors that
shaped both the style of the strikes and sit-ins, and the ambition or reach
of the worker activists.[27] In the first place, many of the protests were
confined to specific sites, such as the factory of a particular company,
generally state owned, where the workers felt oppressed or betrayed by
the management. Second, the thrust of their protests was often against
the fracture of a moral economy that they felt had been undermined
either by management or by the state's reorganization of the industrial
sector. This was significant, since it often determined the forms that
protest took – sit-ins, work-ins, petitions and the refusal of pay cheques,
rather than strikes and walkouts alone. It also meant that the complaints could often be met through local, site-specific concessions, even
if the authorities used force against the workers to make an example of

them. This would explain the curious pattern of repression-concession that was so common in labour disputes during this period.

It was in the 1990s that the Egyptian government pursued a more energetic and radical programme of economic restructuring, extending and deepening the privatization of significant portions of the Egyptian economy. This had the effect of sharpening workers' protests at the impact on their own livelihoods and prospects. Law 203 of 1991 opened the way for the privatization of major state assets on an unprecedented scale. It was soon followed by legal reforms that once again privileged private property – real estate and agricultural land – and rescinded many of the older tenancy rights. Protests, leading sometimes to violence, occurred on a regular basis, as peasants tried to resist the authorities' and the landlords' attempts to implement these laws. By its nature, however, such defiance was generally isolated and limited in scope.

More significant was the enactment of a range of measures designed to conform to prescriptions for 'economic health' drawn up by the international financial institutions. These were meant to draw Egypt more closely into the workings of the global economy by restructuring its price mechanisms, its banking practices and its currency. Some sections of the Egyptian economy made enormous gains, even if unequally shared. For those still tied to the old structures of employment, productivity and reward, the restructuring underlined the precariousness of their positions and the deepening divide between the classes in Egypt. In the decade or so that followed the introduction of the 1991 law, the balance between state and private enterprise changed dramatically, such that by 2005 some seventy per cent of the Egyptian economy was privately owned. While the privatization measures were being implemented and factories sold off to private investors, both Egyptian and foreign, a wave of strikes, sit-ins and protests took place in those industries most directly affected.

Although the 1991 law had expressly forbidden dismissals and lay-offs as a result of privatization, managers found ways to evade this in order to make their industry more attractive to private investment. There was also little evidence that this section of the law was ever enforced. But equally worrying for employees were the new terms of employment. Many of the specified benefits enjoyed under state ownership were now rescinded, new and less secure contracts of employment were drawn up, wage levels fell against inflation and hours of work were often extended. The nature of the inexorable but piecemeal privatization measures meant that resistance was often site-specific. Workers tried to win concessions in the new terms of employment or reassurances from the existing management. It was rarely if ever aimed at resisting or even overturning the very principle of the sale of public assets, nor was it necessarily intended to challenge the authorities.

In the twenty-first century, the full implications of the changes were becoming clearer. It was then that organized, collective resistance began to appear. With it came a new spirit of industrial activism, new ways of organizing labour protests and an agenda that directly challenged the political leadership of the state and the regime's instruments of control. In some areas, the union structure of the corporate state was subverted through the election of more representative union officers intent on making the voice of their members heard at the highest level. Successful as this was in some places and at certain times, the imbalance of power, influence and patronage told against them, and many of the new representatives found themselves, much like their predecessors, co-opted by the state.

The government, apprehensive of the challenge from labour activism, fell back on tried and tested techniques. It strengthened the hold of the senior leadership of ETUF and, in the elections of 2006, ensured that ruling NDP candidates were installed on ETUF's National Council – where they occupied twenty-two out of the twenty-three seats.[28] However, these measures were ineffective against the wave of strikes and industrial action that unfolded across Egypt from late 2006 onwards. It has been estimated that the numbers of workers involved in strike action in state and private industry and in government employ leapt from fewer than 20,000 in 2005 to nearly 90,000 in 2006, with accelerating rates of increase in the years that followed. Those involved in all forms of industrial action – strikes, sit-ins and demonstrations – went from roughly 140,000 in 2005 to more than half a million in 2008, as the number of protests recorded in the same period trebled from about 200 in 2005 to about 600 in 2008.[29]

The figures alone indicate that the old techniques of social control were breaking down. The more the leadership of ETUF had become complicit in economic restructuring policies that were having such an obviously damaging effect on the interests of their members, the more rapid was the erosion of their authority. Membership of the twenty-three unions that comprised ETUF was on the decline, partly due to the non-recognition clauses in the contracts of a number of privatized concerns, and partly due to disillusionment with the ineffective nature of the organizations themselves. In previous decades, wildcat strikes, sit-ins and other demonstrations of workers' protest and resistance had generally been organized without the authorization of the official union leadership and often as part of the workers' indictment of that leadership. After 2006, however, a determined effort to organize collectively outside the framework of ETUF got underway, despite the fact that Law 35 of 1976 explicitly prohibited this.

The most dramatic early expression of this was the organization that emerged out of the strike of the civil servants at the Property Tax Authority in October 2007. Defying their official representatives, these low-paid state employees took direct action. They withdrew their labour and paralysed the state's property tax collection system. They went further and camped out in the middle of Cairo on Hussein Higazi Street, making their presence felt with tents, banners and placards that defiantly stated their demands. These were intended to redress years of neglect. They felt that their services had been taken for granted, and demanded the amalgamation of their agency with the General Tax Authority, as well as the raising of their wages to parity with the employees of the GTA. After about three months of peaceful public protest, unusually free from violent intervention by the authorities, the minister of finance, Yusuf Butros Ghali, negotiated directly with the strikers. Having recognized them in this way, he finally agreed to their main demand and guaranteed them a wage increase of more than 300 per cent.[30]

So heartened were they by this success, watched closely by countless others across Egypt, that they decided to capitalize on this moment of collective organization by establishing a new, independent union to represent and defend their interests. In December 2008, the founding conference of the Property Tax Authority Union was convened in Cairo, and the details of the new union were handed to the minister of labour and migration in the spring of 2009. By July 2009, it was claimed that some 36,000 out of the 55,000 property tax employees had joined the union, undeterred by a lawsuit that was being prepared against its founders by the state-sponsored and ETUF-affiliated banking and finance union that claimed their loyalties – and their dues.[31]

Meanwhile strikes in December 2006 and September 2007 at the Misr Spinning Factory at al-Mahalla al-Kubra generated similar moves. Not only were they organized in defiance of the ETUF-affiliated General Union of Textile Workers, but they also showed all the features of spontaneous collective organization. In defiance of the management and of the union leadership, the workers demonstrated, performed, debated and even negotiated in open assembly that seemed to be in constant session. It was this collective assembly that gave direct approval to those negotiating with the management on their behalf. They would return every now and then to communicate with and gain approval from the assembled workers. A very different and in many ways novel dynamic of power was being played out, as suggested by one of the painted placards that appeared in the open forecourt of the spinning mill, proclaiming 'This is a liberated zone'.[32]

It was an indication that resistance was generating new forms of behaviour. This was seen in the independent collective organization that emerged from the networks of ordinary workers, but could also be read into the messages they were sending to fellow workers and to the authorities. Their concerns had moved beyond the workplace to encompass more ambitious demands concerning the political order in Egypt and the regulation of the economy. New forms of communication appeared, feeding into publications like *al-Ishtiraki* [the Socialist], put out by the Socialist Studies Centre, and new associations emerged, such as Workers for Change and the Workers' Solidarity Committee. These publications and groups encouraged communication among workers themselves, extending the networks that had been so powerful within specific factories and at particular sites, to connect people working in the same industry and in other industries with related concerns and complaints.[33]

At this stage, however, the workers' organizations were wary of associating themselves with some of the opposition parties and organizations that had managed to survive despite constant harassment by the Egyptian authorities. Thus, in April 2009, there was an attempt by the 6 April Movement to call for a general strike on the anniversary of the 2008 strikes at al-Mahalla al-Kubra. It met with a muted response from the property tax collectors' union and from the workers in general. As the journalist and labour activist, Hossam al-Hamalawy, said at the time, 'Not a single political party has the power, even the Muslim Brotherhood ... [to] stop or push the strike wave forward ... Workers aren't just going to wake up and go on the internet and read that some Facebook activist has called for a general strike and obey that. It doesn't work that way'. In part, this may have been because of an enduring suspicion of the motives of political parties: 'Each (political group) is trying to influence people for their ideology', according to Gehad Taman, a labour organizer at one of the mills in al-Mahalla al-Kubra. He went on to say that political activists had, through their efforts, often succeeded in undermining workers' claims.[34]

These claims, as the strikes in al-Mahalla in 2008 demonstrated, included the raising of the national minimum wage, but now extended to calls for the downfall of President Mubarak and his regime. Muhammad al-Attar, one of the strikers arrested at the time, stated unequivocally to a public meeting in Talaat Harb Square in Cairo, 'I want the whole government to resign. I want the Mubarak regime to come to an end. Politics and workers' rights are inseparable. Work is politics by itself. What we are witnessing here right now, this is as democratic as it gets'.[35]

Nevertheless, the strikes were mostly geared to achieving local, often site-specific demands. Generally, they were confined to the workplace, remote therefore from the lives of ordinary Egyptians. They were only sporadically covered in the media and rarely connected with each other. It was considered newsworthy and possibly politically significant when a workers' dispute gained greater visibility. To this end, the workers of the Tanta Linen, Flax and Oil Company staged sit-ins in front of the Cabinet Office in Cairo, both in the summer of 2009 and in February 2010. They were involved in a long-running dispute with the new owners of this recently privatized concern over deteriorating pay and conditions, and then over the dismissal of the local union leader. The workers took the unusual step of making the journey from Tanta to Cairo to gain visibility and to embarrass the government into intervening. In the February sit-in, however, the authorities responded by sending in the riot police to clear the street.[36]

The extraordinary conditions created in January 2011 by the demonstrations in Tahrir Square in Cairo and in other cities across Egypt encouraged the workers' organizations to mobilize and to communicate with each other and with the protestors. This led to a degree of coordination that had not been visible before between those with an obvious national political agenda and the groups of workers whose demands, although often revolving around terms of employment and wages, clearly had political implications. As the dramatic events of late January and early February unfolded, this coordination proved crucial in redoubling the impact of the demonstrations. This was particularly the case during the final week leading up to the reluctant resignation of President Mubarak on 11 February, when there was a real danger that force might be used to clear the demonstrators from Tahrir Square and other public spaces. It was then that the growing wave of strike actions across Egypt was decisive. Culminating in the calling of a general strike on 8 February, the mobilization of workers across Egypt made it clear to the high command of the armed forces in particular that the rejection of the regime had gone much further and deeper than even the impressive numbers of demonstrators might indicate.

These events also gave Egyptian workers the opportunity to form an independent trade union organization. On 30 January 2011, a group of workers from a range of industries and sectors across Egypt – textiles, metals, pharmaceuticals, government employees – held a press conference in Tahrir Square to announce the formation of the Egyptian Federation of Independent Trade Unions (EFITU) [*Al-Ittihad al-Masri li-l-Naqabat al-Mustaqila*]. The spokesmen declared their support for the main political demands of the protestors and announced the formation of committees in factories across the country to coordinate and to plan for a general strike. In the weeks that followed the overthrow of President Mubarak, strikes continued across all sectors of the Egyptian economy. Expectations had been raised that a host of long-suppressed grievances would now be met. It was clear that the workers' resistance was not simply against a particular government or even regime, but against a fundamental systemic shift in Egypt's political economy. The newly founded EFITU, initially comprising four independent unions and encouraging the formation of others, was to be a key player in trying to defend workers' rights in the changing landscape of Egyptian politics. As its conference in March 2011 indicated, one of its first targets was the official state-run federation, ETUF – passionately denounced by El-Badry Farghali, chairman of the Pensions Union, who proclaimed that 'ETUF have sold us out ... we need to rebuild the system and step away from existing corruption'.[37] In the summer of 2011, this goal at least was achieved with the government's dissolution of ETUF.

Despite the manifest displeasure of the new rulers of Egypt, the Supreme Council of the Armed Forces, which made scarcely veiled threats about the dangers of strikes, workers' action continued. In March 2011, the Egyptian government presented a draft law for the approval of the SCAF that banned and criminalized 'demonstrations, strikes, sit-ins or gatherings ... leading to the impediment or the obstruction of any of the state institutions or public authorities from performing their role'. It also outlawed any incitement or calls for strike action.[38] The law came into force in June 2011 and soon workers who took part in sit-ins and strikes in the public sector were being brought before the State Security Courts (the measure was enacted under the still existing State of Emergency laws, in force since 1981) and sentenced to fines and imprisonment. As one of the lawyers for the defendants said, '[the Egyptian authorities] are sending a panic message to all workers that protesting and freedom of assembly is not a right but a crime'.[39]

This did not prevent the continued strikes, sit-ins and demonstrations in the public, as in the private sectors, although such action was still fragmented, tied mainly to local complaints and quite diverse and uncoordinated. EFITU made increasing efforts to assist and encourage independent union activity and found a powerful focus for dissent in the measures that criminalized strike activity in the public sector. The powerful statement released by EFITU in early September 2011, ahead of a planned massive strike at the textile works of al-Mahalla al-Kubra, indicated a degree of organization and a defiance of the law that was likely to overwhelm the existing resources of the government. With some 22,000 textile workers threatening to come out on strike on 10 September, the Egyptian government hastened to negotiate, and the two sides came to an agreement at the eleventh hour. The strike was called off and the textile workers won major concessions on pay, allowances and conditions. For them, as for EFITU, the lesson was clear: 'The victory of the workers at the Misr Spinning and Weaving plant will send a message to all waged workers that the weapon of the strike is the only way to win their rights', in the words of Mustafa Abdul-Aziz, a member of the workers' negotiating committee.[40]

Despite such victories, it was clear that SCAF and many others were determined to restart the Egyptian economy not restructure it. On the contrary, quite apart from the officers' preoccupation with order, they and their advisers, both domestic and international, were determined to set the economy going once again along the lines it had followed for the previous two decades. Apart from anything else, the military as a corporate body and many individual officers had considerable economic interests in the status quo. So the possibility of confrontation persisted. Privatization and the implementation of a market-driven economy would continue to have destabilizing and unsettling effects on the lives of most of those who were supposed to provide the labour for these new projects. Thus, even if it were to be stripped of its association with clannish enrichment and crony capitalism, the neoliberal project was necessarily going to generate resistance from those who were subject to its demands. In addition to the concerns of site-specific workforces, it was this larger preoccupation that underpinned much of the general fear and apprehension about the rights and welfare of the labour force in a system that seemed to prioritize the profitability of capital over the interests of labour.

Even allowing for all the disabilities under which they had to operate, the 'new unionism' of the early twenty-first century suggested a mobilized and increasingly articulate labour force. They were unwilling to acquiesce in their deteriorating position. Instead, they were determined to resist many aspects of the economic reform policies, the neoliberal justifications on which they rested and the intertwined interests of private capital and state authority that promoted them. This growing resistance to the new conditions of labour developing under the terms of globalization tends to support the argument that dominant forms of power generate their own forms of resistance. Indeed, it could be argued that they already contain the seeds of that resistance, structurally and in the imagination. After all, encounters with power are as likely to lead to thoughts of resistance as to ideas of accommodation. It has also been argued that such forms of domination also need a show of resistance as a way of rallying support among those fearful of the alternative.

This gains support from the fact that, in the case of Egyptian workers' organizations, both formal and informal, the government had made enormous efforts not simply to suppress resistance, but also to portray it as embodying the very features that had necessitated economic restructuring in the first place. It was made to stand for the forces of reaction associated with the discredited state-centric system of the 'socialist era'. It was also characterized as incubating the forces of anarchism and disorder – a common feature of capital's portrayal of labour when the workers are thought of as insufficiently disciplined to conform to the logic of the market. In Egypt and elsewhere, workers' sit-ins and demonstrations were often stirred into riots by provocative and brutal police action, allowing them to be used as spectacular proof of this argument by state media in the theatre of the streets of Egypt in the early twenty-first century. In January–February 2011, it was at least partly the ability of the nonviolent protestors to stand this image on its head, recasting the state authorities as the authors of violence and disorder that helped the protestors to prevail.

ALTERNATIVE ECONOMIES: RESISTING THE DOMINATION OF GLOBAL CAPITALISM

Direct confrontation, contestation of public space and attempts to resist the new economic order through collective action were all strategies that had marked the classical struggle between capital and labour elsewhere in the world. It was a pattern of domination and resistance

integral to the capitalist economies of the Middle East as well. It had
been disguised for a time by a corporatist ethos and by a state trying to
safeguard its independence from the demands of external investment. In
some respects, the nationalist regimes had drawn on older ideas of a
moral economy to justify the corporatist state, mobilizing even those
who were disadvantaged around a vision of collective purpose and
social justice. This was, for instance, the case in Egypt in the 1960s
with Nasser's use of 'Islamic socialism' to suggest that he was restoring a
lost order, as much as carrying out a revolutionary project by bringing
all of the economy under state control. A similar language was used by
Abd al-Salam `Arif in Iraq in the 1960s and by Mu`amar Qadhafi in
Libya in the early 1970s before he went off in a more idiosyncratic
direction. It was also very much part of the language of nationalism. In
the wake of independence, governments across the Middle East suggested that the changes they were introducing, placing unmatched
economic power in the hands of the state that they controlled so tightly,
would enhance the welfare of all sections of the national community.

However, in the late twentieth century, regimes from Morocco to
Iraq embraced the dominant neoliberal economic principles of global
capitalism. Correspondingly, a change of rhetoric was required. The
harsher logic associated with economic reform and structural adjustment made redundant much of the earlier emphasis on collective purpose
and benefit. More profoundly, the material effects of these reforms, with
their uncertainties and their threats to the security of provision, violated a
sense of the moral economy among those who were likely to suffer most
from the austerity packages that went with the unleashing of market
forces. It was not surprising, therefore, that public outrage should have
followed. The material costs of lost jobs and rising prices hit hard, as did
the rupture of a sense of order that had sustained people even through
difficult economic times.

For people caught up in these processes, subjected to forces over
which they had no control but which were relentlessly shaping their
world, there was a limited range of options open. As the previous
section indicated, their workplaces could provide some possibilities
for resistance, developing strategies to prevent the erosion of rights
and living standards. For more isolated communities of peasants, direct
action that was both symbolic and sometimes violent could be a strategy
of redress, although in practice it produced mixed results. Peasant
uprisings against unjust or exploitative landlords in pre-revolutionary
Egypt, Iraq and Syria had been frequent if limited in scope. They had

helped to fuel the demand for the redistribution of land and the implementation of rural cooperatives that became part of state policy in each of these countries after the power of the old landowning classes had been broken by the new regimes. The implementation was patchy, however. Often the peasants found themselves similarly subordinated to local party officials and to a state bureaucracy that favoured established figures in the countryside over the small farmers, let alone the landless peasants whose direct action threatened rural order.[41]

This bias of the state authorities became even more marked with the turn towards neoliberal prescriptions in the 1980s and 1990s, particularly when a nominally free market in agricultural land was reintroduced. In Egypt, the law of 1992 that set this process in motion and its implementation after 1997 produced determined resistance in many places. By its nature, however, it was a fragmented resistance, seeking to oppose landlords' plans to claim possession of land in particular places, with all that implied in terms of rent hikes, insecurity of tenure and eviction. Thus, from January to March 2005, there were running battles as the Nawar family asserted its claims to some 2,000 hectares of land around the delta village of Sarando, backed by the full force of the police. Systematic violence was used to intimidate and harass the villagers in an unequal struggle. Similar scenes were played out in May 2006 at Izbet Mersha in the northeast of the delta and indeed across much of rural Egypt during these years.

In an effort at least to record and draw attention to the violence that was being used to enforce these new laws on property ownership, the Cairo-based *Markaz al-Ard li-Huquq al-Insan* [Land Centre for Human Rights] tried to bring these accounts together. Their figures on the casualties inflicted during these years of 'market restructuring' are telling: between 1997 and 2004 there were some 300 violent deaths, nearly 2,000 injuries and about 3,000 arrests caused by efforts to enforce and to resist the new order in the countryside. The accelerating nature of the violence was underlined by the Centre's report that, in the first six months of 2010 alone, there had been 130 violent deaths, 850 injured and 1,234 arrests in disputes caused by the implementation of the land law.[42]

Given these risks and the limited success of direct resistance to the shift in economic values, practices and institutions that so disadvantaged workers and peasants in the face of state enforcement methods, it was not surprising that other strategies were pursued. Some of these, difficult to record but generally believed to be widely practised, involve the kinds of everyday resistance recorded by James Scott in a southeast Asian context.[43] These include various strategies of subterfuge, dissembling and evasion of surveillance by landlords, their agents and state authorities. On one level, this can be seen as an understandable desire to avoid paying the dues or suffering the penalties imposed by an unjust economic system that is backed by the coercive power of the state. On another level, however, it may be related to people's determination to preserve a sphere of social action in which a different set of norms exists. This would be a sphere governed by understandings and practices that define the moral economy and thus, in many ways, help to constitute the self. At this level, questions of identity, of propriety and of effectiveness as an economic and social actor are all intertwined. In practice, they combine to develop strategies that resist categorization by and subordination to an alien and unwelcome order that seeks to control the key aspects of economic life.

Hawala

It was not surprising, therefore, that large numbers of people should have looked to alternative ways of acting. These did not so much confront the dominant economic order, but tried to resist its embrace through evasion. This meant finding ways of acting that corresponded more to people's own sense of the moral economy, whilst also securing their material interests. Some of these practices and strategies had long been established in the Middle East and beyond, overlooked perhaps because they had been tangential to the driving forces of capitalist transformation. Their apparent failure to intersect with the world that had been so radically changed only meant that they had neither been recognized by nor drawn into the financial markets at the heart of capitalist growth. In particular, one of these practices, *hawala*, had long antedated the global capitalist system. It had formed one of the main mechanisms that kept the arteries of commerce open throughout the Middle East and the Indian Ocean in the centuries prior to the coming of the European empires. *Hawala* is a system of transferring funds across distances that depends primarily upon word of mouth and, above all, on the personal trust and social standing of intermediary agents. Although sometimes translated as a system of 'promissory notes', these can be verbal, communicated either in person, or nowadays by phone or via the Internet. Essentially, it involves paying a given sum to an agent who will ensure that it reaches its destination by acting through a trusted contact in the city or village closest to the intended recipient.

Thus a worker in Dubai wanting to transfer funds to his or her family in Lahore would take the funds to the *hawaladar* or agent. The latter would then contact his counterpart in Lahore to pay out the given sum to the designated recipient once this person had provided proof of identify, having been alerted by the family member in Dubai. For the worker and his or her family, this would mean an almost instantaneous transfer of funds, at a much lower rate than through the formal banking system and free of the bureaucratic complications imposed by that system. It would also mean acting through a trusted network, on familiar ground, by a means that had the endorsement of the Islamic authorities, and of custom. The simplicity and speed of the system has ensured its survival both within countries of the Middle East and Asia, as well as between them and the rest of the world.[44]

It was not specifically intended as a means of resistance to global capitalism, but its resilience suggests that it remains a meaningful and practical institution that conforms to the values and sense of propriety of those who use it. This has made it an effective alternative to the system whereby economic transactions are channelled through a limited number of commercial banks, themselves deeply implicated in the alien and sometimes morally repugnant practices, as well as the unequal division of labour that dominates the global economy. *Hawala* is thus resistance by evasion, rather than by confrontation. In itself, it does not challenge the dominant systems of political economy, nor does it represent an alternative means of income generation or financial growth. Instead, it preserves a system of financial transactions more attuned to the concerns of those who make use of it. *Hawala* can therefore be seen as helping to provide a space where a key part of identity formation can proceed free of the otherwise overwhelming practices of the capitalist order.

Of course, the very quality of invisibility or evasion that commended itself to so many hundreds of thousands of workers and traders who have used the *hawala* system so extensively also commended the system to those who had a number of reasons to transfer funds unseen by state authorities. It is for this reason that in the early twenty-first century, security and intelligence forces concerned about the reach of transnational political organizations began to take a close interest in *hawala* practices and networks. The Middle Eastern and Muslim nexus in which it operated merely added to their general suspicions and made the system seem to be a means devised to further a very different kind of resistance – that of transnational Islamist organizations seeking to carry out acts of terror globally.

The 11 September 2001 attacks on New York and Washington had been carried out by members of al-Qa`ida, a group operating in the very countries and milieu that sustained the multiple networks of the *hawala* system. It was in the aftermath of these attacks that Western intelligence organizations became preoccupied by the invisibility of a form of money transfer that seemed designed to evade the regulatory authorities. These in turn depended upon their own technologies of 'paper' trails – literal, as well as electronic – for any kind of financial transaction. They found it increasingly frustrating and disturbing that they were unable to establish a similar regime of scrutiny for the myriads of *hawala* transactions. The sums involved in these could be truly impressive. For instance in 2007–8 alone, $7 billion were calculated to have flowed into Pakistan through the *hawala* system.[45] All of this was being transferred anonymously, hidden from the view of the financial regulators. The vast majority of transactions were innocent of any ulterior motives, and as transactions of migrant workers in the Arab Gulf states in particular, they were vital to the economic life of hundreds of thousands of the least regarded workers within the global division of labour. Their mass reliance on *hawala* suggested disengagement from and refusal to comply with a financial system that had otherwise near universal control. This in itself could be seen as a challenge to its authority.

Efforts by state authorities to bring *hawala* transactions within their purview generally had only limited success. In the 1990s, the Indian government tried to prohibit *hawala* entirely, criminalizing it as an activity, possibly because of the use made of the system by the Kashmiri separatists who had planted bombs in different Indian cities in the 1990s. However, by 2000, it had to acknowledge that the law had had little effect and downgraded *hawala* to a civil offence, believing perhaps that this would be less likely to drive all such activities even deeper underground than had been the case. In the event, this too appeared to have little noticeable effect. Similarly, the authorities in the UAE introduced a system of registration for *hawaladars* in 2003, obliging them to apply for a certificate. It was hoped thereby that the state authorities would have a clearer picture of who was involved in the business. However, it could not tell them anything about the people who used the system, the sums transferred or the recipients, since this remained virtually invisible to the authorities.[46]

Hawala enjoys an Islamic sanction in that it has historically represented, as a term and a mechanism, a financial transaction deemed permissible by all schools of Islamic jurisprudence. At its most simple, it refers in Islamic law to the transfer of debt from debtor to creditor by means of a third party or agent. In many respects, this was a useful innovation, brought by Islamic law to commercial transactions and long-distance trade in the early Middle Ages. It helped thereby to introduce an equivalent practice into Europe, where Roman law had explicitly ruled out the use of agents for the transfer of debt. Ironically, therefore, it can be argued that it helped to create one of the more powerful motors of financial capitalism. In broader terms, however, *hawala* is rooted both in the *fiqh* [Islamic jurisprudence] and in the practice of Muslims historically. As a system based on trust for the transfer of funds over great distances, it is not exclusive to Muslim communities. On the contrary, it has historically been and remains an important part of the ways in which migrant workers, non-Muslim as well as Muslims, in China and Southeast Asia conduct financial transactions and correspondingly goes under a range of different names.[47] But it remains effectively the same institution, developed for much the same reasons and with similar effects, in the sense of retaining a vital sphere of meaningful and productive activity that nevertheless escapes subjection to others.

Islamic Banking

Hawala is a lived practice that has the advantage of being already part of an accepted landscape, preserving a space where the moral economy is not challenged. But the late twentieth century saw a more ambitious effort to build new institutions that would restore the principles of an Islamic moral economy. This was to be through the creation of banks that would operate as alternatives to the conventional banking system, since they would embody distinctive Islamic principles. The emergence of Islamic banking became a feature of the financial world in the Middle East initially, but soon expanded beyond it. Given the growth industry that it became and the recognizable part it now plays in a global financial order, it may seem perverse to include Islamic finance and banking in a chapter on resistance to the dominant economic system of global capitalism. However, as with *hawala* and other non-confrontational forms of 'lateral' rather than direct resistance, so Islamic banking, at least in its early years, constituted for its champions a way of organizing economic life that was consciously trying to disengage from the logic of global capitalism. For some, it even appeared to be an alternative that was set to overturn the dominant financial and economic system in the name of a distinctive Islamic economics.

The early establishment of Islamic banks, starting with the Dubai Islamic Bank in 1975, as well as the Islamic Development Bank under the auspices of the Organization of Islamic Conference, was accompanied by a good deal of optimistic talk about their larger mission. This can be found in the publications of the International Association of Islamic Banks. They declared that this new venture had a very different purpose and ethos than conventional banking and the capitalist order that it underpinned. Islamic banks, from this perspective, were seen as having a dual mission: material increase and profit, certainly, but also the preservation and enhancement of the spiritual well-being of the community of Muslims.[48] Embedded in this was the idea that new and successful practices would themselves reinforce the Islamic ideals which they embodied, challenging a world order founded on the pursuit of untrammelled profit and undermining its claim to be the only plausible route to wealth creation. In the 1970s and 1980s, there was a marked degree of optimism about the new practices and institutions and about their capacity to change the world in significant ways, restoring a moral economy through the power of example.

As a strategy of resistance, this corresponded, in some respects, to the idea of a 'war of position' or 'war of attrition' elaborated in a very different context by Antonio Gramsci. Islamic bankers were far from being the kinds of people normally associated with the more visible and disruptive forms of resistance across the region. However, many did see Islamic banking as a set of practices that would provide an alternative to the dominant forms of interest-based finance. Moral example, as well as commercial success, would provide an alternative to the interest-based financial system associated with the expansion of global capital. It would erode the unchallenged domination that such a system enjoyed across the globe by putting forward institutions that would begin to gain credibility and would finally be seen as more appropriate to the ethical concerns of growing numbers of Muslims. By conjoining the ethical and the practical, it was seen by some as having the potential to constitute a counter-hegemonic force, at least in those parts of the world where Islamic values and sensibilities remained central to people's identities.

In fact, the ambitious statements of intent by the founders were part of the performance of those responsible for keeping up the morale of their members and investors, proclaiming the distinctive nature of the industry to the world at large. It was a rather exaggerated discourse of defiance, but also an expression of the confidence born of the vast revenues flowing into the oil-producing states of the Middle East, thanks to the surge in oil prices in the 1970s. Correspondingly, the steep rise in the price of energy was seen as a crisis for the Western industrialized world where it did indeed set off a recession that eventually drove down energy prices as well. In the early stages, however, it seemed to many that a dramatic shift in the balance of economic power had taken place. It was therefore scarcely surprising that it should have caused some to imagine that an alternative economic system was in the process of being born, resisting entanglement with Western financial institutions and thereby creating a space in which a qualitatively different system could develop.

The Islamic banks themselves meanwhile got on with the task of banking. They expanded their client bases and their business whilst ensuring that their share of an increasingly identifiable market would not succumb either to their Islamic rivals or to the conventional banks. Whether conceived of as such or not, this was indeed closer to the 'war of position': Islamic financial institutions were coming to be seen not as exotic but as serious and practical institutions within a recognized financial world. They appeared to be responding to but also creating a clear demand, and therefore succeeded in attracting substantial sums of capital. The development of new products and the opening up of new markets meant that, within twenty years, Islamic banks were not simply established throughout the Middle East, but also had appeared wherever there were Muslim communities, whether in Muslim majority countries or catering to minority Muslim immigrant populations.

However, it was noticeable that the more successful they became as financial institutions, the more they began to look like conventional banks. Some of their activities, such as the practice of *musharaka, mudaraba* and *bai' salam*, as well as the distinctive organization of insurance, were common to all of them, prescribed by their *shari'a* boards who ruled on the Islamic legality of their activities. However, in many other fields, their assimilation into the conventional banking sector appeared to be complete. In the first place, they were obliged to comply with the banking regulations of their host states. It was also not long before some of the major European and North American banks opened 'Islamic branches' and 'Islamic sections' to tap into a lucrative market. More importantly, the majority of their transactions seemed to be in line with common banking practice. They carefully avoided anything that could be seen as interest-bearing transactions due to the central prohibition of *riba* in Islamic jurisprudence. However, through the development of various other *shari`a*-compliant instruments, such as *murabaha*, they achieved more or less the same effect. They were able to guarantee depositors a known return on their capital and, similarly, could charge a predictable fee on their loans.

The more successful and capital-rich they became, the more it seemed that they had effectively been incorporated into the global financial system. Far from providing a powerful alternative base from which to resist the dominance of interest-based capital accumulation, they had become incorporated players. These were not the pockets of resistance that might have made people think again about the common sense of global capitalism. This change from possible harbingers of resistance to fully integrated players in the dominant system was reflected in the language and behaviour of the federations and associations that grouped the banks together, representing their interests collectively. The associations themselves fragmented as different interest blocs naturally formed within the Islamic banking industry. Furthermore, their language no longer referred to themselves as radical alternatives that would transform the global system. More modestly and more realistically, they geared their appeals instead to the many Muslims who did feel uneasy about investing in or borrowing from interest-based banking systems. Such customers found in the Islamic banks the means not of evading or resisting the dominance of capitalism, but rather of tapping into its ferocious productivity in ways that they could reconcile with their own religious and ethical beliefs.

Possibly by way of compensation, the banks and other financial institutions central to the industry did help to develop institutions that would provide the intellectual rationale for Islamic finance and for the theorization of an Islamic economy. Thus the Islamic Research and Training Institute in Saudi Arabia, the Centre for Islamic Economics in Pakistan or the Institute of Islamic Banking and Insurance in London were all beneficiaries of this larger project. Distinguished from traditional sites of Islamic learning, although drawing upon the jurisprudential and other scholarly resources cultivated there, these were primarily secular institutions seeking to explore both the philosophical foundations and the practical application of Islamic principles in economic practice. Rather than develop an alternative system, they devoted their research and energy to the development of products and techniques that would further integrate distinctive Islamic features of the mortgage, insurance, brokering and other businesses within the mainstream financial world.

In 2008, the banking crisis enveloped much of the financial sector in the major states of the industrialized world, causing heart-searching in various quarters about the precariousness and amorality of such a system. It was then that the Islamic institutions and their backers appeared to come into their own, suggesting that there might be an alternative way of proceeding that would depend upon Islamic principles. Notably, the Islamic banks were generally well insulated from the kinds of investments that had led to the near collapse of so many banks during this period. There was some optimistic speculation at the time about a dramatic change in public trust that would favour the Islamic banking sector, but even at this seemingly most propitious moment, the alternatives proposed were not radically different. They comprised palliatives that would make the dominant system work better whilst encouraging people not to lose sight of the ethical purpose of all economic life.[49] In fact, it soon became apparent that the scale of the bailout and the remarkable recovery of the conventional banks precluded any systemic change. Ironically, it seemed that the logic of the war of position had worked the other way. Far from allowing the development of a counter-hegemony that would gradually displace the dominant system through relentless resistance, it was the Islamic banking alternative that had become subsumed, without noticeable resistance, into the global capitalist system.

RESISTING THE CONDITIONS OF ECONOMIC LIFE

Resisting the conditions created by the dominant forms of economic life is a political project. It engages with the power that stands behind and is enmeshed in the systems of property ownership, of labour management and of profit extraction. Also, as a collective effort, it can involve forms of organization that confront those who have it in their power to make concessions, whether this be in shares of ownership, systems and rates of profit or on rates of pay, conditions of work and security of tenure. In this respect, resistance may be aimed at moderating those conditions, striking bargains with power to implement more equitable arrangements and to provide more humane conditions of economic life in particular workplaces or across a whole sector. It may also be geared to a wider, more ambitious set of goals that would transform the rights of ownership and of labour in such a way that the political system itself would be radically altered.

All of these aspects of a politics of resistance in the economic sphere have been visible across the Middle East. Sometimes they have been connected to larger national political struggles for control of the state and its resources, sometimes they have been based in very specific sites where the struggle may be no less intense, but the resonance is local. Different strategies have been used, suggested both by the kind of power deployed against those who would resist its demands, and by the repertoire or resources that may be available. In all cases, one of the key components has been the capacity for self-organization, the ability to free both the imagination and action from the dominant economic power. In this sense, such resistance is very close to and indeed often forms a key component of the types of civil resistance examined in the preceding chapter. By the same token, it has been the intention of those in power to control all aspects of economic life, not simply through appropriating material surpluses of production, but also by incorporating the forms of organization – both of capital and of labour – as well as by developing a myth that would sustain and justify such control.

Nationalist corporatism provided one such set of structures and rationales, but as the continual struggles of Egyptian workers have demonstrated, the failings of the system in both senses have given birth to movements of resistance. As well as fighting to improve the conditions under which labour is subjected to capital, whether state or private, the independent efforts of factory workers, professional syndicates, transport and government employees have been geared to winning the right to act independent of government cooption or sanction. The attempt by the Egyptian government and its foreign backers and sponsors to restructure the Egyptian economy, with new forms of discipline for the workforce, provoked even sharper resistance.

Not only were these new conditions posing a direct threat to people's livelihoods and welfare, but they were being implemented in a way consistent with the government's attitude towards those it regarded as its subjects. Using the old control mechanisms of the corporate state with its co-opted workers' organizations, but bereft of their former ideological rationale of Arab socialism or welfare nationalism, it is not surprising that they and the government behind them should have encountered a rising tide of labour resistance. The relative if patchy success of these efforts at self-organization and collective action won concessions at various local sites. This reinforced the sense of empowerment among the workers concerned, and also fed into the larger nation-wide protests of early 2011. In this sense, what had begun as localized resistance to particular conditions of labour became part of a general indictment of the government that had introduced and overseen the restructuring of the Egyptian economy. The manner in which it did so, the privileges it reserved for itself and its client base and the apparent indifference to the collective concerns of its citizens epitomized for many the failings of authority, as much as the shortcomings of this economic prescription for Egypt's economic ills.

Bitter as this struggle has been, it has at least produced concessions and victories that have improved the lives of many. More difficult, both imaginatively and organizationally, has been the effort to resist the dominance of the prevailing economic system itself. Its material and imaginative power, as well as its seductions and the promise it appears to hold out, have been hard to resist. This has not been due simply to the advantages it appears to give a particular political regime, but, more insidiously, the ways it has foreclosed or marginalized ways of thinking and acting against the very logic of the global capitalist system that it comprises. Even where, as in the case of the imaginative reconstruction of an economy that draws upon a distinctively Islamic normative tradition, the terms of reference, let alone the fields of possible institutional action, are still shaped by the prevailing financial orthodoxies. These have proved exceptionally resilient, even at times when significant elements of the systems that they have sustained and rationalized have proven so prone to crisis and collapse. In these circumstances, as individuals and associations in the Middle East – and across the globe – have discovered, resistance falls back upon the limited but still meaningful possibilities of alleviating the worst effects of the system, or of carving out a space for autonomous and dignified action, encouraging both evasion and quiet encroachment.

4

Body Politics

Women's Rights and Women's Resistance

On 12 March 2000, the streets of two of the main Moroccan cities witnessed two spectacular but contrasting demonstrations. They were organized in response to a government project to encourage the more complete integration of women into the economic and legal life of the country. The plan, as well as including measures on education and health, also contained proposals for the reform of aspects of the *Moudawana* (*mudawwanat al-ahwal al-shakhsiyya*) [the laws of personal status]. In Rabat, an estimated 70,000 people marched through the streets in support of reforms that promised to improve the rights and status of Moroccan women. Songs, banners and speeches added to the drama of the event, as the avenues and squares of the capital filled with women and men calling on the new king, Muhammad VI, to implement a plan originally put forward in 1999. As the chants and slogans proclaimed, this would not only create a fairer society, but would also enforce the rights of Moroccan women under a constitution that had long stipulated the complete equality of all Moroccans.

At the same time, however, and organized to counter the Rabat event, a demonstration of possibly double the size took place in Casablanca. It filled the streets of Morocco's largest city and commercial capital with hundreds of thousands of people protesting against the plan and especially against any revision of the *Moudawana*. It had been organized by *Jama`at al-`Adl wa-l-Ihsan* (Justice and Charity Association) of Abd al-Salam Yassine, in collaboration with other conservative associations, some Islamist, some secular. The marchers used familiar techniques of dramatic representation to underline their belief that any revision of the *Moudawana* would be against Islamic principles and would allow the culture and identity of Morocco to be dictated by foreign, mainly Western, powers.

The events of that March day in Morocco highlight a key struggle in the contemporary politics of the Middle East. They bring into sharp relief not only a significant site of domination and resistance, but also the reality of resistance in two quite different registers. The site in question is the body, particularly the bodies of women as physical entities and as legal persons. For this reason, issues of women's clothing and behaviour have been used both to reinforce the different status of women and, in the eyes of some, to symbolize their lesser rights. As the Moroccan demonstrators made clear, this also shapes the styles and public statements of resistance. Women who joined the Rabat marches dressed in a variety of ways, showing a range of different preferences, rather than complying with a collective idea of 'correct' dress. By contrast, the majority of women in the Casablanca demonstrations dressed more obviously in conformity with current conservative strictures on 'modesty' and 'propriety', some of them seeing their own forms of 'Islamic' dress as defying the dictates of largely Western conventions and tastes. These variations in dress, not only between men and women but between different groups of women, underline the ways in which symbolic and material resistance makes itself felt through defiance, through subversion and sometimes through disguised conformity.

How resistance is organized and where it is sited largely depend on whether people think that the system of domination is centred in the institutions of the law, the family, the economy, the state or the diffuse forms of culture and ideas – or, more often, a mutually reinforcing mixture of all or some of these. This has also shaped the repertoire of resistance strategies. Thus the demonstrations around the question of the reform of the *Moudawana* pointed to another key battleground. This is the legal abstraction of the body into the 'legal personality', drawing attention in this case to the gendered rights of the citizen. In this respect, the unequal rights enjoyed by men and women are grounded in the same assumptions as those that have led to different rules of behaviour and dress being applied to the female and the male body.

This is the significance of the laws of personal status. They involve rights affecting inheritance and property, regulating relations within the family and covering the custody of children. They can have a direct effect on educational and professional opportunities, supplemented as they often are by laws that discriminate between the genders actively, or by neglect, especially in matters of health provision. In addition, as with questions relating to the body, they become entangled with the class structure of power and the politics of the state. This has effectively meant one set of rules for the elite and one set of rules for everyone else. These factors also affect the ways in which resistance is organized.

In both areas, resistance to entrenched social norms and existing legislation has met ferocious opposition. This presents itself, in turn, as a form of resistance. The claim is that it is resisting an intrusive and alien culture flowing from the West that threatens to encroach on the patriarchal order. In much of the writing about gender-based resistance, there has been a tendency to assume that this equates with struggles where women and men have been battling to overturn existing forms of discrimination and to transform the beliefs associated with them. These present the 'classic' view of resistance as the struggles by the subaltern against a dominant order that is held in place by hegemonic power.

Yet in many parts of the Middle East, the defenders of the very practices that others are trying to end see themselves as valiantly resisting a new hegemonic power that wants to dominate the globe. Whether this is characterized as liberalism, secularism, capitalism or a mix of the three, the 'world-devouring' power of the West, or of Western states and corporations, is seen as the author of a 200-year campaign to dominate the Middle East. What may have begun as outright imperial conquest became, during the post-colonial decades, the entanglement of Middle Eastern economies and societies in the processes that go under the deceptively neutral term of 'globalization'. From this perspective, those who champion 'tradition' – however interpreted – see themselves as the unwilling subjects of a world order that they have not made, have no control over and that appears intent on marginalizing them and their values.

In this struggle to lay claim to authenticity, whether defined mainly in religious terms or those of secular tradition, the forces of local resistance vehemently denounce governments, parties and organizations that appear to be submitting to the dominant global order. Some of this spirit of resistance has found an outlet in movements associated with Islamist politics across the region. Occasionally it has been expressed in acts of violence against targets that appear to symbolize the contours of their struggle.[1] Frequently, though, it has focused on the body, particularly the female body. This has been taken as the site that has come to symbolize and literally to embody the frontline of a struggle between very different conceptions of gender roles and of the power associated with them. In the developing contest in Iran between the clerical leadership and the secular institution of the presidency in the summer of 2011, it was significant that the question of the enforcement of dress codes for women became a burning issue. The attitude that seemed to be summed up in President Ahmadinejad's statement that he would not call for the punishment of women 'who have two strands of hair sticking out from under their scarves' was ferociously denounced by Ahmad Khatami, Friday prayer leader in Tehran. He threatened that 'blood should be shed to solve this issue and eradicate this problem from the society'. Those who demonstrated in support of this view reinforced the violent imagery by shouting slogans declaring that the 'Islamic veil was a "trench" that keeps out rising modernization'.[2]

The forms of such resistance have therefore been various. Sometimes it has been seen in open contests for public space to confront their opponents and to place pressure on government. This was the case of the Moroccan demonstrations against the reform of the *Moudawana*. Sometimes, the effects have been less publicly visible, experienced by women and men in a sphere that is designated as off-limits to the public authorities, but where the hierarchy of the genders is rigorously and sometimes violently maintained. In this sphere, the 'family', either as a kin group or a grouping of like-minded individuals, takes on great significance. It allows the creation of a world in which gender hierarchy can be maintained and in which performances are learned, monitored and played out in a closed or guarded sphere. It thereby resists the troubling innovations that have taken over the exterior, public world of social life within the framework of the state.

Thus there are two registers of resistance. One draws upon universal principles of citizens' rights to fight against the discriminatory practices of social institutions and the laws of the state. The other portrays any such campaign as part of a larger imbalance in a world where Western power works against the identities, religions and cultural traditions of Muslims, Arabs or other subordinated peoples. In some cases, the state authorities stand between the two sides, favouring now one, now the other. Sometimes they enforce a particular kind of conformity because of ideological conviction or on the basis of calculations about the nature of their support base. Whether in the Middle East or elsewhere, state authorities have always concerned themselves with the behaviour of their subjects and citizens, male and female, especially when that behaviour seems to deviate from existing social norms. In some cases, the state becomes intimately involved, spelling out in minute detail how women and men should behave towards each other and what they should wear, as well as assigning them distinct positions in the social hierarchy. It is this system of imposed forms of behaviour, backed up by legal classifications of differential rights – and sanctions – that justifies the term resistance when people organize to change or even overthrow it.

However, it also raises the question that recurs both in the politics of gender and in the politics of resistance more generally. It is a question that revolves around the agency of the individual and the organization of collective action. Here the arguments developed in other contexts for and against the 'weapons of the weak' as strategies of resistance are relevant. As in the matter of gender resistance, they revolve around whether the overall effect of individual acts of resistance is to reinforce the very social order that produces such norms.[3] The nature of family or social pressures on the individual, in terms of their sexuality, may produce a range of reactions that discourage thoughts of resistance. Conformity may not be merely a survival strategy, but can also be internalized as the right thing to do. On the other hand, even where resilient individuals have the chance to free themselves of social inhibitions, provoking ideas of resistance and subversion, the capacity for action may be limited.

Where it is possible to think and to organize collectively, resistance that will have an impact on the balance of power between men and women involves much more than simply open opposition to government policy. Rather, it goes to the root of social gender prejudices, seeking a counterforce strong enough to dismantle the attitudes and practices of discrimination that range from the irksome and demeaning to the violent. This has led to a number of strategies. Systematic petitioning of the state authorities to change the law, or draft laws banning certain social practices, have been used. But so too has direct action in the creation of spaces of sanctuary where women will be safe from the violence of family or tribal codes. A February 2010 seminar on the topic convened by the Tunisian Association for Democratic Women made it clear that not only in Tunisia, but also in Morocco and Algeria, the resources at the disposal of organizations trying to provide such spaces were far outstripped by the demands of abused women.[4]

These cases show up the range and variety of resistance, but also suggest what works and what has been tried in different settings, and suggest what the unforeseen consequences might be. These forms of resistance are geared to changing the structures of power that discriminate against and oppress women. But they go further, trying to change the underlying attitudes, rationales and justifications that keep such forms of unequal power in place. This is effectively an assault on the imaginative aspects of hegemonic power. It is a 'war of position' that may be global but that will also take on distinctive features in particular settings. The targets will be complacent or permissive social attitudes that permit, even applaud, gender discrimination, often held by people who are nevertheless active in resistance to oppression in other spheres. This has sometimes provided opportunies to create intellectual or artistic links between different forms of oppression, as well as to develop practices and performances that begin to change assumptions.

GENDER STATUS AND OPPOSING IDEAS OF RESISTANCE

Morocco: The Struggle for Women's Rights

The struggle to win equal rights for women in Morocco had begun almost as soon as the constitution was promulgated in 1962, containing as it did the promise of equality. The campaign had been launched by women and by women's groups active in the campaign to free the country from the French protectorate. In the newly independent kingdom, they tried to influence the existing political authorities, dominated by King Hassan II. They had focused therefore on the reform of the *Moudawana* – a series of decrees governing personal status that had come into force in 1957–8, following Moroccan independence. For many, these laws embodied and enforced a deeply unequal set of gendered power relations. They invariably placed women at a disadvantage in terms of rights and civil status, since they explicitly gave men power over women, subordinating women's interests to the interests of the male-dominated family.

Drawing on Islamic jurisprudence – and echoing in its name the title of a famous ninth-century treatise of Maliki law – the *Moudawana* also introduced aspects of French and comparative law. However, it was infused by conservative, patriarchal understandings of the roles and rights of women and men. This was evident in the diminished rights it gave women over their own affairs. In many respects, it treated them as legal minors, requiring the approval of a male *wali* [a male blood or marriage relative] to marry, to enter a business contract, to work outside the home or to obtain a passport. In matters of marriage and child custody, it privileged the man, granting him the right to marry more than one wife without informing his first wife, to initiate divorce proceedings without consulting her and in most circumstances to have custody of their children. It further reinforced the spatial segregation of men and women, opening out the public world to men who were held financially responsible for their families, but largely restricting women to the private sphere. Even here, it did not allow women to be free agents. They were assigned clear duties in the home: deference to their husbands and the duty to bring up their children within a framework that placed a higher value on the male-dominated kinship group than on the individual rights of a woman.[5]

A hybrid legal document, therefore, the *Moudawana* was also a political manifesto in some respects, openly declaring that the newly independent Moroccan kingdom was now free from the legal systems of the departing colonial powers and was forging its own legal identity within the framework of a modern state. Quite apart from the religious and customary attitudes that it enshrined, therefore, it became for some a potent symbol of Morocco's political identity and independence – and one which the king, for all the powers vested in him, hesitated to set aside, even had he felt inclined to do so. Understandably, there were many women who resented the fact that they were the ones who were forced to pay the price, through their own subordination, for this assertion of an allegedly authentic Moroccan identity that so devalued them. It is in this context that elements of the Moroccan left and women's groups began to campaign for a reform of the *Moudawana*, indicating not only a desire to remove the inequalities it embodied, but also to contest the power and the right of a religious and conservative establishment to determine what it meant to be Moroccan.

Of course, in this respect, the would-be reformers, whether leftist or not, needed to negotiate the unavoidable fact of the monarch's power in Moroccan politics. As the 1962 constitution made plain, the person of the monarch was considered sacred. He was both a descendant of the Prophet and was granted the title of *Amir al-Mu'minin* [Commander of the Faithful], according him quasi-caliphal powers and making him supreme not only in temporal matters but also in the interpretation of Islamic law. Nevertheless, given the record of the ruling house, it was clear that those who wished to see an improvement in the opportunities and the rights of women would probably find a sympathetic hearing at the royal court. It conformed to the role played by female members of the Alaoui dynasty, separated as they nevertheless were from the vast majority of Moroccan women by class and status. It also matched the desire of the king to project an image of progressive development. Yet it was clear that all reform initiatives would have to be on the monarch's own terms and would have to enjoy his sanction. Anything else would be regarded as undermining the royal prerogative and would be no more tolerated than any other sign of independent political activity.

Consequently, for some thirty years, the main strategy employed by those who tried to reform, even to annul, the *Moudawana* was to petition the king, relying on a variety of techniques to underline their resistance to a system of laws that they felt was effectively stifling at least half of the Moroccan population. Depending upon the vicissitudes of Moroccan politics during those years, these strategies could involve discreet lobbying within the heart of the *makhzen* [the Moroccan state], using the social standing and access of those in established positions of power to take further the project of reform. At other times, reform would be linked to a wider project of political agitation, organized by parties trying to dilute royal absolutism. When such action was allowed, more public manifestations were organized, less in protest, since that would have been to invite repression, than in a spirit of demonstration, with all its attendant theatricality.[6]

Despite the relative success of some of these techniques in moving the king and, through him, the government in the direction of reform, the entrenched power of those who resisted any modification to the laws was greater. In the 1970s, various drafts proposed relatively modest changes in the personal status laws. However, these had been blocked by political inaction or had been rejected by the consensus of a group of *ulama* selected by the minister of justice. Given the symbolic power and weight of the *Moudawana* and what it had become in a barely suppressed struggle over Moroccan identity, the king clearly felt that he needed to balance the possible political cost of radical reform against the price of alienating the reformers. In virtually all cases, despite some modest successes that had led to the redrafting of a few of its more repressive aspects, the weight of conservative and religious opinion carried the day, frustrating those who hoped that a sustained campaign would culminate in a new basis for gender rights in Morocco.

However, the economic and political crises of the 1980s, combined with the significant demographic and social changes that had long been transforming aspects of Moroccan society, opened up the possibility of effective resistance and reform. The apparently overwhelming apparatus of norms and institutions that reinforced patriarchal values at every turn was being undermined by social developments that created greater opportunities for women. Increased urbanization and better educational opportunities that were unevenly distributed nevertheless brought larger numbers of women into the educated workforce. In addition, falling birth rates and the disruptions of migrant labour, both within Morocco and in Europe, combined to shake some of the supports that had kept the power of patriarchy in place. They also confronted the king and his government with a series of crises in the political economy of the country, resulting sometimes in open, violent protest (see Chapter 3), and questioning the competence and thus the authority of the *makhzen* to rule Morocco for the benefit of all its citizens.[7]

Although immediate government response to unrest was repression, the unrest ushered in a period of controlled liberalization during which the king relaxed the rules on associational and representative life. At the same time, the economic crisis made it imperative that Morocco devise and implement development plans that would address the chronic unemployment, high inflation and low productivity that was causing such general hardship. It was in this climate that a flowering of NGOs and other civil society organizations took place across Moroccan society. Many were preoccupied with alleviating some of the worst social hardships of an economy in crisis – and for that reason were all the more encouraged by a government traditionally wary of independent initiative. This was the case with a number of the emerging women's organizations – such as the Association Démocratique des Femmes Marocaines (ADFM) and the Organisation de la Femme Istiqlalienne (OFI). But they also provided a space and an agenda of more focused political activity, sometimes linked to established parties and sometimes independent of them. For these organizations, such as the Union de l'Action Féminine (UAF), founded by Latifa Jababdi in 1987, the aim was not simply to alleviate hardship, but also to reform some of the fundamental inequalities in Moroccan society and law, particularly insofar as they affected women and women's rights.

The UAF's initial attempts to change aspects of the law, especially those that related to divorce, were unsuccessful, but in March 1992, it launched a very public campaign to call for a complete overhaul of the *Moudawana*. This came soon after the king's promise of constitutional reform and was framed within the terms of a petition to the monarch, for which the UAF set itself the goal of achieving at least a million signatures. The 'million signatures campaign' was an unprecedented form of popular mobilization. It involved weeks of intensive organization and coordination between various women's associations and was launched with the formation of the 'National Committee of Coordination to Change the *Moudawana* and to Defend the Rights of Women'. The main demand for a thoroughgoing reform was accompanied by calls for specific measures to ensure equality of rights between men and women in the family regarding children, matters of divorce and the legal age of maturity. It also demanded the ending of the need for adult women to have the agreement of a *wali* in order to marry, the outlawing of polygamy and the enforcement of the absolute right of women to work outside the home. The campaign rapidly gained momentum through seminars, workshops, door-to-door canvassing and an array of techniques of popular mobilization, with tens of thousands of men as well as women adding their names to the petition.[8]

However, the campaign also encountered opposition. Perhaps most disappointing for the organizers was the indifference or criticism levelled at them by the established, secular political parties. It indicated, in the words of Latifa Jababdi, that 'for them [L'Union Socialiste des Forces Populaires (USFP) and the Istiqlal Party] to touch the *Moudawana* was to touch a taboo which would then create problems'.[9] Mistrustful of an initiative that was not associated with their own organizations, the secular parties were positively discouraging. They were more concerned about the promised constitutional reform and elections. As organizations dominated by men, for whom the question of women's rights appeared to be peripheral, the political parties could only see the demand for reform causing controversy among their own male constituents.

More predictable was the increasingly vehement attack launched against the campaigners by various Islamic authorities and Islamist organizations. Investing the clauses of the *Moudawana* with the sanctity of allegedly immutable aspects of the *shari`a*, a number of leading clerics and organizations such as *al-Islah wa-l-Tajdid* (Reform and Renewal) accused the women campaigning for reform of apostasy, 'conspiring against Islam to eliminate it, to remove what is left of Islamic law in the Muslim world in order to facilitate Western domination'.[10] In order to back up their claims, the Islamist organizations set about collecting signatures for a counter-petition that would reject any reform of the *Moudawana* and would reassert 'traditional Moroccan and Islamic values'. By 1993, they had succeeded in putting forward a petition of three million signatures that declared its signatories' opposition to the campaign for reform.[11]

The growing bitterness of the charges and counter-charges, as well as the potential for disorder, revealed the depth of the divide in Moroccan society and impelled the king to intervene. Asserting his powers as *Amir al-Mu'minin*, he declared that it was up to him to determine what was and what was not in compliance with the *shari'a* and that he would establish a commission to look into possible reform of aspects of the *Moudawana*. At the same time, he praised the women for their activism and their concerns, but warned them also against allowing their campaign to be hijacked by 'political interests', declaring, 'you (women activists) should refer such matters to me ... you should not mix up religious matters with civil and political matters'.[12] Through his intervention, the king effectively brought the campaign and counter-campaign to a grinding halt, since all were obliged to defer to the monarch, in a very familiar pattern of Moroccan politics.

A year later, the commission, on which the male clerical establishment was heavily represented and which only included one woman among its twenty-two members, made its recommendations. A series of minor reforms in the provisions of the *Moudawana* were carried out, to the exasperation of the activists who had hoped to build up the momentum for its radical overhaul, even abrogation. Some smaller changes were made in the following years, partly through the effective lobbying of people close to the heart of the *makhzen*, but the dynamism and initiative of the popular campaign had been lost for the moment. The opportunity came again, however, when the larger frame of Moroccan politics changed once more in the declining years of the king's reign, as Hassan II charged the opposition parties with forming a government in 1998, labelled, appropriately enough, 'le gouvernement de l'alternance' [the alternating government].

It was this government, or at least its more liberal and reformist elements, which formulated the 'Plan d'action national pour l'intégration de la femme au développement' [the plan of action for the integration of women into development] in consultation with a range of women's organizations and international agencies, including the World Bank. Much of the plan focused on measures to educate women, to provide for better health care and to ensure a full integration into a trained workforce. But it also envisaged the removal of all the legal disabilities that had so disadvantaged women and which were an integral part of the *Moudawana*. In many respects, the reforms that it proposed corresponded to the demands set out in the million-signature petition of 1992. For that very reason, it provoked the same kind of opposition, from similar clerical and Islamist activist circles, but also from within the coalition government itself where the minister of *habous* [religious endowments] and Islamic affairs came out against it. Drawing upon apocalyptic imagery, the leader of the Islamist Parti de la Justice et du Développement [Justice and Development Party] (PJD), Abd al-Karim Khatib, stated that the struggle over women's rights was 'a war between believers and apostates'. This message was reinforced by those organizing to oppose the plan. Dramatically, they declared that they intended to organize 'an *intifada* against "cultural globalization"'.[13]

It was in this context, encouraged by the accession of the new king, Muhammad VI, in the summer of 1999, that the plan had been presented by the minister for social protection, family and childhood. In January 2000, the opposing sides began to mobilize. They intended to make public, and thus visible to the monarch and to the political establishment, the scope and depth of their support or opposition to the plan for reform. In addition to some forty or so women's associations across Morocco, the main trades unions and the Party for Progress and Socialism coordinated their activities to bring as many people out on the streets as they could for the planned March demonstration in Rabat. Timed to coincide with the weekend closest to International Womens' Day on 8 March, the Rabat demonstrators assembled under a variety of banners and flags, with one slogan in Arabic and French held prominently aloft: 'We share the land, let us share its bounty'.

At the same time, the two main Islamist organizations, the PJD and Yassine's *Jama`at al-`Adl wa-l-Ihsan*, had combined with a number of other conservative associations to form the Organization in Defence of the Moroccan Family which was to coordinate the counter-demonstration in Casablanca. As the very ambivalent attitudes of members of the coalition government indicated, opposition to reform of the *Moudawana* was not confined to Islamist parties, but encompassed secular nationalists and conservatives. Thus the minister of *habous* and religious affairs denounced what he claimed was a campaign to change the 'immutable aspects of the *shari`a*'. The leaders of the Istiqlal Party who nominally supported the reforms were conspicuously absent from the Rabat demonstrations. Even a prominent member of the prime minister's own Union Socialiste de Forces Populaires [Socialist Union of Popular Forces] (USFP) had criticized the reform plan as 'benefiting the imperialist and Zionist offensive'.[14] This was a theme prominently displayed in the placards and slogans used in Casablanca, such as the Arabic banner which read: 'Yes to the integration of women in development. No to westernization and submission'.[15] Religious symbols were to the fore, such as the large copies of the Quran, held aloft by men and women, as well as banners inscribed with various *hadith*.

The effect of the counter-demonstration in particular, given its scale, the speed and efficiency of its organization and the coalition of social and political forces that it mobilized around nationalist as well as Islamist themes, unnerved the young king, Muhammad VI. Using a tactic familiar from his late father's handling of these issues, he urged caution upon the government, discouraging any speedy implementation of the plan and set up a commission to look into the possible reform of the *Moudawana*. In some respects, this was a delaying tactic, but it was also a response to the increasingly active women's organizations which had refused to let the initiative drop, continuing to organize a series of public events to bring to the fore their cooperation in the 'Printemps de l'égalité' [spring of equality]. The king, whose own views were almost certainly closer to those of the reformists, made a point of meeting representatives of women's organizations and listening to their concerns.

In doing so, however, he was aware of some shifts within the Islamist current as well. In particular, a grouping of Islamic feminists had emerged, led by Nadia Yassine (the daughter of Shaikh Abd al-Salam Yassine). She had been prominent in the Casablanca demonstration, but refused to see the *Moudawana* as an immutable sacred text. On the contrary, in the spirit of a distinct strand of Islamic feminism in Morocco, Nadia Yassine was much in favour of wider *ijtihad*. She asserted that women, as much as men, had the right to interpret Islamic law. To do so, she claimed, could provide a corrective to the ways in which men had historically used the texts to justify the discriminatory practices that were such an obstacle to the development of women.[16]

By March 2003, the commission looking into the reform of the *Moudawana* announced that its work would soon be finished, hinting that an entirely new law of personal status would be issued, rather than an altered version of the old law. This created a certain amount of anticipation in reformist circles that a radical overhaul was in the offing, rather than a mere adjustment of the existing law, as in previous instances. In fact, it was rumoured that the commission had provided two alternative sets of recommendations for the king – one which would indeed be a rather modest revision and the other a far more radical set of proposals for a thorough overhaul of the kind that women's groups and others had been demanding over the years. It would then be for the king to decide which of the two versions would gain his support and the weight of his authority, depending on his reading of the politics of the country at the time.

Dramatically, and violently, the king's decision was affected by the bombs that exploded in Casablanca in May 2003. They killed nearly fifty people and had a significant impact on Moroccan political debate. The suicide bombers responsible for these attacks targeted European and Jewish establishments in the city and seem to have come from a radical Islamist group, *al-Salafiyya al-Jihadiyya* – an offshoot of a larger, banned Moroccan Islamist organization, the Groupe Islamique Combattant Marocain [Moroccan Islamic Fighting Group] (GICM). The Moroccan authorities responded vigorously, arresting some 2,000 people and using the state's very considerable machinery of repression. Nevertheless, the shock of these events and the fact that they made gruesomely real some of the rhetorical violence of many of the Islamist associations, allowed the king to move.

He seized the moment. In October 2003, he presented to parliament the more radical plan for the complete replacement of the *Moudawana* by a 'modern Family Law'. This was intended to 'free women from the injustices they endure, in addition to protecting children's rights and safeguarding men's dignity'. He justified this move with reference to his own reading of the Islamic laws and traditions that advocate 'human dignity, equality and harmonious relations'.[17] He was careful, therefore, to frame the revisions within the principles of Islamic law, stressing the ways in which they reflected the true spirit of the original sources of the law and were based upon open *ijtihad* or legal interpretation. But he also made it clear that his view was definitive, underlining his role as king and as Commander of the Faithful. Parliament duly passed the law in January 2004. In most respects, the new law, now named 'The Family Code', embodied all the measures initially proposed in 1999–2000. It made husband and wife jointly responsible in the family, removed the need for women to have a guardian or *wali* once they had reached the age of eighteen and also made this the minimum age of marriage for both men and women. Polygamy was not forbidden but was hedged around with a number of conditions, including the consent of the first wife. Similarly, women's right to divorce was enhanced and men's right to repudiation was restricted. As in the case of polygamy, divorce questions needed judicial oversight and approval, greatly increasing the power of the courts to adjudicate in family matters.[18]

In this sense, therefore, those who had tried to resist the legally sanctioned discrimination against women and the series of oppressive measures to which it gave rise had succeeded in their long campaign to change the law and the attitude of the state. In doing so, of course, they had had to recruit the unlikely figure of the Moroccan monarch as the champion of their resistance. Whatever qualms some may have had about the nature of the king's power in Moroccan politics more generally, they were aware of the fact that he still commanded immense authority, wielded enormous power and could effectively place the reforms beyond public debate. By pursuing the strategy of 'rightful resistance', the reformers had necessarily to acknowledge the overall legal and political framework within which they were operating and to adjust their tactics accordingly.[19] The Islamist and nationalist organizations could not easily mobilize people around their own claimed resistance to Western and anti-Islamic influences when the king himself favoured the reforms. This did not, of course, prevent some in the Islamist movement, most notably Shaikh Yassine, from questioning whether it was permissible for the king to assume such overwhelming religious authority.

However, the reform of the *Moudawana* was only one aspect of a continuing struggle to resist discrimination against and dictation to women, whether within families or in society at large. Those who were determined to champion women's rights and to fight for equality of opportunity were well aware that it was not the law alone which created inequality. Rather, it allowed patriarchy to benefit from the support of the state. The change in the law did not mean that patriarchal attitudes or that discrimination and oppression would simply disappear. Now the struggle was to be carried out on two fronts. One was to ensure that the terms of the law were respected and fully implemented through a reformed and retrained judicial system – a formidable undertaking in itself, given the new structure of family courts. In addition, there were many aspects of Moroccan law that needed further reform if women were to be fully protected in their human rights.

The other challenge was to make women across the country aware of their new rights and to provide them with the means of resisting the still powerful familial and patriarchal forces that continued to shape their everyday lives. This was by far the harder task. It required women's organizations to present themselves as an alternative, even a refuge, for women and to combat social attitudes and prejudices held not simply by men but by women as well. For some twenty years, Aicha Ech Channa had been trying to help single mothers through her organization, Solidarité Féminine. Meanwhile groups such as the Institution of Solidarity with Women in Distress (INSAF), headed by Nabila Tbeur, set up shelters for abused women and for single mothers. By 2010, there were about eight of these across the country, but it was clear that the demand and the need were far greater than could be met by these NGOs with their limited resources.[20]

In this respect, therefore, the struggle to help women resist the accumulated weight of familial, social and official prejudice and discrimination has been an ongoing and a multifaceted one. In Morocco, the relative and limited successes of the public campaigns had won official recognition at a time when the royal house was gradually opening up public space to a greater number of voices. This had come about to some extent because of longer-term underlying social changes that were creating a more mobile and better-educated public. Attitudes were beginning to change, although at a much slower rate than the promulgation of a royal edict or even the passing of a contentious law.

As the dramatic events of the early twenty-first century indicated, there was still a large measure of vocal opposition from those who believed that their national and religious identities demanded that women's rights should be subservient to those of the male-dominated family or religious establishments. Less visible, but much more serious in terms of women's lives, were the multiple forms of oppression that continued to exist in gender relations within families and communities. Here the reach of the state, even one with a reforming agenda, did not extend. Or it was blunted by the conditions of rural and urban poverty and illiteracy, as much as by the efforts of those who believed they had a duty to resist in order to preserve the honour and tradition of the Moroccan family.[21] Against such forces, it was much harder to imagine, let alone to organize, resistance. Patterns of escape tended to be individual, leading to migration to the cities or to Europe with all the problems and vulnerabilities that brought in its wake.

Some forms of resistance organized by women to protect women against everyday violence were clearly too much for the state itself to tolerate. This explains the refusal of the Moroccan government in 2009 to allow the opening of branches of the association 'Ni Putes, Ni Soumises' [neither whores nor submissives]. This organization had been founded in France five years earlier by the French Algerian

Fadela Amara to champion the rights of girls and women in France's North African immigrant communities. It was intended to protect them from coercive pressures to conform and from violence within their families, but it was considered a step too far in Morocco, not only because of its striking name. As the Interior Ministry statement said at the time, '[It] does not conform with the approach adopted in Morocco for dealing with issues relating to women'. At the same time, one of the leading members of the Islamist PJD echoed this sentiment by stating that the organization 'must respect Moroccan particularities'. The president of the association, Sihem Habchi, blamed the ban on 'Islamists and some old-fashioned women's organizations' and wryly commented that the association was even being accused of bringing France's problems to Morocco by having the temerity to raise such issues.[22]

The 'war of position' is one that by its nature extends over time and place. The Moroccan state and the forms of patriarchal power in society at large represent a formidable edifice of structural and imaginative power. Against this, the strategies of resistance could not expect immediate success. Nevertheless, the creation of new spaces and possibilities for public life in Morocco has led to the gradual acknowledgment of the rights of all Moroccans to participate in the public sphere. In the past decade, this has extended to include gender, as well as class and other power differentials. They have not been swept away, of course, but they are in the process of being questioned and tested. Increasing numbers of Moroccan women have become aware of their rights, entering into a conversation of many voices. It certainly does not produce uniformity, but it does hold out the possibility of the understanding of difference, rather than its use as a pretext for subordination. None of this would have been imaginable without the many forms of social and political resistance that have been a constant feature of Moroccan political life during the past half-century.

WOMEN'S RESISTANCE WITHIN NATIONAL RESISTANCE

Iran: Women and the Islamic Republic

Taking their inspiration in part from the Moroccan example, in 2009 Iranian women's organizations began to collect signatures for their 'million signature petition' to reform key aspects of Iranian family law.

This was building on the success that they had achieved in 2008 by helping to block a new draft family law, the 'Family Protection Act', which the conservative Majles had tried to introduce at the behest of President Ahmadinejad. Through intense campaigning, involving peaceful demonstrations, but also information and educational initiatives, women's organizations had conveyed the message that the proposed law was not simply detrimental to women's rights, but would also contravene key aspects of the *shari`a*. Specifically, the intended relaxation of the conditions under which men could marry more than one wife and the clear disadvantaging of women in matters of divorce were retrograde steps in an array of family laws that already placed women at a disadvantage relative to men. Indeed, so discriminatory was it that Ayatollah Yusuf Sanei openly pronounced the draft law to be against the revolution, against women and against Islamic values.[23]

As in Morocco, resistance was most effective when set within the dominant idiom of Islamic values. Secular women had been joined in their opposition to the new draft of the law by organizations such as the Zeinab Association and the Women's Organization of the Islamic Revolution. Indeed, for some of the Islamic feminists of Iran, it was not simply a tactical move to refute the principles that the government claimed were embodied in this law. It was also strategic, since it went to the heart of their project to assert the validity of women's role in the interpretation of Islamic law. Emerging more confidently as an identifiable movement in the 1990s, the writers and activists associated with ideas of Islamic feminism had been very much part of the generation of the revolution. They had been inspired by the same ideals as their male counterparts and were equally critical of the Pahlavi regime for its subservience to the United States and its perceived neglect of Islamic values. However, for them the message of the Islamic revolution was one of equal rights for men and women, as citizens and as beneficiaries of Islamic law. Women such as Maryam Behrouzi, secretary-general of the Zeinab Association, publicly voiced their criticism of narrow-minded men in the Majles. In the pages of *Zanan* (until it was closed down by the government in 2008), Shahla Sherkat continued to argue for a reinterpretation of Islam's basic texts. It would be based on equality between men and women, as interpreters and in the spirit of the interpretation. This meant actively promoting equal access to education, to the labour market and to the legal system, as well as informing women of their rights and ensuring that they were adequately protected within the existing framework of family law.[24]

As the secular feminists had discovered in the early years of the Islamic republic, this was a fiercely contested struggle. Their protests against the new regime's insistence on dictating where women should work, what subjects they should study, how they should behave, what they should wear and how they should submit to male dominance in the family were swept aside. Demonstrations, such as the weeklong sit-in by thousands of women at the Ministry of Justice in March 1979, protested amongst other things at the threat of forced *hijab*. But it came to nothing.[25] The then prime minister, Mehdi Bazargan, did try to defuse the situation by claiming that it would not be a compulsory measure, but he himself was to resign within months, faced by the growing tide of Ayatollah Khomeini's authority and the unparalleled power of his political supporters. By the summer of 1980, not only were women compelled to wear the *hijab*, but a full-scale 'cultural revolution' had been launched. This led to the banning of co-education, the dismissal of thousands of women from the administration, the dismissal of all women judges and women's virtual disappearance from the legal system, as well as the repeal of the Family Code of the previous regime and the barring of women from certain professions and fields of study.

Many of these measures had the enthusiastic support of large numbers of women for whom the appeal of the revolution, the authority of Ayatollah Khomeini and the promised reorientation of Iranian public life towards Islamic values were overriding considerations. Nor, for the majority of Iranian women, did these measures make much of a difference to the lives they had led before the revolution. The rules of a patriarchal society imposed numerous restrictions on women's lives and freedom of action, whether encouraged or merely tolerated by the state. As in other instances, women had long devised strategies of resistance that allowed them a certain freedom of manoeuvre whilst nevertheless avoiding an open challenge to the primacy of patriarchy – the 'patriarchal bargains' so well described by Deniz Kandiyoti in other contexts.[26] In fact, despite the undeniably restrictive nature of many of the measures taken by the new Islamic republican government, for some women other facets of the new order offered opportunities that had not been available beforehand, and they made the most of them.

In many respects, these opportunities were due to the ability of women to exploit the aspects of the revolutionary order that came out of its character as a national liberation movement. Whilst the idiom of the new republic was undeniably Islamic, embodying as it did the principles enunciated by Ayatollah Khomeini, it also shared a great deal with other post-colonial national liberation movements. As such, the government was keen to mobilize all citizens, male and female, in the effort to construct and to defend the new republic, to build up the national economy and to make the most of the resources of the Iranian nation state. Like nationalist movements everywhere, it encouraged a view of women as symbols and as agents of the community's regeneration, combining distinctive aspects of Islamic social thought with the needs of the nation state. It was a synthesis that became even more marked during the 1980s as the country mobilized to fight the eight-year-long war with Iraq.

Thus, on the one hand, the government encouraged women to have children, to stay at home and to nurture the next generation of young Iranian Muslims. On the other hand, it also encouraged women to undergo training and further education, to enter the workforce and to play their part as active citizens in the public sphere. Apart from anything else, it was now important for those standing for elected public office to appeal to women voters. For women who shared the larger goals of the Islamic republic and who wanted to participate actively in the development of Iran, the second part of the message was the key to their increasing involvement in public life. Resistance therefore was geared not to the Islamic republic as such, but towards the restrictive and discriminatory measures that prevented them from playing such a role – measures that sprang from conservative, patriarchal interpretations both of Islamic law and of the nature of nationalism.

In this respect, across Iran, women succeeded in using the official encouragement of the Islamic republican authorities to resist efforts by their families to prevent them from entering further and higher education, to restrict their movements or to make it hard for them to go out to work. Ironically, the restrictive measures imposed upon women by the Islamic republican regime, such as forced segregation or the compulsory wearing of the *hijab*, which many resented as onerous and unjust, allowed women to make the case for active participation in the public sphere. Educational institutions, the workplace, public offices and the city's public spaces were after all now incorporated into an Islamic order which ensured, in theory, that propriety and Islamic values were properly respected. For women seeking to escape the oppressive environment of the patriarchal family, at least temporarily, this was an appealing route and a powerful argument.[27]

Nevertheless, an array of restrictions and legal disabilities remained in force. The story of organized resistance in the years following the death of Ayatollah Khomeini in particular is one in which women tried to reassert and to gain recognition for their rights as women, as Muslims and as Iranian citizens within the framework of the Islamic republic. Already in the 1980s, it was clear that official disapproval of contraception was having little effect, since roughly a quarter of women of childbearing age were using some form of contraception. In fact, by 1989, the government was obliged to recognize this by lifting the ban on contraception at state clinics. Even rates for abortion, which remained illegal and severely punished, were on the increase. Indeed, one of the more prominent Islamic feminists, Azam Taleghani, who was also a member of the Majles, asserted that the right of a woman to control her own fertility and her body is a basic human right.[28]

She saw herself as both a devout Muslim and an ardent defender of women's rights and women's welfare. In this, she was joined by women such as Maryam Behrouzi, Zahra Rahnavard and Faezeh Hashemi who all won seats in the Majles and were thus recognized as 'Islamic women', loyal to the ideals of the Islamic republic. Nevertheless, they were also intent on ensuring, in the words of Behrouzi, that 'some traditions such as patriarchy, anti-woman attitudes and humiliation of women must disappear. These have been fed to our people in the name of Islam'.[29] From their position as 'insiders', they, together with like-minded women, could work in associations such as the Women's Society of Islamic Revolution and the Iranian Islamic Women's Institute. Their aim was to promote the kinds of reforms that would resist attempts by some clerics and laymen to relegate women to a marginal role in the public life of the Islamic republic.[30]

It was through the efforts of people like these, their associations and the alliances they cultivated within the political establishment that aspects of the family laws were reinstated, having been abolished in the early years of the revolution. Family courts, now called Special Civil Courts, were revived and were charged with dealing with divorce issues. This opened the way for women to lobby to ensure that the power of the court would counterbalance that of the male head of the family. In 1992, this resulted in the curtailing of men's rights to divorce. It also imposed upon them the obligation to compensate women – a right which was substantially extended by granting women *ujrat-e mesel* [*ujrat al-mithal*]. This is the right of a woman to claim, as part of a divorce settlement, financial compensation for the housework she had done during the years of marriage, reckoned as wages for work.[31] Furthermore, at the same time, women won the right to reappear in the Iranian court system, both as advisory judges in the civil court and as defence advocates. On the question of polygamy, the diversity of clerical opinion on the proper conditions for its practice allowed the courts to insist on obtaining the first wife's permission before a man could take a second wife.[32]

These processes were reinforced and extended with the changed political climate following the election of Ayatollah Mohammad Khatami as president of the republic in 1997. His more liberal attitudes allowed the appointment of women to some prominent positions in the government, such as Massoumeh Ebtekar, Vice-President in charge of environmental affairs, and Azam Nouri, Deputy Minister of Culture for Legal and Parliamentary Affairs.[33] By the same token, these measures also made women a particular target of a backlash organized by conservatives. They found this aspect of reform a step too far, and tried to negate the progress women had made. They used their majority in the Majles (until 2000) and in the administration to introduce legislation that was in fact so far removed from the realities of Iranian society that it proved impossible to implement. Not just in this sphere but across the whole spectrum of the reformist programme, the conservatives, clerical and otherwise, combined to block much that Khatami and his allies tried to achieve. This generated the feelings of disappointment and frustration that marked the final years of his presidency, demoralizing and fragmenting the movement that had placed so many hopes in him.[34]

However, disappointing as the legislative record may have been, the two terms of Khatami's presidency saw a flowering of women's journalism, literature and artistic expression. A very large part of this addressed social and political issues of concern to women, including marital rights, domestic violence, employment and equality of opportunity, the obligatory wearing of the *hijab*, women's health issues and the necessity for female *ijtihad*. A thriving women's publishing sector developed to give voice to these concerns and to coordinate campaigns to publicize injustices or the need for reform. It brought together secular and Islamist women who found that, although they approached the problems from different perspectives, they nevertheless shared a common set of concerns about many of the problems confronting women in the Islamic republic.

It also stood them in good stead when the conservative backlash produced both a president like Mahmoud Ahmadinejad in 2005 and a reactionary Majles. They seemed intent on reimposing a rigid and discriminatory reading of the rights of Iranians, especially in matters of gender and sexuality. In practice, this proved harder than anticipated. It was true that some of the more ferocious laws governing sexuality and women's behaviour were ruthlessly and prominently enforced. Similarly, there were attempts to tighten up the clothing regulations for women, as the police and other state agencies tried to enforce stricter interpretations of 'proper' veiling and *hijab*. However, in this, as in other areas, the authorities encountered widespread resistance. Iranian women had long been adept at transforming the rules governing *hijab* into something that would indeed demonstrate, as Ayatollah Khomeini himself had claimed in 1979, that it was neither a sign of suppression nor seclusion. For many women in Iran, the *hijab*, whether it took the form of the chador or of some less enveloping form of veiling, such as the headscarf and the manteau, had been used to assert their equal access to public office and to public space. Even Islamic feminists who clearly believed that *hijab* was appropriate to their own circumstance and beliefs were increasingly critical of the laws that made it obligatory for all women, citing frequently the Qur'anic injunction that 'there is no compulsion in religion'.[35]

For those who resented having to submit to the dress code, there were many ways in which it could be subverted. Modifying it to serve self-expression, fashion and indeed gender attraction whilst nevertheless remaining within the strict letter of the law became a fine art. These were multiple acts of individual and social resistance, not collectively organized or intended to have an immediate effect on power relations. Cumulatively, however, the very public and visible effect was to throw into question the capacity of the government to exert authority over a very substantial section of the Iranian population. Equally, efforts to suppress or discourage such open defiance were often counterproductive, opening the authorities up to criticism and even ridicule. Such was the case of Hojjatolislam Kazem Sidiqi, the acting Friday prayer leader in Tehran, who asserted in April 2010 that 'Many women who do not dress modestly lead young men astray and spread adultery in society which increases earthquakes'.[36]

In other spheres, it proved even harder for the government to remove the rights that Iranian women had won over the previous decades, despite the pressures on them to do so. Thus, by 2009, women still represented more than fifty per cent of the students in higher education, even though the Majles Research Centre in 2008 had identified this as an alarming trend. It had called on the government to do something to stop or slow it down before it led to 'social disparity and cultural and economic imbalances between men and women'. This initiated a public debate in which the right of women to higher education was reasserted in a forthright way by women's associations, in the higher education sector more generally and by a number of prominent public figures. Such was the response that it prompted the government to deny that there were any plans to restrict female enrolment in the university entrance exams. Nevertheless, a government spokeswoman did suggest that 'gender discrimination' would apply to certain sectors of the workforce, going back to the idea that women should be helped to achieve the kind of training and education 'suitable' for them – or what the more conservative elements of the government deemed suitable. These vaguely phrased promises, or threats, did not have much substance. Given the Iranian government's general inability to manage the employment sector, let alone to check growing unemployment, there was no official plan of action. However, this in itself often meant that women were the first to be laid off in times of crisis.[37]

In the aftermath of his contested re-election in 2009, president Ahmadinejad showed that he was aware of the price he would pay for alienating the female electorate. He therefore tried to avoid the charge that his administration was one which discriminated against and marginalized women. He nominated three women as government ministers. One of the three, Marzieh Vahid Dastjerdi, was approved by the Majles as Minister of Health, becoming the first woman to serve as a minister since the 1979 revolution. A believer in the strict segregation of men and women in health care, and by no means a reformist, she nevertheless symbolized the public acknowledgment of the right of women to participate fully in public affairs.[38] Nevertheless, this gesture had been preceded and was followed by more concrete measures taken against women's organizations, their publications and websites, as well as against individual women activists such as Maryam Hosseinkhah, Parvin Ardalan, Jelveh Jahaveri and Nahid Kesharvarz who were all sentenced to prison for 'spreading propaganda against the state'.[39] The active involvement of many women in the long-running protests that followed the 'stolen election' of 2009 showed that symbolic gestures did not count for much if the president's authority was itself being questioned by a large section of the Iranian political public. Iranians were reacting not on a gendered basis but as citizens outraged by the violation of their citizens' rights.

Palestinian Women's Struggles for Liberation

There are echoes of many of these themes in the prolonged Palestinian resistance struggle and the roles that women have played. As in Iran, the

larger field of national resistance has thrown into sharp relief some of
the ways in which nationalism, whether secular or Islamist, has tended
to elevate women symbolically whilst marginalizing them in fact and in
terms of their rights. It has presented women in Palestine with a series of
challenges, stemming from the contradictions between their assigned
roles and the roles to which they aspire as activists in the Palestinian
resistance. In seeking to resolve this, women have had to devise strategies within and sometimes against larger resistance movements. They
have tried to change attitudes and expectations, whilst avoiding the
accusation that they are undermining the national or Islamic resistance
movement as a whole. At the same time, they have had to take into
account the conventions governing women's behaviour in Palestinian
society, where failure to conform has often led to ostracism, isolation
and violence.

For some, these experiences have raised the question of whether
women are struggling under a double occupation – that of the Israeli
state and that of a patriarchal Palestinian society. The attitudes that go
with this underpin political movements that have often uncritically promoted certain traditions, or traditional interpretations of Islamic law, in
the name of national or Muslim 'authenticity'. This has had an immediate
impact on the opportunities open to women in contemporary Palestinian
society under occupation. In the longer term, some fear that it will shape
the legal framework of a future Palestinian state in ways that will disadvantage women. This fear has impelled Palestinian women to resist any
attempts to write a gendered conception of power into law.

Historically, women have played an important role in the organization and support of Palestinian resistance since the 1920s. Until
recently, that role has been relatively underplayed in nationalist narratives by comparison with the heroic portrayal of dominant male military and political leaders in the uprisings of the 1920s, or the sustained
insurgency of the 1930s. Yet during the Palestine revolt of 1936–9, in
particular, the widespread organization of civil disobedience, of boycotts, strikes and economic and social mobilization gave women a key
role. Whether organized in families, clans, village associations or political groupings they played a vital part in maintaining the momentum
of a movement that had a powerful political impact, even if it was
eventually defeated on the military front by British counter-insurgency
strategies.[40]

Similarly, in the wake of the *Nakba* of 1948, women in the refugee
camps and elsewhere held together and provided for families displaced

on a massive scale by the forced expulsions and flight from Palestine. The upheaval, loss of lands and livelihoods for hundreds of thousands of Palestinians in 1948 disrupted the balance of power and, more insidiously, of self-worth between men and women. The heroic qualities so highly esteemed as part of the image of masculinity counted for nothing in the face of the forces ranged against the Palestinians. Palestinian men had been unable to defend either their families or their lands, and found themselves herded into refugee camps, dependent on the handouts from refugee relief agencies. As countless testimonies have shown, this did not lessen the often-oppressive demands made of women within the patriarchal family, but it did make women pivotal to the very survival of the family unit. Thus, in many respects, they were pivotal in Palestinian identity itself, in a way that had not been obvious before. The awkward, resented and sometimes violent consequences of this were to make themselves felt and women often bore the brunt. However, it could not obliterate the centrality of women to the story of Palestinian resistance and to the successful iteration of a recurrent theme in Palestinian resistance narratives – that of *sumud* [steadfastness].[41]

Fairly predictably, as Palestinian political society began to re-emerge in the decades following 1948, the nascent liberation movement, adopting both a nationalist and sometimes an Islamist stance, assigned women a symbolically important but effectively marginal role. The exceptions were the socialist and Marxist Palestinian organizations, such as the Popular Front for the Liberation of Palestine (PFLP) and the Democratic Front for the Liberation of Palestine (DFLP). They were sharply critical of traditional, patriarchal values, dismissing their alleged centrality to Palestinian national identity. Instead, they emphasized gender equality and the importance of women's active participation in the struggle of revolutionary liberation. Of course, as products of a certain kind of Marxist discourse, many members of these organizations had gendered understandings of self-determination. Here the 'male' qualities of heroism, activism and military prowess were very much to the fore. Insofar as women could emulate these qualities, there was no barrier to them being admitted at least to the ranks, if not to the leadership circles, of revolutionary Palestinian activism. One of the most dramatic and memorable representatives and symbols of this trend was Leila Khaled of the PFLP. She was a member of the unit that hijacked a TWA airliner in 1969 and who attempted to hijack an El Al airliner in 1970. Her picture, wearing a Palestinian *kaffiyeh* and holding an automatic weapon, became an icon not just of Palestinian resistance but of third-world revolution in the 1970s – and helped to underscore the new roles which women seemed to be carving out for themselves in the Palestinian liberation movements.[42]

The reality, of course, for the vast majority of Palestinian women was very different, whether in exile or in the occupied territories of the West Bank and the Gaza Strip. Women living in refugee camps in Lebanon or in the occupied towns and villages of the West Bank or in the sprawling townships of Gaza tried to ensure that women's issues should neither be ignored nor subordinated to men. As leaders of political organizations, or as the patriarchal leaders of families and clans, men would define the collective national interest, leaving little space for women to express themselves in the larger struggle for liberation. The determination to resist such subordination or marginalization became a feature of women's movements in the 1970s and 1980s. They were not actively setting themselves up to resist the dominant Palestinian political organizations. On the contrary, many were affiliated to those organizations, whether nationalist, socialist or Islamist. In Lebanon, they shared their goals of primarily resisting the political and military forces ranged against the Palestinians. In the territories occupied by Israel, they similarly supported resistance against Israel's efforts to make its occupation permanent and to override the rights of the Palestinians.

In the occupied territories, the DFLP, through the Palestinian Federation of Women's Action Committees (PFWAC), was particularly active. It believed that the organization, education and employment of women were both good in themselves and a key part of a strategy of resistance for the Palestinians living under Israeli occupation. As the activist and academic, Fadwa al-Labadi stated, 'We ... want [ed] to organise women [in nationalist work] *and* we want [ed] to change the social realities that they live in'.[43] Conversely, the women of PFWAC also believed that the active involvement of women in the national liberation struggle was a precondition of and a catalyst for women's liberation in the larger struggle for gender equality. In the words of the PFWAC programme of 1988: 'to the same extent that the organised and the unified women's movement progresses in its confrontation with the policies of the occupation, and to the extent that it can fulfil its role as a crucial part of the nationalist movement, Palestinian women in the occupied territories can establish and develop an imposing presence in their society'.[44]

With a rather different set of priorities and values, but much the same objective of resisting the demoralization and humiliation of Israeli occupation, women's groups associated with the Muslim Brotherhood in Gaza particularly began to organize and to establish self-help groups. In 1981, the Young Women's Islamic Association was set up by the Brotherhood's Islamic Centre (*al-Mujamma` al-Islami*). True to their political affiliation, the organization reproduced the ideas of the Muslim Brotherhood regarding the role and behaviour of women. However, in doing so they laid the groundwork for the Islamic feminism that was to feature in social and political life in Gaza in the twenty-first century. In principle, at least, members of the Brotherhood and of *Hamas* could agree that women should take a full and active political role, whether in a *shura* council or as ministers with government responsibility. Nevertheless, they rejected the idea that a woman could be head of state or commander in chief.[45]

However, it was during and after the first *intifada* (1987–91) that women's organizations – secular, Islamist and of no particular affiliation – began to emerge as key players. They became active in Palestinian national resistance and helped to develop the multiple strategies of the *intifada*. As the campaign of civil disobedience intensified, bringing normal life in the occupied territories to a standstill and disrupting travel, commerce and education, so women's associations became increasingly active. They organized the alternatives that would keep things going for the Palestinians whilst conforming with the pattern of strikes and boycotts that were a key part of the message of the *intifada*. Keeping Palestinian self-sufficiency at the heart of resistance strategy signalled defiance to the Israeli occupiers and to the outside world. It was also a means of building solidarities in Palestine. Here the women's groups, cooperatives, educational and literacy circles, boycott committees, childcare centres and communication networks were central. Just as important, if less spectacular than the barricades of burning tyres and stone-throwing young men, the women's movement was at the heart of the infrastructure of resistance that helped to sustain the *intifada*.[46]

However, the nature of the *intifada* itself began to change as time wore on. It had started as a series of actions that emerged from the grassroots. These had empowered hitherto marginalized or subordinated people, strengthening their capacity for self-help and self-discipline. But the uprising was soon dominated by local political formations that allied themselves with mainstream Palestinian resistance organizations. Whether in association with the PLO or with other parties, this tended to discourage spontaneous and self-generated activities. Instead, it brought all within the orbit of the major Palestinian organizations, whose larger aims and strategies prevailed.[47] In many parts of the occupied territories, women felt the effects of this most sharply. Their behaviour became the subject of close and intrusive interest by the small groups of armed *shabab* [youths] who had graduated from the barricades of the *intifada* to police the towns and villages of Palestine. Women often found themselves in danger, accused of 'moral collaboration' for behaviour that these self-styled guardians of public morals disliked.[48] In Gaza, with the emergence of *Hamas* and other Islamist groupings, women were singled out. For very familiar reasons, they became the targets and main symbolic carriers of a series of distinctive 'Islamic' measures, including the obligatory wearing of the *hijab* – something to which the secular leadership of the *intifada* took a long time to respond. Even though, eventually, the leadership came out against compulsory wearing of the *hijab*, it was clearly unable to protect those women who were subject to physical violence in Gaza if they tried to enter public space 'uncovered'.[49]

The challenge to women's autonomy became even greater following the Oslo Accords in 1993. This led to the establishment of the Palestinian National Authority (PA) with its characteristic patrimonial structure, headed by Chairman Yasser Arafat and his fellow returnees from the PLO. Women in the occupied territories, who were already struggling with an increasingly restrictive social order shaped by *Hamas* and other Islamists in Gaza, now had to contend with the PA. In this respect, they became increasingly apprehensive at the ways in which the PA turned to so-called 'traditional' local structures of authority – clans, kinship groupings, village headmen – with their inbuilt patriarchal biases to establish their control.[50] For many, therefore, the experience of PA rule was deeply disappointing. It provided less support to women and women's concerns than had been promised in the more cosmopolitan settings of PLO exile.

On the contrary, for many, it seemed as if the determination of the PA to control everything was going to frustrate even modest campaigns to protect women's rights. Thus, in 1994, women's groups organized a press conference in Jerusalem to announce the final agreed text (already the subject of some six years of vigorous debate) of the Declaration of Principles on Palestinian Women's Rights. The PA promptly sent one of Arafat's ministers, Umm Jihad (Intisar al-Wazir), to take over the event and to claim the declaration on behalf of her leader. Given Arafat's record and that of many of his closest allies in the drafting of the declaration, this move provoked an immediate protest by many of the

women's organizations present and led to the whole event being suspended.[51] Yet the declaration was seen by many as the key to ensuring
that any draft of a personal status law adopted by the PA would embody
the principles that these organizations believed were fundamental to the
protection of Palestinian women's rights. However, quite apart from
the revealing theatrics of the non-event in 1994, the drafting of a
personal status law for all the Palestinian territories proved too contentious a matter to be resolved within a short span of time. Together
with the PA itself and the occupied territories, its passage was to be
overwhelmed in 2000 by the violence of the *intifadat al-aqsa* and its
consequences in the years that followed.

Ironically, the networks and organizations which Palestinian women
had developed during the years of Israeli occupation and the *intifada*
were to serve them well in trying to resist the patriarchal embrace of
the PA, both in the West Bank and in Gaza. They formed part of a lively
and argumentative civil society in Palestine which confronted both the
Palestinian and the Israeli authorities. Symbolically, Samiha Khalil from
the long-standing, autonomous women's NGO *In`ash al-Usra* [reviving
the family] stood as the sole opposition candidate against Yasser Arafat
in the presidential elections of 1996, although with little realistic hope of
affecting the outcome.[52] In Gaza, where the influence and the political
clout of *Hamas* and Islamic Jihad were felt on the streets and in the
camps, Islamist women's groups aligned themselves with this trend in
relation to the occupation, or to the secular Palestinian nationalists.
However, as in Iran, they were not willing to submit to a wholly male-
dominated, patriarchal interpretation of their duties and rights under
Islam.

On the contrary, through a variety of means – discussion groups,
workshops, Islamic educational institutions and publications – they
contested such measures as the compulsory wearing of the *hijab*. They
felt this should be up to the individual believer. Similarly, they asserted
the need for women to engage in *ijtihad* and criticized the rigid rules of
gender segregation. This led them to develop their own views on such
matters as contraception, women's health issues, social welfare and
women's protection. It was within a distinctive Islamic framework of
norms and beliefs, but based on their own interpretations. They had
effectively re-appropriated the task of interpretation from the male
shaikhs and political leaders of the Islamist movement.[53]

Again, as in Iran and Morocco, male-dominated organizations could
bring power and influence to bear, but it was harder for them to dismiss

or marginalize those women's organizations that were effectively part
of their own movement. Indeed, women played an important role
in the mobilization of support for *Hamas*, carrying out this role through
activities aimed at heightening people's self-awareness as Muslims.
As Samira al-Halayka, one of the successful *Hamas* candidates in
the 2006 legislative council elections, asserted, 'there are numerous
Quranic verses and sayings of the Prophet Muhammad urging women
to be active in politics and in public issues affecting Muslims'. She went
on to cite a relevant *hadith* of the Prophet Muhammad: 'He who doesn't
show concerns for the affairs of Muslims is not a Muslim', making it
abundantly clear in the interview that this applied as much to women as
to men.[54]

To some extent, this was also the case in the more secular nationalist
movements of the Palestinian resistance. Women had found that the PA
was less receptive to progressive ideas about women's rights and equality than its member organizations had been in exile. Nevertheless,
they still worked within the existing parties and through the emerging
institutions, as well as in the burgeoning NGO sector to ensure that
women's voices were heard and their rights were not ignored. In doing
so, they found themselves in the familiar position of trying to seize back
control of women's bodies for the women themselves from a nationalist
movement that claimed them on behalf of the nation. This was under-
scored by the particularly disempowering discourse of the 'demographic
war' that had become such a familiar part of the confrontation between
Israel and the Palestinians.

A constant feature of Israeli public debate – and a virtual obsession
on the Israeli right – was the fear that the Jewish population of Israel/
Palestine would be outnumbered within a matter of decades by the Arab
(Muslim and Christian) population because of Palestinian birth rates.
This had been taken up by Palestinian nationalists, both secular and
Islamist, to argue for the vital importance of Palestinian women's
fertility for the Palestinian cause. This effectively made women's
bodies and their reproductive cycle a common possession of the nation,
no longer of the individual woman herself. Understandably, many
Palestinian women resented this both in principle and for the implications of such an argument for women's control over their bodies and
their lives. It had come under fierce attack by women who, in Hanan
Ashrawi's memorable phrase, resisted the notion that their bodies were
to be the 'hatcheries' of the Palestinian nation. For Rita Giacaman, of
the Community Health Project at Bir Zeit, such an approach directly

contradicted the PLO's insistence that women should also be politically and socially involved, unless by this they meant 'bear more children for the revolution' – a role which she and many others rejected.[55] Organized and articulate resistance to the efforts of a male-dominated political establishment to assign such roles to Palestinian women became a feature of the 1990s. It resulted in the PA adopting the position paper on 'Palestinian Population Policies and Sustainable Development' that had been put before the Cairo UN conference on population and development in 1994.

The second *intifada* – *intifadat al-aqsa* – also witnessed a spectacular and gruesome development that highlighted, in a number of contradictory ways, women's control over their own bodies within the framework of resistance. This was the appearance of female suicide bombers, beginning in 2002. They detonated their bombs against Israeli targets both in the occupied territories and in Israel itself. Frances Hasso's study of four of these women indicates that they had a mixture of motives, but the gender of the bomber and the gendered implications of the act were key elements, even if they were not the only factors at play. On a practical, strategic level, it was calculated that the Israeli authorities would not be expecting women to be suicide bombers and would therefore subject them to less exacting searches than their male counterparts. By the same token, the knowledge that Palestinian women were prepared to kill and to die in this way was believed to redouble the impact, destabilizing Israelis' views of their own security.

Nor were these women simply challenging Israeli stereotypes. One of their number, Dareen Abu `Aisha, a *Hamas* activist, found that neither her own party nor the Islamic Jihad organization were willing to train her for the task, so she turned instead to the secular, Fatah-affiliated Al-Aqsa Martyrs' Brigade.[56] Two prominent leaders associated with *Hamas*, Shaikh Ahmad Yassine and Abd al-Aziz al-Rantissi, found fault with these actions. They argued that a woman, even one intent on *jihad* of this kind, could only leave home lawfully if she were accompanied by a *mahram* [guardian]. They reiterated their belief that the only proper role for a woman in resistance was to look after her male relatives and to bear their loss with fortitude. However, the testimonial videos left behind by three of these women indicated that they were determined to assert that they were fully conscious agents. They decided to use their bodies, in the words of Andaleeb Takatkeh, 'to say what the [male] Arab leaders have failed to say ... my body is a barrel of gunpowder that burns the enemy'.[57]

SEXUALITY AND VIOLENCE: THE LIMITS
OF RESISTANCE

The body has been the target of sanctioned violence but also of attempts
to organize resistance and has become entangled in larger resistance
narratives, nationalist and Islamist. It has therefore highlighted the
rights of men and women to control their own bodies and freely to
enact their own sexuality. This section looks at the possibilities and the
limits of a politics of resistance to violence against women and men
whose sexual behaviour has been judged to go against prevailing social
norms. The judgment can range from social ostracism, through imprisonment and physical assault to death. It is a judgment that is sometimes
enforced by the state, as in Iran and Saudi Arabia, and sometimes by
families acutely aware of social disapproval, as in Palestine, Jordan,
Kurdistan, Lebanon and Iraq. Here the state may tolerate or acquiesce
in a 'privatization of coercion' in a way that would never be counte-
nanced in any other sphere.

'Honour Killing'

In different countries across the region, women's perceived transgres-
sions have been met by violence that, in its most extreme form, has led to
so-called honour killing. The term is used to describe the killing of a
woman by a close male relative because her alleged – often only suspected – sexual conduct is thought to bring shame upon the family. Her
death is seen as a way of restoring the 'lost honour' of the family. As
many women have found to their cost, this has also applied when a
woman has been raped, where the perpetrator may himself be a close
male relative. In countries such as Iran or Saudi Arabia, the state has
taken on the role of executioner in cases where a woman is judged to
have broken laws prohibiting sexual relations outside marriage. It has
also tolerated or turned a blind eye to such killings within the family.

   In Iran, the sentence for adultery – flogging if unmarried, and death
by stoning if married – remains part of the criminal code (Articles 83
and 102). During the 1980s and 1990s, these sentences were carried out
on dozens of people and, although the law applies equally to men and
women, it was noticeable that women formed by far the larger propor-
tion of those stoned to death for adultery. Even within the clerical
establishment, there has been concern about this provision, and plans
have been drawn up for the abrogation of these articles. In the interim, a

nominal moratorium on its practice has been in place since 2002. However, this was an 'advisory' rather than an 'edict' according to a spokesman for the judiciary in 2009. Indeed, a number of men and women have been stoned to death for adultery since 2002.[58] In 2010, this aspect received widespread international attention when Sakineh Mohammadi Ashtiani was sentenced to death for adultery and for complicity in the murder of her husband.[59]

The possibility of resisting such violence against women has been beset by difficulties. As in other spheres, the problem lies in trying to combat a widespread social practice that is rooted in the patriarchal family and reinforced by the state's legal apparatus. In some cases, it is also validated by nationalist and Islamist narratives that hold up this particular model of the family as a bulwark of 'authenticity'. As Nahid Yeganeh has pointed out, this has made sexual behaviour that deviates from the norm a political act in the eyes of the state, aimed not simply at individual sexual gratification or even at relaxing moral standards but at subverting the whole edifice of power. The Iranian authorities' actions against the lawyers and the children of Sakineh Ashtiani have made all too clear their view that challenging the state in the sphere of extramarital sexual relations is on a par with rebellion against the Islamic Republic, carrying with it the same extreme penalties.[60]

Many in Iran are highly critical of a law that they regard as contravening human rights. They condemn it for its criminalization of sexual behaviour between consenting adults, and for the cruel ways in which the death sentences have been carried out. However, they have found it difficult to campaign for its abrogation, faced as they are by a clerical consensus on the absolute prohibition of *zina* [fornication] in Islamic law. This is backed by a state apparatus that believes the restriction of women's sexuality in particular is central to the mission of the Islamic Republic itself. Nevertheless, in October 2006, the Campaign to Stop Stoning Forever was launched in Iran.

The intention was to have the stoning clauses removed from the penal code and, in the interim, to protect eleven people who were then under sentence of death by stoning. As one of the members of the campaign, Mahboubeh Abbasgholizadeh stated, 'The stoning law affects women more than men. So, as feminists, we naturally have to address it as well as other issues ... The nature of the feminist movement in Iran is political because feminists have to target the laws, like [those on] polygamy and stoning, that sustain the patriarchal view of the society. They have to challenge the religious and political establishment that supports those laws'. However, there was no denying the difficulty of the task, since it was obstructed both by state and social forces. As an Iranian journalist said, 'Campaigners have a hard way ahead of them. The response from the society as a whole to the issue of stoning is not so unified. Activists are campaigning to abolish it but there are many, not only religious and political hardliners, who don't mind the law ... In some areas, traditions hold very strong and the stigma against the family of an adulterous woman is compelling. There is little opposition to the idea of stoning in these places because people think a law like that may prevent adultery and stabilise family life. In some cases, the families of the accused women might even take the matter into their own hands and try to wipe off the shame by killing the guilty even before the law takes up the matter. In men's case, if they are not involved with married women, there is much greater toleration'.[61] The same could be said of similarly draconian laws in Saudi Arabia, where there is little space, legally or politically, to contest a law on which the clerical establishment, the ruling state apparatus and substantial sections of society agree.

However, in many countries in the Middle East, it is not the state but the family, the wider clan or kin group, that have taken matters into their own hands. They have imposed sentences ranging from death, through house imprisonment to banishment on those women who are judged to have transgressed the codes of behaviour. Nevertheless, even here the state has played its part. The penal codes of Lebanon, Egypt, Algeria, Jordan and Syria – based on the old Ottoman Penal Code, which was itself based on the French Penal Code of 1810 – all contain articles which effectively exonerate any man who kills his wife, or indeed female relative, if he finds her in an adulterous or extramarital relationship with another man.[62] In some cases, the grounds for exemption are given as the 'passion' of the killer, and in others it is the damage done to his 'honour' that would cause the state to dismiss any case against him. In Saudi Arabia and in Qatar, much the same result is achieved through Hanbali jurisprudence which stipulates that under the *shari`a*, the killer of an adulterer cannot be penalized.[63] Noticeably, this is not a defence that is likely to be accepted if a woman were to kill her husband upon finding him in an adulterous relationship with another woman.

The state has also been complicit through the authorities' failure to investigate or to take seriously the homicidal violence associated with these crimes. In Israel, where no such legal exemption of femicide exists on the statute book, Arab citizens of the state have mobilized to bring this largely concealed or ignored crime to the attention of the state authorities. In the 1990s, women's associations founded the association *Al-Fanar* [the lighthouse] and organized demonstrations in Nazareth, Haifa and Akka to raise awareness of this unspoken crime. They publicized the fact that, in 1991 alone, some forty Arab women had been killed in Israel by their male relatives in order to salvage family 'honour'. In November 1991, in a public protest, women picketed the police station at Ramleh to show their anger at the fact that a girl had been handed back to her family, despite the mortal danger that she faced. Furthermore, they charged the Israeli state with complicity. It stood accused of encouraging a patriarchal system within the Arab minority as a means of reinforcing social control and differentiating that minority from the Jewish majority. But they were equally critical of the Palestinian leadership for its failure to speak out against such crimes. They argued that 'the continuation of these crimes ensures the impulses of regression within our society and will [only] strengthen bigotry and tribalism, and [ultimately] it will be nothing but a barrier upon the road to national independence and equality'.[64]

In the occupied territories, a similar campaign has been under way, especially after the establishment of the PA in 1993. Arafat's preoccupation with social order and control through 'traditional' patriarchal structures reinforced the belief that the woman and her body, and thus her sexuality and morality, were the property of the *hamula* [kin-based clan] and not of the woman herself. It was to prevent any insertion of such a discriminatory set of provisions into the legal code of the emerging proto-state, as well as to ensure an equitable Family Code, that women's organizations mobilized at the time. But they were also aware that this was a society under military occupation, trying to resist the overwhelming power of Israel and its strategies to suppress autonomous political activity. In this context, an obsession with 'honour' and a tolerance of the crimes associated with its 'restoration' made Palestinian women doubly vulnerable. Already in the 1980s, the slogan *'al-ard, wala al-`ird'* ['land not honour'] had been used by some Palestinian resistance groups. It was urging Palestinians to place the recovery of the land, and thus the nationalist struggle, before the inhibiting and debilitating preoccupation with the honour of the family. It was also deliberately recalling a slogan reportedly common in 1948 – *'akhsar al-ard wala al-`ird'* ['lose your land, not your honour']. This sentiment was said to have encouraged Palestinians to flee, fearing that their daughters and wives would be raped by the Israeli forces. The inversion of the slogan was meant to strengthen Palestinian immunity on this score and thus to reduce the vulnerability of Palestinian society.[65]

This had indeed been one of the tactics used in the Israeli authorities' counter-insurgency strategy. Actual or threatened compromise of women's sexual integrity by Israeli interrogators and security officials gave them enormous power over the Palestinian women they detained, knowing the effect any rumour would have on a woman's life. It was used to recruit informers and collaborators precisely because the women concerned could not easily or safely admit to their families that they had been compromised. The silence of self-protection or of shame therefore assisted the Israeli occupation. Known colloquially as the practice of *isqat* [fall], the Israelis used it extensively during the *intifada*. It had serious effects on its organization, but also terrible consequences for some women. It also helped to 'marginalise and to make suspect all women activists' who now lived under the suspicion of their own people that they might be *saqita* [fallen].[66] The women at the forefront of the national resistance movement were more likely to be involved in confrontations with Israeli security forces and to be arrested by them. Ironically, these were the women who then became most suspect in the eyes of their own people. This was a doubly dangerous position for women, possibly threatened by their own family and by the self-appointed guardians of public morality and security.

Even where such an added element of risk was not present, the danger of 'honour crimes' was redoubled where social convention also cast a veil of silence over it. It was to break this silence that women's publications and organizations started a debate on the topic not only in Palestine, but also in Lebanon and Jordan, opening up a hitherto taboo topic for discussion. They hoped thereby to make people confront the horrors of a crime in which many were complicit, if only through their silence, as well as to put pressure on governments to change the laws which appeared to condone such behaviour. One of the most prolonged and active of these campaigns was in Jordan where, from the late 1990s, a concerted effort has been made to address this question head-on. Public demonstrations, marches and educational campaigns involved members of the royal family, including Princess Basma, sister of the late King Hussein, and Queen Rania, as well as other prominent Jordanians in order to give the cause wide publicity and legitimacy.

The National Jordanian Campaign to Eliminate So-Called 'Crimes of Honour' aimed at the repeal of Article 340 of Jordan's Penal Code.

This effectively exempted men from prosecution for killing their wives or female relatives in cases where they judged that the women's conduct had brought shame upon them and their family. Although there was support for such a move in the Jordanian parliament, it ran into opposition from the over-represented rural, tribal deputies. They, in alliance with the Islamic Action Front, rejected the government's proposed repeal of the article in 2000. Echoing their Moroccan counterparts, they accused those agitating for reform of acting on behalf of foreign, Western powers. They used a series of arguments which claimed that any such change would both be harmful to Jordanian values and would violate the *shari`a*. In respect of the latter, however, there were others in the Islamist movement who argued, on the contrary, that Article 340 itself was in direct conflict with the *shari`a*, since it appeared to elevate protection of honour and reputation above Islamic teachings about the sanctity of human life.[67]

However, the campaign did not end there. During the following decade, King Abdullah II added his voice to the campaign. Perhaps surprisingly, this did not succeed in having the infamous article rescinded. It did, nevertheless, help the government push through measures that effectively restructured the legal system with the result that, after July 2009, so-called 'honour crimes' were treated as regular criminal cases. Rather than receiving the token two- or three-month sentences that had been imposed up to that point, those found guilty of these crimes were sentenced to between seven and fifteen years in prison. Nada Husseini, a journalist and activist who had done much to expose the true extent and nature of 'honour killing' in Jordan, voiced her concern that the failure to change the law made sentencing policies vulnerable to the interpretation of the judges. Nevertheless, there was some satisfaction that in the first nine months of the new policy's operation, some ten men were given lengthy prison sentences. However, it was also clear that such crimes were still being condoned in society at large. In nearly all the cases of 'honour crimes', the families of the victim drop the charges, allowing the sentence to be halved.[68]

As in the case of the *Moudawana* in Morocco, those who were trying to resist the coercive power of 'honour killing' found 'rightful resistance', supplemented by publicity campaigns and public demonstrations to be an effective strategy of resistance. By tackling the problem within the established law and by enlisting the support of powerful figures within the elite, there was some hope for change. This strategy did bring its own problems, but it succeeded in at least changing the formal framework. It also sent out the signal that the state no longer condoned this particularly violent and discriminatory social practice. In Lebanon, for instance, the efforts of more than a decade of campaigning were rewarded with success in August 2011 when the Lebanese parliament annulled the notorious Article 562 of the criminal code. As in other Middle Eastern states, it had specifically mitigated the sentence of any-one who harmed a family member who had allegedly compromised the 'honour' of the family. The campaigners made clear that there remained numerous other articles that explicitly discriminated against women and which they wanted to see annulled, but as Nadya Khalife of Human Rights Watch said, 'For years attempts to eliminate honour as an excuse for violence have fallen on deaf ears . . . Finally, all murders will be treated alike and so-called honour related crimes will be seen for what they are: simply crimes'.[69]

The public performances of those who defended such formally repres-sive legislation also followed a similar pattern. They would invoke 'tradition' and 'Islam' as integral to laws which in fact owed more to the French Penal Code of the early nineteenth century, via the Ottoman legal codes, than to the *shari`a*. Nevertheless, as those organizing against these practices were only too well aware, there was a limit to the degree to which such legal reform could change social practices. By the nature of their predicament, the fate of the women involved was often hidden from the public gaze and repressed or silenced within the family.

The campaign to publicize honour killings therefore was as much about giving women and their relatives the opportunity to speak out about what had happened and what was likely to happen. There were, however, clear limits to what could be achieved in terms of getting inside families and persuading them to speak publicly about a topic that was surrounded by so many issues of honour and shame. An alternative strategy of direct action, used to good effect in Europe and elsewhere during the past forty years, was the construction of women's refuges. These were intended for women who feared domestic violence, whether driven by 'honour' or by other motives. In Morocco, shelters or safe houses were created from the late 1990s onwards. The difficulty had been to ensure that women knew of this possibility of safe internal flight, without allowing that information to become general knowledge, avail-able therefore to their male relatives. In these 'republics of cousins', as the kin networks of Moroccan society have been called, this has been a challenge.[70]

The need, however, has been felt across the region and nowhere more so than in Iraq, following the U.S.-led invasion and occupation of 2003. In the chaos of the years that followed, levels of violence in Iraq soared, claiming hundreds of thousands of victims, both men and women. Women, like men, shared the danger of being in the wrong place at the wrong time when bombs or shooting were claiming so many lives. But for women, there were added dangers. The militias of the Islamist parties, both Shi`i and Sunni, used violence to impose their ideas of 'Islamic propriety' on women, forcing them to dress and behave in public in ways that would satisfy the militias of their piety. This was in addition to the demands made upon women within the home by male relatives, trying to exercise the control within the family that they had lost in the public sphere. Furthermore, the growing numbers of widows, the unemployment and the destitution that were the cumulative results of years of war, sanctions, military occupation and social breakdown meant that women were increasingly vulnerable.[71]

In response to this, the Organization of Women's Freedom in Iraq (OWFI) was founded to try to protect women against violence, as well as to advance a wider agenda that would ensure the protection of the rights of women in the emerging legal system as the Iraqi state was rebuilt. OWFI established a number of women's shelters across Iraq and at the same time set up organizations that could help women reach these shelters or that could help them even to escape the country. Immediate protection from violence was often vitally necessary and the only way of resisting the forces that were bearing down on women in the short term. In the longer term, as the founder Yanar Muhammad said, the project of resistance was more wide-ranging: 'Either we organize and demand our social and political freedoms, or we give way to a theocracy and the institutionalized, legalized oppression of women in Iraq'.[72]

The problems involved in organizing resistance to a coercive set of social codes were not due simply to the difficulty of intervening in the closely guarded sphere of the family. There was also the challenge of trying to communicate to women and men the need to imagine the possibility of resistance, or to think that escape was morally, as well as practically, feasible. There is evidence to suggest that women themselves have sometimes been staunch defenders of such a system of organized violence, despite the personal costs to them and their families. Even some of those who had been identified as the likely targets of such treatment, often as victims of sexual crime in the first place, have internalized the social stigma. They have tended to judge themselves as harshly as they would be judged by their family and community.[73] For the more resilient and confident, the idea of resistance was possible. However, even they could only use individual strategies of escape, of dissimulation, of suppression, of subversion in isolation – using the 'weapons of the weak' to avoid a fate that appeared to be collectively mapped out for them.

SITES AND STRATEGIES OF RESISTANCE

In the Middle East, as in many other parts of the world, women have found that when they try to fight against the forms of oppression that are imposed upon them as women, they have had to struggle on many fronts. The patriarchal family at the centre of rural and much of urban society becomes the guardian and enforcer of rules that are sanctioned by 'tradition' and by religion. Both men and women have helped to maintain it, believing it to be fundamental to their security, their identity and the rules of social life. It has also been a key feature in the division of labour and thus in the organization of family-based economies. However, in the context of a modern state and a developing economy, it has become a zone of conflict. It is here that gender roles are being redefined, and because of their implication in the myths of state power, it is also a site for an emerging politics of resistance.

The laws of the state, particularly the laws of personal status that regulate key aspects of women's and men's relations with each other, have become central to particular forms of resistance. These have been pursued, whether in Morocco or Iran or Lebanon, through the existing legal and political systems. 'Rightful resistance' is thus very much to the fore as a strategy, often accompanied by direct action, such as protests and demonstrations, to influence those who have the power to reframe the law. By focusing on these forms of resistance, the women involved, acting as citizens in pursuit of their rights, take on far more than simply the question of gender difference and discrimination. They are also asserting their rights as politically active citizens to determine the laws that have such an impact on their lives. In some places, such as Iran, this can mean defiance of the gendering of power itself in public office and in the authoritative interpretation of Islamic *fiqh* (jurisprudence) – a sphere that the Islamic Republic has strenuously reserved not simply for men but for an exclusively male clerical establishment.

The determination of women from Morocco to Egypt, Turkey and on to Iran to assert their rights, as Muslims, to interpret the *fiqh* has come from conviction. However, it is also a strategy to expand the scope for women's autonomy without being drawn into unequal battles over 'authenticity'. Here the larger resistance struggle on behalf of the 'nation' or 'Islam' against cultural and political domination by the 'West' has been used as a way of isolating women's organizations. Their campaigns for gender equality based on a human rights discourse originating in – although by no means exclusive to – Western ideas of female emancipation have been charged with furthering the aims of neo-imperialism.

In this context, Islamic feminism, disconcerting as the idea may appear to some, can be seen as a form of resistance to patriarchy's appropriation of the sacred texts. By challenging men's exclusive rights to interpretation, women are trying both to lay claim to a right and to introduce understandings that avoid misogyny. A similar struggle has also been taking place within nationalist resistance movements. Here women have discovered, as in other parts of the world, that the struggle for national self-determination tends to be dominated by gendered visions of the self. Almost exclusively, male leaders and theorists have assigned different roles to men and women that are disturbingly similar to patriarchal and ultimately oppressive ideas about the 'proper' sphere of women's action. Understandably, women have been to the fore in obliging their compatriots to question those features of the 'nation' that stem from unthought and, for men, comforting 'traditions' privileging men over women.

It is here, at the level of the personal and the familial, that a politics of resistance for women becomes more problematic and more dangerous. It is problematic because women have sometimes internalized norms that disparage and prohibit a wide range of behaviour. This can make it harder for women's organizations to make them see that these are states of unequal power that can and must be resisted. It can also be dangerous to resist. Women and men alike have frequently shown a ferocious determination to preserve the 'guarded sphere' of the family. This puts at risk members of women's organizations who try to educate and protect those they believe are in need of protection. In places where social and geographical mobility as well as educational opportunity for women have vastly expanded, it can also be dangerous to them individually. Social attitudes may not have adapted to these changed circumstances. A woman may therefore still be seen as an adjunct of the family or the clan, subordinate to its members' view of her 'honourable' behaviour and subject to their violence should she act otherwise. In these circumstances, a strategy of resistance can take two forms. It can either revolve around a collective campaign to ensure that the state neither sanctions nor turns a blind eye to family violence against women, whether in the name of 'tradition' or 'religion'. Or it can lead to the establishment of women's shelters that need to be protected also against the violence sometimes used against them. Taking refuge in such places is obviously not open to all women. For them, resistance may take the form of negotiating individual strategies of survival to reduce the risks they run from the kind of power to which they are perennially subject.

5

History Wars

Contesting the Past, Reclaiming the Future

In April 1989 at the Dayan Centre of Tel Aviv University, a two-day conference on the war of 1948 – known as the war of independence by most Israelis and as *al-Nakba* [the catastrophe] by Palestinians – provided the setting for a skirmish in another war. This was the 'war' for Israel's history and, to some extent, for the identity of the nation state. In an engagement joined by historians and social scientists who nevertheless observed the usual conventions of academic propriety, it revealed the bitterness of the divide between different interpretations not simply of the events of 1948 but also of Israeli history itself. Broadly speaking, on one side there were those who defended the commonly accepted and often heroically presented story of Israel's establishment and conduct as a state. Confronting them were those who challenged this version of the state's beginnings, turning a critical light on the behaviour of its political leaders and of its armed forces in 1948 and in the years that followed.

Nor was the battle fought out only within the confines of the university campus or of academic journals. It was a matter of public debate as well, filling newspaper columns and becoming the subject of media interest and interpretation. Writers such as Shabtai Teveth (the official biographer of Ben Gurion, seen as a champion of the 'authorized version' of Israel's past) used the occasion of the conference to publish a series of four long articles in the daily paper, *Haaretz*. In these, he vehemently accused the revisionists of traducing not only the memory of the former prime minister, but also the very foundation and raison d'être of the state of Israel.[1]

Some treated this as normal historical revisionism, very much to be expected in the writing and rewriting of history. For others, however, more seemed to be at stake. This was particularly noticeable amongst those who objected to the ways that historians and sociologists had begun to question the received, conventional wisdom about the nature of Israeli society and the origins of the Israeli state. Of course, those who championed the various forms of revisionism felt equally strongly, but they came at it from a variety of different directions and with a number of purposes. Nevertheless, whatever their ultimate objectives, they were bound together by a determination to interrogate the given, to resist a version of Israel's past that had been so dominant for so long and that many felt would compromise its future. For some, the struggle signified nothing less than the radical transformation of Israel as a state. For others, it was more a case of establishing an accurate and credible historical narrative unconnected to any specific political cause.

Precisely because of the public debate that surrounds it and the political implications that have been so much to the fore, the Israeli case is a good example of resistance to dominant narratives of power in Middle Eastern politics. In particular, it opens the way for an examination of the importance and centrality of *nationalist* narratives in the politics of state formation in the modern Middle East. This is a key feature of the political landscape of the region, as in so much of the rest of the world, where the territorial nation state has become the chief form of political organization, embodying the sovereign powers of distinct communities. Nationalism is not simply an ideology, but also defines a field of struggle in which various groups fight it out for the right to determine the character of the nation and their own power to define it. This has been a marked feature of Europe's long and bloody centuries of wars, revolutions and civil wars. It has also been prominent in post-colonial Asia and Africa, where struggles over imbalances of power and stories of belonging have occurred between and within states and communities.

In the post-colonial Middle East, developing a convincing national story was part of the resistance to colonialism. It was also a conscious strategy of state building used by the new elites that held power after independence. They were determined to define the distinguishing features of a community and to 'discover' it as an actor through time – historical continuity being assumed to give it certain rights in relation to others, among them sovereignty over a specific territory. Nationalist histories have therefore given birth to numerous myths, to narrative invention and to strategic silences. Some of these have been more self-consciously developed than others, but all to some extent have been the product of the creative art of historical writing within a context of national imagining. Challenges to any aspect of this can be deeply disturbing. They can shake people's sense of themselves and their identities, as well as the political order that they have taken for granted and indeed have integrated into their moral universe.[2]

Resisting particular versions of the past that help to underpin regimes of power in the present becomes mired in political struggle as the links between power and knowledge are laid bare. Telling an alternative story, a version that does not conform to that of the state establishment, can be politically explosive. It may expose the way in which the story has been told to suit the interests of a particular section of society, in ethnic, class or institutional terms. More radically, it may force a reassessment of historical rights, the renegotiation of access to resources or the recognition – and reclassification – of hitherto marginalized people. A narrative of resistance thus opens the way for voices that have been written out of history, giving them the chance to reassert themselves and their rights in the present, overcoming the silences that form the unspoken part of any narrative.[3]

In the retelling of the past, a larger political movement may be born. This was, after all, one of the major achievements of resistance movements during the period of decolonization. Narratives that asserted the place of hitherto unrecognized national communities were geared to mass mobilization and to the goal of winning sovereign power. However, in most cases, this assertion was achieved at the expense of alternative versions that might have had equal historical validity but did not mesh with the ideas and concerns of the leaders of the political struggle at the time. Ironically, history itself ensures that these dominant narratives are always vulnerable to the passage of time – changing conditions may make it harder to sustain a story that begins to lose authority and credibility. It is not surprising, therefore, that recent decades should have witnessed the emergence across the Middle East of resistance to the narratives that have been so deeply implicated in the initial constitution of established power.

In particular, two successful nationalist movements in the Middle East, the Zionists in Palestine and the FLN in Algeria, are worthy of closer study for the ways in which excluded histories, strategic silences and untold stories have come back to haunt the intellectual and political establishments – and to shake the apparent certainties not simply of the nationalist narrative but also the identity and the political destiny of the nation itself. They are not unique in this regard, either in the region or elsewhere. In the Middle East alone, the retelling of national history and the redefinition of national identity have been associated with nationalist revolutions and political upheavals in Turkey, Iran, Iraq and Yemen. In some cases, this may involve an assertion of the identity and rights of a particular linguistic or religious community, such as the Kurds of Turkey, the Arabs of Iran or the Shi`a of Lebanon. But even where the aim is not the assertion of claims of this kind, people may be resisting versions of history that appear to justify the existence of a discredited political order. Resistance in this sense can have both a political and a disciplinary agenda.[4] It is political in that it engages with established power, presenting a critique of the ways in which a perceived misuse or imbalance of power has been used to perpetuate injustice and possibly planning its redress. It is disciplinary in that it seeks to displace what may be perceived as 'bad history' or simply practices routine historical revisionism.

The grammar of myth making and historiography, whether in the hands of the powerful or of those trying to resist, is significantly close – significantly, because it allows a particularly intimate struggle to take place, in which certain code words and certain sites of performance are charged with symbolic meaning and thus fiercely contested. It is this that allows such struggles to be thought of as instances of political resistance. It is not that they are aiming to overthrow a particular government. More ambitiously, they are aiming to dismantle a dominant common sense that lets a certain regime of truth flourish. In doing so, they can undermine the credulity that has led to the acceptance of power without serious question.

A central issue in these struggles has been the attempt to give weight to a particular narrative by conforming to the rules of a particular discipline. By the same token, it has often provoked the accusation that those who hold to a different version flout those same rules. This may account for some of the bitterness and the ad hominem nature of these disputes. The charge that a hidden, possibly malign political agenda is being served can shift the terrain away from a debate about the writing of history to an argument about conflicting political interests. In both Israel and in the case of the assertion of Amazigh (Berber) identity in North Africa, such charges have envenomed much of the debate. They have also been indicators of the seriousness of what is believed to be at stake.

ISRAELI 'CRITICAL SOCIOLOGISTS' AND 'NEW HISTORIANS' – AND THEIR CRITICS

The interest and relevance of this case lies in the fact that, since the 1980s, increasing numbers of Israeli scholars – historians, sociologists and political scientists – have been holding up for scrutiny and critically examining aspects of Israeli history and society. Since the foundation of the state and even before, these same aspects had formed part of many Israelis' views of themselves, of their national identity and of their national institutions, as well as of their political and military leaders. By revisiting, revising and critically deconstructing the recent past, these scholars were arguing against a dominant, even hegemonic narrative. It was adhered to in most of its particulars by the full spectrum of Zionist parties in Israel and reproduced in numerous places and by different means. There had, of course, been criticisms of the past actions, accounts and justifications associated with the dominant forces in Israel since the time of its foundation, but these had not had a serious impact on public consciousness. In part, this was because of the numbers involved, but it was also due to the location of many of these critics in parties or organizations that limited their ability to enter the mainstream of Israeli debate.[5]

From the 1980s onwards, the dramatic and significant changes in Israeli society and the developments in its domestic and international politics that had taken place in previous decades had helped to stimulate a critical turn among scholars and journalists. They also provided an increasingly receptive audience for the retelling of Israeli history. Dissatisfaction with the given version of the past and growing wariness of the uses made of this in the present by political parties whose authority was in decline provided a willingness amongst the public to contemplate, at the very least, alternative views of apparently well-known events. For some, whose personal identities and histories had been deeply involved in the existing, hitherto accepted version of the past and its elaboration, this seemed like an attack that was both personal and against the very nation state itself.

This had made itself felt, initially within the confines of the small but lively field of academic sociology in Israel, with those who came to be called the 'critical sociologists'. The targets of their criticism were the functionalist and integrative claims about the nature of Israeli society that had dominated the discipline up to the 1970s, notwithstanding the mounting evidence of profound social conflict. The critique went further, however. It took issue with the role of the discipline, or rather of some of its main practitioners, in not simply analysing Israeli society, but also in advising government on the very social policies that, in the view of the critical sociologists, had become part of the problem. The charge was that they had lent their authority to policies that had helped to impose on a disparate and powerless population of immigrants a version of Israeli identity and society that suppressed and marginalized the immigrants' own varied cultures. This was particularly the case with regard to the many immigrants who had arrived in Israel from the countries of the Arab world in the 1950s – and whose disadvantages in and alienation from mainstream, largely European, Israeli society were producing a new and restive politics by the 1970s.

Gershon Shafir, one of the critical sociologists, reflected on his own intellectual formation. He confessed that his critical view of Israeli sociology and of the picture it had painted of Israeli society came from a variety of sources: intellectual dissatisfaction with functionalism as a mode of explanation, since he was aware that it was being questioned within the discipline in the wider world; a feeling that social conflict needed to be explained and that this meant taking seriously the concerns and interests of the protagonists; a wariness of the uncritical admiration for the state and of the étatism that the leading sociologists shared with the political elite who tended to see the state as the 'utmost expression of nationhood and community and sole trustee for the welfare of its citizenry'.[6]

Equally, the erosion of his faith in the Labour Zionist establishment led him to question much of the mythology surrounding it and, by association, the founding stories of the state of Israel. It was only reinforced by the behaviour of the Israeli authorities in the territories occupied in 1967 where, far from behaving in the democratic and egalitarian spirit that had been part of the founding myth, the state resembled a colonial power. This in turn provided the incentive to re-examine Labour Zionism and to see in its early decades not only an elitism in relation to the working class, but also an internal colonialism, based on European and modernist prejudices, vis-à-vis the *Mizrahim* – the Jewish immigrants from 'Eastern', mainly Arab countries.[7]

These charges were met with vehement rebuttal. Particularly resented was the suggestion that much of the sociological establishment had been for decades in the pocket of the state administration, acting as courtiers to the Labour Zionist movement and thus losing their autonomy as scholars. Those like Moshe Lissak, who attacked the critical sociologists, denounced them for suggesting that Israeli society and state were essentially colonial in origin and character, 'born in sin' as he colourfully put it. He claimed to see in their criticism a distinctly anti-Zionist agenda, disguised in fashionable post-modernism that, he suggested, refused to recognize that any theorization could be free of ideological bias. Echoing some of Shafir's original critique of the way in which sociology in Israel was narrowly defined to exclude the study of topics like the varied social impact of the Arab–Israeli conflict on Israeli society, those who attacked Shafir and his fellow sociologists suggested that the critical sociologists were preoccupied with questions of ideology, politics and identity – none of these, it was suggested, were fitting subjects for sociological study.[8]

It was scarcely surprising that with a focus on power and its links with knowledge, identity and belief, the critical sociologists should have made those who subscribed to the dominant narrative of Zionism as Jewish nationalism extremely uneasy. One of the intriguing aspects of the emergence of critical sociology was the degree of acrimony that seemed to be associated with sociologists performing the very role that their discipline demanded of them: their duty to 'pierce through the facades that each society sets up about itself'.[9] They seemed to represent no more than the expected 'debunking tendency of sociology' itself. Yet they were accused of anti-Zionism, of rejecting the entire Zionist enterprise and thus, implicitly, of throwing into question the very legitimacy of the state of Israel.[10]

The significance of the varied challenges of the critical sociologists – they were and are highly diverse as a group, holding a variety of views and espousing different methodologies – was that all of them, in one way or another, challenged some of the hitherto comforting assumptions about Israel and Israeli society. The earlier approaches of Eisenstadt and his followers had been so serviceable for the Labour Zionist establishment in the early decades possibly because of ideological and political proximity, but also because 'functionalism as sociological perspective and functionality as political practice went hand in hand'.[11]

The fact remained, however, that the silences of establishment sociology matched the silences of the dominant Zionist narrative, and the assumptions of the sociologists mirrored the exclusive and largely European prejudices of many Zionist ideologues. Thus the diversity and particularity of the non-European Jewish immigrants and their customs were either dismissed or classified as dysfunctional 'traditions' that impeded their development as modern Israeli citizens. The Zionist and sociological goal was to ensure greater 'functionality' by obliging these new migrants to fit in to a society shaped and dominated by a European elite – for their own good, it was claimed. But it was clearly for the enlightened nationalist modernizers to determine what that good might be. The critical sociologists not only subjected these often highly authoritarian policies of the 1950s and 1960s to intense scrutiny, but also suggested that such policies had produced a host of social problems in contemporary Israel – problems with direct political consequences, since the original policies had been the product of and had themselves reproduced severe imbalances of power.

Quite apart from the implications of this for the profession itself and the attention it drew to the complicity of some of its practitioners, it also undermined one of the assertions of Zionism as Jewish nationalism: that there was a Jewish identity that superseded all others. On the contrary, the critical sociologists had drawn attention to the fact that the identity of Jews in many respects was as diverse as the cultures and values of the societies in which they had lived and been brought up. This had two disturbing implications for the nationalist myth of Zionism. First, it suggested that Zionism should be seen as the expression of a particular European ethnicity that had overcome other possible expressions of what it meant to be Jewish in order to assert hegemonic control through its domination of the Yishuv and of the Israeli state.

Second, precisely because the focus was on the *Mizrahim*, the Jewish immigrants of Arab culture and origin, it blurred the lines of distinction between the Jews and the Arab 'other' – something which Israeli sociology up to that point, as well as state ideology, had been careful to maintain. By reintroducing this unsettling aspect of *lack* of difference, the critical sociologists opened up the field to a more meaningful and open recognition of Arab Israelis – hitherto largely neglected in sociology – as well as the Arab, Palestinian inhabitants of the territories occupied in 1967. They had received little or no attention, since the whole issue had been deemed by the discipline to be 'too political'. It was not surprising, therefore, that the critical sociologists had such a disturbing effect. They had blurred the lines of exclusive Jewish identity and thus faced charges of anti-Zionism, of undermining the state itself and indeed of posing 'the greatest danger to sociological research in Israel'.[12]

If this was the case with the critical sociologists, it was even more so when Israeli historians began to examine Israel's history, especially in the context of its relations with the original Arab inhabitants of Palestine and with the surrounding Arab states. In doing so, many of the commonly held beliefs about the foundation of the state of Israel, its conduct in war and its place in the region, as well as its vigorous state and nation-building strategies, came under close and critical scrutiny. To some degree, this had been prefigured in the works of writers like Gabriel Sheffer or Yehoshafat Harkabi. The latter's change of heart had had considerable impact, since he had not only been the head of military intelligence in the 1950s, but had also been a sometimes outspoken representative of the consensus within the civilian and military establishments.[13]

Some writers, such as Simha Flapan, explicitly intended to question what he regarded as the principal myths in the official Israeli version of the history of 1947–9. Indeed, his book, published in 1987 – *The Birth of Israel – myths and realities* – was organized to address seven such myths, including 'Myth One: Zionists accepted the UN partition and planned for peace', 'Myth Three: Palestinians fled voluntarily, intending reconquest' and 'Myth Six: Defenseless Israel faced destruction by the Arab Goliath'.[14] Others re-examined specific aspects of this history, such as the historians Benny Morris in *The Birth of the Palestinian Refugee Problem, 1947–1949* (1987), Avi Shlaim in *Collusion Across the Jordan: King Abdullah, the Zionist Movement and the Partition of Palestine* (1988) and Ilan Pappé in *Britain and the Arab–Israeli Conflict* (1988). Basing their research on newly released official archives of these years, both in Britain and in Israel, they came to a variety of conclusions which were by no means uniform, but which differed markedly from the versions of these events that had hitherto been dominant in Israel.

These established versions had been championed not only in academic circles but by political leaders who ensured that they became part of the defining narrative of the Israeli state, propagated in school textbooks, in the media and in public discourse generally. Essentially, although there were differences of emphasis and interpretation here as well, the dominant version of history stressed the heroic and moral aspects of the state's foundation – intentionally so, as far as those commissioning school history texts were concerned. Michael Ziv, head of high school education in the Ministry of Education in the 1950s, stated explicitly that 'It is essential that the values underlying the official historical narrative ... coincide with society's principal accepted values. No society can afford a conflict between these two value systems'. Similarly, his successor, Naftali Zon, who was in charge of the same department until the early 1970s, stated that it was the duty of teachers to 'select those facts indicating the existence of the values of sacrifice and heroism which would enable [the student] to identify with the actors'.[15] Indeed, as successive education laws and curricular revisions indicated, there was a determination from the outset to reinforce young people's attachment to a version of Jewish and of Israeli history that would inspire their admiration, bind their loyalties to the state and shape the collective memory of the nation.[16]

Consequently, when the 'new historians' – the label applied to those who were critically re-examining and re-evaluating Israel's past – came to conclusions that differed markedly from these versions of history, it was not surprising that the critical and even hostile reception of their work was not confined to other professional historians. On the contrary, it sparked a public debate of great intensity and complexity. In many respects, by scrutinizing the motives and outcomes of the actions of the leaders of the Zionist parties, as well as the conduct of Israeli forces in the violent events surrounding the establishment of Israel, they removed the fog of heroism from individual and collective actions and allowed them to be assessed in a harsher but clearer light. Some of the behaviour thereby revealed was so far from heroic as to be morally repugnant, particularly when seen forty years after the event. Nevertheless, much of it was perfectly understandable if the foundation and consolidation of the state of Israel were seen as examples of the ruthless realpolitik associated with most successful political projects.

However, for those who still held to the heroic and mythic versions of the past, some of the developments that were coming to light proved difficult to accept. For instance, many were unsettled by Morris's contention that a large part of the Palestinian refugee problem had been the result of deliberate policies pursued by Ben Gurion and other leaders of the Zionist movement before, as well as after the formal declaration of Israeli independence in 1948. Brought up to believe that the 'flight' of the Palestinians had been due either to Arab leaders' instructions to the population to leave whilst the Arab armies occupied Palestine, or merely to the impersonal misfortunes of war, it was unsettling to be presented with contradictory evidence. This tended to show that the bulk of the Arab inhabitants of Palestine had not fled simply as a by-product of the fighting, but because of policies carried out by the Zionist leadership in the chaos of Britain's hasty withdrawal and by the Israeli authorities under the cover of war, supplemented by the actions of particular military units seeking to 'cleanse' or 'purify' [in Hebrew, *tiher*] Arab villages and neighbourhoods for tactical reasons.[17]

Ilan Pappé's thesis that the wholesale destruction of Palestinian Arab society and the expulsion of the great majority of Palestine's Arab population was the result of a conscious policy of 'ethnic cleansing' was an even more radical statement of this general argument, not shared by all.[18] Nevertheless, in either case, Israelis were obliged to face up to the responsibility of the Zionist movement and the state of Israel in the creation and perpetuation of the Palestinian refugee problem. As a writer in *Haaretz* commented, 'the establishment of the State of Israel was justice for the Jews, but it was accompanied by a terrible injustice for the Palestinians'.[19]

The unsettling aspect of this was twofold. First, the plight of the Palestinian refugees could no longer be ascribed to some impersonal phenomenon such as 'war', but was now traced in many instances to the particular actions of named units and individuals who had hitherto formed part of the tableau of the heroic generation of Zionism. Second, acknowledgement of even partial responsibility would have direct political implications since Israel was to embark in the 1990s upon negotiations with the Palestinians and amongst the key issues to be discussed was the question of the status and future of the Palestinian refugees. It was noticeable, for instance, that when the then prime minister, Ehud Barak, made an unprecedented declaration before the Israeli Knesset in October 1999 in which he 'expressed, on behalf of the State of Israel, his regret and sympathy for the suffering of the Palestinian people', he was careful neither to apologize nor to accept any Israeli responsibility for their plight.[20]

Focusing in on the micro-history of the events surrounding the flight of some 250,000 Palestinians from the territories occupied by the Zionist forces prior to the withdrawal of the British from Palestine, the fighting that took place in 1948 and the exodus of a further 450,000 Palestinians from their towns and villages thereafter meant also that the spotlight was turned on the behaviour of the Israeli armed forces themselves. The massacre of villagers at Deir Yassin in April 1948 had long been acknowledged but was portrayed as the responsibility of the Irgun and Lehi militias and could thus be disowned by the official forces of the Haganah. Indeed, some alleged that the atrocities had been exaggerated by Ben Gurion precisely to discredit the political leadership of these militias.

However, with the opening of the archives and with the close scrutiny of the record of the Israeli fighting units, other incidents came to light. In some cases, it appeared that the Israeli armed forces had themselves been responsible for killings of civilians that could not be attributed simply to the heat of battle. One particular incident at Tantura, an Arab coastal village near Haifa, in May 1948, became a cause célèbre in Israel in the year 2000. The author of an MA thesis at the University of Haifa, Teddy Katz, had claimed that there had been a massacre of villagers by soldiers of the Alexandroni Brigade. When these findings were publicized in the press, he was sued by survivors of the Brigade and, although his dissertation had been passed with distinction and appeared to have been based on a wealth of oral testimony from both Jewish and Arab witnesses of the events, he came under intense pressure and retracted his claim that a massacre had taken place. The university, far from supporting him, annulled his degree and effectively disowned him. This, in turn, was to lead to the resignation of Ilan Pappé who had supported him and endorsed his account of the killings at Tantura.[21] Some contemplated these developments with a good deal of satisfaction, seeing them as a 'watershed event that has begun to put Israeli historiography back on track' and thus marking the 'turning of the tide as the post-Zionists' hold over Israeli historiography wanes'.[22]

This seemed like wishful thinking. Quite apart from the findings of the first grouping of 'new historians' whose methodologies were in fact very much in the conventional mould, new trends in historiography and social science were becoming prevalent in Israel, as elsewhere. As the editor of one of the more important historical journals in Israel, *Zmanim* (Times), stated, by the mid-1990s, the journal may have begun with a positivist approach in the conventional historiographical sense but had now become a forum for critique and reflection on the art of historical narrative itself. Thus, as elsewhere, the writing of history had become more self-consciously aware of the intimate links between the relationships between power and knowledge. The assurances of the old nationalist narrative could no longer be sustained, not simply because of the coming to light of new evidence and the intervention of hitherto silenced voices. It was also because of the successful resistance of many to the idea and reality of an unexamined and hegemonic 'truth', especially one that seemed to be so intimately linked to a political project that was itself the subject of contention.[23]

It was despair at this state of affairs that seems to have provoked impassioned outbursts like that of the writer Aharon Megged in the pages of *Haaretz* in June 1994 under the eye-catching title of 'The Israeli Suicide Drive'.[24] In this, he attacked the historians and sociologists whose re-examination of Israel's past seemed to him to show contempt for the myths that had inspired the early Zionists. He berated them for undermining the legitimacy of Zionism itself and for throwing into doubt the very enterprise of state building in Israel. For him, it appeared that the real danger of those who had emerged to contest the accepted versions of Israeli history was indeed the impact they were having on power relations – by undermining the main nationalist narrative, they were eroding both the solidarity of the national community and unsettling the ideological foundations of the state. Fearful of the effects of this in the future, he was also concerned that the work of the new historians was destroying the faith of young Israelis in the hitherto barely questioned justice of the Zionist cause.

Interestingly, the writings of those who were effectively debunking the nationalist myths surrounding the early years of the state seemed to be more unsettling for people generally associated with the old Labour left in Israeli politics than for those on the right. Some of the latter had fewer problems about much of the research, since they saw expulsion as the natural result of war and even reproached Ben Gurion for being insufficiently aggressive in his territorial aims. Others even came out in support of the findings of the 'new historians'. For instance, Emunah Eilon from one of the more intransigent settler movements had no difficulty in accepting some of the 'difficult, even shocking discoveries' that the new historians had made. They had revealed for her in a clearsighted and unsentimental way, undisguised by Labour Zionist moralizing, the harsh realities of the basic struggle between the Jews and the Palestinian Arabs for possession of the land. True to her political beliefs, this did not shake her faith in the Jews' right to the land or in the need to 'chase away anyone who needs to be expelled'. It simply underlined the ruthless realpolitik at the heart of Israel's history – a feature she found encouraging.[25]

This was an extreme case. In fact, the right, as represented by the Likud party, was vociferous in denouncing what it regarded as pernicious and malign attacks on Israel's reputation. This became vividly apparent when the Israel Broadcasting Authority broadcast a documentary series, *Tekuma* ('rebirth'), in 1998 to mark the fiftieth anniversary of the founding of the state, looking back at its history. In the series, it incorporated many of the findings of those historians who had been part of the movement to re-examine the myths of Israel's history, some of whom acted as advisers to the programme. This provoked outrage from Ariel Sharon, then a senior government minister himself, who protested to the Minister of Education that the series 'distorts the history of the rebirth and undermines any moral basis for the establishment of the state of Israel and its continued existence' and called for it to be taken off the air, or at least to be banned from schools. Similarly, his colleague, Limor Livnat, Minister of Communications, as well as saying that she was forbidding her teenage son to watch the series, complained that it 'depicts the Palestinian side sympathetically, systematically distorts the great Zionist deeds and causes severe and probably irreparable damage to our image'. However, despite the complaints and the fact that the government of Netanyahu was uneasy about the whole enterprise, *Tekuma* achieved record viewing figures, and as Gideon Drori, the editor of the series, said, 'We didn't choose to shatter myths. The myths were already shattered'.[26]

This was essentially true. However, this may be less a testimony to the power of the new historians and critical sociologists to resist and to break the ideological dominance of the Zionist establishment. It was perhaps more due to the fact that the very circumstances that had caused scholars to re-examine Israeli national life in the first place were also affecting the Israeli public more generally. The war of 1967 had led to the occupation of all of historical Palestine by Israel, bringing under Israeli rule some 1.5 million Palestinians, many of them refugees from the war of 1948. Military occupation was hardly conducive to a free flow of people and ideas across old boundaries, psychological as well as physical, but it did bring increasing numbers of Israelis into contact with large numbers of Palestinians. Whether as a growing part of the Israeli labour force or as subjects of the military administration or as the majority of inhabitants in the newly annexed eastern section of Jerusalem, the Palestinians could no longer be marginalized or ignored, as had been largely the lot of the 150,000 Palestinian Arabs who had remained within the state of Israel after 1948. There was clearly another side to the stories that Israelis had come to believe. For some, whether through the experience of military service in the occupied territories or through a range of personal encounters, this was enough to begin questioning whether the narrative that the state had so carefully constructed was but a partial account of events.

At the same time, within Israeli society itself, a new generation, children of the Mizrahim – the Jewish immigrants from Arab countries in the 1940s and 1950s – began to question their status within Israeli society. It was not simply that the egalitarian claims of the Labour Zionist establishment rang hollow to those who found themselves on the lower rungs of the ladder. It was also that they seemed to be blocked from advancing any further largely because of their ethnic origin. Thus it was noticeable that the upper and even middle echelons of society were occupied principally by Jews of European origin, whether relatively recent immigrants or those born in Palestine or Israel during the preceding decades. In this sense, the myths of assimilation and integration into an Israeli society founded on the Zionist assertion that all Jews were equal clearly did not match the lived experience of being a Mizrahi Jew in Israel. This awareness gave birth to political organizations that began to voice the demands of this section of Israeli society. Furthermore, general awareness of the hollow nature of the foundation myths of Labour Zionism contributed to the dramatic upset of Labour's defeat in the 1977 elections. It also bred an understandable scepticism about other stories that appeared so supportive of the imbalance of power and opportunity inherent in the status quo.

Of equal impact in another key area of nationalist mythology, the 1982 invasion of Lebanon threw into question both the legitimacy of Israel's use of armed force and the conduct of the armed forces themselves. The message of the unprecedented and massive demonstrations in Israel against the war at a time when Israeli forces were still fighting in Lebanon was reinforced by the refusal of increasing numbers of men to serve in the armed forces during the war. To this was added growing moral revulsion at the cost in terms of Lebanese and Palestinian civilians' lives as the numbers of casualties became known, both during the campaign and in the Palestinian refugee camps of Sabra and Shatilla under Israeli occupation. Above all, these events shook the faith of many who had hitherto unquestioningly accepted Israel's use of force on the understanding that two principles governed its deployment: *'ein breira'* [no alternative] and *'tohar haneshek'* [purity of arms]. These two catchphrases had been integral to the stories of 1948 and indeed of the other wars fought by Israel since then. They express, first, the belief that Israel only goes to war in self-defence, when it has no choice but to do so, and second, the claim that, in all cases, Israel's use of violence is governed by a strict moral code. Both claims looked threadbare to many in the aftermath of 1982.

By the end of the 1990s, the notion that there might indeed be more than one narrative at work in shaping Israeli history became unarguable, underlined by developments such as the *intifada* of 1987 onwards, the emergence of Shas as a powerful political force for the Mizrahim, the increasingly vociferous settler movement in the occupied territories, as well as the 1979 peace treaty with Egypt, the 1993 Oslo Accords with the PLO and the peace treaty with Jordan in 1994. For some, the developing peace process of those years meant that if it were to work, a real effort needed to be made to understand the concerns and collective memories of the Palestinians. This helps to explain the statement which Prime Minister Barak made to the Knesset in 1999, as well as the similarly sympathetic statements by the Minister of Education, Yossi Sarid. He also commissioned a revision of the school textbooks to incorporate some of the alternative narratives of 1948, taking the Palestinian stories seriously and giving them a voice in history. Even so, they did not go far enough for some in the correction of the painfully one-sided version of history presented in earlier textbooks, whilst for others they represented a shameful and dangerous retreat from basic Zionist values and myths. This ensured that when the Barak government fell, to be replaced by a Likud government led by Ariel Sharon, the 'revisionist' textbooks were all withdrawn.[27]

In this respect, the exposure of Israeli scholars, and to some extent the educated public, to the increasingly authoritative writings of Palestinian scholars re-examining their own history provided interlocutors who could not simply be dismissed as part of a political project aimed at the dismantling of Israel. This did not of course prevent some in Israel from making just such allegations, often classifying the critical Israeli historians and sociologists as enemies of Zionism and of the state as well. Nevertheless, works by Walid Khalidi, Rashid Khalidi, Nur Masalha, Sami Hadawi, Edward Said and others gave voice to alternative narratives of the events not simply of 1948 but also of the preceding century and of the decades that followed. It was a voice, or a variety of voices, that could not be ignored and that countered many of the key features of the dominant Zionist myths clouding Israel's history. Just as with the Israeli historians, the Palestinians had differing interpretations and approaches to historiography, and they by no means agreed with each other or with the Israeli historians on all particulars. However, they had helped to open the field to a dialogue that was increasingly productive but that undermined and displaced the version of Israeli history that had been so influential not only in Israel for the preceding fifty years but also in much of the rest of the world.[28]

Thus, by the turn of the twenty-first century, the once-dominant Zionist narrative of Israel's founding and history was seen as merely one version among many. Those who had felt dissatisfied with it and had resisted its overarching claims had succeeded through critical scrutiny in fragmenting the monolithic façade it had presented in the preceding decades. This had coincided with and had helped to reinforce the efforts to reach a political agreement between Israel and the Palestinians that had gained momentum in the final decade of the twentieth century. Thus the recasting of the historical narrative might have helped to open the way for negotiations by addressing some of the concerns of those silenced by the nationalist narrative of Zionism. In fact, Pappé refers to the fact that, at the beginning of the Oslo process of 1993, Yossi Beilin, the chief Israeli negotiator, had produced an array of books by the new Israeli historians to demonstrate to his wary Palestinian counterparts that things had changed and that Israelis did now acknowledge Israel's part in the dispossession of the Palestinians.[29] Furthermore, as Israel's then foreign minister, Shlomo Ben-Ami, admitted, the work of the new historians had a direct influence on the Israeli–Palestinian negotiations in 2000 and 2001. For the Palestinians, research in the Israeli archives on the origins of the Palestinian refugee problem proved that Israel was partially responsible for the plight of the refugees of 1948. For their part, the Israelis, in Ben-Ami's words, 'came to the negotiating table with perspectives that were shaped by recent research ... the introduction of new and powerful arguments on the 1948 war into the public debate in Israel became part of the intellectual baggage of many of us, whether we admitted it or not'.[30]

This development had been made possible by the cumulative effect of events that had created receptive grounds for those who were becoming increasingly sceptical of the myths of the given nationalist narrative. It did not substitute one such narrative for another. On the contrary, it was in the very spirit of the critical approaches to Israeli history and society to develop multiple stories, based on a range of methodologies. In many respects, this too reflected the visible pluralism of Israeli society, the enduring perplexity of how to reconcile various conflicting calls on the power and resources of the Israeli state, and the competing views in Israel about the fundamental requirements for Israeli security and sovereignty. Thus, in 2000, with the collapse of the peace talks and the outbreak of the second *intifada* and all that it brought in its train, the receptivity that had once characterized attitudes to the critical work of historians and sociologists alike began to recede. It was in this atmosphere that the Katz 'trial' took place.

Similarly, with the eruption of armed conflict, characterized by Israel's military incursions into areas nominally under Palestinian control, targeted assassinations in the Palestinian territories and a Palestinian campaign of suicide bombings in Israel itself, attitudes hardened and polarized. Where once it had been thought that resistance to the power of the dominant narrative should take place in the very sites that had validated it – Israel's universities – as well as in the society at large, it seemed to some that more active efforts were needed to make an impact on the hardening of attitudes.[31] Resistance to the stories that established power in Israel was using to frame the problem and to justify its actions spread out to multiple sites. It was no longer confined to academic debate, to television programmes or to scholarly publications. Instead, the focus shifted to publicized performance – sometimes literally so in films like *The Lemon Tree* or *Paradise Now*.[32] It also took the form of demonstrations against the building of the wall that was to separate the occupied territories from Israel, or public acts of commemoration, as in the activities of *Zochrot*, marking the disappeared villages of Arab Palestine.[33]

At the same time, the critical re-examination of various aspects of Israeli and Jewish history continued. The movement might have begun by revisiting 1948 and the events surrounding it – especially the expulsion of the majority Arab population of Palestine to secure a Jewish majority in the state of Israel. Over the years, however, it extended to the re-examination of many facets of Zionist historiography, including the relationship with the diaspora, the uses made of the telling of the events of the Holocaust in the consolidation of a certain kind of national identity and the very question of the existence of a 'Jewish nation' as an ethnic unit with a continuous if dispersed history.[34]

Of course, there were multiple purposes and politics at work. Many of the historians and social critics differed greatly, or came to do so, both in their political outlooks and in their intentions. They did not constitute a 'movement', even loosely, nor did they see themselves as such. Therefore it could not be said that they had a political goal that they pursued collectively, despite the accusations of many of their critics. Indeed, for a number of them, political engagement, in the narrow sense of projects relating to the legitimacy of the state of Israel, the tenure of the government of the day or the political agenda of negotiations between Palestinians and Israelis, were never part of their purpose.[35] The cumulative effect, however, was that these historians, sociologists and political scientists did, in their different ways, challenge a powerful set of dominant ideas. In resisting its power, they had helped to fragment it, and had succeeded in opening up a space for many voices to be heard – voices which might have been discordant but which presented a more plural, sometimes ambiguous and thus truer set of narratives relating to Israeli society and its troublesome legacies than had been available before. As they would be the first to acknowledge, this did not in itself transform Israeli politics, nor even lessen the antagonisms that had fuelled the conflicts between Israel, some of its neighbours and the Palestinians over whom it ruled. But it did help to lay the groundwork for a wider, better-informed discussion of the issues, making it clearer what was at stake both in terms of realpolitik and of moral jeopardy.[36]

RECLAIMING HISTORY IN ALGERIA: 'BERBERISM' AND THE FLN

In March 1980, a police roadblock 10 km outside the Algerian city of Tizi Ouzou stopped a car in which two Algerian academics, Mouloud Mammeri and Salam Chaker, were travelling. They were two of the leading authorities on Berber or Amazigh language and culture and had driven south that day so that Mammeri could give a lecture at the Centre Universitaire de Tizi Ouzou on ancient Kabyle poetry in the city that is the capital of the predominantly Berber province of Kabylia.[37] Instead, the police took them to the office of the provincial governor who told them that the authorities had cancelled the lecture 'because of the risk of public unrest'. Whatever the imagined risk of holding the lecture might have been, its cancellation provoked the very thing the governor said that he wanted to avoid. Public protests first broke out on the campus of the university, but within a month had spread not only throughout the province of Kabylia but also to Algiers itself.

Unnerved by the speed and vehemence of the protests, the authorities responded by arresting dozens of students and lecturers, especially those who had studied in France, convinced that they were the ringleaders. In fact, it was a largely spontaneous protest movement, provoked by the often brutal actions of the authorities themselves, even if it did draw upon longstanding grievances that the Algerian government had been unwilling to address. These events and the unfolding sequence of protests that followed became known as the 'Berber Spring'. Despite its label, the protests were not confined to 'Berberist' issues and represented the first major crack in the edifice of power of the FLN, the sole political party that had ruled Algeria since independence in 1962.[38]

The significance of this was that although many of those who came out on the streets in the spring of 1980 were making the specific demand that the government recognize Tamazight (the name given to the standardized version of Berber language that was emerging), many others were demanding official recognition of Algerian Arabic, as well as a variety of freedoms of expression, long denied by the ruling party. Thus while the 'Berber Spring' did primarily engage the Berbers – at least those living in or originating from the province of Kabylia – it represented a more general challenge to the authority of the ruling regime of the FLN. It was an open expression of mass resistance to a party and a regime that had dominated Algeria since independence, rooting its power not only in its command of the armed forces, but also in its attempts to control the intellectual and cultural life of the country. Indeed, one of the principal objectives of the FLN government since winning independence had been to develop a historical narrative and a collective memory that would conform with its idea of the Algerian nation.

In this, it did not differ much from many post-colonial governments that were trying to distance themselves from the humiliations and repressions of the colonial past. This was to be achieved through a dominant, unifying national narrative that would provide the basis of a national identity, benefiting those who held power. In this sense, even if the circumstances were very different, the logic was broadly similar to that which had shaped the dominant Zionist narrative of origins and identity. It too had been highly serviceable for the ruling establishment in the first decades of Israel's independent existence. In the case of the FLN, this exercise involved drawing a sharp dividing line between the Algerians and the French colonizers who had ruled over and settled in Algeria for more than 100 years. The million or so European settlers may have left since independence in 1962, but the imprint of French language and culture was still powerful especially amongst educated Algerians. Furthermore, for the FLN the political identity and destiny of Algeria lay within the larger Arab and Muslim spheres, not as an outpost of Europe in North Africa.

For the faction that came to dominate the movement for Algerian independence in exile and for the leaders of the resistance army (ALN), three priorities rapidly arose: the assertion of an Arab–Islamic and socialist identity for Algeria; the insistence that this would be the dominant expression of Algerian unity, marginalizing or suppressing other ways of being Algerian; and the enactment of legislation to ensure that the vehicle for this unified identity would be the sole legal political party – the FLN. Through its hold on government, its monopoly of the media and its control of the education system, it ensured that no other version of Algerian identity would be tolerated. The official FLN view of the Algerian nation would be the framework in which all Algerians would be obliged thenceforth to think themselves into history and into world politics.

These aspirations had already been evident in the Tripoli Programme of the FLN in June 1962, immediately prior to Algeria's formal independence. In April 1964, in the Algiers Charter, produced by the First Congress of the FLN, the vision of the Algerian nation which the new government was determined to implement was made even clearer: 'Algeria is an Arab and Muslim country . . . the Arab and Muslim essence of the Algerian nation has been a solid rampart against its destruction by colonialism'. For Ahmed Ben Bella, the first president of Algeria, this expressed both his own view of Algerian identity and history and the programme that the FLN must implement in transforming Algerian society from one scarred and divided by colonialism into a unified socialist, Arab and Muslim republic. Houari Boumedienne, who ousted Ben Bella in 1965 and ruled as president until his death in 1978, as well as his successor, Chadli Benjedid, who was president at the time of the 'Berber Spring' in 1980, all subscribed to these views – and ensured that this was the only narrative permitted not simply in the state education system but more generally in the closely controlled forums of public life in Algeria.

Under the auspices of the FLN regime, 'Arabization' campaigns were initiated from the outset. They aimed not simply at displacing French as the common language of business, intellectual life and government in Algeria but also at spreading mass literacy. This proceeded gradually, such that, by the late 1970s, Arabic had become the sole medium of instruction throughout the Algerian school system, with only the highest educational grades, particularly in the sciences, retaining bilingual teaching that combined French and Arabic. Even so, the lingering power of French caused resentment and tension, since students who only spoke Arabic found themselves at a disadvantage when it came to applying for jobs in business and law, where French was still regarded as an asset. Student strikes and demonstrations impelled the government to accelerate the Arabization programme at the higher levels. However, this in turn angered many Algerians of Kabyle origins. Their first language was Tamazight and their preferred second language was French, for historical reasons connected with sustained emigration over the decades. Anger at these moves had indeed been one of the contributing factors in the riots in Kabylia and Algiers during the 'Berber Spring'.[39]

In this respect, therefore, the 'Berber Spring' of 1980 was tied up with and found expression in the question of linguistic rights and privileges – and the unwillingness of the authorities to tolerate any assertion of Algerian Amazigh/Berber identity. However, the authorities' ban on the proposed lecture on ancient Kabyle poetry that had sparked these events was a kind of recognition. The FLN saw the public expression of an alternative narrative of Algerian identity as a danger to the kind of order they had imposed on the country. The authorities' reaction was testimony to the unease within the party and the regime when confronted by forces that disputed the received version of Algeria's history and identity. Implicitly, therefore, in the view of the FLN, this challenge threatened its own hold on power. As the events of 1980 and subsequent years demonstrated, the FLN government could meet such threats in the short term, but it could not so easily compensate for the gradual erosion of its authority. This was by no means solely due to the emerging Amazigh/Berber language and cultural movement. However, it was an important tributary – especially in Kabylia – of the growing torrent of protest and resistance in different sectors of Algerian society in the 1980s. It not only defied the forces of the regime on the streets of Algeria's cities, but also challenged its claimed monopoly on truth, eventually fracturing that monopoly and presenting a variety of different – and often bitterly opposed – views of Algerian national history and identity.

In this sense, therefore, the dominance of the FLN was coming under fire from all directions, fuelled by the deteriorating economy and by the miserable job prospects of the majority of young Algerians, whatever their ideology or linguistic background. This was provocation enough for those who had been systematically denied any say in how they should be ruled and who found themselves on the receiving end of policies devised by a small and privileged elite. But the economic failure of the government also belied the FLN's claim that its exclusive rule was in the interests of all Algerians. Inevitably, it led to profound questioning of those claims. This gave rise to a crisis of legitimacy that soon engulfed those who had tried to use such claims to justify their hold on power. The same documents that had asserted the Arab–Islamic character of the Algerian nation had also claimed that the retrieval of a national culture would 'contribute to the emancipation of the people by liquidating the after-effects of feudalism' (Tripoli Programme, 1962) and had promised 'The exercise of power by the people...' and 'the building of socialist democracy, and the fight against every form of exploitation by man' (Algerian Constitution, 1963). Since, in Algeria of the 1980s, it was manifestly clear that none of these promises had been kept, the young in particular rebelled.

From the point of view of many who took to the streets in the 1980s, their protests were intended to expose the lie behind the façade of the regime. For some, their indictment of the FLN was couched in the idiom of Islam. This provided a powerful vocabulary of moral outrage and social justice, sanctified through direct validation by the word of God and used in countless sermons by the leaders of the various movements that were eventually to coalesce into the Front Islamique du Salut [*Al-Jabhat al-Islamiyya li-l-Inqadh*] (FIS). They not only denounced the highly visible social inequalities that existed in allegedly egalitarian Algeria, but also upbraided the FLN for having the temerity to appropriate Islam as a key part of Algerian national identity whilst doing nothing to implement its precepts for the organization of society. Thus, if Algerian identity was indeed Muslim, the FLN and its narrative of unity and its monopoly of power were unfit to rule in the eyes of the growing number of Islamists and their supporters. In one of Ali Benhadj's 1989 sermons at the al-Sunna mosque in Bab el-Oued, he used vivid language to indict the existing order for a growing gap between wealth and poverty and for the use of Algeria's resources to promote activities that in his view failed to comply with Islamic principles: 'Dear brothers! I know houses, I know empty houses! Houses which are occupied only on Thursdays and Fridays to practice depravity and sin! Villas! Palaces! Empty . . . How can such places be built? Where are Algeria's finances? Where is the people's money?'⁴⁰

This last question was one that was being asked by most Algerians, regardless of ideological alignment. It is not surprising, therefore, that similar feelings of resentment towards and resistance to the rule of the FLN appeared in Kabylia. It was not the first time in the history of the republic that this region had been the site of determined opposition to the leadership of the FLN. In September 1963, Hocine Ait Ahmed, a leader of the FLN who had resigned in 1962 in protest at the crisis that led to the installation of Ben Bella as president, raised the standard of rebellion in Tizi Ouzou. He had called for armed resistance against the FLN dictatorship and for greater accountability, as well as for democratic pluralism, and, with another former commander in the ALN, Mohand Oulhadj, he had founded the Front des Forces Socialistes (FFS) to pursue the struggle. The crisis that this precipitated during the following twelve months led to the military occupation of Kabylia by some 50,000 troops, led by Colonel Houari Boumedienne, who went on to overthrow his former ally Ben Bella in June 1965. Ait Ahmed himself had been captured earlier in 1965 (he was to escape from prison in 1966 and flee into exile) and the rebellion crushed, but this crisis formed part of the indictment of Ben Bella's presidency from within the regime. It was a rebellion that had largely been confined to Kabylia, partly because of old links and networks from the war of independence, even if the grievances of the FFS had been phrased in national terms, criticizing the autocracy of Ben Bella, the lack of accountability and the monopoly of power in the one-party state.

This might not have had much resonance in the rest of Algeria in the first optimistic years of independence, but in Kabylia they found a more receptive audience. Here, the principle of local government, combined with a belief that the 'outsiders' (i.e. the FLN units which had been working in Tunisian or Egyptian exile during the war of independence) had seized power in 1962, displacing and in some sense disinheriting the 'insiders' who had fought so hard to keep the war going, were strongly felt. Kabylia, after all, had been one of the main theatres of war. These factors combined to cause the Kabyles to look critically at the version of Algerian nationalism that was being championed by the FLN, just as they were sceptical of the histories of the war of independence itself that seemed conveniently to assign prominence to those who now exercised power in Algiers – a number of whom could be considered 'les résistants de la dernière minute' ['last minute resisters'] – a category of 'heroes of the resistance' well known in France itself after 1944.

As Kabyle Berbers/Imazighen, there was one particular feature of the FLN's version of Algerian identity which jarred with their sense of themselves as Kabyles but also as Algerians: the writing out of Amazigh/Berber identity from all the proclamations of Arab–Muslim Algeria. Ben Bella's 1962 declaration that 'We are Arabs, Arabs, Arabs', after his release from French captivity, rang hollow to those who knew themselves to be Algerian but also not Arab – although it is unknown whether or not it was an aide of Berber origin who allegedly whispered in Ben Bella's ear immediately after this pronouncement, 'Ça va finir par être vrai!' ['That will eventually be true!'][41] Kabyle resentment of the heavy hand of Algiers was in part, therefore, resentment of undemocratic centralism and of a regime dominated by the security forces (*Le Pouvoir*).[42]

But it was also partly due to their understandable resistance to the denial of their own history, language and cultural identity throughout the story of Algeria, whether in the distant past, or in the troubled period of decolonization. It was not particularly reassuring for the Amazigh/Berber peoples of contemporary Algeria to read in the Algiers Charter of 1964 that the FLN's definition of Algeria as an Arab and Muslim country 'excludes all references to ethnic criteria and does not imply an underestimation of the stock existing before the Arab penetration'. As time passed, this became increasingly irksome. The label 'Arab' was clearly an ethnic designation that privileged the majority ethnic group (those speaking all varieties of Amazigh/Berber languages constitute about twenty-five to thirty per cent of the total population of Algeria), since Arabic was the only language recognized as the official and national language of the state. Furthermore, it seemed to relegate Amazigh/Berber identity to ancient history, no longer relevant after the Arab–Muslim invasions of the eighth century.

Quite apart from the personal prejudices of individuals in the FLN concerning Kabyle or Amazigh/Berber identity in general, there was also a particular problem in Algeria, a legacy of its colonial past. Many Algerians regarded the assertion of Amazigh/Berber identity as a perpetuation of the French colonial project to divide and rule the Algerians. Thus the study of Berber languages and cultures, the very definition of it as a legitimate field of study in contemporary Algeria, was seen as a 'Trojan Horse' of colonialism, preparing the way for internal division and encouraging the separation of Algerians from pan-Arab solidarities. These fears led to the abolition of the Chair of Berber Studies at the University of Algiers in 1973 and the further restriction of any publications that dealt with Berber culture, let alone ones that were published in Tamazight. Significantly, this interdiction applied equally to those who were calling for the official recognition of the distinctive form of Arabic spoken in much of Algeria. The ruling FLN insisted that classical or modern standard Arabic were to be the only versions of the language to be applied in the Arabization programmes. However rare it was to hear this spoken outside academic or literary circles, the authorities took pains to enforce this ruling throughout the country.[43]

With such an attitude towards any manifestation of Amazigh/Berber linguistic or cultural activities, it was not surprising that the authorities should have acted towards those calling for greater recognition of the language as if they did indeed represent the beginnings of overt political resistance. Thus, throughout the 1960s and the 1970s, the security forces would make periodic arrests of students and others who may have gathered for poetry readings, to put on a play in Tamazight or who had had the temerity to organize themselves independently of the FLN's cultural committees. Although not part of a specifically Amazigh/Berber movement, the artistic project of the 1960s, *Aouchem*, by challenging the monologue and the aesthetic orthodoxy of the FLN's version of 'official' Algerian culture, came in for similar treatment. In its case, the acts of censorship and suppression were often carried out by fellow artists, members of the state-backed National Union of the Plastic Arts who ripped down many of the paintings during its first exhibition in 1967. This was not simply because the artists of *Aouchem* had deliberately rejected the modernism and socialist realism of the dominant schools, but also because they had reinterpreted the artistic and historical traditions of Algeria, consciously reconnecting them with the symbols and colours of an unmistakable Amazigh/Berber tradition (see Chapter 6, section on Algeria). The state authorities meanwhile seized and censored publications, closed down the Tizi Ouzou radio station and barred well-known singers such as Taos Amrouche and Ait Manguellet from giving public performances.

In such circumstances, the expression and exploration of Amazigh/ Berber language, culture and history became displaced, finding the space and opportunity to develop among the large Kabyle element in the Algerian immigrant population in France. This redoubled the suspicions of the Algerian authorities, but it did lead to a thriving cultural and intellectual milieu of Amazigh/Berber studies in Paris and elsewhere. In 1967, the association that was to become the core of the Académie Berbère/Agraw Imazighen in 1969 was founded in Paris. It was set up by a group of intellectuals of Kabyle origin, such as Mouloud Mammeri, Taos Amrouche, Abdelkader Rahmani and Bessaoud Mohand Arab. Their explicit aims were twofold: to study and to disseminate Amazigh/Berber history in order to retrieve for the Berbers their proper place in the making of North Africa; and to promote Amazigh/Berber culture and language as a living force, not simply a legacy of antiquity. This was to be achieved in large measure through its monthly publication *Imazighen*, by turns informative, erudite, satirical (as far as official Algerian cultural policies were concerned) but also increasingly polemical as it became identified with a more strident form of Amazigh/Berber self-assertion.[44]

In 1973, a course on Berber civilization and language was established at the University of Vincennes (Paris VIII), run by a breakaway group from the Académie Berbère, calling itself La Groupe d'Etudes Berbères (GEB). It was a more explicitly political grouping, radical in its indictment of the regime in Algeria, which it denounced systematically in the pages of its occasional publication, *Bulletin d'études berbères*, replaced in 1978 by the journal *Tissuraf*. It was soon followed by the foundation the same year of the Ateliers Berbères de Production et Diffusion (ABPD) by members of the GEB who felt that it was important to undertake practical work, such as publishing, as well as the organization of cultural events beyond university campuses. It was also geared to a political programme, much of which was incorporated in the platform of the party of Ait Ahmed, the FFS, revived (in exile) in 1979. This continued to call for greater freedom and democracy in Algeria as a whole, but it now incorporated clear demands for the official recognition of Tamazight and for the restoration of Amazigh/ Berber culture and identity to its rightful place in the ongoing narrative of the Algerian nation, based on, but not confined to its historical roots in Algeria.[45]

These various currents, encouraging an increasingly self-confident assertion of a specifically Amazigh/Berber identity among the Algerian Kabyles in France, naturally had an effect on sentiments among Kabyles in Algeria itself, both in the capital and in the province of Kabylia. They provided many young Kabyles with an idiom for their grievances, some of which may have been specific to their region but many of which they shared with other young Algerians. Out of this came the Mouvement Culturel Berbère/Amazigh (MCB/A), a rather loose grouping, operating clandestinely through its network of students and sympathizers. It acted as a diffuser of the literature produced in France that promoted the writing of Amazigh/Berber culture and language into the history of Algeria. It also acted as a focus for specifically political demands inside Algeria. In this respect, it campaigned to oblige the Algerian government not only to recognize the identity of the Imazighen in Algerian society and history free of colonial association, but also to make Tamazight both a national and an official language of the state on a par with Arabic. This became the aim of the mobilization and agitation that followed the 'Berber Spring' of 1980.

For about a year, until the authorities decided to crack down with mass arrests and the break-up of all discernable Amazigh/Berber cultural associations, the young Kabyle militants stood up to the regime. Through strikes, demonstrations and the open challenge of popular protest, they showed their defiance and caused the regime to hesitate in its response. According to Salam Chaker, 'the cultural militants, relatively young and weakly or recently politicised, managed to do what no "classic" political party had succeeded in doing before them: to oppose openly and in a sustained way the authority of the State, leading it – in spite of everything – to show relative moderation in its repression'.[46] The significance of this was underlined by Benjamin Stora when he stated that 'The effect of the "Berber Spring" was to produce, for the first time since independence and from within Algeria, a public counter-discourse of real import, in a country operating on the principle of unanimity [*l'unanisme*]'.[47] The power of the regime was still formidable, despite its initial hesitation, and the Kabyle/Amazigh campaigners were confronted by the FLN Central Committee's restatement in the summer of 1981 of the intransigent assertion of Algeria's Arab–Muslim identity.

Organized mass protests became impracticable, and energies were turned instead towards laying the groundwork for cultural reaffirmation and, as one of those involved said: 'not to get power to make concessions, but to construct, through daily work at the base, an incontrovertible and irreversible social fact, i.e., an autonomous Berber culture facing the future'.[48] Partly in response to such activities and to the unrest of the preceding years, the president of Algeria, Shadhli Benjedid, caused a certain ripple of excitement when he used a speech to the FLN party congress in December 1983 to assert that all Algerians had Berber ancestry.[49] Encouraging as this might have seemed, for Amazigh/Berber activists it simply confirmed their view that, for the regime, their identity could safely be consigned to ancient history. In other words, there were to be no contemporary implications of such a statement. Thus, while it did accord a certain kind of historical recognition, it did not contradict the regime's continued suppression of anyone campaigning for cultural or language rights. This was the explosive issue that continued to land Imazighen in jail.

However, Amazigh/Berber activists were also able to make use of their arrest and trial to publicize not simply their cause but also that of all Algerians suffering under the repressive regime of the FLN. Jane Goodman's detailed study of the trial of twenty-three political prisoners in 1985 demonstrates how they turned the courtroom in Medéa into a public space for the dissemination of their opinions and, as she puts it, turned the court into 'a forum for the performance of the very discourse that is tolerated in no other public venue'.[50] The twenty-three had been charged not with 'Berberist' activity but for founding the Algerian League of Human Rights without the permission of the state authorities. In answering these charges, the mostly Kabyle defendants managed to link issues of Amazigh/Berber identity and expression to the larger questions of the condition of freedom of expression and of human rights in Algeria. Their performances and their successful and rapid dissemination of the transcripts of the four-day trial ensured maximum resonance. As one of the accused, Said Sadi, stated. 'What is at the heart of the matter here? It is none other than the "Berber plot" in whose name all abuses are permissible. It's well known, *Messieurs de la cour*, that Berber is the "bogey-man" (*croque-mitaine*), the ultimate target when the clannish interests of *Le Pouvoir* are threatened'.[51]

It was only with the ending of the FLN monopoly on political organization in 1989 that a more varied expression of identity politics became possible. With it came the explorations of Amazigh/Berber histories in the narrative of Algerian and indeed North African history – narratives that would engage directly with the politics of rights and the allocation of power in Algeria. New political organizations sprang up, not simply those expressing variations of Amazighité. However, in this sphere, Kabyle and Amazigh/Berber politics became more complex. It produced rival organizations voicing different understandings of what an Amazigh/Berber narrative of Algerian identity might mean in practical terms. The prohibition of works in Tamazight no longer applied, broadcasts in the language were allowed and, in the constitutional revision of 1996, Amazigh/Berber identity, together with Arab and Islamic identities, were explicitly recognized as the three elements that went to make up Algerian national identity. In addition to a series of other measures recognizing the public use of Amazigh/Berber names and places and initiating Tamazight instruction in certain schools in Berberophone provinces, President Bouteflika agreed in 2001 that Tamazight should be recognized as a 'national language' in the constitution, a pledge implemented in 2002. This recognition fell short of the demand by a number of campaigning organizations that Tamazight should be accorded the status of an official language on a par with Arabic, but it still represented a marked advance on the position confronting the Imazighen twenty years previously.[52]

However, the 'Black Spring' of April 2001 indicated that the authorities – *Le Pouvoir* – had lost none of their repressive edge. In that month, the death of a high school student, Guermah Massinissa, while in the custody of the gendarmerie in Kabylia, led to widespread rioting in the region and beyond. The weeks of rioting that followed came to be known as *la protesta* and spread across many different regions of Algeria. The protestors were met by ruthless violence on the part of the gendarmerie, particularly in Kabylia and other rural areas. By July 2001, some fifty young Berbers had been shot in the violence, and some 200 or more wounded. The Issad Commission, set up by President Bouteflika in May 2001, confirmed that this was a worryingly high toll, especially since there were no gunshot casualties suffered by the security forces. However, the commission avoided coming to the conclusion that the violence was sanctioned at the very highest level of the security services, despite widespread suspicions that the behaviour of the gendarmerie could only be explained by the orders they received from senior officers in the regime. By April 2002, it was reported that some ninety protestors had been killed with thousands wounded, and, by the end of the disturbances, a total of 126 had apparently been killed and many thousands injured or tortured by the gendarmerie.[53]

However, as the extent and the substance of the riots indicated, this was not simply a 'Berberist' protest, let alone one that pitted Imazighen against the forces of an Arabized state. In fact, in Kabylia, the upheavals had little to do with the culturalist policies championed by the principal Kabyle Berberist parties, the FFS and the RCD. On the contrary, these associations tended to be avoided by a new generation of activists who believed that the old forms of culturalist nationalism and identity politics and the strategies thought appropriate to achieving their goals were largely irrelevant to their own lives. These were dominated by the chronic unemployment and underinvestment in the region, by the visible inequalities, favouritism and patronage that stemmed from a regime regarded as corrupt and patrimonial and by the everyday violence and contempt shown by the authorities and especially the security services to ordinary Algerian citizens, whatever their background.

The term *hogra* (an Algerian expression for the contempt and disdain of the authorities for ordinary people) was an apt summation of the condition that was so resented by young people who had no voice in their governance and little chance of work in their hometowns. But *hogra* was not something experienced by Kabyles or by Imazighen alone – it was a general and enduring complaint coming from a disenfranchised and unemployed generation across the country.[54] In Kabylia, with its long history of resentment of direct and repressive control by Algiers, the protests did give rise to movements, even organizations, such as the Aarouche and the Mouvement de l'Autonomie Kabyle (MAK) which talked openly of regional autonomy, based in part on linguistic and cultural difference from those who ruled the state. But it seemed chiefly aimed at escaping the mixture of neglect and brutality that the region had suffered at the hands of Algiers ever since independence. It was meant therefore to bring power down to the localities where people could finally hold it accountable.

In this sense, something that had begun as resistance to the narrative hegemony of the FLN had developed over the decades into a more determined resistance to the structures of the state and to the forms of power associated first with the FLN, and subsequently with the Rassemblement Nationale Démocratique (RND)–Presidential Alliance–military domination of Algeria. The bloody civil war of the 1990s between a number of Islamist organizations and the forces of the state had lasted for more than a decade and had cost the lives of an estimated 120,000 Algerians. It was proof of the power of the state establishment and its resilience, even when confronted by the direct armed resistance of well-organized and socially rooted opponents. It also indicated that there were now multiple narratives circulating and in some sense competing in Algeria. The Groupe Islamique Armé (GIA) and the Armée Islamique du Salut (AIS) were unsuccessful in military terms, but their own endurance showed that they enjoyed widespread support, if not always for their methods then for their objectives.

The Islamists' ferocious attacks on Amazigh/Berber organizations, or on figures associated with the reassertion of Amazigh/Berber legacies in the national life of Algeria, made even the actions of the government and its agents pale in comparison. There were many in fact, not simply in Kabylia, who suspected a degree of encouragement and collusion by *Le Pouvoir* when the Islamists targeted Amazigh/Berber movements. It was seen as a ploy not only to suppress the Kabyle voice, but also to drive home the common argument of authoritarian governments that a firm hand is needed to prevent social discord from tearing apart the fabric of society and state. Whatever the truth behind acts such as the murder of the Algerian Kabyle singer Lounès Matoub in June 1998, the fact was that the challenge of the Amazigh/Berber movement in all its variety to the hitherto accepted Arab and Islamic narratives of Algerian history unsettled many. As the late Franco-Algerian scholar, Mohammed Arkoun (himself of Kabyle origin), remarked, 'Jacobin ideology wedded to the spiritual cement of the Islamic *ummah* have given a certain cast to historiography ... Nationalist logic, reinforced and transcendentalized by Islamism, has rendered intolerable and unacceptable any attempt to think the unthinkable in the Maghreb'.[55]

For those seeking to resist this enforced narrative of history, whether Amazigh/Berber or other, the opposition they encountered could be ferocious. But it also opened up the field within Algeria for debates about the nature of Algerians' history and identity that became part of the disintegrating control of the post-colonial state. Nor were the 'Berberist' revival movements immune to the many voices that they had themselves encouraged. In part, this took the form of class and generational questioning of the older generation of interpreters of what it meant to be Amazigh/Berber. Typically, as in any movement seeking to reclaim and reinstate its history, different narratives emerged, emphasizing a range of possibilities – gender roles, subaltern identities, religious symbols – that had more resonance with some than with others.

In Algeria, it also had regional implications in that there were concerns amongst some that the Kabyles were taking the lead as the principal initiators and articulators of Amazigh/Berber reassertion. The concern was that they were imposing upon other Berber populations of Algeria what was effectively a Kabyle identity. This was felt particularly sharply in the mountains of the Aurès, in eastern Algeria. Historically, the Aurès had been the site of the realm of the Kahina Dihya Tadmut or Damya, who had ruled in the late seventh century and whose military prowess had temporarily kept in check the Arab–Islamic invasion of the Maghreb. As the reassertion of a distinctive Amazigh/ Berber voice began to be heard, many in this region felt that their own identity was being subsumed and marginalized in a narrative that now appeared to equate Amazigh/Berber with Kabyle.

In the first decade of the twenty-first century, the various cultural associations of the Aurès became more active. Notably, in 2003, the Association Aurès El-Kahina succeeded not only in erecting a statue to the Kahina in Baghai in the province of Khenchela, but also in persuading the president of Algeria, Abdelaziz Bouteflika, to attend the ceremony.[56] Furthermore, as numerous websites and publications indicate, there was a determined effort to resuscitate the particular historical legacies of the Aurès, to encourage their own variant of the Berber language, Shawia, as well as to underline the key role that the region's inhabitants had played in the modern history of Algeria, particularly in the war of independence. As the Aurèsian playwright, Slimane Benaissa, stated, 'Mes ancêtres sont une mémoire qui ne dort jamais' [my ancestors are a memory that never sleeps], and, in a phrase that could stand for the whole Amazigh/Berber project to make their voice heard, the effort was 'en hommage à notre histoire et contre l'oubli...' [dedicated to our history and against forgetting].[57]

Whilst the president, the RND and the security forces hold the state and enjoy power unrivalled by any other organization in Algeria, they no longer exercise the kind of overall control that was once the chief political project of the FLN in post-independence Algeria. In some respects, they and the other forces at work in the more plural and openly contentious politics of Algeria today have inherited a situation created by the initial resistance to that once powerful hegemony. This resistance came from those who felt that, in being written out of history, they were also being excluded from any chance of controlling their present or indeed the future of the country of which they were citizens. This may have begun with the attempt of one section of the population to reconnect with a history that was indubitably Algerian but was also Amazigh/Berber. However, it had a resonance for hundreds of thousands of young Algerians, from many different backgrounds, who experienced a state that was either indifferent to or contemptuous of their own concerns. It can plausibly be argued therefore that the revision of Algerian history to take in the forgotten and suppressed narratives of its people was both a symptom of the decay of the hegemony of the FLN and contributed to its disintegration. In this sense, resistance was intertwined, as was dominant power, with the versions of history that seemed to reinforce a particular kind of politics.

The outcome of historical revisionism and the puncturing of the myths of power in Algeria, as in Israel, did not lead to the complete reversal of the dominant national narrative. On the contrary, it helped to open up the field to multiple voices, many of which were in sharp disagreement with each other. These, in turn, were taken up by a range of political organizations, some of them closely allied to the dominant forces in the state, others openly challenging them for political power. In the middle of this, the call for the revision of national history to take into account the identity, language and culture of the Amazigh/Berber peoples was not simply a call for their reinstatement as a historical curiosity. It aimed to counter the process of historical forgetting, certainly, but it was also aimed at shaping the way Algerians as a whole, and especially their national institutions, saw and projected their history. In this respect, by comparison with the decade when these efforts first became noticed, there was little doubt that the movement, fragmented as it became, did have some effect. In addition to the catalytic effects of the 'Berber Spring' on the FLN's hold on power, there was also the visible relaxation, in some spheres, of the earlier suppression of Berber language and history. Indeed, it became an accepted part of Algeria's story.

Thus, since 2003, Tamazight has been taught in middle schools across Algeria, and acknowledgement of the Amazigh/Berber contribution to Algeria's distinctive history has been more visible in the public domain.[58]

The basic disparity of power remains, however. This is not so much between Arab and Berber but between *Le Pouvoir* – those around the president, the leading cadres of the RND and the security forces – and the citizens of Algeria as a whole.[59] Concessions to the cultural expression and historical revision of the Amazigh/Berber story have taken time. However, it has been more difficult to win from the regime concessions that might affect its hold on the resources, administration or coercive potential of the Algerian state.[60] As the long-running but limited riots and demonstrations of late 2010 to early 2011 showed, the causes of discontent were as powerful as ever, but so was the determination of the regime not to succumb as had the regimes of Tunisia and Egypt so dramatically in January and February 2011. These were nationwide events in which Amazigh/Berber parties, such as the secularist RCD of Said Sadi, participated along with countless other Algerian organizations protesting against the indifference, brutality and ineptness of the government. They were met by a daunting show of force on the part of the authorities. The streets of Algiers were flooded with tens of thousands of riot police when major demonstrations were threatened, effectively preventing the coalescing of the forces of opposition.

NARRATIVES OF POWER

The recognition that the writing of history reflects but also moulds the present – and thus shapes the future too – has long played a central role in the understanding of its power. It has therefore been a common concern of governments to exercise some control over versions of their countries' history. The more authoritarian the government, the tighter will that control become, moving out from the realm of school curricula and textbooks to the censorship of books, plays, films and even poems that build up the narratives of historical memory. Whether through direct intervention or through the versions reproduced in the official academy, in the mass media or in the subsidized institutions of culture, narratives that validate the dominant order will form the daunting edifice of official history.

This has been particularly visible in the post-colonial Middle East where the definition of national identities has been integral to the struggle for power. To claim to rule in the name of the nation makes it imperative that those who rule should ensure that their views of its identity and its interests should be paramount. This has been accompanied by equally tight control over the spaces in which alternative versions of the national interest might find expression. Thus the restriction of political space and imaginative space go hand in hand. Narratives of power that stress the dominance through history of particular ethnic or religious groups, social classes, military formations, clans and families, or regional groupings have been part of the way in which hegemony has been reproduced. It seeks to mould the imagination of the subjects, interwoven with and reinforcing the material forms of power that are part of the landscape of domination.

As the Israeli case shows, this need not be through blatant or unmediated coercive power nor under the aegis of an undemocratic government. On the contrary, many can contribute to the construction of a national mythology that helps to define a field of conformity beyond which few will venture. In the collective task of state building and of defining the nation, particularly in a situation that is represented as a struggle for national survival, common assumptions emerge, embed themselves in the media, the academy and elsewhere. They become the 'common sense' version of a country's past, informed by and informing its present. The power of the narrative in this sense is that it can act as the prism through which political relations are seen. It is reinforced and reproduced through countless small images, acts and publications, significantly reducing any incentive to look beyond the prism and to cast a very different light upon these same events. Although by no means universal, a dominant consensus emerges, shaped by the institutions of knowledge, buttressed by prevailing political ideologies and seemingly preserved by a sense of beleaguered isolation that is itself both product and cause of this view of history and of destiny.

Resistance in this sense may take the form initially of going against the grain, of taking up counter-narratives that had been associated with fringe movements or those seen as hostile to the national consensus and its political project. By the same token, however, the decay of the original consensus and the demographic, as well as intellectual changes that brought this about, are part of the mutable nature of politics, laying bare conflicting or contradictory elements within the dominant narrative. This may explain the sometimes ferocious reaction to those who would cast a different, critical eye on a country's history, as was evident in the controversies surrounding the 'new historians' in Israel. The accusation that those involved have as their goal the negation of the very state itself is a symptom of the intimate links between the telling of history and the exercise of power. When a particular version of the past validates present attitudes, policies and political arrangements, it shows how vulnerable power is. Or perhaps, more accurately, it is a testimony to the power of historical narrative. Changing it and obliging people to look at their past in a different light can shake the reassuring beliefs and myths that have led people to think that this is the way things have always been and must continue to be. As in many other cases of resistance, resisting the dominant political myths by questioning their historical foundations is both a product and a cause of the sideways look, the distanced view that can be so unsettling to established power.

In the case of a more authoritarian system, there is one central apparatus that claims the exclusive right to determine people's future. Part of this claim rests on its exclusive control of the narrative of history that justifies both its own dominance and the future it has mapped out. As the Algerian case showed, the propagation of an official version of Algerian history that largely excluded the Amazigh/Berber role in that history, and thus in Algerian national identity, was bound up with the systems of restrictive and authoritarian power characteristic of the FLN. The expression of an identity and an interest that did not conform to the official line, that questioned its dominance and that resisted by inserting diverse narratives into the story of Algeria was not confined to Amazigh/Berber cultural militants.

It was also part of the general uprising against and resistance to FLN domination. It came from different sources and comprised those who were demanding a distinctively Islamic form of government or those who were asking for more democratic accountability, the fairer distribution of the oil wealth and an end to the violence of the security forces. All of these counter-narratives threatened the FLN hold on power in that they represented not simply imaginative divergence from the official line, but also the mobilization of publics over which the FLN could only exercise power through physical intimidation. The loss of the capacity to tell the history of Algeria was a signal that its power was declining and fragmenting when faced by a more fractured society than the official version of Algerian national unity had been willing to acknowledge.

In fact, as the trajectory of both Israeli and Algerian politics has demonstrated, power is as resourceful as resistance. The new versions of history may have discredited some of the professional guardians of the discipline and may have unsettled some who held to the heroic visions of power that the older narratives reproduced. They have certainly made it harder to take for granted a number of the myths that were intertwined with dominant strands of national thought in both countries. However, nationalism is a field of contestation and opening up debates about national origins and national destiny does not in itself resolve the question one way or the other. Nor does it seek to install an alternative meta-narrative to displace the old. Indeed, in both Israel and Algeria, that would have gone against the spirit and intent of many of the revisionists and the dissidents. The purpose was to open up the debate about history in the same way as the debate about the political future was to be opened up. This did not privilege one version or another. It was for the conjuncture of political events to determine what kind of history, and what kinds of myth, were to be the most congenial to the emerging politics of these states.

In the twenty-first century, this has produced a more assertive, even strident and often religiously inflected nationalism in Israel, drawing upon threads and reservoirs of ideas in Zionism that may have long been present but that have received a new salience and plausibility under the pressure of events. It has drawn in even those who once were critical of such views, including some of the 'new historians' themselves. This trend, although by no means uncontested in everyday politics or in intellectual life in Israel, is relatively indifferent to the debunking of the old myths that had such an unsettling effect on a particular generation of Zionists. Rather, it has pressed ahead with the forging of new stories and narratives that have received support, and come in for criticism, in a contested field of power. They are bolstered by the knowledge that some of the main pillars of the edifice of power itself – such as the identity, security and destiny of their construction of the Jewish people – remain largely unshaken by recent history wars and retain their powerful hold on the imaginations of significant numbers of Israelis. By the same token, although in a very different setting, the rulers of Algeria, inheritors of the FLN and embodiments of *Le Pouvoir*, have found that they too can accommodate narratives of Algerian history and identity that once appeared to threaten the whole edifice of their power. By incorporating their elements into a new story of Algerian destiny that allows for different voices, they have found new ways of retaining control of the central apparatus of the state.

6

Symbolic Forms of Resistance

Art and Power

ART SPEAKS TO POWER

In the summer of 2002, in the middle of the Palestinian uprising known as *intifadat al-aqsa*, the Palestinian artist Vera Tamari set up an art installation in a field at al-Bireh near Ramallah. She organized a line of cars, nose to tail on a curved tarmac road laid down especially for the purpose. The striking feature was that the cars were crushed and flattened. Tamari had had them dragged there from the streets of al-Bireh and Ramallah where they had been squashed by Israeli tanks during one of the Israeli army's military operations in April of that year. Ironically entitled 'Mashin?' ['Going for a ride?'], the crushed cars, some with radios still playing and adorned with the usual mirror charms that had so obviously failed to protect them, stood as strange and haunting, but also eye-catching, reminders of everyday violence in occupied Palestine. In the words of Vera Tamari, the cars had taken on a new reality: 'They metamorphosed from once practical objects to become subjects of vengeful voodooism. Do we hurt the Palestinians more by destroying their cherished personal belongings? ... I simply wanted to make a statement how a mundane logical reality becomes totally illogical through the violence of the war machine ... This act of destruction became like *action art*, disturbing the status quo of matter'.[1] Someone could wake up one morning to find that tanks had rolled down their street and over their car. But at the same time, in the layout of the exhibition in a sunny field and with jaunty music playing over the radios, the installation itself asserted something about those subject to this violence. Self-consciously, by transforming the cars into an

FIGURE 1. Vera Tamari: '*Mashin?*' [Going for a ride?], Ramallah (2002)
[© Vera Tamari. Photo courtesy of Vera Tamari]

artwork, it signalled their refusal to be intimidated by Israeli military power. Tamari had shown her public defiance of the occupation, and had done so in a way that struck a chord with the many Palestinians who passed by or wandered around among the wrecked cars.

As an example of the art of resistance, this installation at al-Bireh had a power that was lost on neither the Palestinians nor the Israelis. Indeed, so potent was it that an Israeli military unit took it even further, amplifying its effects unwittingly by themselves becoming part of the installation. The day after the exhibition opened, in June 2002, the Israeli army launched another military operation, 'Determined Path', invading al-Bireh and Ramallah with predictably destructive effects. To the surprise of the artist herself, who lived close to the installation and witnessed the event, two Israeli tanks rolled into the field. They went backwards and forwards over the already crushed cars, and even shelled them, flattening them further. This performance ended only when the cars were utterly destroyed. Some of the tank crews then urinated on the twisted metal for good measure. The irony was that, from the perspective of what the installation was trying to achieve, this new dimension of performance art laid on by the Israeli army and filmed by Tamari only reinforced the power of its many messages. As Tamari said, 'This was the ultimate metamorphosis for my work'.[2] Needless to say, once the tanks had gone and normal life had resumed in al-Bireh, the installation, with its new video addition, became an instant draw for all those now made aware of the intimate connection between art and life.

Of course, in this as in other artistic endeavours, it is easier for the observer to assess the aesthetics of the work of art itself and the intentions of the artist than to be certain of the effect it might have on the spectators. In the case of Tamari's 'Mashin?' at least, the reaction of the unintended audience of Israeli soldiers did give some sense of the power of the work, or at least its capacity to unsettle and annoy. In terms of the arts of resistance, this is important. Underlying the artistic effort is the attempt to challenge political hegemony, harnessing the power of art to make people look again at the status quo, enthusing them or aggravating them. But their reaction may also be affected by their own aesthetic judgements. These will depend on what they bring to their encounter with a work of visual art, literature or film in terms of tastes shaped by their own backgrounds, as well as by their personal preferences.

It is this dual aspect that is so characteristic of the art of resistance. Art may be explicitly linked to a political resistance movement. A work of art may also, in itself, be intended to bring about a shift in the way the world is viewed, through the development of a new, possibly radical aesthetic. Here the challenge is both to artistic conventions and to the systems of power that have used these conventions to buttress their own claims to authority. Such an approach may also be at odds with the prevailing conventions of any organized resistance movement. It can open out radically different possibilities, but may also throw into question some of the ways that the resistance movement has tried to portray itself.

The deliberate flouting of convention has a particular power to disturb, disrupt and to mobilize. However, it may also lose its power to communicate by departing too far from commonly understood conventions. Like art more generally, it can be poised between the shock of the new and the incomprehension of the unfamiliar. Its power will be tied to the resonance it can strike in an audience that may itself be changing, transformed by its own experiences and for whom therefore the old aesthetics are already losing their grip. In this respect, posters, graffiti and cartoons have an impact that may depend upon existing forms of recognition, sometimes using already familiar idioms and sometimes juxtaposing the unexpected to satirical and powerful effect.[3] This is particularly the case when they take on, and transform, the artistic conventions and symbolic vocabulary of the ruling establishment. By radically changing the message that 'official art' is trying to convey, it can serve a more disrespectful and possibly subversive purpose.

In this respect, the visual arts have a key role to play, through paintings, sculptures, drawings, installations, photography and videos. There are crossovers between what some would call 'fine art' and more popular forms, through poster design or the use of graffiti in paintings.[4] Equally important is the role that artists can play in forging a new visual vocabulary. This is not simply a new way of looking at the world. It is also a way of representing half-remembered things, perhaps long suppressed. They help to create a powerful mnemonic for collective memory and to establish a presence that demands recognition. This in itself is troubling enough for those who want to maintain a status quo that depends upon the suppression of alternatives and the non-recognition of those who are demanding a wholesale political realignment. However, when it takes concrete form through powerful and moving artistic expression, it can touch not only the hitherto voiceless but also the regime's own constituency. In some settings, it can affect a broader international audience, acting as a check on officially sanctioned propaganda. Potentially, therefore, it can help to mobilize a counterforce, breaking the silence of those subordinated to the dominant power.

Striking as this may be in the sphere of the visual arts, the same principles apply in the arts of performance, whether through song, poetry, theatre or film, as well as in literary output more generally. The formidable apparatus of censorship in many countries testifies to governments' obsession about the public expression of dissonant and subversive messages and their fear of the power of art. It also testifies to the care that government takes of its own image and its perennial anxiety about the fragility of that image and its vulnerability to gifted and determined resistance. This reinforces the notion that power contains within it the outlines of its own resistance, suggesting both the key sites and the principal means for its own negation – as the examination of any censorship regime will tend to show.[5]

For those art forms that demand space and freedom to develop their own voice, resistance is often geared initially to carving out that space. The substance of the messages may vary. They might be explicit denunciations of the ruling political order. More obliquely, they may be trying to get people to reflect upon values and conventions they have taken for granted, unsettling the habitual comforts of the everyday. However, the very act of publicizing ideas that go against the grain of conventional thinking, that create an audience and a following willing to contemplate alternatives, indicates a shift in the parameters of power. In some form, those in authority have ceded ground to others whose activities may lead to the erosion of established power, intentionally or not.

In this sense, the effects of the art of resistance can often be assessed through the reactions of those who feel most threatened. The response of those who find themselves and their values questioned and resisted through visual, dramatic, musical or literary images can show up the vulnerability at the heart of power. This may justify examining such artistic expressions as an art of resistance, not merely of dissent or protest, although that may be a question of degree, depending on the context and on what is believed to be at stake. Here judgement about the intention of the artist is important. It focuses on how that intention is expressed and thus on the relationship between the medium and the message in a performance that is searching for some kind of recognition. On the other hand, it is also necessary to assess the environment in which the act is conceived and executed – the pool, as it were, in which the stone will fall, creating ripples. This means studying the capacity of artistic perform-ance (in its widest sense) to unsettle, to mobilize, to undermine the claims of authority and to help in the creation of an impetus that itself is part of a larger process challenging established power.

Two distinctive features of the art of resistance emerge in this context. The first is the way in which such artistic performances begin to create new collective understandings of histories, rights and identities through a variety of techniques. This goes back to the potential of art – whether visual, aural, dramatic or literary – to develop a new vernacular, an idiom that can give voice to the voiceless, representing and even giving reality to forms of collective experience and identity. The capacity of art to impose coherence on multiple memories, 'standing in' for half-remembered and sometimes chaotic lived experiences, is precisely the resource on which many try to draw, whether defending or attacking established power.

Through visual representation, music, song, poetry and literature, or through the built environment itself, people can be persuaded to see themselves in a certain way. The ingenuity and appeal of artistic experi-ences can lead people to accept a certain kind of history and to embrace an emerging identity. It is not surprising, therefore, that there is an urge in politics to control this process, to ensure an absence of internal contra-diction and a congruence between the form and the message being con-veyed. The result has been conflict and artistic contestation, not only between established power and those who want to resist and undermine it, but also among the organizers of resistance where each may seek to lay their hand and place their stamp on the dominant narrative of the cause.[6]

In this sense, therefore, the art of resistance plays its part in giving substance to contentious politics, helping to define and to make it recognizable.

By the same token, asserting collective identities and claims demands public space for their expression. It is here that artists, singers, graffiti writers and others have been prominent, asserting the right to a voice and a presence in the public sphere. Through such a public presence, a common language, often a vernacular of solidarity and defiance, will be established. Whether it mobilizes people directly for a specific political cause is perhaps less significant than the steady erosion that can take place as established authorities find themselves outflanked, superseded, mocked and derided. It becomes harder in such circumstances to maintain the kind of unthought domination that is at the heart of hegemonic power. It can no longer be assumed that the traditional symbols and techniques of authority are creating the conditions for even an outward show of obedience. On the contrary, each poster, graffito, song, play, painting or cartoon becomes part of a spectacle of public defiance and derision. The more vigorously the authorities try to put a stop to this by arresting artists and singers, closing down plays, raiding art exhibitions and seizing artworks, or blacking out graffiti, the clearer it becomes that they have failed to establish their own version of the truth.

In this sense, therefore, the art of resistance is closely connected to the public protests associated with civil disobedience and demonstration. Indeed, it can be used directly to amplify the force of a demonstration. As the example of Cairo's Tahrir Square in 2011 vividly showed, banners, posters, songs and street theatre were key ways in which the mobilized citizens defied the authorities and reclaimed public space.[7] In other places, the 'art of destruction' is used to signal defiance and to encourage resistance. The public flouting of authority is organized by targeting public artworks that symbolize the power of the existing order, sometimes literally turning those images on their head.[8] In both cases, the reclaiming of public space, together with visible defiance of established power, constitute an artistry of resistance, helping to communicate with, to enthuse and to mobilize an emerging political public.

POSTERS AND GRAFFITI

One of the most obvious artistic expressions of resistance has been the political poster. Intended for public display on demonstrations or in public spaces, it has been a key feature of campaigns of political protest and mobilization. Darkness and anonymity allow fly-posters to transform the city streets in time for startling public exposure with the coming of daylight. The same is true of graffiti, the painted and sprayed symbols, slogans and deflating satires that can make buildings into sites of public art, blazoning defiance and resistance, often by their very presence. Laila Shawa, the Palestinian artist who has incorporated graffiti into some of her most powerful pictures, acknowledged this fact. Observing that the Oslo Accords between the PLO and Israel had not changed the quality of people's lives in Gaza, she did remark wryly that it did seem to have brought brighter and more striking colours to the graffiti on its walls.[9]

Political posters, by the very nature of their production and the processes involved, tend to be associated with organizations, parties or movements. As examples of the art of resistance, posters have therefore reflected the concerns of organizations involved in immediate and urgent struggles. The struggle itself, played out in a larger arena, determines the messages of the posters and may also influence the images and symbols used. Precisely because of the infrastructure needed for poster production, their appearance in the Middle East as instruments of resistance, rather than simply as political statements, has generally taken place only where the power of established authority is already weak. For this reason, major concentrations of posters have been produced by Palestinian resistance organizations in Lebanon and as part of the upheaval and defiance of the Iranian revolution of the late 1970s.

Palestinian Posters

In the Palestinian case, the production of defiant, mocking or encouraging posters that challenged the status quo in the occupied Palestinian territories themselves was always difficult. Until 1967, the grip of the Jordanian and Egyptian authorities made it virtually impossible to produce and distribute posters critical of these regimes, and after that date, the Israeli military authorities were equally intolerant. As a result, until recently, energy and creativity went into producing posters extolling Palestinian resistance mainly outside Palestinian territory. Lebanon, with its dynamic art movements, the weakness of its central government and the presence of powerful political forces championing the Palestinian cause, became the main field of production. It was here that some of the most striking posters appeared, despite the debilitating restrictions under which most Palestinians actually lived in that country.

In the hundreds of posters produced since the 1970s, Palestine was the linking theme and the cause that was being promoted. Inevitably, however, different visions of Palestine dictated the messages and to some degree the iconography of the posters themselves. In fact, the sequences of posters championing Palestinian resistance over the years serve as a powerful visual reminder of the fact that they represented very different ideas about mobilization, action and even of Palestine itself. Nevertheless, they all supported the liberation of Palestine and affirmed the identity and rights of the Palestinian people as a national community. This involved evocation of the land of Palestine, using the national flag, supreme symbol of national sovereignty. It also used other symbols of Palestine, such as the black-and-white chequered *kaffiyeh* of the Palestinian male peasant or the embroidered dresses of Palestinian village women. In this sense, there was a strong assertion of a Palestinian identity that was distinct as well as populist. This can be seen, for instance, in a poster of 1982 that called rather optimistically for solidarity between the people of southern Lebanon and the Palestinians. The two communities are represented by their distinctive clothing, with the Palestinian portrayed as a guerrilla in a *kaffiyeh* and the Lebanese wearing a version of the national dress of the mountains.

FIGURE 2. Ismail Shammout: '*One People, One Path*', PLO, Beirut (1982) [Photo courtesy of the Palestinian Poster Project]

On the other hand, the very style of the posters, the ways in which the images and shorthand of resistance and liberation were used, had a cosmopolitan flavour. They used the vernacular of an internationally recognizable poster art.[10] Many were also produced by artists outside Palestine and in European languages as well as in Arabic. This raises the question of the purposes of the poster and the role it is meant to play in any strategy of resistance. In virtually all cases, the Palestinian posters produced over the years were signals. They affirmed the existence of the community and the presence not simply of an abstract Palestinian nation but also of the organization claiming to speak in its name. The appearance of the posters in a street, a square or any other public space reassured those who were denied an identity and defied those who tried to deny it. The shorthand of the gun or the grenade was frequently used to signal determination to resist and a readiness to use force to regain lost lands and rights. They also in many cases commemorated those who had been killed in the armed struggle.

FIGURE 3. Archichoda Italia – Collectif de Peintres des Pays Arabes – Atelier F.A.P. '*Fateh: revolution until victory*' (for Fatah c. 1983) [Photo courtesy of the Trustees of the British Museum]

FIGURE 4. Muwaffaq Mattar: '*The giant has escaped from the bottle*', 16th anniversary of the outbreak of the Palestinian revolution Ashbal al-Thawra – Quwat al-ʾAsifa, Fatah (1981) [Photo courtesy of the Trustees of the British Museum]

Many Palestinian posters also took up the theme of steadfastness [*sumud*]. They used the common imagery of popular revolutionary and resistance movements to suggest that the people's endurance and indeed their sheer numbers would win the struggle against occupation. Some combined both themes, such as 'the giant has escaped from the bottle' poster of the armed *shabab* emerging from the miserable conditions of the refugee camps, produced in Lebanon in the 1980s.

At the same time, very different visions of Palestine were being evoked. Common themes, such as the beauty of the lost lands, the need for popular, often armed struggle and the brutality of Israeli occupation and dispossession were featured. However, in the more recent posters of Islamist organizations like *Hamas*, or of their regional sympathizers in Lebanon and Iran, the Palestine that was and yet might be emerges as a distinctly Islamic space, signalled by Islamic symbols and buildings, as well as through Qur'anic quotations. Even for the more straightforwardly and generally secular nationalist posters produced by the PLO or indeed by Fatah, the frequent use of an image of the Dome of the Rock in Jerusalem lent a distinctly Muslim aura to the representation of Palestine. In the posters of secular leftist organizations such as the PFLP, this image was scarcely in evidence at all. Instead, they drew attention to the people of Palestine, portrayed as contemporary workers, citizens and fighters dedicated to the task of state building and armed struggle. This generally replaced the idealized and picturesque peasantry that the fine arts department of the PLO's Unified Information Office in Beirut had encouraged in many of the posters that they commissioned.[11]

The portrayal of Palestinian women and their role in the resistance followed a similar pattern. Their relatively rare appearance in *Hamas* and Islamist posters portrays them in a role of support and steadfast solidarity with the struggle, naturally abiding by the conventions of 'modest' Islamic dress. In PLO and Fatah posters, women appeared sometimes as fighters, represented as equal to their male counterparts. But they also featured as idealized peasants, mothers and supporters of the struggle or of the lost idyll of a free Palestine. In this guise, they wore traditional embroidered Palestinian dresses, with the embroidery itself sometimes standing in for both the women and the land. These idealized portrayals of Palestinian womanhood shared many features with the symbolic representation of women in nationalist discourse more generally, including the representation of Palestine itself as a woman.[12]

Correspondingly, in the posters of the PFLP, DFLP and other socialist Palestinian organizations, women were shown as the equal of men, engaged in the same tasks of political and military struggle. This became particularly prominent when one woman, Leila Khaled, took on iconic status in the 1970s due to her role in the PFLP's hijacking of aircraft. Posters featuring her image, wearing the black-and-white *kaffiyeh* of Palestine and holding a Kalashnikov, became universally known. They drew attention to the Palestinian cause and to the determination of the Palestinian movements to pursue armed struggle. Memorable as this was for the PFLP and the Palestinian cause, it took its toll on the subject herself. After the hijackings, she underwent plastic surgery because, as she told an interviewer in January 2000, she 'refused to wander round with the face of an icon'.[13]

The Palestinian organizations, whether nationalist, Islamist or socialist, were not simply trying to promote images of Palestine that would resonate among and mobilize the Palestinian people, scattered as they were. The posters were also meant to help in the struggle to gain international recognition of the Palestinian people and their rights. As so many of the posters show through their languages and their iconography, the intention was to create international awareness of the plight of the Palestinians, stressing the need for global solidarity in the ongoing struggle with Israel. Regional and international allies of the Palestinians often had their own motives for promoting the cause of Palestine at certain times and used this opportunity to demonstrate their own solidarity and to attack those who opposed a just solution to the Palestinian question.

Thus in March 1978, at the Beirut Arab University, the PLO organized an exhibition of posters – The International Exhibition for Palestine. This was specifically intended to display the range of global support enjoyed by the Palestinians. The following year, the Baghdad International Poster Exhibition chose two themes for its competition – 'The Third World Struggle for Liberation' and 'Palestine – a Homeland Denied' – encouraging both the linkage of these themes and the participation of an international artistic community in the production of the posters. The Palestinian exhibition was transferred to the Iraqi Cultural Centre in London, where visitors could see the winning poster, created by Jacek Kowalski of Poland. Indeed, the poster advertising the exhibition itself had been designed by Pedro Laperal of Spain.

Posters were seen by Palestinians as important ways of affirming Palestinian identity and Palestinian rights. For this reason, many of the posters have featured the *Nakba* of 1948 to underline the fate that overtook the Palestinians and the need for international action to

FIGURE 5. Jacek Kowalski [Poland] (1979) [Photo courtesy of the Palestinian Poster Project]

redress this injustice. The continuing attempt by the Palestinian Authority to negotiate a settlement that would include compensation for the refugees of 1948 also creates the setting for the Al-Awda [the return] Award competition. Organized annually since 2007 in Ramallah and in Gaza by the Badil Centre for Palestinian Residency and Refugee Rights, 'the award aims to foster Palestinian talent and creativity and to raise the profile of the Palestinian *Nakba* and the right of all forcibly displaced Palestinians to return to their homes and lands'.[14] Planned as part of the ongoing commemorations of the *Nakba*, these were not posters designed to be pasted up on the walls and public spaces of the occupied territories. It was more that the event itself and the posters on display were meant to create media interest, drawing attention to the *Nakba*, to the depth of feeling it aroused and to the kinds of memories that Palestinians associated with it.

Iranian Posters

The long Palestinian struggle to gain recognition and to establish a Palestinian state seemed to require a poster art that proclaimed resistance not simply or even principally in the Palestinian territories themselves but rather on the international stage. It was here that some of the major forces were at work that would shape the political fate of the Palestinians, and it was here, accordingly, that their energies were increasingly focused. By contrast, in Iran, another extraordinarily productive site for the imaginative and powerful development of poster art within the framework of resistance, the audience and the messages were largely internal ones. The tumultuous events of 1978 served both to inspire those who had long resented the dictatorship of the Shah and to undermine – and eventually to paralyse – much of his feared security apparatus. In these circumstances, some Iranian artists used the relative sanctuary of the campus of Tehran University to set up a workshop that would provide the facilities for people to design and produce posters, regardless of their political affiliation. The output of the workshop began to find its way onto the walls of Tehran, acting as an accompaniment to the increasing pace of demonstration and proving, in the best tradition of poster art, that the security forces were unable to prevent this public expression of defiance and resistance.[15]

In the same vein, commemorative posters appeared, dedicated to those who had fallen when the armed forces fired on the crowds or to those who had been executed in the Shah's prisons.

„ از خون جوانان وطن لاله دميده ،،

FIGURE 6. Morteza Momayez: *'Tulips have bloomed from the blood of the nation's youth'*, Tehran (1978–9) [Photo courtesy of Nicky Nodjoumi]

FIGURE 7. Behzad Shishehgaran: *'Long live Iran'*, Tehran (1978) [Photo courtesy of the Trustees of the British Museum]

More noticeable perhaps than the wall posters of that year were the poster portraits that were carried aloft, portraying Ayatollah Khomeini, Imam Hussein, Lenin and Mossadeq, depending on which organization had called the people out on the streets. In some cases, for example in December 1978, these unlikely allies were spotted at the same mass demonstration in the streets of Tehran. Equally prolific and prominent as an art signalling defiance and resistance were the banners held aloft at the demonstrations, the power of which lay often in their words but sometimes also in the calligraphic beauty of their phrasing. The calligraphic poster in Iran, as in the Arab world, was a direct descendant of the hand-painted calligraphic cloth banners [*al-yafta* (Arabic) – *pardeh* (Persian)] that had long been part of the urban landscape, used to publicize events of all kinds, sometimes hung across the street, sometimes carried in procession. Pressed into the service of political resistance, it amplified the power of the slogans shouted by the crowds that so successfully reclaimed public space in Iran during the months of revolutionary upheaval in 1978 and 1979. It also had a familiarity that conveyed its meaning immediately to those watching the events, in person or on television, seeking to draw them in and to mobilize them in the escalating trial of strength on the streets of Tehran and Iran's other major cities.[16]

By February 1979, the uprising against the Shah and his regime had succeeded, but other trials of strength were to follow. During the early years of the revolutionary regime, the public art of resistance took on two principal forms. The first was the official sponsorship by the new government of a vast array of posters and murals replaying the themes of the revolution and projecting them onto a regional and global arena. Seeing itself as the beacon of Islamic revolution, the government of the Islamic Republic was determined to proclaim its radical stance and the changed position of Iran in global politics. Thus a stream of imaginative and powerful posters were produced, taking up themes of anti-imperialism, the determination of the republic to overthrow the tyranny of kings and of Western puppet rulers and, increasingly, the universality of Islamic revolution.[17] In many respects, this was part of the new government's promise that it would bring about a new political order in the Middle East, fighting for the oppressed and shaking the status quo to its foundations. It was making itself very self-consciously a focus of resistance regionally and globally. For instance, aware of the power of the art of resistance, the Iranian government was reported to have sent Iranian graphic artists to Lebanon in the 1980s to assist Hizbullah in the

FIGURE 8. Logos of the Hizbullah and of IRGC 2011 [Photo courtesy of Emily Tripp]

design of its posters and even of its now-famous logo – based on that of the Islamic Revolutionary Guard Corps.[18]

Like all post-revolutionary governments, that of the Islamic republic was convinced that the great powers, their regional allies and those who still supported the old regime inside the country would try to undermine them. The memory of Western intervention to overthrow the government of Mohammad Mossadeq in 1953 was a vivid reminder of what might happen. Consequently, the replaying of the revolution in all its gory detail, as well as the graphic portrayal of the evil forces trying to undermine the Islamic republic, were meant to alert people to imminent danger. It would remind them of the cause they had been fighting for and rally them, in the name of the martyrs, of Islam and of the Iranian people, around the revolutionary government. This was particularly the case after the Iraqi invasion of Iran in 1980. The 'imposed war', as the Iranian government labelled it, was portrayed as a conspiracy by Iraq, the United States and others to destroy the Islamic Republic. For eight long years of war, much of the sponsored artistic output of the Islamic Republic therefore was geared to these themes in an effort to rally the Iranian people to resist the invader by all means possible in the name of Islam, the revolution and of Iranian patriotism.

FIGURE 9. Mahmood Hemati Turabi: Basij Resistance force poster of Hosein Fahmindeh, alleged to have blown himself up in 1981 in order to destroy an Iraqi tank, Tehran (c. 2002) [Photo courtesy of the Trustees of the British Museum]

In propagating these images, it became apparent that, as power shifted within the new regime, and as the Islamic Republican Party became Ayatollah Khomeini's favoured organization, the portrayal of what the revolution had really been about began to change. Correspondingly, its symbolic and graphic portrayal, the imagery used and the anniversaries celebrated emphasized the role of Islam and of Khomeini and his associates. Through the posters and murals of the time, it is possible to see a new hegemonic power in the making. It was excluding, displacing and eventually eliminating other participants in the revolutionary process and their versions of what it had been about. Domestically, therefore, what had begun as an art of resistance became increasingly identified with the emerging power of a state, controlled by a small number of people, intolerant of opposition and determined to exclude from power those whose views challenged their own authority.[19]

Those who were gradually and often violently excluded not simply from the narrative of the revolution but also from representation in the Islamic Republic tried to resist by various means. They used posters and graffiti to signal their presence as much as to convey a particular message. As in other theatres, defiance and resistance were acted out in public to contest the growing dominance of the government and to assert the existence of other stories, other participants and other ideas in the revolution. However, as the repression of dissidents intensified after 1980 and even those who differed modestly from the followers of the 'Imam's line' were expelled from positions of power, such art, whether on posters or banners, found fewer and fewer opportunities to show itself in public. Posters became too difficult and dangerous to produce within the borders of the Islamic Republic. The covert art of graffiti seemed to be the main medium left to those who were trying to resist what the republic was becoming, signalling their resistance in the public sphere on the walls of Iran's streets. Graffiti, whether written as slogans on walls, as pictures and murals or as stencilled images and messages could be quickly executed, were difficult to eliminate and often had a subversive impact as striking as that of a poster. Above all, they signalled the presence of dissenting voices and created a kind of anonymous solidarity in the cities of Iran that often succeeded in eluding the authorities.

For that very reason, the authorities cracked down on graffiti artists, concerned about the possibility of any dissent that might undermine the claim not simply of political conformity but also of social conformity as defined by the guardians of public morality within the regime.[20] They also tried to appropriate the public space of the street walls for their own

FIGURE 10. Outer wall of the former U.S. Embassy, Tehran (2008) [Photo courtesy of Li-Chiao Chen]

'street art' in the form of giant murals depicting their own chosen themes of anti-imperialism, martyrdom, Iranian history and the triumph of the Islamic revolution. In this sense, as well as arresting and imprisoning the dissident artists of resistance, the government was also seeking to drown out their messages with their own appropriation of public space.

Palestinian Graffiti

In occupied Palestine, the Israeli authorities had exercised similar forms of restriction on public space, prohibiting any kind of Palestinian cultural production that defied or even subverted the military occupation or which expressed sympathy for political organizations opposed to Israeli occupation. Inevitably, just as it limited and inhibited the production of printed material like books and newspapers, censorship of this kind made it virtually impossible for Palestinians under occupation to practice the art of the poster, at least not in any developed way. It was under these circumstances that graffiti became a marker of defiance and an art form that began to fill the walls of the occupied territories, reaching an unparalleled intensity and proliferation during the first Palestinian *intifada* of 1987–91.

As in other environments, the graffiti that appeared throughout the occupied territories served a number of purposes, chief amongst them being the assertion of dissent. As an act of civil disobedience, explicitly challenging Israeli military regulations, the very act of painting or spraying graffiti in a public place left a permanent mark of defiance. This remained even when the Israeli authorities obliterated the words or pictures themselves or obliged the unhappy owner of the wall on which they appeared to paint over them. The series of black or sometimes purple oblongs and patches across the walls served as reminders of the original act of defiance and in that sense continued at least part of the message of the graffiti, even after the content had been erased.[21] Of course, the content was also important. It was meant to convey not just a message of resistance through a broadcast presence of Palestinian dissent, but was also intended to signal the existence of distinct political organizations, with messages that generally gave an indication of their origins. In this respect, they were aimed at engaging the Palestinian public, not simply at aggravating the Israeli forces of occupation. Indeed, the sometimes tangled, nearly illegible graffiti that appeared as one organization tried to overpaint the efforts and slogans of another were testimony to the many strands of political resistance in Palestine. As Julie Peteet put it, 'Palestinians "thought out loud" in the graffiti'.[22]

The messages were various. They included the name of the organization responsible – PLO, PFLP, *Hamas*, and so on – inscribing slogans long associated with a particular faction, as well as non-partisan expressions of hope in victory or the ending of oppression. This was supplemented by plays on words, humorous deflation of the claims of power, as well as by commemorations of those who had been killed or imprisoned by the Israeli security services. Occasionally, graphic images were used to drive home a point or to memorialize a person or to blazon a logo, but, given the longer time and higher risk involved in such productions, it is understandable that these were less widespread than the hastily sprayed slogan. The increasing use of stencils, however, allowed graphic images to be reproduced much more quickly and safely across walls, doors, shop shutters and virtually all surfaces that stood still long enough in the public spaces of Palestine to be used as a public canvas.

As with many of the posters produced elsewhere, some of the graffiti of the *intifada* were aimed at an international, as well as a Palestinian audience, as the frequent use of English proved. The *intifada* had itself attracted the attention of the international press, providing vivid images of civil disobedience and of the marked imbalance of forces in the occupied territories, but also, crucially, reminding people of the political aspirations and predicament of the Palestinians. In such circumstances, it was clearly part of the strategy of resistance that the international community should be made aware of the strength of feeling in Palestine and of the hatred of Israeli occupation. The graffiti were an immediate way of conveying these feelings to the outside world, especially when the graffiti themselves became as much a focus for photojournalists and television crews as the young men and boys throwing stones at Israeli soldiers and armoured vehicles.[23]

With the ending of the *intifada* and the signing of the Oslo Accords in 1993 allowing a limited form of self-government in some enclaves within occupied Palestine, the graffiti did not cease. Some continued to denounce and to resist any form of Israeli control, but in some respects, the edge had been blunted. As often as not, they expressed intra-Palestinian political rivalries, less as part of the art of resistance and more as mundane political competition with one group – figuratively – trying to shout down another. Also, in many parts of occupied Palestine, painting or spraying graffiti in public places was no longer the dangerous act of civil disobedience that it had once been. Israeli patrols no longer policed many of Palestine's urban areas, reducing the risk of confrontation and, after 1993, many of the slogans, images and symbols used to assert Palestinian identity and to champion Palestinian political organizations were no longer considered illegal by the Israeli military authorities. Consequently, the painting of a Palestinian flag or the spraying of a slogan extolling Fatah and the Palestinian revolution were not acts of resistance in the same way. Affirmative they might have been, but they did not place the act and the actor in the same category of dissent as had been the case during the *intifada*. For some, this was seen as the banalization of graffiti, following a path trodden by those graffiti artists in the West whose work had moved from the field of edgy urban protest to become commodities in a market ruled by the capital and consumer taste of the affluent.

However, as Fatah's domination of the PA became more rooted, maintained by familiar authoritarian methods, and as dissatisfaction with the agreement of 1993 began to grow, the graffiti echoed the public protests visible in Gaza in particular. These reflected the growing strength of *Hamas* and Islamic Jihad in the Gaza Strip, presenting these organizations as resisting not only Israeli occupation but also the rule of Fatah and indeed the very notion of a government that was not sanctioned by Islamic values. With the outbreak of the *intifadat al-aqsa* in 2000, the intensification of political competition between *Hamas* and the PLO and, finally, the break of 2007 that saw a separate *Hamas*-led administration in Gaza, the 'battle of the graffiti' gave way to a form of graffiti in the streets of the Gaza strip that was effectively sponsored by the Hamas administration. So concerned was the Hamas administration that the graffiti, especially of Quranic verses, should be calligraphically appropriate and grammatically correct that it was reported to have opened a school for graffiti calligraphers in Gaza. It was also clear that they were determined to control the forms it took and images it conveyed.[24] Of course, much of the writing on the walls of Jabalya and other refugee quarters was not specifically concerned with political subjects. Nevertheless, as a form of public expression, even the most personal messages of congratulation or Quranic verses took on a political dimension. They were the acts of people asserting their identity and presence in the public sphere.

The art of resistance in Palestinian graffiti was to take another turn in the occupied West Bank after the outbreak of the *intifadat al-aqsa* in 2000. The violence of the years that followed witnessed repeated armed Israeli incursions into Palestinian territory, with corresponding casualties, as well as a campaign of suicide bombing that brought the fight to the heart of Israel's cities. It was also responsible for the Israeli government's decision to build a barrier between Israel and the occupied West Bank. The government needed to be seen by the Israeli public to be protecting them against further suicide bombs and thought to achieve this by building a physical barrier that would severely control access to Israel from the occupied territories. In 2002, work began on the barrier, but, rather than following the path of the Green Line (Israel's border with the West Bank from 1948–67), it pursued a twisting line that swallowed up nearly ten per cent of Palestinian territory. Testimony to this is the length of the wall itself. Whereas the Green Line measures 315 km, the Wall will measure roughly 750 km. It has isolated Palestinian villages, cutting many off from their agricultural lands, making movement even harder than it already had been.[25] Since East Jerusalem and much of its environment had been annexed by Israel in 1967, it also ensured that the city was now physically cut off from its Palestinian hinterland.

The Separation Wall or Barrier – called by the Israeli authorities the 'separation fence' or the 'security fence' and by the Palestinians 'the racial segregation wall' [*jidar al-fasl al-unsuri*] – was made up, particularly in urban areas, of eight-metre-high concrete slabs, patrolled on the Israeli side but unguarded on the Palestinian side. As in the case of the Berlin Wall that had also served as a free surface for artistic expression for nearly forty years, this had the effect of creating a massive canvas that

FIGURE 11. Section of the wall near Qalandia checkpoint, Ramallah (July 2011) [Photo courtesy of Emily Tripp]

FIGURE 12. Section of the wall near Qalandia checkpoint, Ramallah (July 2011) [Photo courtesy of Emily Tripp]

invited graffiti artists. They now had a clear focus for resentment and for the expression of resistance. Their message was no longer simply against Israeli occupation and domination in general, but against this most physical manifestation of the ills that the occupation had brought in its wake – and the messages could be painted and sprayed on the very symbol itself. It was not long before slogans, denunciations and a vast repertoire of mocking and derisory graffiti appeared.

This was in part a Palestinian effort, but it also became a focus for international attention in a way that many, though not all, Palestinians encouraged. As William Parry's book shows, the wall became the focus and the canvas on which anyone who had the opportunity to visit the occupied territories could express their solidarity and support for Palestinian rights, their opposition to the wall and their denunciation of Israeli government policies, and often of Israel itself. Graffiti appeared in all the languages of those who visited the wall, supplemented in many cases by paintings and murals, small and large, that amplified this show of solidarity and used images to undermine the power of the wall and of those who stood behind it.

This did not make the everyday life of Palestinians trying to negotiate the permits, the checkpoints and the intrusion of the wall any easier, but it did serve to draw attention internationally to what many regarded as yet another imposition on Palestinians living under occupation. In that sense, it is debatable as to whether the graffiti sprayed onto the wall or the massive and looming form of the wall itself had the greater effect on how people outside the region were coming to see the plight of the Palestinians. In many senses, the brute ugliness of the high concrete wall needed no further adornment to make the case of those who lived in its shadow. This was certainly the view of some Palestinians, wary of the fact that something that was for them a real, material and oppressive factor in their lives had become a symbolic space for a stream of passing visitors in which to act out their fantasies, aesthetic and political. It was a sentiment captured in an exchange experienced by the British graffiti artist, Banksy. As William Parry recounts, his visual humour and irony was lost on an elderly Palestinian who watched him work for some time and then remarked, 'You paint the wall, you make it look beautiful', for which Banksy thanked him, but the old man replied, 'We don't want it to be beautiful. We hate this wall, go home'.[26]

VISUAL ARTS

Palestine

Depictions of the wall itself, as well as the graffiti written on the walls of occupied Palestine, have also entered the imagery of Palestinian artists. Their audiences might be more limited – and some would argue more self-selected – than the crowds that take in the posters and graffiti that feature in public spaces. But they play an important role in cultural production, as well as in the diffusion of the works of Palestinian artists through international networks of artists and intellectuals. It is they who have helped to ensure a wider reception for many of these works, both in the sense of places where they can be exhibited, as well as the community of support that has drawn attention to the histories and experiences from which Palestinian art has emerged. Thus a work such as Abed Abdi's 'The Wall', with its textured surface and shadowy figures before a phantom landscape imagined beyond the wall and under that ubiquitous Palestinian symbol, the *kaffiyeh*, conveys the sense of loss, interruption and imprisonment that many Palestinians feel.[27]

Equally, Laila Shawa's powerful 'Walls of Gaza' series, as well as the '20 Targets' picture underlining the child victims of the suppression of the *intifada*, and the ambivalent 'Children of War, Children of Peace' sequence that again highlights the effect of the violence on the children of Gaza, all incorporate graffiti from the streets of Gaza itself. The messages of the graffiti and the subject of the pictures succeed in

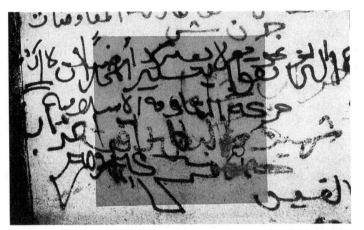

FIGURE 13. Laila Shawa: '*A Gun for Palestine*' from *Walls of Gaza* (1992)
[© Laila Shawa. Photo courtesy of the Trustees of the British Museum]

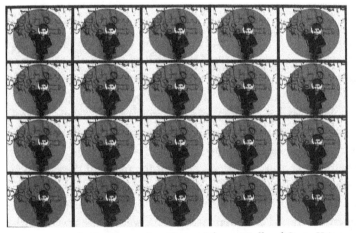

FIGURE 14. Laila Shawa: '*20 Targets*' from *Walls of Gaza II* (1994) [© Laila
Shawa. Photo courtesy of Laila Shawa]

drawing attention to the predicament that Palestinians are resisting, and
also give an indication of the forms of that resistance, as well as its
consequences.

In this respect, Abdi, Shawa and, of course, Tamari with her installation 'Mashin?', as well as many other Palestinian artists, are acting out
Boris Taslitzky's call to 'carry the museums into the streets'. An associate of Picasso at the time that the famous picture 'Guernica' was being
painted, Taslitzky was an advocate of the potential of art to inform, to

mobilize and to shape the way in which people see power, whilst at the same time provoking passionate responses. Such indeed was the intention behind 'Guernica' itself. It had commemorated the bombardment of the Basque town of Guernica by Fascist forces during the Spanish Civil War through its graphic representation of the violence of modern warfare. Powerful as the picture is, it was significant that the responses to it in Europe, where the struggle with Fascism was very much to the fore, were reportedly very different to those in the United States. There the press concentrated more on the forms used by Picasso, discussing the avant-garde technique of the work, rather than the political issues it raised. This underlines the fact that art 'presupposes active involvement from people outside the purely artistic sphere. This is particularly true of an art which seeks to be politically effective'.[28]

Many Palestinian artists, therefore, have been determined to portray or to evoke key themes in the experiences of the Palestinian people, often seen through their own personal encounters with violence, loss, flight, exile and repression.[29] It is not always represented as such and often depends on who is reading the work and decoding it, but for many the themes of a lost, often idyllic land, of the rupture of the *Nakba* and of the endurance of those who remain have been powerfully repeated. They have been taken up by very different artists in a variety of ways. Some have been working within the occupied territories and within the refugee camps in Lebanon and Gaza, while others have been active in various sites of exile in the Middle East, Europe and North America. Although sometimes close to the poster art of a more directly or obviously political kind – and there was a good deal of interchange between the two, as in the cases of the artists Ismail Shammout and Mustafa al-Hallaj – the works of many Palestinian artists have succeeded in conveying powerfully, in a variety of ways, key aspects of the Palestinian political experience.

In doing so, they have not only drawn attention to the fact of loss and the poignancy of dispossession, but have also asserted through individual interpretation some of the key features of what it means to be Palestinian, in terms of identity, memory, rights, aspirations and presence. These are the messages communicated through the works of artists as diverse as Jumana al-Husseini with her dreamy and stylized Jerusalem as an imaginary city,[30] the extraordinary series of murals painted by Ismail Shammout and Tamam al-Akhal, capturing the violence and trauma of the *Nakba* of 1948,[31] or the powerful series of drawings and paintings entitled '99 martyrs' by Raed Issa that reflect the contemporary experience of the violence of occupation and siege in Gaza.[32] Similar themes of loss and steadfastness can be seen in Vera Tamari's allegorical photos and ceramics entitled 'Tale of a Tree' (referring to the uprooting of so many of the olive trees of Palestine by Israeli forces or by settlers), and in the film made by the diaspora Palestinian artist, Rosalind Nashashibi, *Dahiyet al-Bareed* [Post Office District]. It focuses on a district of Jerusalem, the fate of which captured much of the poignancy of life under occupation.[33] Using humour and surrealism, similar effects have been achieved by Khalil Rabah's installation 'United States of Palestine Airlines' or the subversive photographs of Raeda Saadeh in which she recreates classical pictures by herself posing in appropriate costumes against the background of a forbidden Palestinian arcadia.[34]

Kamal Boullata, the Palestinian artist who has done so much in his own works and in his writings to situate Palestinian art in the full context of Palestinians' lived experiences, takes his cue from John Berger's observation that 'we live in a world of suffering in which evil is rampant, a world whose events do not confirm our Being, a world that has to be resisted. It is in this situation that the aesthetic moment offers hope'.[35] Boullata thus sees the very act of producing art under occupation and particularly under the Israeli military retaliations during *intifadat al-aqsa* as an act of defiance and resistance in itself. He portrays it as an affirmation of identity and solidarity that refused to be erased by the efforts of those whose political projects would be made easier by the denial of Palestinian identity and rights.[36] Both before and after the Oslo Accords of 1993, this had been part of the struggle of Palestinians to assert the 'aesthetic moments' that would testify to their resilience and to their aspirations, often in the face of determined suppression by Israeli occupation forces.

Since the 1970s, Palestinian artists in the occupied territories had tried to create public spaces in which their art could be seen. Thus, in 1972, the League of Artists was established in the occupied West Bank against the wishes of the Israeli forces of occupation. Nevertheless, it met and organized exhibitions and was finally given official recognition in 1980. This did not, however, protect it or its members from harassment and arrest. Nor did it prevent the confiscation and destruction of their works when the Israeli military authorities judged that these had contravened the sweeping prohibitions contained in the censors' charter that was the Israel Defence Forces Order No. 101 of 27 August 1967, relating to the 'Prohibition of Incitement and Hostile Propaganda Actions'.

When Gallery 79 was established in Ramallah in 1979 as a place for Palestinian artists to exhibit their work, it became a target for the Israeli authorities, convinced that it was encouraging resistance and subversion through the exhibitions it mounted. In September 1980, the Israeli military governor himself appeared, flanked by a platoon of soldiers, and seized posters and paintings that were considered offensive. It was finally closed down by the military authorities during an exhibition by Sulaiman Mansour. Ironically, he had tried to avoid the intervention of the censors by ensuring that the paintings on display contained no overt political symbolism or message. As Mansour said, in some bewilderment, 'For this exhibit, I tried to put myself in the mind of the military governor. So as not to enrage the authorities, I did not exhibit anything I thought he would think political. We wanted the work of the gallery to continue'. However, it seemed that the very fact of the exhibition was too political an act for the occupation authorities to tolerate and his paintings were seized, the gallery closed down and he was to find himself subject to persistent harassment thereafter.[37]

At the time of the Oslo Accords in 1993 and the limited autonomy they promised, as well as the relaxation of some aspects of Israeli censorship, new public spaces were opened up by Palestinian artists and gallery owners to exhibit the growing body of Palestinian art. Not all of this, of course, was consciously geared to the political goals of resisting the occupation. In fact, at the 2002 competition for young Palestinian artists, the Cuban member of the jury was heard to express a certain surprise at the absence of 'pamphleteer art or nationalistic paintings' and his admiration at the individuality and complexity on display.[38] However, the establishment of spaces such as the Al-Wasiti Art Centre and Al-Ma'mal Foundation in East Jerusalem, the Khalil Sakakini Cultural Centre in Ramallah and the Qattan Foundation, as well as the institution of prizes for Palestinian artists and the initiation of the Ramallah Biennale in the year 2000, testified to the determination of Palestinians to resist the cultural erasure with which they had been threatened over the years. As the violent events of 2002 demonstrated, when Israeli forces ransacked the Sakakini Centre in Ramallah (and unsuccessfully tried to erase Vera Tamari's art installation), this was a threat which was to remain ever present and which appeared to target precisely the symbolic features of the arts of resistance that had helped to define a distinct Palestinian presence in the world.[39]

The publicity surrounding the travelling exhibition 'Made in Palestine' during the years 2003–6 showed that the international recognition and presence of Palestine through the medium of its many artists was something that could not be suppressed. This was despite the restrictive conditions of occupation in Palestine itself and the unease shown by so many museums in the United States at the prospect of hosting such an exhibition.[40] Vera Tamari, one of the artists exhibiting in the show, explained, 'I think it's an important reflection that there is a people and that the people have a right to express themselves. They have issues that they want to tell the world, stories that they have to tell the world. Many of the works here are not directly political, but they are political in the sense that we want to tell the story of what's happening in Palestine. People ignore the fact that there are Palestinians who have the same potential as other people in the world, that Palestinians are like other people, that they can live, can produce art and music'.[41]

Algeria

These examples from Palestine have been representative of the arts of resistance to foreign military occupation and the violence that it unleashes in people's daily lives. However, there is another context in which it also makes sense to speak of an art of resistance. This is represented by the works of artists who have used images, installations and performances to assert a different view and to challenge dominant social and political hierarchies. By defying taboos, by raising issues and aspects of social and historical existence that have hitherto been successfully repressed or rendered voiceless, the hegemony of power is being resisted. Sometimes this art is produced in conjunction with a political campaign or movement that is trying to raise such issues and to build a platform based on the call for the redress of historical wrongs. But sometimes it is the work of an individual artist, alienated from the dominant order, intellectually, emotionally or physically. This distance allows the artist to turn a critical eye on the taboos that have kept so many people in thrall for so long. This means confronting head-on the substance of the myths themselves, sometimes obliquely, but enhancing the radicalism of the message through artistic innovation that itself represents a break with the conventions of 'acceptable' expression.

Just such a combination appeared in Algeria in the late 1960s, long before the more public social protests that were to erupt in the 1980s. In this case, it took the form of the movement *Aouchem* ['tattoo' – referring to the popular art of body decoration and its repertoire of ancient magical symbols]. Co-founded by Hamid Abdoun, Denis Martinez,

Rezki Zérarti and Mustafa Akmoun, it comprised a number of Algerian artists who organized an exhibition in 1967 that so outraged other members of the official National Union of the Plastic Arts (UNAP) that they intervened directly and removed the pictures from the walls. As the manifesto of the group proclaimed, 'We want to show that, magical always, the sign is stronger than bombs' ['Nous entendons montrer que, toujours magique, le signe est plus fort que les bombes']. They saw themselves as a movement of resistance, against Western abstraction as much as against the Orientalist picturesque that had so informed the leading artists of Algeria up to that point. But it was also against the dominant patriotic realism of the UNAP promoted by the FLN government. *Aouchem* saw this as no more than a bogus corporatist nationalist narrative fabricated by the state. This, they proclaimed, was the production of 'the rearguard of aesthetic mediocrity' ['l'arrière-garde de la médiocrité esthétique'].⁴²

Aouchem drew upon thousands of years of popular symbols, forms and colours in order to bring into the open a suppressed history of the Algerian people who had preserved them 'despite all the conquests that have intervened since that of the Romans' ['malgré toutes les conquêtes intervenues depuis la romanisation']. It was thus a precursor of the Amazigh/Berber movement that was to emerge to challenge the official Arab–Islamic narrative of Algeria's history and identity some fifteen years later. However, it was not an Amazigh/Berber revivalist movement. Rather, *Aouchem* insisted that the Arab–Berber and African heritages of Algeria should be acknowledged and should inspire a cultural revival. It demanded that the pre-Islamic and pre-Arab elements should be reinscribed into Algerian identity and into the common idiom of its arts. Drawn towards the 'magic' symbols of popular and often Berber culture, *Aouchem* called for a new aesthetic and a new language in the arts that would free Algerians from the baneful legacies of Western colonialism and of monoglot Arab nationalism.

Although the group did not long survive as an organization, its influence did endure and fed into emerging cultural production in Algeria. In particular, its legacy was visible through the currency of some of the signs and symbols that so marked many of its members' works, as well as through the very public nature of its 'street actions' with a variety of public spaces – walls, pipelines, street surfaces – becoming the canvases on which many of the works were painted. It unsettled both the art establishment and the authorities, but clearly resonated with large numbers of people who saw the signs of popular culture reclaiming public spaces of Algeria.[43] In this respect, it was one of the streams that fed into a more general movement that first questioned, then resisted and in some cases violently challenged the dominant order that the FLN regime had imposed on Algeria since the war of independence.

As the events of the 1990s demonstrated, the movements of resistance were by no means harmonious. On the contrary, such was the bitterness of their antagonism that one of the founders of *Aouchem*, Denis Martinez, was forced to flee Algeria in the early 1990s having received death threats from elements of the armed Islamist resistance of the time. He was targeted precisely because of the artistic vision that he espoused and the popular aesthetic he sought to revive. This so unsettled those who held to a narrow view of Algeria's Islamic identity that they could only think of silencing him. In fact, it spurred him on to produce work of a kind that remained true to the original manifesto of *Aouchem*, using it to express his feelings of exile and longing and to reassert his attachment to his country. In 2002–4, with the ending of the violence that had torn the country apart for a decade, he returned with the striking performance and interactive installation 'La Fenêtre du Vent' [the window of the wind].[44]

Turkey

Although the setting and the political context were very different, a similar spirit of defiance and resistance informed a number of Turkish artists in the 1980s and 1990s. They were reacting against the imposition of military government in the early 1980s, followed by a series of civilian governments shadowed and overseen by the Turkish military high command. But they were also reacting to what some saw as the everyday acceptance of this state of affairs by large numbers of their compatriots. They were therefore resisting a common complacency that not only failed to question the need for military oversight, but also subscribed to a uniform version of Turkish nationalism that was at odds with the plural nature of Turkish society.

It was precisely such passive acceptance of domination that Hale Tenger's work at the 1992 Istanbul Biennale challenged. It urged people to resist their mute acquiescence in their own repression, all in the name of Turkish nationalism. In her work, 'I Know People Like This II', she arranged brass statuettes of an ancient Anatolian god with a small body and large phallus in the shape of the crescent and star of the Turkish flag, surrounded by small brass representations of the three monkeys that 'see no evil, hear no evil, speak no evil'. The title – drawing attention to the way the regime referred to the Turkish Kurds as 'these people' or as 'mountain Turks' – and the eye-catching symbolism, indicting patriarchy, militarism and society's complicity, were not lost on the public or on the authorities. Tenger was prosecuted for 'insulting the Turkish flag', but, since there was no actual flag involved, the charge was altered to 'insulting the emblems of the Turkish nation' – a charge that carried the possibility of a term of imprisonment. The case lasted for about a year before the charges were dropped. Her lawyers had argued 'that star and crescent are present in many other nation's flags and the work is about women being oppressed by men universally'. However, even though the charges were dropped, Tenger was disconcerted to be told as late as 2007 that, if she tried to exhibit the work again at a show in Istanbul, she ran the risk of being prosecuted once more. As she says, 'because freedom of speech is still restricted, I simply don't show the piece in Turkey. Instead I talk about it in public lectures and show images of it and tell the audience that I don't/can't show the piece. Not a great situation but it saves me from headache'.[45]

In 1997, a similar fate awaited Halil Altindere whose exhibition entitled, appropriately enough, 'Dances with Taboos', led to a lawsuit. This was provoked by works that included a giant banknote for a million Turkish lira with the iconic portrait of Ataturk seeming to

FIGURE 15. Hale Tenger: '*I Know People Like This II*', Istanbul (1992) [© Hale Tenger. Photo courtesy of Hale Tenger]

cover his face in shame. It also included an installation of giant ID cards that served as a public indictment of the erosion and suppression by the state of a distinctive Kurdish identity. This was represented by his self-portrait that began conventionally enough in the first large blow-up but became increasingly obscure until, in the sixth and final card, it disappeared altogether. For Turkish viewers, the place of birth given on the card – Sürgücü, between Diyarbakir and Mardin – made it clear that he was born in the southeast of Turkey and that this was consequently referencing the predominantly Kurdish region of the country. Altindere's description of a police raid on his flat gives a flavour of the reactions to his work. As he told an interviewer in 2007, speaking of the police, '"Where are they", they said, "show us your artwork". When they entered my room, they saw my banknote-work with Atatürk covering his face. A young policeman, he said, "Chief, take a look at this", showing him the identity card, where I covered my face with my hands, my work on identity titled "Dance with the Taboos". "Where are you from", they asked, "are you ashamed of your Turkish identity?" I told them that it, too, was a work of art. "Get dressed, we're off", they replied' and took him off to the police station at Kadiköy.[46]

Despite the outrage this caused, and the lawsuit which it generated but which Altindere succeeded in defending himself against, he continued to develop an art that provoked and tried to make people think twice about an order that they thoughtlessly accepted. Possibly as a result of his experiences, as well as those of Tenger and others, Altindere curated the exhibition 'When Ideas Become Crime' in Istanbul in the autumn of 2010. Here he brought together nearly fifty Turkish artists whose work directed a critical gaze on much that was taken for granted in the Turkish political and social order: nationalism, gender politics, boundaries, militarism, as well as the very field of production and consumption of art itself.[47]

In fact, as an interview with Altindere indicated, part of the thinking behind such an exhibition was his criticism of and resistance to the infamous Article 301 of the Turkish penal code, introduced in 2005, which makes it a crime to 'publicly denigrate Turkishness' (amended in 2008 to 'the Turkish nation') or to 'publicly denigrate' the republic, the Grand National Assembly, the government, the judicial institutions of the state or the military and security organizations. At the same time, it states that 'expressions of thought intended to criticize shall not constitute a crime' (helping to suggest the title of the 2010 exhibition).[48] Writers and journalists were to feel the full force of this law. Although lawsuits were brought against some artists, this was relatively rare compared to the fate suffered by writers and editors who had the temerity to challenge state taboos by raising such issues as the Armenian massacres of 1915, the question of civil rights in the Kurdish regions or the conduct of the security forces. These were the public voices that the security arm of the state authorities found difficult to tolerate.

As far as the artists were concerned, their limited audience, the largely bourgeois milieu in which they operated, the sometimes allusive and even obscure nature of their works, as well as the changing political climate in Turkey meant that the authorities tended to be more relaxed when considering their output. This appeared to be the case, even when it displayed anger against the hegemony of state, national and religious authority. When this moved into a more public realm, targeting particular politicians, there was a sharp reaction. This was illustrated by the case of the cartoon in *Cumhüriyet* newspaper in 2004 that portrayed the Turkish prime minister, Recep Tayyip Erdogan, as a cat tangled up in a ball of wool, representing measures on religious education that he was trying to get through parliament. Erdogan sued the cartoonist, Musa Kart, for publicly humiliating him and won a very modest sum in damages. When the satirical magazine *Penguen* in protest published a cover in which the prime minister was portrayed as an array of different animals, he sued its editors as well, claiming 'mental anguish'. However, Erdogan's reaction was counterproductive. It gave the images greater publicity and did little for his reputation. In the event, the judge threw the case out of court.[49]

Lebanon

Many of the Turkish artists are concerned to resist both the heavy-handed behaviour of the state and the complacency of a society that they see as accepting of this kind of behaviour. By contrast, in Lebanon where the state is scarcely present, the art of resistance has targeted other forms of unequal power. These have included obvious political targets such as the forces that have repeatedly intervened in Lebanon – Israel, Syria, but also Iran and the United States, regarded by various sections of the Lebanese population as wanting to dominate the country. Of course, this has also reflected the internal divisions in Lebanese society. Resistance by some has been viewed as collaboration by others, often graphically displayed in Lebanese poster and street art.[50] However, there is a thread linking the works of a number of Lebanese artists where resistance is not set within a partisan framework. Rather, it has been an indictment of all those forces, Lebanese as well as foreign, that have used Lebanon as their battleground, regardless of the cost in Lebanese lives. It is in this sense an art of resistance against those who have made violence part of the everyday experience of the Lebanese for much of the past thirty years, particularly during the worst episodes of the civil war. It can be seen as a protest against a moral economy of violence, as well as against its political economy.

This is the sentiment captured in the work of Etel Adnan, dramatically portrayed in her art book 'Blessed Day', using the words of the poet Nelly Salameh Amri as the basis for a poignant indictment not simply of the violence but also of the social attitudes and norms that continue to fuel the ruthless inhumanity of civil conflict. Opening with the chilling words 'Today is a blessed day. It is a day of rest for the snipers...', the poem goes on to retell the story of Antigone who died 'due to her compassion for the dead not out of love for the living'. In the Greek myth, Antigone was killed because she had defied Creon, King of Thebes, by giving her dead brother an honourable burial, despite the stigma of treachery that attached to him.

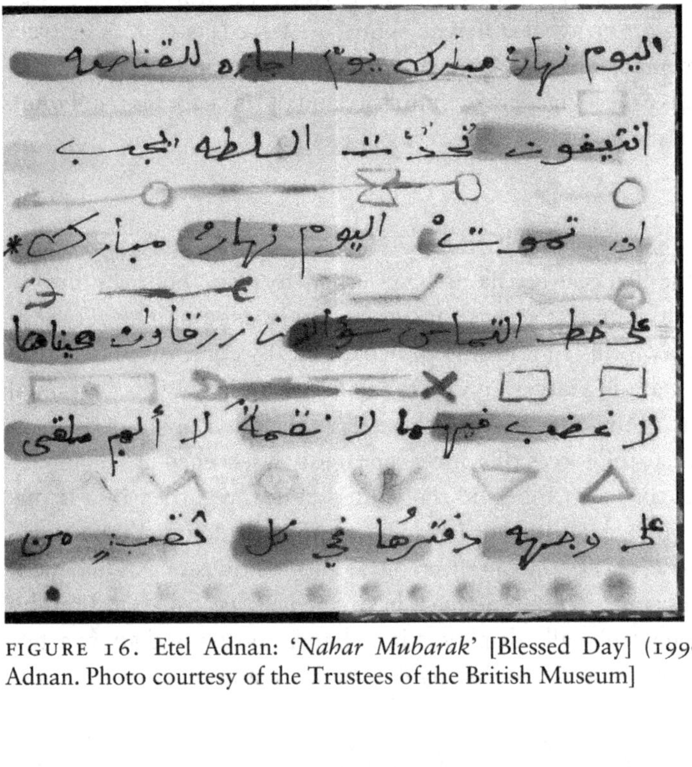

FIGURE 16. Etel Adnan: '*Nahar Mubarak*' [Blessed Day] (1990) [© Etel Adnan. Photo courtesy of the Trustees of the British Museum]

A similar although very differently conceived commentary on and protest against the violence to which the Lebanese have been subjected during the past decades is the work of Walid Raad. He produced an archive of the civil war through the writings of a fictional character, Dr. Fadl Fakhouri. One set of these files records all the colours and makes of the cars used as car bombs throughout the civil war, detailing the amount of explosive used, the numbers of killed and wounded and the damage done. Through this almost obsessive, meticulous recording of the bare facts, accompanied by pictures of cars taken from catalogues and advertisements, he succeeds in emphasizing the objective horror of those years. This is the everyday nightmare of the Lebanese, catalogued and recorded inescapably as a testimony to the violence they have inflicted on themselves and others have inflicted upon them.

This is not simply an indication of despair at the inhumanity of the conditions of the war, but also an implicit protest against a situation that was allowed to reach such a pitch of violence. That it might have benefited those who were in theory responsible for conducting the affairs of state, or at the very least charged with the protection of their communities, is well captured in the work of the Lebanese-American artist, John Jurayj. His gallery of thirty Lebanese, Israeli, Syrian, American, Libyan, Iraqi, Saudi and Palestinian leaders, in the work *Untitled Men (We could be heroes)*, is digitally printed in negative on vellum. The eyes of the portraits are burnt out, suggesting that they have looked upon – and presumably commanded – things too terrible to be borne. As Jurayj himself says, 'the eyes are burned in a uniform gesture

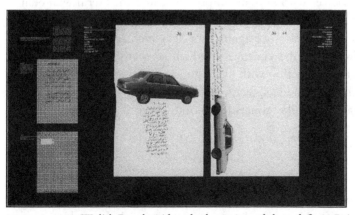

FIGURE 17. Walid Raad: *'Already been in a lake of fire'*, Beirut (2007) [© Walid Raad. Photo courtesy of the Trustees of the British Museum]

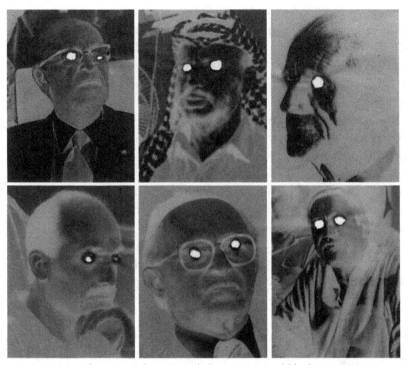

FIGURE 18. John Jurayj: from *Untitled Men (We could be heroes)* [Top row, L to R: Suleiman Franjieh; Yasser Arafat; Pierre Gemayel, Bottom row, L to R: Samir Geagea; Menachem Begin; Nabih Berri] (2007–2011) [© John Jurayj. Photos courtesy of John Jurayj]

across countries and interests, without bias. The burning of the eyes leaves the viewer with both an empty space and the literal wall behind the image'.[51] A work of this power is an indictment of an entire political class – an art of resistance against the very hierarchies that have used and profited from the violence in which so many were killed. When exhibited in conjunction with his haunting portraits of people killed in the war and of buildings, again burnt, holed and spotted with a substance that looks like congealed blood, there is little doubt of the message.

Iraq

As in Lebanon, so in Iraq – another country marked by war, invasion and civil strife. Here too artists have expressed themselves against the surrounding violence, mediating it through their art, but thereby heightening the effects of the horror. This is not a photographic record, but a graphic representation of violence in which the presence of the suffering individual is suggested, making the image more haunting than any literal representation could have done. Thus the Iraqi artist Walid Siti's book, *Dark Interludes*, seeks to come to terms with and to convey the terror of the fighting during the Iran–Iraq war (1980–8). In thirteen harshly contrasting black-and-white woodcuts, with accompanying text by Kanan Makiya, they throw into question 'those fictitious nationalist and religious goals of the 1980s, and whose cost is to this day still being paid for by the people of Iraq'. As Makiya says, 'There are no people in Dark Interludes: flags, crescents, broken monuments, sculpted heads fallen off their pedestals, sharp arches that cut and pierce and the dreadful all-too-familiar machinery of 20th-century warfare are the literal subject matter of these thirteen images'.[52] But they also represent, symbolically, the power and the violence that exacted such a terrible human toll and, when seen through the unflinching gaze of Siti, stripped of heroics or glory, they confront the viewer with a bold statement, defying those who would make war serve their political purposes.

A similar message is contained in the work of Salam Khedher, responding to the next war to overtake the people of Iraq in 1991, following upon the invasion and occupation of Kuwait in 1990 by the

FIGURE 19. Walid Siti: *'Moonlight'* from *Dark Interludes* (1988) [© Walid Sitti. Photo courtesy of the Trustees of the British Museum]

FIGURE 20. Salam Khedher '*Intahat al-harb*' [The war is over] (1992)
[© Salam Khedher. Photo courtesy of the Trustees of the British Museum]

Iraqi armed forces. These events gave rise to a series of seven prints that
again depict the desolation and cruelty of war, one of which he entitled –
ironically – 'The war is over'. Burning oil fires in the desert, a crashed
plane and crows pecking at the outstretched hand of a corpse show the
harsh aftermath of the fighting. As Khedher was to say of this picture, 'it
says that the war is continuously going on, whether in Halabja or in
another place in Iraq ... My prediction is the war will go on. It is a
negative conclusion, but it is cutting my heart and making my future a
grim one'.[53]

For Kareem Risan, the aftermath of that war was destroying the
people of Iraq, as he wanted to convey in his powerful and disturbing
book of paintings *Uranium Civilization* (2001).[54] It speaks of his anxiety not only about the effects of the war on Iraqi culture and society, but
more specifically about the danger that depleted uranium shells used by
American and British forces in southern Iraq represented for the health
of Iraqis across the south of the country. Dark and grim, shaded by red
and black, the work demands attention, engaging its audience and possibly, therefore, seeking to bring closer an international investigation
into the conditions that had led to such suffering.[55]

This was not to materialize before the people of Iraq were engulfed
by the next war, with all its attendant horrors both during the fighting

and in its aftermath. Echoing the Lebanese artists of an earlier period, although in his own particular style, Risan responded with complex and troubling books that were virtually installations, protesting against the everyday violence faced by Iraqis. Thus at the centre of the book entitled *Every Day* (2005) lie two pages that look distressingly like the aftermath of a car or suicide bomb, with tyre tracks, the impression of cast-off spectacles and a torn banknote impressed into a blood-red street.[56] Bombings of this kind and the pools of blood and a scattering of ordinary and pathetic possessions were to be common sights in the streets of Iraq during the years following the U.S.-led invasion of 2003. The helplessness of individuals and the knowledge that there were those who were profiting from this violence only intensified the alienation of many from what Iraq had become.

For Hanaa Malallah, one aspect of the horror of the war of 2003 was represented by the destruction and burning of many of Baghdad's libraries and archives. While the U.S. and allied forces of occupation watched and did nothing, not only government ministries but also many of Iraq's cultural institutions were looted and burned, including its national museum and its libraries. In a powerful statement of protest and loss, Malallah also created a book, charred and torn with scarcely recognizable words appearing through its blackened and defaced pages. Entitled *Conference of the Birds* after the classic poem

FIGURE 21. Hanaa Malallah: *Mantiq al-Tayr* [Conference of the Birds] (2007) [(© Hana Malallah. Photo courtesy of the Trustees of the British Museum]

by the twelfth-century poet Farid al-Din al-Attar, it represents the
desolation of Baghdad in the wake of the invasion and thus directly
gave the lie to the claims of the new military occupiers that they had
acted in the interests of the Iraqi people.

The violence of the U.S.-led military occupation of Iraq in 2003 and
of its aftermath in the subsequent years when 150,000 American,
British and other foreign forces seemed unable to bring an end to a
civil war, often driven by sectarian politics, provoked another kind of
resistance art. This was not the fruit of long, slow-burning rejection of
hegemonic power, but an impassioned attack on the forces that now
appeared to be devouring Iraq and its people. It was essentially an art
that resisted through stripping away some of the myths that had been
used to justify the establishment of a new order in Iraq. For some, such
as the exiled Iraqi artist, Wafaa Bilal, the principal audience was the
American public itself. He used a variety of techniques and installations
to bring home to an American audience both the forces at work in the
war and the price that ordinary Iraqis were paying for this. Thus,
already in 1999, in the wake the first Gulf War and the periodic bombardment of Iraq in the decade that followed, particularly the attack on
Baghdad in December 1998, he had created a series of striking installations. In one of these, the burnt figure of a mother holds out her child, in
another a coffin lies within a sacred space reminiscent of a jail and from
the coffin comes the cry of a child, while in another the well-suited figure
of a wild boar sits amidst sand and oil fields guffawing at videos of
Baghdad's destruction.[57] These prescient images of suffering, of power
and of the ruthlessness with which the people of Iraq would be treated
were accompanied by a video playing a soundtrack of official U.S.
government justifications for the attack on Baghdad while showing
some of the destruction it had caused.

It was the invasion and occupation of Iraq in 2003 which impelled
Bilal in 2007 to mount even more dramatic installations, with one
work – *Domestic Tension* – combining the technology of videogaming,
interactive programming and performance art. Originally entitled
Shoot an Iraqi, the performance involved Bilal himself. He shut himself
in a room for a month, with cameras watching his every move, allowing
people to interact with him by webcam through conversations or, more
controversially, by shooting him with a paintball gun attached to the
camera. It was informed by his own personal sorrow at the death of his
younger brother in Najaf, killed by a random piece of flying shrapnel,
but also by his awareness that airborne drones operated by U.S. military

personnel based thousands of miles away in Nevada could fire missiles that would kill people in Iraq. Above all, it was meant to bring home to Americans the violence of a war that could be portrayed on television as a virtual war in cyberspace but which had real effects, killing Iraqis. Whether this was quite the message that got through to the multi-national audience that took part in this online performance remains a moot point. At one stage, some 40,000 paintballs were being fired at him every day, and by the end of the month, it was estimated that about 60,000 people across the globe had participated. From the accompanying blog, it seemed that many were doing so because they admired the technology or because they were hostile to what they saw as his anti-war message.[58]

Iran

Iranian artists had also responded to the years of war undergone by their country, directly opposing their views of violence and pain to the heroic style of the posters produced by the Iranian government's licensed artists. In this sense, their visions were analogous to the responses of their counterparts in Iraq. The grim paintings by Khosrow Hassanzadeh of shrouded corpses, based as they were on his own experiences as a teenage soldier in the Iran–Iraq war, have much in common with others who have wanted to debunk the heroism and glorification of war. Nevertheless, for the Iranian authorities, this was far from troubling. On the contrary, such images conformed to official representations of the martyrdom encouraged within the framework of the 'imposed war' as it was officially labelled. Thus the emphasis on death, self-sacrifice and the suffering caused by war fitted well into the narrative developed by the Iranian government itself, even if the overall effect of such paintings was hardly to encourage thoughts of paradise.[59]

More relevant to the theme of an art of resistance has been the focus on women and gender difference in the work of a number of Iranian artists. Key symbolic fields for the government of the Islamic Republic of Iran were women's bodies. The 1979 constitution stipulated the legal requirements for women's clothing, enabling the regulations that have since become the norm for the policing of women's behaviour and their dress in public. So central have these preoccupations become to the government of Iran that the enforcement of these regulations, or their relaxation, have been used as barometers of the political complexion of the government of the day. This has served to draw attention to the

FIGURE 22. Khosrow Hassanzadeh: from 'War' (1998) [© Khosrow Hassanzadeh. Photo courtesy of Khosrow Hassanzadeh]

ways in which women are categorized and gender differences maintained. Of course, underlying this state of affairs are the legal and political frameworks that govern the rights of women, relating to personal status, autonomy and equality of opportunity.

In many respects, the visibility of women and the governing of their bodies in public space have become measures of the authority of the Islamic republic itself for the Iranian authorities. It is not surprising, therefore, that this has become a contested terrain in daily life, open to a variety of ingenious forms of everyday resistance by women challenging state dictation. It has also invited symbolic challenges in a developing art of resistance. Some of this is produced within Iran, although under difficult circumstances for most of the years that have followed the establishment of the Islamic republic. Much is also produced outside the country by exiles whose work is nevertheless transmitted back into Iran itself, largely by electronic means.

One of the more prominent Iranian women artists (living in the United States since the revolution), Shirin Neshat, has become known for her powerful if ambiguous portrayals of women dressed in full chador and thus impeccably conforming to the body codes of the Islamic republic. Yet they are also subverted by various techniques. As she said of her *Women of Allah* series, 'We are confronted with threatening images of women embracing the gun, yet there is something terribly submissive, erotic and sensual about the female bodies and gazes'. Sometimes the subversion of the image of the 'Muslim woman' is achieved through the calligraphic phrases inscribed on their bodies, suggesting that they have become vehicles for text but not necessarily of the kind sanctioned by the ruling religious authorities of Iran – as in the use of a poem by the Iranian feminist Forough Farokhzad on the eyeball of the subject in the work *Offered Eyes*. In doing so, Neshat is defying both the imposed 'type' required by the Islamic Republic and the stereotype of veiled Muslim women so prevalent in the West.[60]

For Farkhondeh Shahroudi, another Iranian artist living in exile, the focus on women's bodies and their dress has taken the form of ironic commentary through stitched work, either in books or as articles of clothing. Her work *Gloves* displays a pair of the black gloves that are often encouraged by a strict reading of the requirements of 'Islamic dress' for women in Iran, stitched together at the fingers so that they become useless or act like handcuffs – and the stitching, in green thread, takes the form of calligraphic writing, too dense and tangled to read. Nevertheless, as with the books she has stitched and painted, they leave no doubt about the power of the text to shape women's public being and to constrain her behaviour. By drawing attention to the limitations visually and powerfully, she is also making a statement of protest and resistance.[61]

It is not only women artists who have responded ironically and defiantly to the state's attempt rigorously to maintain gender difference through its close control of women's bodies and their dress. The Iranian artist Ramin Haerizadeh has also used women's dress and the role of women in the public sphere in Iran as a prominent theme in his work. His strategy for subverting the official position, however, has been to insert himself into the pictures, allowing his bearded face to peer out of the headscarves and chadors that are used to signal officially sanctioned gender difference. For good measure, in his work *Bad Hejab*, he has also placed his face beneath the peaked hat of a policeman, in street scenes where women are being reprimanded or apprehended for failing to

FIGURE 23. Ramin Haerizadeh: *Bad Hejab* (1) (2008) [© Ramin Haerizadeh. Photo courtesy of Gallery Isabelle van den Eynde, Dubai and Ramin Haerizadeh]

abide by the stricter codes of 'Islamic dress'. The mixing up of genders through the manipulation of dress and dress codes has a comic effect, but it also serves to underline the arbitrary nature of any such regulations – a defiant act of resistance when the government claims that such rules are sanctioned by divine authority. This blurring of the lines of difference between genders was reinforced in the recent work *Men of Allah* (2008) in which it becomes difficult to disentangle the fleshy show of male and female bodies, complicated as ever by the appearance of his own bearded face attached to apparently female bodily forms.[62]

In a development that may well have gratified Haerizadeh and which certainly drew attention in a remarkable way to the very points he was seeking to make in his art, the protests of 2009 threw up a striking series of representations of dress and gender in Iran. The state authorities tried to use women's dress to ridicule and humiliate one of the leaders of the student protests, Majid Tavakoli, who had been arrested during a demonstration and sit-in at Tehran's Amirkabir University in December 2009. Not long after his arrest, official news websites put up pictures of him dressed in a chador, accompanied by a story that he had tried to escape undetected from the campus by wearing women's clothes. This was denied by those who had witnessed his arrest. Instead, it appears

FIGURE 24. Ramin Haerizadeh: *Bad Hejab* (2) (2008) [© Ramin Haerizadeh. Photo courtesy of Gallery Isabelle van den Eynde, Dubai and Ramin Haerizadeh]

to have been a ploy by the security forces to ridicule and humiliate him in front of his large student following. If this was the case, the plan backfired spectacularly. Within a matter of hours, Tavakoli's supporters filled Internet sites with pictures of Supreme Leader Ayatollah Ali Khamenei and of President Ahmadinejad photoshopped to appear dressed in the same clothes.[63]

Encouraged by this, the protesters went further and demonstrated both their solidarity with Tavakoli, as well as their contempt for those who would use women's dress to signify humiliation. Opening up a website on Iranian.com, they invited men to post pictures of themselves wearing varieties of headscarf and chador prescribed for women in the Islamic republic.[64] The response was overwhelming, turning a strategy of repression into an act of resistance through the medium of art and gave rise to an extraordinary Youtube performance entitled 'We are all Majid'. To a stirring musical accompaniment, the film focused in on hundreds of images of men dressed in various kinds of head and face covering, some traditional and others imaginatively improvised.[65]

THE INTERNET AND THE ART OF RESISTANCE

The struggle in Iran draws attention to another site of public display that generates its own conventions and aesthetics. This is the digital world of online expressions of resistance to various forms of power across the Middle East. Through the versatility and immediacy of digital photography, the Internet provides striking resources that draw on already familiar techniques of Internet advertising, transmitting the image with the message in a combination of picture, logo, printed word and sound. Geared by its very nature to those with access to computers and to an audience that crosses national boundaries, it has often been used by those who believe they are resisting more than simply a local hegemony or who are trying to enlist international support for their struggle. This, in turn, has often determined the range of symbols, as well as the format and the aesthetic used to convey messages of defiance, resistance and solidarity.

Thus the English language Palestinian solidarity site, The Electronic Intifada (EI),[66] which carries news items, commentary and a range of information about occupied Palestine, made an arresting photograph by the Dutch photographer, Johannes Abeling, one of its key symbolic images. Featuring graffiti on a wall in Gaza, it also became the image that EI used on its products, such as T-shirts and mousepads in its online shop. Given the nature of its intended audience in the United States and Western Europe, it is scarcely surprising that this globalization of graffiti from Gaza features words written in English.

Echoing the use of Palestinian Arabic graffiti in the work of Laila Shawa, this image is put to much the same use, amplifying the original act of defiance and resistance that led to these words being written on a wall and ensuring their visibility in a vastly expanded if diffuse public space.

FIGURE 25. Johannes Abeling: *Khan Yunis, Gaza Strip* (2005) [© Johannes Abeling. Photo courtesy of Johannes Abeling]

The same is true of a number of websites that publicize and support Palestinian rights against Israeli occupation and in the face of international indifference, such as the largely U.S.-based *Al-Awda*, representing the Palestine Right to Return Coalition.[67] Videoclips, posters, cards, a range of products and images use the various symbolic or documentary representations of Palestinian history and identity to mobilize international support. Similarly, the site Liberation Graphics, through its online collection of posters on behalf of Palestine and the Palestinians, is taking the art of the poster from the local and limited public space in Palestine to the vast public space that is the World Wide Web.[68]

The same phenomenon was visible after the invasion and occupation of Iraq in 2003. A number of websites appeared (and disappeared) that graphically depicted the many facets of Iraqi resistance to foreign occupation. Some tried to uphold the image and memory of Saddam Hussein and the overthrown Ba`thist regime, whilst others signalled their presence with titles and graphics that referred to the Islamic heritage and future of Iraq. Some of the sites mixed Iraqi nationalist and Islamic slogans and images, using both Arabic and English to establish themselves as representatives of resistance within the country, in the eyes of the foreign occupiers and across the Arabic and English speaking worlds. As well as bringing the printed and sometimes audio messages of resistance activities in Iraq to the attention of a wider world, they also developed the graphics of resistance. They did this through photo galleries, posters and logos, and used videoclips to capture moments when U.S. or other forces were under fire, in attacks claimed by the posting organization.[69] By and large, they drew upon and helped to reinforce the common idioms of a politics of defiance and resistance, derived from the poster art of earlier generations and other struggles, both in the Middle East and elsewhere.

However, in the context of the Iraqi resistance, another kind of aesthetic was soon to appear. This was a mixture of the graphic representation of defiance, performance art and the theatre of cruelty. In well-publicized videoclips that achieved worldwide notoriety, and in screen-grabs that were seen on a large number of websites, Iraqi resistance organizations' practice of filming themselves with their hostages became a standard feature of the art of resistance in Iraq. The presentation seemed to follow very similar lines, even if the group holding the hostage differed: in front of a black banner blazoning the Muslim profession of faith, the hostage would be kneeling, blindfolded before a line of masked, black-clothed armed men. In some cases, the murder of a hostage was also filmed in the same setting, driving home the ruthlessness and ferocity of the resistance in a way that no mere poster or painted representation could hope to do.[70]

In this performance, Iraqi resistance groups were following the example of the Pakistani group, the National Movement for the Restoration of Pakistani sovereignty, which had abducted and murdered the American journalist Daniel Pearl in Karachi in 2002, later releasing a film of his murder and decapitation, accompanied by text associating him not only with the U.S. government but also with Israel. This in turn had been influenced by the emerging genre of self-presentation that accompanied the video recordings that had been used so powerfully by numerous suicide bombers in Palestine. Although obviously testifying to individual acts of violence that could be portrayed in the framework of resistance, they shared a common grammar, intended to indicate both the inspiration and the intention of the individual, as well as the social and political forces that this individual represented.

So powerful had these images become that they were taken up by others, further afield, who tried to emulate the violence and determination that they witnessed in the Middle East. The self-representation of radical Islamist suicide bombers and those who admired the spirit of resistance they were believed to embody created a certain style that gave rise to a recognizable aesthetic of distinctively 'Islamic resistance'. This can be seen, for instance, in Abu Musab al-Zarqawi's video address in 2004, but also in the video made by Mohammed Sidique Khan, one of the men who blew themselves up in the London underground system in July 2005. It can also be seen in the video made by Ahmed Abdulla Ali, one of the men convicted in the UK for conspiring to blow up airliners in the summer of 2006, as well as in one transmitted by al-Qaida in the Arabian Peninsula from its base in Yemen in 2009. All of them conform to a very similar pattern, in the graphics, the dress and posture of the participants and the settings they have chosen.[71]

In this sense, a recognizable art of resistance was emerging, geared to the digital age in which it was produced. As with the common stock of images used in the production of political posters, with their own idiom and symbolic graphics of popular resistance, it become equally easy to recognize these productions by organizations that wanted to present themselves as champions of Islamic resistance against infidel world powers. They too borrowed from the earlier repertoire of nationalist iconography. Although they obviously made use of distinctive Islamic slogans and banners, they tended to adopt similar ways of signalling authenticity and resolve, using modes of dress, background and often weapons to deliver their messages and make their demands.

Indeed, it was a style that lent itself to caricature, so recognizable did it become. As in the case of resistance to the violent predicament of many in the region seen in the works of Iraqi and Lebanese artists, 'Islamic resistance' became itself the target of an art of resistance. For Wafaa Bilal, the situation in which the world was caught between videogames that, on the one hand, urged players to join the 'Quest for Saddam' and, on the other, encouraged – although one presumes a different set of players – to experience the 'The Quest for Bush – the Night of Bush Capturing' could not go without comment.

Accordingly, in 2008, he produced an art installation as a videogame: 'Virtual Jihadi'. Its graphics paralleled closely, but in a deliberately exaggerated way, the art of 'Islamic authenticity' adopted by so many Islamist resistance groups. He also placed his own face in the outfit of the suicide bomber whose mission in the game is to kill President Bush. Bilal had been appalled by the way in which the extremism and violence that had sucked in and destroyed the defenceless in real life were now being treated by videogamers as material for a new and exciting game in the fantastic space of virtual reality. He wanted to draw attention to the fact that although 'Al Qaeda's game where Bush is hunted down and killed generated much international outrage, the U.S. Army's own free on-line game is equal to the *Night of Bush Capturing* in its propaganda motives ... I want to show how civilians in war zones find themselves switching allegiances as a means of self-preservation as the balance of power shifts. Their cities are turned into battlegrounds, and survival is often a matter of obeying the power that exists at any given time regardless of any ideology ... It's the fundamentalists – Islamic and evangelical – who fuel this violence, and force civilians to ally with them in order to survive'.[72] Clearly not everyone got the message. Initially at least, his attempts to show the installation in various American institutions were frustrated when university administrators or city authorities closed it down, perversely claiming to see in it an incitement to terrorism.

THE POWER OF ART

Censorship is the tribute that ruling authorities pay to the unsettling power of art. Similarly, the resources and the effort that governments, whether autocratic, oligarchic or democratic, put into the patronage of visual arts, particularly those that have a public presence, testify to the belief that art has a unique power to move and to persuade. The more plural the vision of power, the more diverse the artistic forms. Even the expression of artistic diversity itself projects a particular image that is meant to have an effect on those who behold it. By the same token, the more restricted the circles of power, the more artistic expression will be expected to conform to standards set and monitored by the political authorities. Yet there will be the same assumption that the symbolic order will not only reflect but also help to support the order of power.

When art is used against the established order, in symbolic reversals that form part of a project of resistance, it shows all the intimate familiarity with power that has been apparent in other spheres. Thus, quite apart from the ironic and comic satires upon the official face of power, as well as its defacement, there is the subversion of the very images that the rulers have tried to project as evidence and instrument of their dominion. At the same time, the everyday can be transformed into something strange and disconcerting, jolting people's acceptance of the world 'the way it is' and possibly causing them to see it, and the power relations that are interwoven in and sustained by it, in a new and different light. As the examples from the Middle East have shown, these acts of artistic intervention have three powerful links to a politics of resistance.

In the first place, the act of producing art, whether in the form of posters, graffiti or publicly accessible artistic events, has been a power-ful way of signalling presence. An enraged mass public, an increasingly self-conscious and restive ethnic or national movement, a revolutionary organization – all have used these means to declare their opposition, their presence and their determination in the face of established power. It was this spirit that the Egyptian artist, Ganzeer, wanted to mobilize when he called for a 'Mad Graffiti Week' in January 2012. It was intended that 'the streets of Egypt will see an explosion of anti-military street art'. Exasperated by the continuing rule of the SCAF and its repressive instincts, he and others proclaimed that 'our only hope right now is to destroy the military council using the weapon of art'.[73] This is a call that has been echoed by other Egyptian artists, such as Keizer, Sad Panda, KIM, Husny and Ammar Abo Bakr, whose paint-ings, along with those of Ganzeer, have featured so strikingly in Egypt's public spaces since January 2011. Reflecting the continuing political struggles in the country, and the mistrust of the military and of the *fulul* [remnants of the old regime], their works have been a dramatic part of the public debate about Egypt's future.

Graffiti, as well as posters, have been ways of reclaiming public space, not with the physical mass of bodies seen in the politics of demonstration but with the symbolic capture of the walls and surfaces of city streets. The act itself is an act of defiance against authorities that want to assert their own unchallenged control of such spaces, forcing those who challenge that control to risk paying with their lives or with their freedom. The messages conveyed by the writing on the wall, by the images and symbols, signal alternative sources of authority, disrespect for established power and, implicitly, its loss of control. By standing out for all to see, it shows the limits of state capacity and suggests the existence of a mass public that rejects the authority of those in power.

In this respect, such an art of resistance can also help to create or sustain collective solidarities, colluding against the powers that be and potentially forming the core of a dissenting public. This may be through a growing sense of civic rights and collective action aimed at reclaiming those rights. Or it may be in relation to any kind of grouping – ethnic, national, sectarian or class- or gender-based – that is asserting itself collectively to contest its status. As with music, songs and literature in general, so the impact of the visual arts may be to create or foster solidarities. Posters and graffiti can resonate with people's experiences, epitomizing in visual images or memorable phrases a sense of shared experience. In fact, they can create a powerful, shared vocabulary, a visual idiom that becomes an accepted way of expressing both identity and political determination. Furthermore, in the act of reading, interpreting and commenting, the very encounter with art can foster such solidarities. In this respect, although less publicly accessible or visible than political posters, the visual arts more generally can generate a sense of identity by creating the visual reference points for shared historical memories.

The part played by artistic representation in all its forms constitutes the third important link with a politics of resistance. As with the writing and rewriting of history, so the visual arts can harness the power of the aesthetic to the persuasive force of a particular story. In the case of the visual arts, the 'summing up' of a narrative of identity and power, as well as the representation of key moments, can impress themselves indelibly upon the eye. They can thus form part of collective memory and imagination, displacing or overriding thousands of individual memories to stand as the epitome or summation of historical experience. Established power has always used this technique. It has deployed film, the plastic arts and other means to create a common, mutually reinforcing imagery that will shape the present and the future, convincing people that this 'was the way it was'. The countervailing power of resistance follows the same path. As with historical narratives written against the grain of power, so too can the power of art express a story suppressed and so give voice to the voiceless.

The art of resistance may not in itself change the balance of power, but it is a factor that shapes the environment in which attitudes to power are formed. It can counter the 'official version' that may have become part of an unthought 'common sense' that persuaded people to accept the status quo. By making people look at power sideways, it can shake the certainties that may have allowed those who rule to get away with it for so long. Art opens up a space for the possibility of debate and critical engagement with power. In doing so, it contributes to the creation of a politics that calls power to account to a public that it may have successfully ignored up to that point. Regardless of the forms and representations – and these may be various, discordant and by no means tied to a single political project – the very fact of their expression can both outline the contours of resistance and unsettle the arrogant complacency of established power. Whether the regime will be successfully undermined or not will depend upon an array of other factors and the force they can bring to bear, but within it all, the imaginative and aesthetic power of art will have made a contribution.

Conclusion

Completing the manuscript of this book during the year 2011 was a strange and sobering experience. The dramatic events that began in Tunisia, tearing across North Africa and the Middle East, 'from the ocean to the Gulf', as the old Arab nationalist slogan had it, provided an exhilarating but also moving and sometimes desperately sad accompaniment. Writing about resistance, its many forms and its historical as well as contemporary manifestations is one thing. But watching it daily in action as people rise up against long-established systems of repression that have become complacent in their contempt and cruelty has been something very different. It has also given the generic term 'resistance' a human face, linked to tales of exceptional courage and resilience. The stories of apparently ordinary people become extraordinary through their behaviour under pressure and in the midst of exceptional events. Across the region, men and women have risked everything to stand up and to reclaim long-denied rights as human beings and as citizens. Many have paid for this with their lives.

These events have also encouraged reflection on some of the major questions raised by this book and its thematic treatment of the subject. In reality, in any given country, these themes come together, reinforcing each other and shaping the resistance movement at a particular moment in history. Whether in Tunisia, Libya, Bahrain, Syria, Egypt or Palestine, those who defied the status quo have needed to deal with the problem of armed force, have explored the possibilities of collective civil action, have mobilized labour and have recaptured the space where men and women can act in common as citizens – and all of this at the same time. In doing so, they have been drawing on the narrative resources of resistance. Through histories, imaginings and identities, as well as through artistic and symbolic representations that both epitomize and help to build a changing consciousness, they have drawn upon memories and have fostered an awareness that things need not be like this – they can and must be otherwise.

It is this feeling of compulsion to stand up against the established order that gives resistance its political drive. Whether energies are devoted to changing the way people look at power or to collective organization for defence or indeed to direct confrontation, a politics of resistance is contesting the many forms of domination that maintain and justify a status quo. This goes to the heart of the imaginative project of power, its portrayal of itself, as well as challenging the more directly material and coercive instruments used to sustain it. In doing so, successful resistance not only shatters the illusion of authority that allows power to reproduce itself, it can also provoke a response that adds to its own unravelling, in which those in command of coercive force become unwitting collaborators in the dismantling of their own authority.

A vivid, individual example of this was presented in the autumn of 2011 when the attorney general of Hama province in Syria, Adnan Bakkour, publicly resigned his post and sided with the growing opposition to the regime of President Bashar al-Asad. Having witnessed the security forces' torture and execution of dozens of protestors during the largely peaceful demonstrations of the preceding months, he finally reached breaking point in September and denounced the regime. The regime's immediate response was ferocious. They sent armed forces and militias to hunt him down, killing several of his associates in the process but failing to silence or catch him. The violence of the reaction was testimony to growing concern that the contagion of dissent and resistance was now affecting senior levels of the regime's servants.[1]

Whether in the events of 2011 or in the long histories of resistance movements, successful and unsuccessful, this intimacy between established power and those who resist has been striking. The peoples of the Middle East have had a long and bitter experience of rule imposed by force of arms and have often resisted accordingly. The modern state, first in the guise of European imperial ventures and then as a form of power enthusiastically taken up by nationalists, socialists, Islamists and others across the Middle East, was resisted with varying degrees of success. The violence of the initial enterprise met armed resistance that defied but was unable to match the massive resources at the disposal of the industrial, organizational and military power that stood behind this 'violent modernity', in the words of Abdelmajid Hannoum.[2] Nevertheless, it was with the gradual encroachment of modern state power, the practices it enforced, the myths it created, the architecture of its public face and the conformity it demanded that resistance began to follow the lines that the state had itself established. Categories that lay at the heart of the new order – citizen, nation, public – were taken up and used to reinforce obedience, but were at the same time to become the basis for alternative readings, subversive of the existing order. These drew both upon the multiple meanings inherent in these terms and practices, as well as on the memories and narratives of other ways of ordering power. As the Algerian and other examples showed, this was to be the undoing of colonialism and the making of national self-determination.

For those who inherited the colonial state and then proceeded to claim the exclusive right to rule it, the very languages and practices of power that gave them dominion were eventually turned against them. Idioms that had been used to buttress the power of a restrictive elite were taken up by their opponents and given a very different significance, whilst retaining their potency. Nowhere was this more visible than in the extraordinary trajectory of the speech made by Mu`ammar Qadhafi in February 2011. It was then that he had tried to recapture the revolutionary spirit of his early years by using the slogans that his people had heard so often about power and the revolutionary masses. Faced by a rising tide of opposition and an uprising in the east of the country that threatened to cut Libya in two, he denounced the 'vermin' of the resistance and called on his countrymen to 'march to purge Libya, inch by inch, house by house, alley by alley [*zanga li-zanga*]'.[3] The video of the speech was taken up by an Israeli musician, Noy Alooshe, who then created a remix entitled '*Zenga, zenga*' set to hip hop. The remix went viral on the Internet, achieving more than 2.5 million viewers in the first week of its release. It spread rapidly throughout the Arab world and was adopted by the Libyan resistance not only for the catchiness of its tune, but also for the delicious irony of the fact that Qadhafi and his revolutionary slogans – 'The Libyan people and the popular revolution will control Libya' – appeared to be endorsing the very uprising that was aiming to unseat him.[4]

Resistance has made itself felt not only by subverting the language and the myths propagated by state power. In other ways too, resistance has emerged from and within the organization of power, in the Middle East, as elsewhere in the world, intertwining itself with the very systems of power, the better to subvert them. In this respect, the elaborate systems of the bureaucratic state may be the mechanisms for enforcing a conformity that in time becomes an unthought habit. Reaching out to all sectors of the population, entangling them in the procedures that amplify the power of the centre, they are part of the capillary power of the modern state, disciplining their subjects' bodies and shaping their imaginations. However, they can also be prime sites of resistance. This may be a daily occurrence that shows itself through the quiet acts of resistance, go-slows, disrespect and pilfering so well described by James Scott in the lives of peasants in Southeast Asia. It may be more systematic, in the sense of the gradual infiltration of the bureaucracy by alternative associations and networks, effectively negating the hierarchy of bureaucratic command by superimposing a different map of power and status. When this comes within the orbit of a directing central force, it can form the basis of the 'shadow state' that has been so integral to many systems of power.[5]

Everyday resistance of this kind might not have an explicitly political aim, other than the pursuit of individual and sometimes family or clan advantage. However, when linked to a larger movement of political protest and upheaval, these same techniques and sites can give a resistance project intimate access to the very sinews of power. In the Middle East, this has been used effectively and even devastatingly. Such actions have included the strikes and go-slows of Palestinian Arab civil servants in the administration of Mandate Palestine in the 1930s, the participation of the bureaucrats in Iran's finance sector that contributed to the downfall of the Shah in 1978–9, recent developments in Egypt, such as the land tax collectors' prolonged strike in 2008 and the civil service strikes that accelerated the departure of President Mubarak in February 2011.

There is an added intimacy in the relationship between state power and resistance, frequently embedded in the very hierarchy of power itself. All forms of power are based on exclusions and inclusions of different categories of people, defined in terms of categorical rights of access to representation, justice and resources. The more consensual the pattern of rights, the more chance there is of debate to extend them and redress to adjust them. Where such debate and adjustment are prevented, often through the consensus of a majority, sometimes through a dominant 'common sense', a movement of protest and resistance is likely to emerge. This was the case with the prolonged campaign for women's suffrage in the early decades of the twentieth centuries in Europe and North America. It also gave rise to civil rights movements in the United States in the 1950s and 1960s and in Northern Ireland in the late 1960s. The mobilization of those who had been excluded through the tyranny and prejudice of the majority in these last two cases, in countries that portrayed themselves as advanced democracies, signalled the presence of excluded minorities that were now reclaiming their rights to equality as citizens. They took the public legitimating language of authority and insisted that it be taken seriously, thereby disrupting the complacent 'common sense' of racial and sectarian discrimination.

The same has been the case in the Middle East. Countless protest and resistance movements have been driven by a determination to assert the rights of the excluded. They have directly challenged the very systems of power that have so ruthlessly denied to whole categories of their subjects some of the most fundamental rights, as citizens and as human beings. In doing so, those who have benefited from such a system of exclusion and denial have not only provoked the anger of thousands, but have created the very categories that have formed the basis of collective organization, both actually and rhetorically. In the 1970s, the call for the restoration of the rights of the dispossessed [*al-mustada`afin* – literally, 'those deemed weak'] in Lebanon and Iran was a potent rallying cry. It helped to define and to mobilize the movement led by Ayatollah Musa al-Sadr in Lebanon who sought redress for the largely ignored and poor of the Shi`a community. In Iran, it became one of the main aims of the revolution, articulated both by Ayatollah Khomeini and by the secular resistance movements.[6]

Similarly, it can be argued that one of the contributing factors in the resurgence of Palestinian resistance after 1948 was a growing awareness amongst the scattered Palestinians that wherever they were, they were discriminated against and excluded *as* Palestinians, whether subject to Israeli control or to that of the surrounding Arab states. The same applies to the uprisings of 2011. Identical slogans of defiance rang out across the Arab world, voiced by hundreds of thousands in different countries miles apart who nevertheless shared a common experience of subjection to regimes contemptuous of their rights and often violent in the exercise of power. In this sense, therefore, the very systems of exclusion through which power operates become the mechanisms for the mobilization of resistance.

As the women's suffrage movement of the early twentieth century demonstrated, this operates also in the realm of gendered power. In this respect, however, women's continuing struggle against discrimination and subordination, even in countries where the battle for formal civic rights has been won, has been a good illustration of the multilayered nature of power itself. Not simply in the Middle East but also globally, the hierarchies, exclusions and differential rights and entitlements attached to constructions of gender have been at the heart of the way power has been experienced by millions. This may be integral to the power of the state, but it can equally be simply encouraged by those in authority or even merely ignored and thus allowed to flourish. The effects, however, can be individually and collectively devastating.

For this very reason, resistance will follow and target the systems of power – familial, social or state-sponsored – that maintain an order resting on these categorical exclusions. In doing so, it will not be generated by the mere fact of discrimination and oppression but by a growing awareness amongst women, however dispersed they may be, that they have a common cause. It is on this basis that a sense of collective political consciousness is created, in opposition to and resisting entrenched attitudes amongst women and men concerning rights and entitlements. As the examples from Morocco and Iran have shown, this continues to be a prolonged struggle, fought out by individuals and by collective bodies in the many sites where gendered power holds sway. In all these arenas of resistance, the challenge has been to persuade women and men that things can be otherwise and that the diminution of the rights of some can diminish the rights of all.

It is in this connection that symbolic, artistic, narrative and imaginative forms of resistance can exercise such power against an accepted yet unequal order. The difficulty of measuring their effects in any positivist sense, the problems of correlating their production with observable and dramatic shifts in power and, sometimes, the over-inflated claims of artists themselves have often combined to generate scepticism about this realm of activity. Yet it is here that the idea of a different reality, of an alternative ordering of things, can take root. This can be of immense power in two distinct ways. First of all, whatever the medium, artistic expression can give people a language that captures a sense of themselves – as a community, as citizens, as a class or gender grouping – and that voices their interests and concerns. Second, it can lead people, through drama, shock, parody and all the many techniques of artistic and narrative engagement, to look again at the accepted stories of power and to question their own habitual obedience. This does not happen in a blinding moment, striking and inspiring as art can be. More importantly, it lays the groundwork for different ways of looking at power, preparing through narrative and the imagination the resistance that may in the future materialize to shake a complacent order. In combination with other developments that also encourage defiance, it can epitomize what the struggle is about, representing therefore an alternative understanding of power.

This is a key to its importance in a politics of resistance. The narrative and artistic imagination has not only a catalytic effect. It also has the capacity, precisely through its ability to 'take people out of themselves' and to imagine power differently, to encourage people to think about power outside the categories used by an established order. This can be crucially important for opening up a space that may help to prevent resistance from becoming so like the power with which it is intimately entwined that it ends up reproducing many of its most oppressive features. Such an outcome has been a common enough occurrence through history in the Middle East and elsewhere. It has been a particularly marked feature of the aftermath of successful armed resistance.

Here the logic of clandestine organization, the habits of command and the practice of violence can lead to outcomes that are as authoritarian and as exclusionary as the order that has been displaced, whatever the initial hopes may have been. In these circumstances, the intimate familiarity with the techniques of established power, visible in successful resistance, may serve to shape the movement itself, influencing its priorities as well as its methods. Equally, the communicative power of violence can make all other languages seem redundant, as Fadhil al-Jamali, a former prime minister of Iraq, remarked at his trial before the 'People's Court' in 1958. Citing the lines of the ninth-century Abbasid poet, Abu Tammam – 'The sword is a more trustworthy form of communication than books; in its cutting edge lies the boundary between seriousness and frivolity' – he was accurately predicting the course the Iraqi revolution would take, as military force became the prime instrument of power.[7]

The drama and the speed of events across the Middle East in 2011 caused participants and observers alike to reflect upon the inherent dangers of success. In the aftermath of the overthrow of a president, the dismantling of a regime or the winning of concessions from those in power, it is important to think about the consequences, the paths not taken and the choices ahead. In this respect, there has been a tendency in much of the coverage to swing between hope and despair: hope that resistance creates a new beginning, ushering in a different, more humane dispensation of power; despair that the apparent victories of the resistance have only dislodged a small fraction of the powerful and left unaffected the habits of power, leading the victors to become co-opted into a system that does not differ substantially from its predecessor. Underlying this are general attitudes that tend, on the one hand, to romanticize resistance, wherever and however it shows itself, as well as those that see any form of resistance as incapable of escaping the hard logic of coercive state power that success may bring under its control.

Outcomes are, of course, always uncertain, but it is in the understanding of a movement of resistance that it differs from mere opposition or criticism by potentially, at least, opening up different fields of power and alternative ways of imagining power. It is for this reason that new narratives, forms of expression and imaginative departures can play such a key role. It is not that they can immunize people against the harsh binaries of coercive power. However, they can both cause people to think of power differently and serve as a reminder of the alternative visions that informed and generated resistance in the first place. Whether through fiction, the telling of history or artistic representation, the art of resistance can stimulate the imagination of a system free of the exclusions and inclusions of the old order. In doing so, it can contribute towards a resistance that may reflect power and doggedly follow it, but will stop short of mimicking it, since it will be here, in the realm of imaginative possibility, that the independence of resistance from the established order will be manifest.

How and whether this takes place in any given situation will depend, as it must, on the contingency of human choice, pragmatic and moral. As in all politics, so in the politics of resistance, opportunity, chance and human actions play their part. This can transform the project of resistance into a truly alternative ordering of power or it can cause it to succumb to the techniques of a displaced regime for any number of reasons, an obsession with order and personal ambition being foremost among them. Even in those cases where the expectations generated by active resistance have been disappointed, the experience, stories and historical memory of a politics of struggle can lay the groundwork for a cycle of resistance. This is not only virtually impossible to eradicate but may provide the repertoire for new generations of defiance, nurtured by memories that reject and undermine the imaginative dominance of the established political order.

Whether the road taken is truly alternative will depend upon the moral choices involved in all human agency. Thus one should neither romanticize resistance nor pessimistically suggest that it can never escape from the very power that has provoked it into being. An example of such a set of choices, with markedly different consequences, would be the contrast between the responses of different Holocaust survivors to the terrible experiences they had undergone. A man like Primo Levi, for instance, saw the bearing of witness to these events as the prime duty of those who survived: 'We, the survivors are not the true witnesses ... we are those who by their prevarications or abilities or good luck did not touch bottom. Those who did so ... have not returned to tell about it or have returned mute, but they are ... the submerged, the complete witnesses ... We speak in their stead by proxy ... I could not say whether we did so or do so because of a kind of moral obligation towards those who were silenced, or rather in order to free ourselves of their memory; certainly we do it because of a strong and durable impulse'.[8] For others, such as those who threw themselves into the fight for the establishment of Israel in 1948, war was seen as 'the revenge of rebirth'.[9] Both had experienced the unimaginable suffering and inhumanity of the Holocaust, but the means by which they chose to resist the annihilation of their communities and their memory could not have been more different.

The course of resistance, therefore, whatever its origins, is shaped by the decisions of those who commit themselves to it. At its heart, there lies the conviction that the existing order is oppressive and unjust in a fundamental way. Springing from a source that may have led to actions provoked by the dominant power, it is by no means beholden to that power. On the contrary, it draws upon a repertoire of normative and narrative possibility that owes nothing to the imaginative hegemony of the established order and stands in opposition to it. It is this that helps to make it so potent as an inspiration for others to re-evaluate their situation, to begin to see power in a new and unflattering light, stripped of its customary authority. In these circumstances, power and the fight to preserve it can be reduced to the crudest of coercive means. Resistance, having got under the skin of power, symbolically and organizationally, can oblige it to show itself for what it is.

Of course, this is far from being a guarantee of success. On the contrary, violence can be relentlessly persuasive even in the absence of acknowledged authority. It can also be sustained over decades in a way that convinces people of the prudence of compliance and conformity.

In doing so, it is capable of generating rationales to justify collaboration. This is where any number of contingent aspects in the experience of the politics of resistance come into play: the ingenuity and ruthlessness of those in power; the morale and competence of those who would resist; the nature of the resources, both material and symbolic, at the disposal of both parties; the calculations of human suffering; and the effects of demonstrative cruelty – all of these can shape the outcome in any given struggle at a particular moment in history and in a specific place.

Nevertheless, uncertain as the outcomes may be, the fact of resistance underlines the enduring nature of a politics of contention. Some might argue that this is at the heart of politics everywhere, whatever the system of power or the place and epoch concerned. In the Middle East, as the case studies have shown, the relentless imposition and maintenance of forms of government on the peoples of the region both by outside powers and by local elites has devalued consent and stigmatized dissent. In fact, one might argue that the very definition of the region itself has been a task unilaterally carried out, privileging the strategic preoccupations of others, rarely of those who inhabit the various countries that have been labelled in this way. It is a testimony to the resilience of the human spirit and to the subversive possibilities of resistance that those who have been categorized as 'Middle Eastern' have used the label to assert their identities as actors in the shaping of their own fates. Across the region, not only outside powers but also collaborative elites have been confronted by defiant citizens who have demanded that they be held to account.

Mobilized citizens of countries from Morocco to the Gulf have demonstrated their scepticism about authority's claims and their anger at the denial of their rights. In doing so, they are linked inextricably, in terms of aims and tactics, with movements of social and political protest across the world. These have shown in their own countries the resolve and defiance that has been part of a pattern of global resistance. The comforting and complacent stories that established power and vested interests had told themselves about the 'exceptional' passivity and occasional 'fanatical' outbursts of the peoples of the region have been blown apart. Instead, we have seen how the organization of power itself, through the exclusive and often oppressive practices of the nation state, through a globalized economy that brings unequal benefits and class appropriation of public resources, has bred a resistance that shares much in common with similar movements in Europe, Asia, Africa and the Americas. Of course, the specifics differ, as do the trajectories, but the basic impulse to assert an autonomous way of being has been at the root of much of the resistance in the Middle East, as it has elsewhere, varied and often conflicting as many of these movements may be. It is a plurality of politics and a spirit of defiance that has resonated across the region, forcing strategic recalculations by local regimes and by outside powers. The 2011 song, '*Ezzay?*' [How?] by Muhammad Munir, addressing his beloved Egypt, captured this spirit: 'And [I swear] on your life I'll keep changing you until you're satisfied with me' [*wa-hayatik li-fadl aghayyir fiki li-hadd ma tarda `alayi*].[10]

Notes

Introduction

1 BBC World News – Middle East, 23 April 2011, http://www.bbc.co.uk/
news/world-middle-east-13175677 [accessed 23 April 2011].

2 George Woodcock, *Anarchism* (Harmondsworth, England, 1973) pp. 279–
94; Emma Goldman, *Anarchism and other essays* (Minneapolis, MN, 2005)
pp. 39–65.

3 David Forgacs (ed.), *The Antonio Gramsci reader – selected writings 1916–
1935* (New York, 2000) pp. 53–75; Georg Lukács, *History and class consciousness* (Cambridge, MA, 1999) pp. 46–82.

4 Daniel Miller, Michael Rowlands and Chris Tilley, *Domination and resistance* (London, 1989) pp. 10–16; Pierre Bourdieu, *Acts of resistance – against
the new myths of our time* (Cambridge, 1998) pp. 98–104; John Chalcraft
and Yaseen Noorani (eds.), *Counterhegemony in the colony and the postcolony* (Basingstoke, England, 2007) pp. 7–12.

5 Lisa Wedeen, *Ambiguities of domination – politics, rhetoric, and symbols in
contemporary Syria* (Chicago, 1999) pp. 67–86.

6 Michel Foucault, *Power/knowledge: selected interviews and other writings
1972–1977* (tr. and ed. C. Gordon) (Brighton, England, 1980) pp. 78–107.

7 Rania Abouzeid, 'Syria's revolt: how graffiti started an uprising', *Time*, 22
March 2011, http://www.time.com/time/world/article/0,8599,2060788,00.
html [accessed 20 April 2011].

8 Khalil Mutran, 'Boycott' [*Muqat`a*]

'Hadha jahdukum
Fa-bihi munjatuna . . . fa-shukran'

Khalil Mutran, *Diwan al-Khalil* (Beirut, 1967) Vol. 2, p. 9.

9 James Scott, *Weapons of the weak: everyday forms of peasant resistance*
(New Haven, CT, 1987) pp. 28–41.

10 Robert Darnton, *The great cat massacre and other episodes in French
cultural history* (New York, 1985).

11 BBC World News – Middle East, 'Hezbollah leader Nasrallah makes rare
public appearance', 6 December 2011, http://www.bbc.co.uk/news/world
-middle-east-16048832 [accessed 7 December 2011]. See the two very different accounts of Hizbullah and its relationship to 'resistance' in Alistair
Crooke, *Resistance: the essence of the Islamist revolution* (London, 2009)
and Mona Harb, *Le Hezbollah à Beyrouth 1985–2005: de la banlieue à la
ville* (Beirut, Lebanon, 2010).

12 Kevin J. O'Brien, 'Rightful resistance', *World Politics* 49/1 (1996) pp. 31–55.

13 Asef Bayat, *Life as politics: how ordinary people change the Middle East*
(Stanford, CA, 2010) pp. 51–65.

14 Michel Foucault, *Histoire de la sexualité*, Vol. 1, *La volonté de savoir* (London, 1976) pp. 125–6.
15 Hossam al-Hamalawy to Al-Jazeera, 'Egypt's Mubarak hospitalised', 12 April 2011, *Al-Jazeera*, http://english.aljazeera.net/news/middleeast/2011/04/20114121675 5944186.html [accessed 24 April 2011].
16 This refers to the leaders of the eighteen sectarian communities recognized in the Lebanese constitution.
17 Jocelyn A. Hollander and Rachel L. Einwohner, 'Conceptualizing resistance', *Sociological Forum* 19/4 (2004) pp. 537–49.
18 The Algerian term '*hogra*' comes from the word *haqqara* which means to hold in contempt, to despise or to humiliate – all meanings packed into that one word *hogra* that summed up the public's view of the attitude of those in authority towards themselves. Those in authority, ironically, have been labelled '*le pouvoir*' [the power] since the war of independence – denoting the web of security officials that determine the course of politics in Algeria, regardless of the public institutions or rhetoric of the state – the 'shadow state' in other words.
19 *Les taches d'huile* [oil spots] were used to describe the colonial counter-insurgency strategies pursued by the French generals Hubert Lyautey and Joseph-Simon Gallieni in their 'pacification' campaigns of the late nineteenth and early twentieth centuries in southeast Asia and North Africa; Robert B. Asprey, *War in the shadows: the guerrilla in history* (London, 1976) pp. 150–8.

1. State Capture and Violent Resistance

1 Benjamin C. Brower, *A desert named peace – the violence of France's empire in the Algerian Sahara 1844–1902* (New York, 2009) pp. 81–4; Julia Clancy-Smith, *Rebel and saint: Muslim notables, popular protest, colonial encounters – Algeria and Tunisia* (Berkeley, CA, 1994) pp. 254–64.
2 Charles-Robert Ageron, *Modern Algeria: a history from 1830 to the present* (London, 1991) p. 53.
3 Sartre quoted in Robert Young, *Postcolonialism: an historical introduction* (Oxford, 2001) p. 294.
4 Frantz Fanon, *The wretched of the earth* (London, 2001) pp. 66–9; Young, *Postcolonialism* (2001), pp. 295–9; Nigel C. Gibson, *Fanon: the postcolonial imagination* (Cambridge, 2003) pp. 103–15.
5 Ferhat Abbas, *Autopsie d'une guerre: l'aurore* (Paris, 1980) pp. 104–8; Gibson, *Fanon* (2003) pp. 108–9.
6 Abbas, *Autopsie* (1980) p. 105.
7 Sir Edmund Allenby's official proclamation following the fall of Jerusalem, 9 December 1917.
8 *The Times*, 9 November 1917.
9 Leonard Stein, *The Balfour Declaration* (New York, 1961) p. 470.
10 Zeina B. Ghandour, *A discourse on domination* (London, 2010) pp. 122–3.
11 Jacob Metzler, *The divided economy of mandatory Palestine* (Cambridge, 1998).
12 Ghandour, *Discourse* (2010) pp. 105–20.

13 Charles Townshend, 'The defence of Palestine: insurrection and public security, 1936–1939', *The English Historical Review* 103 (1988) pp. 917–49; Matthew Hughes, 'The banality of brutality: British armed forces and the repression of the Arab revolt in Palestine, 1936–39', *English Historical Review* 124 (2009) pp. 313–54; Matthew Hughes, 'From law and order to pacification: Britain's suppression of the Arab revolt in Palestine, 1936–39', *Journal of Palestine Studies* 39/2 (2010) pp. 1–17.

14 Official British estimates suggested that about 2,000 Palestinian Arabs were killed by British forces, more than 100 were hanged and nearly 1,000 died as a result of intra-Palestinian and Zionist violence. Rashid Khalidi, building on the work of Walid Khalidi, gives a much higher total for Arab Palestinian casualties, estimating that more than 5,000 died, nearly 4,000 at the hands of the British, and that by the end of the revolt 'over 10 percent of the adult male population [of Arab Palestinians] was killed, wounded, imprisoned or exiled'. Rashid Khalidi, 'The Palestinians and 1948: the underlying causes of failure', in Eugene Rogan and Avi Shlaim (eds.), *The war for Palestine* (Cambridge, 2007) p. 26; Hughes, 'Banality of brutality' (2009) pp. 348–9; Walid Khalidi (ed.), *From haven to conquest: readings in Zionism and the Palestine problem until 1948* (Washington, DC, 1971) pp. 846–9.

15 Bruce Hoffman, *Inside terrorism* (New York, 2006) pp. 47–53.

16 Avi Shlaim, *Lion of Jordan – the life of King Hussein in war and peace* (London, 2007) p. 276.

17 Abu Iyad interviewed by Lutfi al-Kholi, June 1969, for *Al-Tali'a*, quoted in Leila Kadi, *Basic political documents of the armed Palestinian resistance movement* (Beirut, Lebanon, 1969) p. 49.

18 Yezid Sayigh, *Armed struggle and the search for state* (Oxford, 1997) pp. 1–24.

19 *The Sunday Times*, 15 June 1969.

20 George Habbash interviewed by Gerard Chaliand, late 1969/early 1970, in Gerard Chaliand, *The Palestinian resistance* (London, 1972) p. 166.

21 Al-Fatah Central Information Bureau weekly bulletin, No. 12, 7 July 1969, in Kadi, *Basic political documents* (1969) pp. 112–13.

22 Bishara Khader and Naim Khader (tr. and eds.), *Textes de la révolution palestinienne 1968/74* (Paris, 1975) pp. 108–9.

23 Cited in David Hirst, *Beware of small states: Lebanon, battleground of the Middle East* (London, 2010) p. 86.

24 George Habbash interviewed in 1970, quoted in David Hirst, *The gun and the olive branch* (London, 1977) p. 304.

25 Hamas communiqué, 14 December 1987, quoted in Robert A. Pape, *Dying to win – the strategic logic of suicide terrorism* (New York, 2005) p. 31.

26 Pape, *Dying to win* (2005) p. 70.

27 Alastair Crooke, *Resistance – the essence of the Islamist revolution* (London, 2009) pp. 200–3.

28 Fathi al-Shiqaqi, in *Al-Quds*, 11 April 1995, cited in Pape, *Dying to win* (2005) p. 32.

29 Abdel Karim, in Joel Greenberg, 'Suicide planner expresses joy over his missions', *New York Times*, 9 May 2002, cited in Pape, *Dying to win* (2005) p. 31.

30 Nasra Hassan, 'An arsenal of believers: talking to the human bombs', *The New Yorker*, 22 November 2001, cited in Luca Ricolfi, 'Palestinians, 1981–2003', in Diego Gambetta (ed.), *Making sense of suicide missions* (Oxford, 2005) p. 79.

31 Beverley Milton-Edwards and Stephen Farrell, *Hamas* (Cambridge, 2010) pp. 91–103, 123.

32 Frances Hasso, 'Discursive and political deployments by/of the 2002 Palestinian women suicide bombers/martyrs', *Feminist Review* 81 (2005) pp. 25–9.

33 Mia Bloom, *Dying to kill – the allure of suicide terror* (New York, 2007) p. 27.

34 Menachem Klein, *The Jerusalem problem: the struggle for permanent status* (Gainesville, FL, 2003) p. 97.

35 Between 2000 and 2005, it was estimated that 1,080 Israelis and 3,570 Palestinians had lost their lives in the violence; Milton-Edwards and Farrell, *Hamas* (2010) p. 107.

36 Khalid Mish'al, 'This brutality will never break our will to be free', *The Guardian*, 6 January 2009, p. 26.

37 Ma`an News Agency, 'Exclusive: PFLP in Gaza on peace, resistance and unity', 17 January 2009, http://www.maannews.net/eng/ViewDetails.aspx?ID=207912 [accessed 13 July 2009].

38 Amnesty International, *Israel/Gaza – Operation 'Cast Lead': 22 days of death and destruction* (London, 2009).

39 Nir Rosen, *Aftermath* (New York, 2010) p. 17.

40 *The Guardian*, 27 October 2009, guardian.co.uk; http://news.bbc.co.uk/1/hi/8327352.stm [accessed 2 November 2009].

41 This was loudly proclaimed as the rationale behind the bombardment of Baghdad in the early days of the invasion: 'shock and awe', as the policy was called, was a way of linking political spectacle with violence in the hope of bringing about significant political change; Harlan K. Ullman, James P. Wade, et al., *Shock and awe: achieving rapid dominance* (Washington, DC, 1996) p. xxiv.

42 Ahmed S. Hashim, *Insurgency and counter-insurgency in Iraq* (London, 2006) pp. 23–4.

43 Nir Rosen, *In the belly of the green bird* (New York, 2006) pp. 151–7.

44 Dominic Streatfield, 'How America armed al-Qaida', *The Guardian*, 7 January 2011, G2, pp. 4–10 [extract from Dominic Streatfield, *A history of the world since 9/11* (London, 2011)].

45 Patrick Cockburn, *Muqtada al-Sadr and the fall of Iraq* (London, 2008) pp. 181–4.

46 Hashim, *Insurgency and counter-insurgency* (2006) p. 178.

47 During the period 2003–11, 4,792 U.S. servicemen died in Iraq and 32,159 were wounded, although not all of the casualties were due to hostile action by insurgents. It was noticeable, however, that from the autumn of 2007, there was a significant drop in the number of U.S. casualties, leading to totals in 2008 that were about two thirds lower than in 2007; The Iraq Coalition Casualty Count, http://icasualties.org/iraq/index.aspx [accessed 28 August 2011].

48 'Iraq Shia Cleric Muqtada Sadr urges Iraqis to Unite', 8 January 2011, http://www.bbc.co.uk/news/world-middle-east-12141874 [accessed 8 January 2011].

49 *Iraq Body Count* website, http://www.iraqbodycount.org/database/ [accessed 4 December 2011].

50 Human Rights Watch, *World Report 2011: Iraq*, http://www.hrw.org/en/ world-report-2011/iraq [accessed 10 February 2011]; Human Rights Watch, 'Iraq: secret jail uncovered in Baghdad', 1 February 2011, http:// www.hrw.org/en/news/2011/02/01/iraq-secret-jail-uncovered-baghdad [accessed 10 February 2011]; Amnesty International, *New order, same abuses – unlawful detentions and torture in Iraq* (London, 2010).

51 Umar Abd Allah, *The Islamic struggle in Syria* (Berkeley, CA, 1983) pp. 107–9.

52 *Al-Nadhir*, 7 April 1980, cited in Abd Allah, *Islamic struggle* (1983) p. 109.

53 Brynjar Lia, *Architect of the global jihad: life of al-Qaida strategist Abu Mus'ab al-Suri* (London, 2007) pp. 35–50.

54 Thomas Mayer, 'The Islamic opposition in Syria, 1961–1982', *Orient* 4 (1983) pp. 589–90.

55 'Bandits kill 2 officers, Damascus says', UPI website, 11 April 2011, http:// www.upi.com/Top_News/Special/2011/04/11/Bandits-kill-2-officers-Damascus-says/UPI-58251302543621/?rel=34491302783420 [accessed 25 April 2011]; Martin Chulov, 'Syrians join the Arab protests', *The Guardian*, 29 March 2011, http://www.guardian.co.uk/world/2011/mar/ 29/syria-bashir-al-assad-protest [accessed 25 April 2011].

56 'Syrian army kills 6 "terrorists", arrests 149 in Daraa', AP news website, 1 May 2011, http://apnnews.com/2011/05/01/syrian-army-kills-6-terrorists -arrests-149-in-daraa/ [accessed 4 May 2011].

57 This may have been the case of the attack on the Air Force intelligence building in Harasta, north of Damascus, in November 2011, but the circum-stances suggested to some that this had more to do with conflicts within the regime itself; BBC World News – Middle East, 'Syria defectors "attack military base in Harasta"', 16 November 2011, http://www.bbc.co.uk/ news/world-middle-east-15752058 [accessed 3 December 2011].

58 http://www.lccsyria.org/ [accessed 15 December 2011].

59 BBC World News – Middle East, 'Syrian opposition to co-ordinate with Free Syrian Army', 1 December 2011, http://www.bbc.co.uk/ news/world-europe-15984682 [accessed 4 December 2011]; Cecily Hilleary, 'Free Syria Army leader asks Obama for decisive action on Syria' Middle East Voices – Arab Spring 2 December 2011, http:// middleeastvoices.com/2011/12/exclusive-free-syria-army-leader-asks-obama -for-decisive-action-on-syria/ [accessed 4 December 2011]. In June 2012, indicating frustration at the lack of progress, the SNC elected a new chairman, Abdul-Basit Sida, an exiled Syrian academic of Kurdish origins.

60 BBC World News – Middle East, 23 December 2011, http://www.bbc.co .uk/news/world-middle-east-16313879 [accessed 2 January 2012].

61 John Bulloch and Harvey Morris, *No friends but the mountains* (London, 1992) pp. 150–9.

62 Human Rights Watch/Middle East, *Iraq's crime of genocide: the Anfal campaign against the Kurds* (New Haven, CT, 1995).

63 Charles Tripp, *A history of Iraq* (Cambridge, 2007) p. 248.

64 See the striking story of the goldsmith of Marw in Michael Cook, *Commanding the right and forbidding the wrong in Islamic thought* (Cambridge, 2000) pp. 3–10.

65 Chris McGreal, 'Go to hell, Gaddafi', *The Observer Magazine*, 24 April 2011, pp. 34–41; Evan Hill, 'The day the Katiba fell', Aljazeera website, 1 March 2011, http://english.aljazeera.net/indepth/spotlight/libya/2011/03/20113175840189620.html [accessed 3 March 2011].

66 'Libya protests: Gadhafi's son warns of civil war', BBC World News – Middle East, 21 February 2011, http://www.bbc.co.uk/news/world-middle -east-12520586 [accessed 3 March 2011].

67 'Gadhafi's friend turns foe', Aljazeera website, 1 March 2011, http://english .aljazeera.net/news/middleeast/2011/02/2011228232312771972.html [accessed 3 March 2011].

68 'Libya: Gaddafi loyalists mount onslaught', BBC World News – Middle East, 11 March 2011, http://www.bbc.co.uk/news/world-africa-12708687 [accessed 21 March 2011].

69 Chris McGreal, '"If he wins, we're dead". The rebel mood darkens amid fears revolution has stalled', *The Guardian*, 10 March 2011.

70 'Defiant Gaddafi vows to fight on', Aljazeera website, 23 February 2011, http://english.aljazeera.net/news/africa/2011/02/2011222164589913596. html [accessed 10 April 2011].

71 UN Security Council Resolution 1973 (2011), 17 March 2011, http://www .un.org/Docs/sc/unsc_resolutions11.htm [accessed 28 April 2011].

72 David Kirkpatrick, 'Egypt premier, warning of economic dangers, pleads for peace', *The New York Times*, 22 December 2011, http://www.nytimes .com/2011/12/23/world/middleeast/egypts-prime-minister-adds-more -blame-on-protesters.html?_r=1&ref=egypt [accessed 2 January 2012].

2. Contesting Public Space: Resistance as the Denial of Authority

1 La Place des Martyres in Beirut was the site of the hanging of a number of Lebanese nationalists by the Ottoman authorities in 1916. In Tehran, Jaleh Square had been renamed Martyrs Square to commemorate those who had been killed by the Shah's forces in an anti-regime demonstration in September 1978. Tahrir Square was so named to commemorate the liberation of Egypt from British rule, and had been a contested space for decades with the British authorities since it fronted the British Kasr al-Nil barracks.

2 Tom Finn, 'Yemen protests see tens of thousands of people take to the streets', *The Guardian*, 4 February 2011; International Crisis Group, *Popular protest in North Africa and the Middle East (II): Yemen between reform and revolution*, Report 102, 10 March 2011, http://www.crisisgroup.org/en/regions/ middle-east-north-africa/iran-gulf/yemen/102-popular-protest-in-north-africa -and-the-middle-east-II-yemen-between-reform-and-revolution.aspx [accessed 24 April 2011].

3 Faleh Jabar, 'Le leviathan et le sacré: le Baas et les chiites', in Chris Kutschera (ed.), *Le livre noir de Saddam Hussein* (Paris, 2005) pp. 236–7; W. Thom

Workman, *The social origins of the Iran–Iraq war* (Boulder, CO, 1994) pp. 77–8; Hanna Batatu, 'Iraq's underground Shi'i movements', MERIP 12/1 (1982) p. 6.

4 Benjamin Smith, 'Collective action with and without Islam', in Quintan Wiktorowicz (ed.), *Islamic activism: a social movement theory approach* (Cambridge, 2003) pp. 213, 228–33.

5 The bazaar, so important as a site of public defiance of the Shah's government during these years, was not exactly a public space but one that belonged to the bazaaris. Indeed, it was the unwarranted intervention into this space by the state authorities and the Rastakhiz Party cadres that they were protesting against. Nevertheless, as a site of public sociability and visibility developments there had a resonance far beyond the physical spaces of the bazaar itself. Arang Keshavarzian, *Bazaar and state in Iran – the politics of the Tehran marketplace* (Cambridge, 2007) p. 96.

6 Charles Kurzman, *The unthinkable revolution in Iran* (Cambridge, MA, 2004) pp. 33–7.

7 Kurzman, *The unthinkable revolution* (2004) p. 46.

8 Mansour Moaddel, *Class, politics and ideology in the Iranian revolution* (New York, 1993) pp. 1–25; Ervand Abrahamian, *Iran between two revolutions* (Princeton, NJ, 1983) pp. 496–529.

9 Charles Kurzman, 'The Qum protests and the coming of the Iranian revolution, 1975 and 1978', *Social Science History* 27/3 (2003) pp. 287–325.

10 Kurzman, *The unthinkable revolution* (2004) pp. 49, 63.

11 Ali Ansari (ed.) with Daniel Berman and Thomas Rintoul, *Preliminary analysis of the voting figures in Iran's 2009 presidential election*, Chatham House and Institute of Iranian Studies, University of St Andrews, 21 June 2009; Ali Ansari, *Crisis of authority: Iran's 2009 presidential election* (London, 2010).

12 Ian Black, 'Iran elections: Ahmadinejad and Moussavi rallies bring Tehran to a halt', *The Guardian*, 8 June 2009, p. 15.

13 Ian Black, Saeed Kamali Dheghan and Haroon Siddique, 'Iran elections: Mousavi lodges appeal against Ahmadinejad victory', *The Guardian*, 14 June 2009, http://www.guardian.co.uk/world/2009/jun/14/iran-election-mousavi -appeal [accessed 4 November 2010].

14 Kevin O'Brien, 'Rightful resistance', *World Politics* 49/1 (1996) pp. 31–5; Kaveh Ehsani, Arang Keshavarzian and Norma Claire Moruzzi, 'Slaps in the face of reason: Tehran 2009', in Nader Hashemi and Danny Postel (eds.), *The people reloaded – the Green Movement and the struggle for Iran's future* (Brooklyn, NY, 2010) pp. 29–36.

15 Black, Dheghan and Siddique, 'Iran elections', *The Guardian*, 14 June 2009, http://www.guardian.co.uk/world/2009/jun/14/iran-election-mousavi-appeal [accessed 4 November 2010].

16 Ervand Abrahamian, '"I am not a speck of dirt, I am a retired teacher"', in Hashemi and Postel (eds.), *The people reloaded* (2010) pp. 65–8.

17 Nahid Siamdoust, 'Tehran's rallying cry: "We are the People of Iran"', *Time*, 15 June 2009, http://www.time.com/time/world/article/0,8599,1904764 -1,00.html [accessed 4 November 2010]; Ian Black, 'Shots fired as more

than 100,000 Iranians defy march ban', *The Guardian*, 15 June 2009, http://www.guardian.co.uk/world/2009/jun/15/iran-opposition-rally-banned -mousavi [accessed 4 November 2010].

18 Khamenei's Friday sermon at Tehran University mosque, Friday 19 June 2009, http://pastebay.com/23186 [accessed 4 November 2010].

19 Pedestrian blog, http://www.sidewalklyrics.com/?p=1567; http://www .irannewsdigest.com/tag/qods-day/page/2/ [both accessed 6 January 2011]. Of course, all these slogans sound a good deal better – and funnier – in Persian where the rhymes and plays on words have full scope.

20 Jason Athanasiadis, 'Iran regime drums up its own sounds to oppose Green Movement', *The Christian Science Monitor*, 30 December 2009.

21 Nader Hashemi and Danny Postel, 'Introduction', in Hashemi and Postel (eds.), *The people reloaded* (2010) pp. xvi–xvii.

22 Issandr El Amrani, 'The murder of Khaled Said', *The Arabist*, 14 June 2010, http://www.arabist.net/blog/2010/6/14/the-murder-of-khaled-said.html [accessed 14 April 2011].

23 http://www.youtube.com/watch?v=DaxepUuCFFM

24 Ahmed Zaki Osman, 'Egypt's police: from liberators to oppressors', *AlMasry AlYoum*, 24 January 2011, http://www.almasryalyoum.com/ node/304946 [accessed 14 April 2011].

25 This did not stop them arresting a number of individuals whom they identified – wrongly – as the key organizers of protest, largely on the basis of their known oppositional activity in previous years or their familiarity with the new electronic forms of communication or simply because they appeared so frequently in the demonstrations.

26 *Al-Ahram*, 17 January 2011, http://english.ahram.org.eg/NewsContent/ 1/2/4115/Egypt/Society/In-Egypt,-man-sets-himself-on-fire,-driven-by-econ .aspx; 'Egyptian man dies after setting himself alight', BBC News – Middle East, http://www.bbc.co.uk/news/world-middle-east-12214090 [both accessed 14 April 2011].

27 There has been some suggestion that the plans of the riot police for countering demonstrations had become known, either through electronic hacking or through inside information. This allowed false trails to be laid, convincing the police that a demonstration was going to be taking place in one place, only for them to assemble and to find no one there, but that it was happening elsewhere.

28 Alaa Al-Aswany, 'Police alone can't keep rulers in power. Egypt's battle is on', *The Guardian*, 28 January 2011.

29 Ian Black, 'Leaflets being circulated in Cairo give blueprint for mass action', *The Guardian*, 28 January 2011; *Kaif tathawr bi-hida'a* [how to revolt peacefully], http://www.tahrirdocuments.org/wp-content/uploads/2011/03/ thawra2011_lo.pdf, English translation at http://www.theatlantic.com/ international/archive/2011/01/egyptian-activists-action-plan-translated/ 70388/ [both accessed 12 April 2011].

30 *The Guardian*, 29 January 2011.

31 *The Guardian*, 31 January 2011; 'Istimrar al-muzahirat bi-l-suwis' [dem-onstrations continue in Suez] *al-Masry al-Yawm*, 31 January 2011, http:// www.almasryalyoum.com/node/307911

32 *The Guardian*, 29 January 2011.

33 *The Guardian*, 1 February 2011.

34 BBC News – Middle East, 1 February 2011, http://www.bbc.co.uk/news/
mobile/world-middle-east-12331520 [accessed 6 February 2011].

35 *The Guardian*, 3 February 2011; 'Egypt PM "sorry" for violence', Al
Jazeera website, 3 February 2011, http://english.aljazeera.net/news/
middleeast/2011/02/2011231335518585868.html [accessed 6 February
2011].

36 BBC News – Middle East, 4 February 2011, http://www.bbc.co.uk/news/
world-middle-east-12362826 [accessed 6 February 2011].

37 Chris McGreal, 'Mubarak is still here, but there's been a revolution in our
minds', *The Observer*, 6 February 2011.

38 Amnesty International, 'Egyptian military urged to halt torture of detainees', 17 February 2011, http://www.amnesty.org/en/news-and-updates/
egyptian-military-urged-halt-torture-detainees-2011-02-17 [accessed 27
February 2011]; *The Guardian*, 10 February 2011.

39 Egypt State Information Service, 10 February 2011, http://www.sis.gov.eg/
En/Story.aspx?sid=53690 [accessed 5 July 2011].

40 *The Guardian*, 11 February 2011. A report by an official investigating panel
in Egypt stated that in the course of the January/February uprisings, 846
civilians and twenty-six policemen had lost their lives across the country.
The toll of the wounded was calculated to exceed 6,400. 'Egypt unrest: 846
killed in protests – official toll', BBC News – Middle East, 19 April 2011,
http://www.bbc.co.uk/news/world-middle-east-13134956 [accessed 25
April 2011].

41 Inigo Gilmore, 'Egypt erupts into new violence as dozens injured during
Cairo protest', *The Guardian online*, 24 July 2011, http://www.guardian
.co.uk/world/2011/jul/24/egypt-violence-tahrir-square-protest [accessed 12
October 2011].

42 'Cairo clashes leave 24 dead after Coptic church protest', BBC News –
Middle East, 10 October 2011, http://www.bbc.co.uk/news/world-middle
-east-15235212 [accessed 20 October 2011].

43 Jack Shenker, 'Tahrir Square crowds vow "fight to the death" for end of
military rule', *The Guardian*, 21 November 2011, p. 4.

44 There has been no official census to indicate the balance between Shi'i and
Sunni communities in Bahrain since 1941 – when it was estimated that of
the Muslim population, 52.5% were Shi'i, whilst 47.5% were Sunni.
Since then it has been assumed that the Shi'a comprise 60–70% of the
population. This is disputed by some, not least because the Bahrain
government has been pursuing a policy of *al-tajnis* [granting nationality]
that has led to the naturalization of some 90,000 Sunnis during the past
ten years – representing about 16% of the present population: Justin
Gengler blog, http://bahrainipolitics.blogspot.com/2011/04/facts-on
-ground-reliable-estimate-of.html [accessed 14 April 2011]; Fahim
I. Qubain, 'Social class and tensions in Bahrain', *The Middle East
Journal 9/3* (1955) pp. 269–71.

45 Toby Matthiesen, 'The Shi'a of Saudi Arabia at a crossroads', *Middle East
Report*, 6 May 2009, http://www.merip.org/mero/mero050609 [accessed
7 March 2010].

46 Bill Law, 'Bahrain Shi`a call for activists' release', BBC News – Middle East, 28 February 2008, http://news.bbc.co.uk/go/pr/fr/-/1/hi/world/middle_east/7268820.stm [accessed 15 November 2008].

47 Habib Toumi, 'Planned peaceful Sitra protest ends in violence', *Gulf News*, 8 March 2009.

48 Michael Slackman, 'Sectarian tension takes volatile form in Bahrain', *New York Times*, 29 March 2009.

49 Joe Stork, *Routine abuse, routine denial: civil rights and the political crisis in Bahrain* (New York, 1997).

50 Human Rights Watch, Bahrain: elections to take place amid crackdown, 20 October 2010, http://www.hrw.org/en/news/2010/10/20/bahrain-elections-take-place-amid-crackdown [accessed 15 April 2011].

51 Ian Black, 'Bahrain election puts Shia opposition as largest single group', *The Guardian*, 24 October 2010, http://www.guardian.co.uk/world/2010/oct/24/bahrain-poll-shia-opposition [accessed 15 April 2011].

52 Facebook page: *Thawra 14 fibrayir fi al-Bahrain* [14 February revolution in Bahrain].

53 Ian Black, 'Mourner dies as Bahrain police open fire on funeral procession', *The Guardian*, 16 February 2011; International Crisis Group, *Popular protests in North Africa and the Middle East (III): the Bahrain revolt* (Report 10) 6 April 2011 (Brussels, 2011) pp. 6–9.

54 Interview with Martin Chulov, *The Guardian*, 17 February 2011.

55 Martin Chulov, 'Bahrain's quiet anger turns to rage after brutal attack', *The Guardian*, 18 February 2011.

56 Ned Parker, 'Bahrain protestors celebrate as police, soldiers withdraw from Pearl Square', *Los Angeles Times*, 19 February 2011, http://articles.latimes.com/2011/feb/19/world/la-fgw-bahrain-square-20110220 [accessed 7 March 2011].

57 Zoi Constantine, 'Bahrainis pour on to the streets of Manama once again', *The National*, 23 February 2011, http://www.thenational.ae/news/worldwide/middle-east/bahrainis-pour-on-to-streets-of-manama-once-again [accessed 5 April 2011].

58 Omar al Shehabi, 'The community at Pearl Roundabout is at the centre', *The National*, 1 March 2011 http://www.thenational.ae/thenationalconversation/comment/the-community-at-pearl-roundabout-is-at-the-centre [accessed 5 April 2011].

59 Bill Law, 'Bahrain protestors facing "death threats"', BBC News – Middle East, http://www.bbc.co.uk/news/world-middle-east-12720537 [accessed 18 April 2011].

60 *The Guardian*, 14 March 2011.

61 Martin Chulov, 'Saudi Arabian troops enter Bahrain to help regime quell uprising', *The Guardian*, 15 March 2011.

62 Bahrain Center for Human Rights list of people killed in Bahrain since 14 February 2011 – extrajudicial killing 13 April 2011, http://bahrainrights.hopto.org/en/node/3864 [accessed 18 April 2011]; Human Rights Watch, 'Bahrain: wounded prisoners beaten, detained', 20 March 2011, http://www.hrw.org/en/news/2011/03/30/bahrain-wounded-protesters-beaten-detained [accessed 18 April 2011]; Amnesty International, 'Bahrain

witnesses describe bloody crackdown', 17 March 2011, http://www
.amnesty.org/en/news-and-updates/bahrain-witnesses-describe-bloody
-crackdown-2011-03-16 [accessed 18 April 2011].

63 Human Rights Watch, *Bahrain's human rights crisis*, 1 July 2011, http://
www.hrw.org/sites/default/files/related_material/Bahrain's%20Human%
20Rights%20Crisis.pdf [accessed 12 September 2011].

64 Anthony Shadid, 'Bahrain boils under the lid of repression', *New York
Times*, 15 September 2011, http://www.nytimes.com/2011/09/16/world/
middleeast/repression-tears-apart-bahrains-social-fabric.html?_r=2&hp
[accessed 9 November 2011].

65 BICI, *Report of the Bahrain Independent Commission of Inquiry*, Manama,
Bahrain, 23 November 2011, http://files.bici.org.bh/BICIreportEN.pdf
[accessed 30 November 2011].

66 Toby Jones, 'We know what happened in Bahrain: now what?', *Carnegie
Endowment for International Peace*, 1 December 2011, http://
carnegieendowment.org/2011/12/01/we-know-what-happened-in-bahrain
-now-what/7yfo [accessed 2 December 2011].

67 James Gelvin, *The Israel–Palestine conflict: one hundred years of war*
(Cambridge, 2007) p. 220.

68 See, for instance, George Baramki Azar, *Palestine: a photographic journey*
(Berkeley, CA, 1991) or Mustafa al-Kurd's famous song, 'A stone and an
onion and a bucket of water' from his popular cassette *Awlad Filastin*
[children of Palestine] (Nazareth, 1988) cassette recording.

69 F. Robert Hunter, *The Palestinian uprising* (Berkeley, CA, 1993) pp. 58–71.

70 Hunter, *Palestinian uprising* (1993) pp. 120–33; Mazin Qumsiyeh, *Popular
resistance in Palestine – a history of hope and empowerment* (London,
2011) pp. 139–52.

71 Qumsiyeh, *Popular resistance in Palestine* (2011) pp. 109–33.

72 Julie Peteet, 'Male gender and rituals of resistance in the Palestinian intifada:
a cultural politics of violence', *American Ethnologist* 21/1 (1994)
pp. 31–49.

73 'The Separation Barrier', *B'Tselem*, http://www.btselem.org/separation_
barrier [accessed 27 August 2011], and detailed map of the route followed
by the barrier (June 2011), http://www.btselem.org/sites/default/files/
download/20110612_btselem_map_of_wb_eng.pdf

74 A film about these incidents, entitled *Budrus*, was made by Julia Bacha, co-
produced with Rula Salameh and Ronit Avni and released in 2009, http://
www.justvision.org/budrus [accessed 2 November 2010]; Amira Hass, 'The
village against the fence', *Ha'aretz*, 11 February 2004, http://www.haaretz
.com/print-edition/features/the-village-against-the-fence-1.113619
[accessed 2 November 2010].

75 Amira Hass, 'Bil'in and Na'alin declared closed military areas each Friday
for months', *Ha'aretz*, 16 March 2010, http://www.haaretz.com/print
-edition/news/bil-in-na-alin-declared-closed-military-areas-each-friday
-for-months-1.264808 [accessed 2 November 2010].

76 As in the case of the death of Jawaher Abu Rahmeh in December 2010 in
Bil'in, http://www.awalls.org/topics/recent_activities; Isabel Kershner,
'Israeli military officials challenge account of Palestinian woman's death',

New York Times, 4 January 2011, http://www.nytimes.com/2011/01/05/
world/middleeast/05mideast.html?_r=1&partner=rss&emc=rss   [both
accessed 7 April 2011].

77 Martin Asser, 'West Bank village hails victory', BBC News – Middle East, 5
September 2007, http://news.bbc.co.uk/1/hi/world/middle_east/6979923
.st [accessed 7 April 2011].

78 'Bil`in residents cautious following Supreme Court order to move the
annexation wall', http://www.bilin-village.org/english/articles/press-and
-independent-media/Bilin-residents-cautious-following-Supreme-Court
-order-to-move-the-annexation-wall [accessed 7 April 2011].

79 Sami Awad, 'Non-violence from the bottom up', *Foreign Policy*,
1   June   2010,   http://mideast.foreignpolicy.com/posts/2010/06/01/
nonviolence_from_the_bottom_up [accessed 4 January 2011]; Josh
Mitnick, 'Borrowing from Gandhi? Palestinian passive resistance
gains followers', *Christian Science Monitor*, 28 April 2010; Ethan
Bronner, 'Palestinians try a less violent path to resistance', *New
York Times*, 6 April 2010.

80 Al-Haq, 'From Palestinian olive groves to Canadian courtrooms: resisting
Israel's land annexation policies in the West Bank – the case of Bil`in village'
2008, http://www.alhaq.org/etemplate.php?id=440 [accessed 7 April
2011].

81 Canadian Centre for International Justice 'Bil`in', http://www.ccij.ca/
programs/cases/index.php?WEBYEP_DI=11 [accessed 7 April 2011].

82 BDS Movement, http://www.bdsmovement.net/bdsintro#.TttDdnOvNr9;
see also the Boycott Israeli Goods, http://www.bigcampaign.org/; Omar
Barghouti, 'Besieging Israel's siege', *The Guardian online*, 12 August
2010,   http://www.guardian.co.uk/commentisfree/2010/aug/12/besieging
-israel-siege-palestinian-boycott [accessed 14 April 2011].

83 *Proposed bill to prevent harm to the state of Israel by means of boycott*, 27
June 2011; 'Knesset passes boycott law; ACRI plans to appeal', 12 July
2011, Association for Civil Rights in Israel (ACRI), http://www.acri.org.il/
en/?p=2766 [accessed 19 September 2011].

84 Qumsiyeh, *Popular resistance* (2010) pp. 177–201.

85 Ethan Bronner, 'Palestinians try a less violent path to resistance', *New York
Times*, 6 April 2010.

86 'Eyewitness: Lebanon protests', BBC News – Middle East, 2 March 2005,
http://news.bbc.co.uk/1/hi/4308217.stm [accessed 17 March 2010].

87 'Syrian troops leave Lebanese soil', BBC News – Middle East, 26 April
2005, http://news.bbc.co.uk/1/hi/4484325.stm [accessed 17 March 2010].

88 'Huge Beirut protest backs Syria', BBC News – Middle East, 8 March 2005,
http://news.bbc.co.uk/1/hi/4329201.stm [accessed 17 March 2010].

89 Magda Abu Fadil, 'Live from Martyrs' Square: Lebanon's reality TV turns
coverage of peaceful protests into a media battle', *Transnational
Broadcasting Studies* 14 (2005), http://www.tbsjournal.com/Archives/
Spring05/abufadil.html [accessed 17 March 2010].

90 Elisabeth Eaves, 'Syria squeezed', *Lebanon Wire*, 19 April 2005, http://
www.lebanonwire.com/0504/05041901SLT.asp [accessed   17   March
2005].

91 Michael Young, *The ghosts of Martyrs' Square: an eyewitness account of Lebanon's life struggle* (New York, 2010).

92 'Protestors set up camp in Beirut', BBC World News – Middle East, 2 December 2006, http://news.bbc.co.uk/1/hi/world/middle_east/6201084 .stm [accessed 17 March 2010].

3. Imposition and Resistance in Economic Life

1 Jeremy Harding, Review of Gilles Kepel, *Jihad: the trail of political Islam* (London, 2002), *London Review of Books*, 24/14, 25 July 2002, pp. 6–9.

2 See the essays collected in Edmund Burke and Ira Lapidus (eds.), *Islam, politics and social movements* (Berkeley, CA, 1988).

3 Donald Quataert, *Social disintegration and popular resistance in the Ottoman Empire, 1881–1908: reactions to European economic penetration* (New York, 1983) pp. 64–5.

4 Quataert, *Social disintegration and popular resistance* (1983) pp. 14–24.

5 Kohei Hashimoto, 'Lebanese population movement 1920–1939', in A. Hourani and N. Shehadi (eds.), *The Lebanese in the world: a century of emigration* (London, 1992) pp. 82–3.

6 John Chalcraft, *The striking cabbies of Cairo and other stories: crafts and guilds in Egypt 1863–1914* (Albany, NY, 2004) pp. 42–3, 165–75, 187.

7 Quataert, *Social disintegration and popular resistance* (1983) pp. 91, 86–92.

8 Robert Vitalis, *When capitalists collide: business conflict and the end of empire in Egypt* (Berkeley, CA, 1995) pp. 32–4.

9 Nikki Keddie, *Religion and rebellion in Iran – the tobacco protest of 1891–92* (London, 1966).

10 Vitalis, *When capitalists collide* (1995) pp. 42–4.

11 Eric Davis, *Challenging colonialism* (Princeton, NJ: Princeton University Press, 1983) pp. 123–35; Vitalis, *When capitalists collide* (1995) p. 45.

12 Joel Beinin, 'Islam, Marxism and the Shubra al-Khayma textile workers: Muslim Brothers and Communists in the Egyptian trade union movement', in Burke and Lapidus (eds.), *Islam, politics and social movements* (1988); Richard Mitchell, *The society of the Muslim Brothers* (Oxford, 1969) pp. 43–8.

13 Ellis Goldberg, *Tinker, tailor, textile worker: class and politics in Egypt 1930–1952* (Berkeley, CA, 1986) pp. 139–72.

14 Joel Beinin, *Workers and peasants in the modern Middle East* (Cambridge, 2001) pp. 126–7.

15 The Solidarity Center (Joel Beinin, principal author), *The struggle for worker rights in Egypt* (Washington, DC, 2010) p. 10; Joel Beinin, 'Egyptian textile workers: from craft artisans facing European competition to proletarians contending with the state', in Lex Heerma van Voss, Els Hiemstra-Kuperus, and Elise van Nederveen Meerkerk (eds.), *The Ashgate companion to the history of textile workers, 1650–2000* (Farnham, England, 2010), pp. 172–97.

16 Larbi Sadiki, 'Popular uprisings and Arab democratisation', *International Journal of Middle East Studies* 32/1 (2000) pp. 79–85.

17 Solidarity Center, *Struggle for worker rights* (2010) p. 10.

18 James Toth, 'Beating plowshares into swords: the relocation of rural Egyptian workers and their discontent', in Hopkins and Westegaard (eds.), *Directions of change in rural Egypt* (Cairo, Egypt, 1998) p. 72.

19 Fatemah Farag, 'Chronicles of an uprising', *Al-Ahram Weekly Online*, 18–24 January 2007, Issue 828, http://weekly.ahram.org.eg/2007/828/special.htm [accessed 13 November 2009].

20 Jim Paul, 'Riots in Morocco', *MERIP Reports* 99 (1981) pp. 30–1.

21 David Seddon, 'Riot and rebellion: political responses to economic crisis in North Africa, Tunisia, Morocco and Sudan', in Berch Berberoglu (ed)., *Power and stability in the Middle East* (London, 1989) pp. 114–35.

22 Eberhard Kienle, *A grand delusion: democracy and economic reform in Egypt* (London, 2000) pp. 77–88.

23 Marsha Pripstein Posusney, *Labor and the state in Egypt: workers, unions and economic restructuring 1952–1996* (New York, 1997) pp. 73–4.

24 Assef Bayat, 'Populism, liberalization and popular participation: industrial democracy in Egypt', *Economic and Industrial Democracy* 14 (1993) pp. 77–8; see also Pripstein Posusney, *Labor and the state in Egypt* (New York, 1997).

25 Marsha Pripstein Posusney, 'Irrational workers: the moral economy of labor protest in Egypt', *World Politics* 46/1 (1993) pp. 102, 117.

26 Omar El Shafei, *Workers, trade unions and the state in Egypt 1984–1989* [Cairo Papers in Social Science, Vol. 18, Monograph 2, Summer 1995] (Cairo, Egypt, 1995) pp. 22–5.

27 Pripstein Posusney, 'Irrational workers' (1993) pp. 102–4, 109–14.

28 Anne Alexander, 'Leadership and collective action in the Egyptian trade unions', *Work, Employment and Society* 24/2 (2010), p. 246.

29 Solidarity Center, *Struggle for worker rights* (2010) pp. 16–18; Joel Beinin, 'A workers' social movement on the margin of the global neoliberal order, Egypt 2004–2009', in Joel Beinin and Frédéric Vairel (eds.), *Social movements, mobilization, and contestation in the Middle East and North Africa* (Stanford, CA, 2011) pp. 186–91.

30 *Research briefing: Egypt's strike wave* (text: Anne Alexander; photos: Hossam el-Hamalawy) 2009 Creative Commons Attribution noncommercial share alike http://www.harakat.org/ngpa_egybriefing0909.pdf [accessed 23 November 2009].

31 Alexander, 'Leadership and collective action' (2010) p. 251.

32 Alexander, 'Leadership and collective action' (2010) p. 250.

33 Omar Said, 'Egypt: lessons from the labor movement', 26 August 2009, *Menassat*, http://www.menassat.com/?q=en/news-articles/7171-egypt-taking-lessons-labor-movement [accessed 8 October 2009]; Beinin, 'A workers' social movement' (2011) pp. 191–6.

34 Alastair Sharp, 'Analysis: Egypt workers fight for pay, not against the state', *Reuters*, 13 July 2009, http://www.reuters.com/article/2009/07/13/idUSLC693674 [accessed 8 October 2009].

35 Liam Stack and Maram Mazen, 'Striking Mahalla workers demand government fulfil broken promises', *The Daily News*, 27 September 2007, http://www.thedailynewsegypt.com/archive/striking-mahalla-workers-demand-govt-fulfill-broken-promises-dp1.html [accessed 16 October 2009].

36 Center for Trade Union and Workers Services 'Tanta Linen, Flax and Oil Co Workers in front of Egyptian Cabinet', 10 February 2010, http://www.ctuws .com/default.aspx?item=417 [accessed 15 November 2010]; BBC News – Middle East, 'Unions and police clash in Egypt', 11 February 2010, http:// news.bbc.co.uk/go/pr/fr/-/1/hi/world/middle_east/8510131.stm [accessed 15 November 2010].

37 Quoted in Yassin Gaber, 'Egypt workers lay down demands at new trade union conference', *Al-Ahram online*, 3 March 2011, http://english.ahram .org.eg/~/NewsContent/1/64/6901/Egypt/Politics-/Egypt-workers-lay-down -demands-at-new-trade-union-.aspx [accessed 17 September 2011].

38 Human Rights Watch, 'Egypt: revoke ban on strikes, demonstrations', 25 March 2011, http://www.hrw.org/news/2011/03/25/egypt-revoke-ban -strikes-demonstrations [accessed 17 September 2011].

39 Khaled Ali to *Al-Masry al-Yawm*, cited in William Rogers, 'Five sentenced in Egypt for violating anti-strike decree', 6 July 2011, *Left Labor Reporter*, http://leftlaborreporter.wordpress.com/2011/07/06/five-sentenced -in-egypt-for-violating-anti-strike-decree/ [accessed 17 September 2011].

40 Hisham Fouad, 'Egypt: Mahalla workers win big concessions', *MENA Solidarity Network*, 8 September 2011, http://menasolidaritynetwork .com/2011/09/12/egypt-mahalla-workers-win-big-concessions/ [accessed 19 September 2011].

41 Beinin, *Workers and peasants* (2001) pp. 132–6; Leonard Binder, *In a moment of enthusiasm: political power and the second stratum in Egypt* (Chicago, 1978) pp. 226–300.

42 Land Centre for Human Rights, *Land and peasant*, report 55, http://www .lchr-eg.org/index.htm [accessed 15 January 2011]; Beshir Sakr and Phanjof Tarcir, 'Rural Egypt returns to the ancien régime', *Le Monde Diplomatique* [English Edition], October 2007.

43 James C. Scott, *Weapons of the weak: everyday forms of peasant resistance* (New Haven, CT, 1987).

44 Roger Ballard, 'A background report on the operation of informal value transfer systems (hawala)' (2003), http://www.casas.org.uk/papers/ pdfpapers/hawala.pdf

45 Benedetta Berti, 'The economics of counterterrorism: devising a normative regulatory framework for the hawala system', *MIT International Review* (2008) p. 15.

46 See the Abu Dhabi declaration on Hawala made at the First International Conference on Hawala 16 May 2002, p. 94, in IMF Monetary and Financial Systems Department, *Regulatory frameworks for hawala and other remittance systems* (2005); *MIT International Review* (2008) pp. 19–21.

47 Berti, *MIT International Review* (2008) p. 17; Maryam Razavy, 'Hawala etc', *Crime, Law and Social Change* 44/3 (2005) pp. 277–99.

48 Charles Tripp, *Islam and the moral economy – the challenge of capitalism* (Cambridge, 2006) pp. 137–9.

49 Mohammad al-Hamzani, 'Islamic banks unaffected by global financial crisis', *Al-Sharq al-Awsat*, 30 September 2008, http://www.asharq-e.com/ news.asp?section=6&id=14245 [accessed 12 December 2009].

4. Body Politics: Women's Rights and Women's Resistance

1 See, for instance, the demonstrations and violence across Afghanistan in April 2011, following the publicized 'trial' and burning of a Quran by a Christian pastor in the U.S. state of Florida, http://www.bbc.co.uk/news/world-south-asia-12949975 [accessed 4 April 2011].

2 Thomas Endbrink, 'Ahmadinejad and clerics fight over headscarves', *The Washington Post*, 20 July 2011, http://www.washingtonpost.com/world/middle-east/ahmadinejad-and-clerics-fight-over-scarves/2011/07/12/gIQAhoqJPI_print.html [accessed 20 July 2011].

3 See Timothy Mitchell, 'Everyday metaphors of power', *Theory and Society* 19/5 (1990) pp. 545–59.

4 Jamal Arfaoui, 'Demand exceeds capacity at Maghreb abused women's shelters', 21 February 2010, http://www.magharebia.com/cocoon/awi/xhtml1/en_GB/features/awi/features/2010/02/21/feature-01 [accessed 19 April 2010].

5 Léon Buskens, 'Recent debates on family law reform in Morocco: Islamic law as politics in an emerging public sphere', *Islamic Law and Society* 10/1 (2003) pp 70–7.

6 Laurie Brand, *Women, the state, and political liberalization – Middle Eastern and North African experiences* (New York, 1998) pp. 46–68.

7 Brand, *Women, the state, and political liberalization* (1998) pp. 35–45.

8 Josep Lluis Mateo Dieste, '"Demonstrating Islam": the conflict of text and the Moudawanna reform in Morocco', *Muslim World* 99 (2009) p. 144.

9 Brand, *Women, the state, and political liberalization* (1998) p. 70.

10 Brand, *Women, the state, and political liberalization* (1998) pp. 71–3.

11 Dieste, '"Demonstrating Islam"' (2009) p. 145.

12 Fatima Harrak, 'The history and significance of the new Moroccan Family Code', Working Paper 09–002 March 2009 (Institute for the Study of Islamic Thought in Africa, Buffett Centre, Northwestern University) p. 3, http://www.cics.northwestern.edu/documents/workingpapers/ISITA_09-002_Harrak.pdf

13 Bruce Maddy-Weitzman, 'Women, Islam and the Moroccan state: the struggle over the Personal Status Law', *Middle East Journal* 59/3 (2005) p. 403.

14 Dieste, '"Demonstrating Islam"' (2009) pp. 145–6.

15 Buskens, 'Recent debates' (2003) pp. 103–4.

16 Dieste, '"Demonstrating Islam"' (2009) p. 147.

17 Maddy-Weitzman, 'Women, Islam and the Moroccan state' (2005) p. 404.

18 Maddy-Weitzman, 'Women, Islam and the Moroccan state' (2005) pp. 404–6.

19 On the idea of 'rightful resistance', see Kevin J. O'Brien, 'Rightful resistance', *World Politics* 49/1 (1996) pp. 31–55.

20 Jamal Arfaoui, 'Demand exceeds capacity at Maghreb abused women's shelters', 21 February 2010, http://www.magharebia.com/cocoon/awi/xhtml1/en_GB/features/awi/features/2010/02/21/feature-01 [accessed 19 April 2010].

21 Loubna Skalli, 'Women and poverty in Morocco: the many faces of social exclusion', *Feminist Review* 69 (2001) pp. 73–89.

22 Naoufel Cherkaoui, 'Morocco issues pre-emptive ban on renowned French feminist group', 26 February 2009, http://www.magharebia.com/cocoon/awi/xhtml1/en_GB/features/awi/features/2009/02/26/feature-02 [accessed 21 April 2010].

23 Bernard Gwertzman and Isobel Coleman, 'Reform and women's rights movements intertwined in Iran', 24 June 2009, *Council on Foreign Relations* http://www.cfr.org/iran/reform-womens-rights-movements-intertwined-iran/p19694 [accessed 4 April 2011]; 'Women fight polygamy proposal', 8 February 2010, http://fairfamilylaw.in/spip.php?article418 [accessed 4 April 2011].

24 Shahla Sherkat, *Zanân: le journal de l'autre Iran* (Paris, 2010).

25 Valentine Moghadam, *Modernizing women: gender and social change in the Middle East* (Boulder, CO, 2003), p. 195.

26 Deniz Kandiyoti, 'Gender, power and contestation – rethinking bargaining with patriarchy', in Cecile Jackson and Ruth Pearson (eds.), *Feminist visions of development* (London, 1998) pp. 135–54.

27 Shahin Gerami and Melodye Lehnerer, 'Women's agency and household diplomacy: negotiating fundamentalism', *Gender and Society* 15/4 (2001) pp. 562–4.

28 Moghadam, *Modernizing women* (2003) pp. 208, 216.

29 Moghadam, *Modernizing women* (2003) pp. 216–7, quoting interview in *Zan-e Rouz*, 1994.

30 Fereshteh Ahmadi, 'Islamic feminism in Iran: feminism in a new Islamic context', *Journal of Feminist Studies in Religion* 22/2 (2006) pp. 33–53; Ziba Mir-Hosseini, 'Women and politics in post-Khomeini Iran: divorce, veiling and emerging feminist voices', in Haleh Afshar (ed.), *Women and politics in the third world* (London, 1996) pp. 142–70; Louise Halper, 'Law and women's agency in post-revolutionary Iran', *Harvard Journal of Law and Gender* 28/1 (2005) pp. 110–42.

31 Moghadam, *Modernizing women* (2003) p. 219; Halper, 'Law and women's agency' (2005) p. 100.

32 Ziba Mir-Hosseini, 'Conservative-Reform conflict over women's rights in Iran', *International Journal of Politics, Culture and Society* 16/1 (2002) p. 39; Nahid Yeganeh, 'Women, nationalism and Islam in contemporary political discourse in Iran', *Feminist Review* 44 (1993) pp. 10–11.

33 Moghadam, *Modernizing women* (2003) p. 215.

34 Mir-Hosseini, 'Conservative-Reform conflict' (2002) p. 40; Ziba Mir-Hosseini, 'How the door of ijtihad was opened and closed: a comparative analysis of recent family law reforms in Iran and Morocco', *Washington and Lee Law Review* 64/4 (2007) pp. 1504–5.

35 Moghadam, *Modernizing women* (2003) p. 217, citing Faeza Hashemi.

36 'Iranian cleric blames quakes on promiscuous women', BBC News – Middle East, http://news.bbc.co.uk/go/em/fr/-/1/hi/world/middle_east/8631775.stm [accessed 14 May 2010].

37 Iraq Gorgin, 'Does the Iranian government fear educated women?' http://www.iran-press-service.com/ips/articles-2008/february-2008/does-iranian-government-fear-educated-women.shtml [accessed 21 April 2010].

38 'Iran backs first woman minister', BBC News – Middle East, http://news.bbc.co.uk/1/hi/8235264.stm [accessed 14 May 2010].

39 Amnesty International Report 2009, http://report2009.amnesty.org/en/
   regions/middle-east-north-africa/iran [accessed 4 April 2011].

40 Rashid Khalidi, *Palestinian identity* (New York, 1997) pp. 26–7; Ellen
   Fleischmann, *The nation and its 'new women': the Palestinian women's
   movement 1920–1948* (Berkeley, CA, 2003) pp. 115–36.

41 Laleh Khalili, *Heroes and martyrs of Palestine* (Cambridge, 2007) pp. 182–3;
   Julie Peteet, *Gender in crisis: women and the Palestinian resistance movement*
   (New York, 1991); Kathy Glavanis-Grantham, 'The women's movement,
   feminism and national struggle in Palestine – unresolved contradictions', in
   Afshar (ed.), *Women and politics* (1996) pp. 171–85.

42 Leila Khaled, *My people shall live – autobiography of a revolutionary by
   Leila Khaled as told to George Hajjar* (Toronto, Canada, 1975);
   Rajeswari Mohan, 'Loving Palestine: nationalist activism and feminist
   agency in Leila Khaled's subversive bodily acts', *Interventions* 1/1
   (1998) pp. 52–80.

43 Frances Hasso, 'The "Women's Front": nationalism, feminism and modernity in Palestine', *Gender and Society* 12/4 (1998) p. 446.

44 Hasso, 'The "Women's Front"' (1998) p. 449.

45 Jeroen Gunning, *Hamas in politics – democracy, religion, violence* (London,
   2009) pp. 30–1, 62; Maria Holt, 'Palestinian women and the intifada – an
   exploration of images and realities', in Afshar (ed.), *Women and politics*
   (1996) pp. 186–7, 193–203.

46 Rabab Abdulhadi, 'The Palestinian women's autonomous movement: emergence, dynamics and challenges', *Gender and Society* 12/6 (1998) 656–7;
   Philippa Strum, 'West Bank women and the intifada: revolution within the
   revolution', in Suha Sabbagh (ed.), *Palestinian women of Gaza and the West
   Bank* (Bloomington, IN, 1998) pp. 63–77.

47 Cheryl A. Rubenberg, *Palestinian women: patriarchy and resistance on the
   West Bank* (Boulder, CO, 2001) pp. 214–47.

48 Frances Hasso, *Resistance, repression and gender politics in occupied
   Palestine and Jordan* (Syracuse, NY, 2005) pp. 122–6.

49 Abdulhadi, 'Palestinian women's autonomous movement' (1998) p. 657.

50 Fadwa Allabadi, 'Secular and Islamist women in Palestinian society',
   European Journal of Women's Studies 15/3 (2008) pp. 185–6.

51 Abdulhadi, 'Palestinian women's autonomous movement' (1998) pp. 666–
   8; 'The women's document: a tool for women's empowerment and struggle –
   an interview with Eileen Kuttab', pp. 121–6, in Suha Sabbagh (ed.), *Arab
   Women – between defiance and restraint* (New York, 1996).

52 Nathan Brown, *Palestinian civil society in theory and practice* (paper presented at the International Political Science Association, Washington DC,
   May 2003) p. 16. She won 11.5% of the vote against Arafat's 88.2%, http://
   www.sog-rc27.org/Paper/DC/Brown.doc [accessed 16 May 2010].

53 Islah Jad, 'Between religion and secularism: Islamist women of Hamas', in
   Fereshteh Nouraie-Simone (ed.), *On shifting ground: Muslim women in the
   global era* (New York, 2005) pp. 172–98.

54 Interview with Samira al-Halayka conducted by Khalid Amayreh February
   2010, Khalid Amayreh, *Islamist women's activism in occupied Palestine*
   (Conflicts Forum Monograph, 2010) p. 3.

55 Abdulhadi, 'Palestinian women's autonomous movement' (1998) p. 664.

56 Frances S. Hasso, 'Discursive and political deployments by/of the 2002 Palestinian women suicide bombers/martyrs', *Feminist Review* 81 Bodily Interventions (2005) p. 28.

57 Hasso, 'Discursive and political deployments' (2005) pp. 29–33.

58 Thomas Erdbrink, 'Iran stones 2 men to death; 3rd flees', *The Washington Post*, 14 January 2009, http://www.washingtonpost.com/wp-%20dyn/content/article/2009/01/13/AR2009011302174.html [accessed 3 April 2011].

59 Ian Black, 'Sakineh Mohammedi Ashtiani may not face death by stoning, says prosecutor', *The Guardian*, 2 January 2011, http://www.guardian.co.uk/world/2011/jan/02/sakineh-mohammadi-ashtiani-iran-sentence [accessed 3 April 2011].

60 Yeganeh, 'Women, nationalism and Islam' (1993) p. 16.

61 Kimia Sanati, 'Stoning for adultery – more a women's issue', Inter Press Service 4 December 2006, http://ipsnews.net/news.asp?idnews=35701 [accessed 3 April 2011].

62 In Lebanon, a draft law criminalizing violence against women was approved by the Council of Ministers in 2010, but it was delayed in its passage through parliament by the political upheavals in the country and by the vocal opposition of both the Sunni Muslim Dar al-Fatwa and the Higher Shi`a Islamic Council on the familiar grounds that the law 'intends to destroy the social construct of the family … built on a Western way that is incompatible with the norms and values of [Lebanese] society', http://www.hrw.org/en/news/2011/07/06/lebanon-enact-family-violence-bill-protect-women [accessed 26 July 2011]. However, in early August 2011, the Lebanese Parliament finally annulled Article 562 of the criminal code which had mitigated the sentence of those found guilty of killing a female relative on account of 'family honour', http://www.stophonourkillings.com/?q=node/8175 [accessed 15 September 2011].

63 Fadia Faqir, 'Intrafamily femicide in defence of honour: the case of Jordan', *Third World Quarterly* 22/1 (2001) pp. 72–4.

64 Elizabeth Faier, 'Looking in/acting out', *Political and Legal Anthropology Review* 20/2 (London, 1997) p. 7; Abdulhadi, 'Palestinian women's autonomous movement' (1998) p. 665.

65 http://users.ox.ac.uk/~metheses/MabuchiNoImages.pdf [accessed 3 April 2011]; Bouthaina Shaaban, *Both right and left handed: Arab women talk about their lives* (London, 1991) p. 170; Samira Haj, 'Palestinian women and patriarchal relations', *Signs: Journal of Women in Culture and Society* 17/4 (1992) pp. 761–78.

66 Abdulhadi, 'Palestinian women's autonomous movement' (1998) pp. 655–6, 658.

67 Faqir, 'Intrafamily femicide' (2001) pp. 74–5.

68 Tom Peter, 'Jordan honor killings draw tough response. Finally', GlobalPost, 7 April 2010, http://www.globalpost.com/dispatch/jordan/100323/honor-killings-jordan?page=0,0 [accessed 23 April 2010].

69 'Law reform targets "honor" crimes', Stop Honour Killings, 11 August 2011, http://www.stophonourkillings.com/?q=node/8175 [accessed 22 August 2011].

70 Germaine Tillion, *The republic of cousins: women's oppression in Mediterranean society* (London, 1983).

71 Nadje al-Ali and Nicola Pratt, *What kind of liberation? Women and the occupation of Iraq* (Berkeley, CA, 2009) pp. 46–80; Human Rights Watch, *At a crossroads: human rights in Iraq eight years after the US led invasion* (2011) pp. 6–29.

72 'Iraq: the Organization of Women's Freedom in Iraq', MADRE website, http://www.madre.org/index/meet-madre-1/our-partners-6/iraq-the -organization-of-womens-freedom-in-iraq-37.html [accessed 8 April 2011], and 'Iraq: an underground railroad for Iraqi women', MADRE website, http://www.madre.org/index/meet-madre-1/our-projects-20/iraq-an-under ground-railroad-for-iraqi-women-57.html [accessed 8 April 2011].

73 Nadera Shalhoub-Kervorkian, 'Re-examining femicide: breaking the silence and crossing "scientific" borders', *Signs: Journal of Women in Culture and Society* 28/2 (2002) pp. 586–91, 602–4.

5. History Wars: Contesting the Past, Reclaiming the Future

1 These were later published in the U.S. journal under the title 'Charging Israel with Original Sin', *Commentary*, September 1989, http://www .commentarymagazine.com/article/charging-israel-with-original-sin/. The battle continued in its pages – see Avi Shlaim's and Benny Morris's letters to the editor and Shabtai Teveth's letter in riposte, 'The Founding of Israel', *Commentary*, February 1990, http://www.commentarymagazine.com/ article/the-founding-of-israel/ [both accessed 10 August 2010].

2 Ernest Renan, in his famous lecture 'What is a Nation?' at the Sorbonne on 11 March 1882, accurately foretold some of the consequences of subjecting national myths to scrutiny: 'Forgetting, I would even say historical error, is an essential factor in the creation of a nation, and thus the advance of historical studies is often dangerous for [the idea of] nationality. Indeed, historical investigation brings to light those acts of violence which have occurred at the beginnings of all political formations...'. Ernest Renan, 'What is a nation?', in Geoff Eley and Ronald Suny (eds.), *Becoming national: a reader* (Oxford, 1996) pp. 41–55.

3 Michel-Rolph Trouillot, *Silencing the past – power and the production of history* (Boston, 1995) pp. 22–30.

4 As the Algerian political scientist, Fanny Colonna, remarked, 'one thing has struck me [thinking about Algerian history and politics] and that is the violence which is done to people when imposing (or offering) a version of history that does not belong to them'. Fanny Colonna, *Les versets de l'invincibilité* (Paris, 1995) p. 366.

5 Avi Shlaim, 'The debate about 1948', *International Journal of Middle Eastern Studies* 27/3 (1995) pp. 287–304.

6 Uri Ram, *The changing agenda of Israeli sociology* (New York, 1995) p. 41, cited in Gershon Shafir, 'Israeli society: a counterview', *Israel Studies* 1/2 (1996) pp. 205–6.

7 Shafir, 'Israeli society' (1996) pp. 190, 208–10; Yehuda Shenhav, 'Jews from Arab countries and the Palestinian Right of Return: an ethnic community in

the realms of national memory', *British Journal of Middle East Studies* 29/1 (2002) pp. 27–56.

8 Moshe Lissak. '"Critical" sociology and "Establishment" sociology in the Israeli academic community: ideological struggles or academic discourse', *Israel Studies* 1/1 (1996) pp. 247–94; Eliezer Ben-Raphael, 'Critical vs non-critical sociology: an evaluation', *Israel Studies* 2/1 (1997) pp. 175–89.

9 Peter Berger, cited in Chaim I. Waxman, 'Critical sociology and the end of ideology in Israel', *Israel Studies* 2/1 (1997) p. 194.

10 Waxman, 'Critical sociology' (1997) pp. 196–201.

11 Uri Ram cited in Shafir, 'Israeli society' (1996) p. 205.

12 Lissak cited in Ben-Raphael, 'Critical vs non-critical sociology' (1997) p. 178.

13 Gabriel Sheffer (ed.), *Dynamics of a conflict: a re-examination of the Arab–Israeli conflict* (Atlantic Highlands, NJ, 1975); Yehoshafat Harkabi, *The Bar Kochba Syndrome* (Chappaqua, NY, 1983) and *Israel's fateful decisions* (London, 1988) – contrast these books with his *Arab attitudes to Israel* (London, 1972).

14 Simha Flapan, *The birth of Israel – myths and realities* (New York, 1987).

15 Elie Podeh, *The Arab–Israeli conflict in Israeli history textbooks, 1948–2000* (Westport, CT, 2002) pp. 22–3.

16 Podeh, *The Arab–Israeli conflict* (2002) pp. 25–6.

17 Ilan Pappé, 'The Tantura case in Israel: the Katz research and trial', *Journal of Palestine Studies* 30/3 (2001) p. 20.

18 Ilan Pappé, *The ethnic cleansing of Palestine* (Oxford, 2006); Benny Morris, 'Politics by other means', *The New Republic*, 22 March 2004.

19 Cited in Silberstein, *The postzionism debates: knowledge and power in Israeli culture* (London, 1999) pp. 1–2.

20 Avi Shlaim, 'The war of the Israeli historians', Lecture at Georgetown University, Washington DC, 1 December 2003, p. 6; an abridged version of this talk is available in Avi Shlaim, 'La guerre des historiens israéliens', *Annales* 59/1 (2004) pp. 161–9.

21 Pappé, 'The Tantura case' (2001) pp. 19–39.

22 Yoav Gelber, *Palestine 1948: war, escape and the emergence of the Palestinian refugee problem* (Brighton, England, 2001) pp. 326–7.

23 Uri Ram, 'Postnationalist pasts: the case of Israel', in J. Ollick (ed.), *States of memory* (Durham, NC, 2003) pp. 236–50.

24 Aharon Megged, 'The Israeli suicide drive' (in Hebrew), *Haaretz*, 10 June 1994, and 'One-way trip on the highway to self-destruction', *Jerusalem Post*, 17 June 1994.

25 *Yediot Ahronot*, 29 September 1999, cited in Daniel Gutwein, 'Left and right post-Zionism: the privatization of Israeli collective memory', *Journal of Israeli History* 20/2 (2001) p. 27.

26 Silberstein, *Postzionism Debates* (1999) p. 1.

27 Ethan Bronner, 'In Israel, new grade school texts for history replace myths with facts', *New York Times*, 14 August 1999; Amnon Raz-Krakotzkin, 'History textbooks and the limits of Israeli consciousness', *JIH* 20/2 (2001) pp. 155–65; Podeh, *The Arab–Israeli conflict* (2002) pp. 61–2.

28 In this respect, Ilan Pappé's article about setting up the Palestinian–Israeli Academic Dialogue in 1997 – and its vicissitudes – is indicative of some of

the dynamics involved. 'Histories and historians in Israel and Palestine', *Transforming Cultures* 1/1 (2006) http://epress.lib.uts.edu.au/journals/TfC [accessed 11 August 2010].

29 Pappé, 'Histories and historians' (2006) p. 37.

30 Avi Shlaim, 'When historians matter', *Prospect* 147, 29 June 2008, http://www.prospectmagazine.co.uk/2008/06/whenhistoriansmatter/ [accessed 28 January 2011].

31 Assaf Likhovski, 'Post-post-Zionist historiography', *Israel Studies* 15/2 (2010) p. 15; Ofira Seliktar, '"Tenured Radicals" in Israel: from new Zionism to political activism', *Israel Affairs* 11/4 (2005) pp. 722–7.

32 *Paradise Now* [*Al-Janna al-An/Gan Eden Akhshav*] (2005), directed by Hany Abu-Assad – a Palestinian/Israeli/French/German/Netherlands production; *The Lemon Tree* [*Etz Limon/Shajara Limun*] (2008), directed by Eran Riklis – an Israeli/German/French production.

33 *Zochrot/Dhakirat* [remembering] http://www.zochrot.org/index.php ?lang=english [accessed 15 April 2010].

34 See, for instance, Idit Zertal, *Israel's holocaust and the politics of nationhood* (Cambridge, 2005); Shlomo Sands, *The invention of the Jewish people* (London, 2009).

35 As the historian Avi Shlaim stated, 'I am a historian – my aim is to write about the [Arab–Israeli] conflict as fully, accurately and interestingly as I can' [interview, Oxford, 21 January 2011].

36 An interesting – if ambivalent – opinion poll was carried out in Israel in 2009: 'The Israeli–Jewish Collective Memory of the Israeli–Arab/Palestinian Conflict', by Professor Daniel Bar Tal and Rafi Nets-Zehngut. This suggested that amongst the segment of the Jewish Israeli public questioned in the poll, 47.2% believed that the Palestinians had been expelled in 1948 by Israeli forces, whereas 40% subscribed to the old version that they had left of their own accord, and more or less equal percentages ascribed responsibility for continuation of the conflict to the Arabs and to the Israelis respectively. Nevertheless, 40% were unaware that the Arabs were a majority in Palestine at the beginning of the twentieth century or that the UN 1947 partition plan offered the 1.3 million Arab inhabitants of Palestine 44% of the territory, compared with the 55% it offered to the 600,000 Jewish inhabitants. Furthermore, the overwhelming majority of respondents subscribed to the government's version of more recent history when it came to the breakdown of negotiations, the eruption of the second *intifada* and the Lebanon war.

37 'Berber' is the anglicized form of the Arabic *al-barbar* which was itself taken from the Greek term '*Barbaros*' (foreigner). This seems to have been used in the period of the Byzantine Empire to refer to the majority of the inhabitants of North Africa, although in classical times, Herodotus, for instance, used the term *Maxyes* to refer to them, and in Latin they were generally referred to as *Mazyces*. It is thought that this is derived from the term *Amazigh/ Imazighen* (sometimes translated as 'free men' or 'noble men') used locally to refer to themselves. This has now become the term used by those asserting a distinctive indigenous non-Arab, Amazigh/Berber identity, although more particular local identifying terms are also used, such as Kabyle, Chaoui or Touareg, by different groups across North Africa.

38 Mohand Salah Tahi, 'The struggle for linguistic rights and democratic pluralism: the case of the Kabyle Berbers in Algeria', in B. Isaksson and M. Laanatza (eds.), *About the Berbers: history, language, culture and socio-economic conditions* (Uppsala, 2004) pp. 218–9.

39 Jonathan Hill, 'Identity and instability in postcolonial Algeria', *Journal of North African Studies* 11/1 (2006) pp. 5–7, 9–10.

40 L. Martinez, *The Algerian civil war 1990–1998* (London, 2000) p. 31, fn 29. Ali Benhadj [Ali Bin al-Hajj] was one of the founders of the FIS.

41 James McDougall, *History and the culture of nationalism in Algeria* (Cambridge, 2006) p. 205.

42 *Le pouvoir* – 'the power' – means the network of state security and intelligence agencies that, in the view of many Algerians, constitute the real power in the state, lurking behind and manipulating the public institutions.

43 Salam Chaker, 'Langue et identité berbères (Algérie/émigration): un enjeu de société', in Jean-Robert Henry (ed.), *Nouveaux enjeux culturels au Maghreb* (Paris, 1986) pp. 173–4; Mohand Salah Tahi, in Isaksson and Laanatza (2004) pp. 212–14.

44 Tahi, in Isaksson and Laanatza (2004) pp. 214–17.

45 Tahi, in Isaksson and Laanatza (2004) pp. 217–18.

46 Chaker, in Henry (1986) p. 177.

47 Stora, cited in Maddy-Weitzman, 'Berber/Amazigh "memory work"', in Bruce Maddy-Weitzman and Daniel Zisenwine (eds.), *The Maghrib in the new century: identity, religion and politics* (Gainesville, FL, 2007) p. 114.

48 Chaker, in Henry (1986) p. 178.

49 International Crisis Group, *Algeria: unrest and impasse in Kabylia*, Report 15, 10 June 2003, p. 7.

50 Jane E. Goodman, 'Imazighen on trial: human rights and Berber identity in Algeria, 1985', in Katherina E. Hoffman and Susan Gibson Miller (eds.), *Berbers and others: beyond tribe and nation in the Maghrib* (Bloomington, IN, 2010) p. 106.

51 Goodman, 'Imazighen on trial' (2010) p. 118.

52 ICG Report No 15, 10 June 2003, pp. 7–8.

53 McDougall (2006) pp. 184–5, 212–13; ICG Report No 15, 10 June 2003, pp. 9–10. For the text of the Issad Report of 7 July 2001, see http://www.tamazgha.fr/Rapport-Issad,240.html [accessed 18 April 2010].

54 Said Ould-Khadra, '"Hogra" is the lot of all young Algerians', Algeria-interface.com, 14 June 2001, http://www.algeria-watch.org/en/articles/2001/hogra.htm [accessed 18 April 2010].

55 Mohammed Arkoun, 'Langues, société et religion dans le Maghreb indépendent', in Marial-Angels Roque (ed.), *Les cultures du Maghreb* (Paris, 1996) pp. 88–9.

56 Maddy-Weizman, 'Berber/Amazigh memory work' (2007) p. 116.

57 See the website http://aureschaouia.free.fr [accessed 23 February 2011].

58 Mohamad Benrabah, 'Language in education planning in Algeria: historical development and current issues', *Language Policy* 6 (2007) p. 235 [pp. 225–52].

59 The historical connection between the construction of 'Berber' and 'Arab' in Algeria and the dominant power of the day is well brought out by James

McDougall in his close examination of this question in Algerian historiography and society in his chapter, 'Histories of heresy and salvation: Arabs, Berbers, community and state', in Katherina E. Hoffman and Susan Gibson Miller (eds.), *Berbers and others: beyond tribe and nation in the Maghrib* (Bloomington, IN, 2010) pp. 15–37.

60 Miriam R. Lowi, *Oil wealth and the poverty of politics* (Cambridge, 2009) pp. 126–44.

6. Symbolic Forms of Resistance: Art and Power

1 From a presentation by Vera Tamari at a conference 'Art and War' in Ramallah in November 2004 – personal communication from Vera Tamari 3 September 2011.

2 Kamal Boullata, *Palestinian art – from 1850 to the present* (London, 2009) p. 286.

3 See the fairly well-established idiom of symbolic representation in poster art of the twentieth century in Jeffrey T. Schnapp, *Revolutionary tides: the art of the revolutionary poster 1914–1989* (Milan, 2005).

4 See Paul Guiragossian's posters for the Communist Party and the Lebanese National Resistance in 1982. Zeina Maasri, *Off the wall – political posters of the Lebanese civil war* (2009) figs. 1.8. 1.9. 1.10; also Laila Shawa's paintings in the series 'Walls of Gaza' of 1990s (see Figs. 13 and 14).

5 See, for example, the Israel Defence Forces Order No. 101 of 27 August 1967 following the occupation of Jerusalem, the West Bank and Gaza, relating to the 'Prohibition of Incitement and Hostile Propaganda Actions' B'tselem website, http://www.btselem.org/english/Legal_Documents/19670827_Order _Regarding_Prohibition_of_Incitement_and_Hostile_Propaganda.pdf [accessed 17 October 2010].

6 This is well exemplified in the role of art in emerging nationalisms and the political-aesthetic struggles associated with this. See Partha Mitter, *Art and nationalism in colonial India 1850–1922* (Cambridge, 1994).

7 Some examples of this are well illustrated in Karima Khalil (ed.), *Messages from Tahrir – signs from Egypt's revolution* (Cairo, Egypt, 2011) and on the website http://www.tahrirdocuments.org

8 Such as the tank commander who fired at Saddam Hussein's portrait in Basra in 1991, the demonstrators' defacing of the posters of President Ben Ali in Tunisia in January 2011, or the destruction of the statue of Hafiz al-Asad by protestors in Dar'a in March 2011. See also Dario Gamboni, *The destruction of art – iconoclasm and vandalism since the French revolution* (London, 1997) pp. 51–90.

9 Laila Shawa talking about her picture 'Children of war, children of peace' said that there had been 'no change in these children's lives and the trauma and the dispossession has carried on. The only apparent difference ... was the change in the colour of the graffiti which became brighter'. Venetia Porter, *Word into art – artists of the modern Middle East Dubai 2008* (Dubai, 2008) p. 137.

10 Jeffrey Schnapp, *Revolutionary tides – the art of the political poster* (Milan, 2005).

11 Maasri, *Off the wall* (2009) p. 38 and fig. 1.1 – 'Land Day 1980'.

12 Beth Baron, *Egypt as a woman: nationalism, gender and politics* (Berkeley, CA, 2005).

13 Interview with Katherine Viner of *The Guardian*, 26 January 2000, on PFLP website, http://www.pflp.ps/english/?q=interview-leila-khaled-guardian -2000 [accessed 3 November 2010].

14 http://www.badil.org/annual-al-awda-award/itemlist/category/135-2010 [accessed 7 October 2010].

15 Balaghi, 'Iranian visual arts' (2002) p. 33.

16 The *pardeh* had the added resonance in Iran of being used in the `ashura ceremonies, marking the martyrdom of the Prophet Muhammad's grandson, Imam Hussein bin `Ali. Peter Chelkowski and Hamid Dabashi, *Staging a revolution: the art of persuasion in the Islamic Republic of Iran* (London, 2000) pp. 39–40, 98–105.

17 Chelkowski and Dabashi, *Staging a revolution* (2000) pp. 140–75.

18 Maasri, *Off the wall* (2009) p. 50.

19 Haggai Ram, 'Multiple iconographies...'; Balaghi and Gumpert, *Picturing Iran* (2002) pp. 97–100.

20 France 24, 'Spray cans in Tehran – risky but increasingly popular', 19 November 2009, http://observers.france24.com/en/content/20091119 -spray-cans-tehran-risky-increasingly-popular-graffiti [accessed 8 October 2010].

21 The ironic prominence of the purple patches that were intended to obscure the graffiti has been highlighted by the Palestinian artist Laila Shawa in some of her 'Walls of Gaza' series of paintings.

22 Julie Peteet, 'The writing on the walls: the Graffiti of the Intifada', *Cultural Anthropology* 11/2 (1996) p. 141.

23 Peteet, 'Writing on the walls' (1996) p. 145.

24 Toufic Haddad, 'Gaza's writing on the wall', Aljazeera website, 29 December 2009, http://english.aljazeera.net/focus/gazaoneyearon/2009/ 12/2009122710591848555 7.html [accessed 17 October 2010]; Mia Gröndahl, 'Writing for both heart and mind' http://www.miagrondahl .com/calligraphy.htm [accessed 21 October 2010]; Gaza Graffiti blog, http://gazagraffiti.wordpress.com/ [accessed 21 October 2010]; Mia Gröndahl, *Gaza graffiti – messages of love and politics* (Cairo, Egypt, 2009).

25 William Parry, *Against the wall – the art of resistance in Palestine* (London, 2010) p. 11.

26 Parry, *Against the wall* (2010) p. 10.

27 See the website of Abed Abdi – Palestinian visual artist from Haifa http:// abedabdi.com/index.php?option=com_phocagallery&view=category&id=8 &Itemid=50&lang=en [accessed 28 October 2010].

28 Jutta Held and Alex Potts, 'How do the political effects of pictures come about? The case of Picasso's "Guernica"', *Oxford Art Journal* 11/1 (1988) p. 36.

29 This has been echoed elsewhere in the region – for instance, in the works of the Kurdish artist, Osman Ahmed, whose powerful series of drawings evoke the suffering but also the steadfastness of the Kurdish people during the unimaginable violence of the Anfal operations launched against them by the

Iraqi government of Saddam Hussein in 1988–9 https://profiles.google.com/osman962/photos/5451070038908872113http://www.kurdmedia.com/article.aspx?id=15018 [accessed 28 August 2011].

30 Kamal Boullata, 'Artists re-member Palestine in Beirut', *JPS* 32/4 (2003) pp. 26–9, 31–2.

31 Ismail Shammout and Tamam al-Akhal, *Jadariyat al-sira wa-l-masira al-filastiniyya/Palestine: the Exodus and the Odyssey* (Amman, Jordan, 2000).

32 http://www.eltiqa.com/raed/e_2000.htm [accessed 28 October 2010]; Kamal Boullata, 'Art under siege', *JPS* 33/4 (2004) p. 76.

33 Boullata, 'Art under siege', *JPS*, 33/4 (Summer 2004) pp. 75–8.

34 Rose Issa, 'Weapons of mass discussion' in *Reorientations – contemporary Arab representations* [catalogue of an exhibition at the European Parliament Brussels, November 2008] pp. 10, 24–31.

35 John Berger, *The sense of sight* (New York, 1985) p. 8.

36 Boullata, 'Art under siege', *JPS* 33/4 (2004) p. 82.

37 Joseph Massad, 'Permission to paint: Palestinian art and the colonial encounter', *Art Journal* 66/3 (2007) p. 130; Muhammad Hallaj, 'Palestine – the suppression of an idea', *The Link* 15/1 (1982) pp. 11–12.

38 Boullata, 'Art under siege', *JPS* 33/4 (2004) p. 74.

39 Massad, 'Permission to paint: Palestinian art and the colonial encounter', *Art Journal* 66/3 (2007) p. 132; Adila Laidi-Hanieh, 'Arts, identity and survival: building cultural practices in Palestine', *JPS* 35/4 (2006) pp. 28–43.

40 http://www.stationmuseum.com/Made_In_Palestine/Made_In_Palestine.htm [accessed 28 October 2010].

41 Omesh Roychoudhuri, 'Made in Palestine', *Mother Jones*, 11 May 2005, http://motherjones.com/media/2005/05/made-palestine-1 [accessed 28 October 2010].

42 http://www.founoune.com/articles/index.php?mode=detail&id=554 [accessed 30 October 2010].

43 Ali Silem, 'Mouvement Aouchem: signes et résistance', in Noureddine Sraieb (ed.), *Pratiques et résistance culturelles au Maghreb* (Paris, 1992) pp. 197–200.

44 Cynthia Becker, 'Exile, memory and healing in Algeria', *African Arts* 42/2 (2009) pp. 24–31; the effect of this installation is best captured on the website Dailymotion http://www.dailymotion.com/video/xb856i_la-fenetre-du-vent_creation in Guillaume Fortin's film of Denis Martinez and a number of villagers at Ait Yenni, Kabylia, Algeria in 2004 [accessed 10 September 2011].

45 Personal communication from Hale Tenger Erden, 3 October 2011; Kosova, 'An extra struggle', *Bidoun* (2005) p. 71.

46 Halil Altindere, interviewed by Süreyya Evren, March 2007, 'An incident in Kiziltoprak', http://halilaltindere.wordpress.com/about/ [accessed 2 September 2011].

47 http://www.depoistanbul.net/en/activites_detail.asp?ac=37 [accessed 30 October 2010].

48 'If this exhibition doesn't wake them up it's not my fault!' interview with Halil Altindere by Isil Egrikavuk, *Boot Print* 1/ 2 (2007) p. 22.

49 Erden Kosova, 'An extra struggle', *Bidoun* (2005) p. 70; Helena Smith, 'Turkish PM sues over animal cartoon', *The Guardian*, 26 March 2005, http://www.guardian.co.uk/world/2005/mar/26/turkey.helenasmith [accessed 30 October 2010].

50 See Maasri, *Off the wall* (2009).

51 Personal communication with John Jurayj, 30 November 2011. All thirty portraits that comprise the work itself are also in the collection of The British Museum, London.

52 Venetia Porter, *Word into art – artists of the modern Middle East* (London, 2006) p. 110.

53 Porter, *Word into art* (2006) p. 113.

54 This can be seen on the Arteast website at http://www.arteeast.org/pages/ artists/article/122/?artist_id=10 [accessed 8 April 2011].

55 Porter, *Word into art* (2006) p. 112.

56 Kareem Risan, *Every day* (2005) is in The British Museum collection, accession number AN266062001.

57 Wafaa Bilal's website http://www.wafaabilal.com/html/sorrowBaghdad .html [accessed 21 October 2010].

58 Kari Lydersen, 'Shot more than 40,000 times, an Iraqi artist spreads a message with a paintball gun', *Alternet*, 22 June 2007, http://www.alternet .org/world/54537/?page=1 [accessed 28 October 2010].

59 Mirjam Shatanawi (ed.), *Tehran studio works – the art of Khosrow Hassanzadeh* (London, 2007) pp. 50–61.

60 Shirin Neshat interviewed by John LeKay 2005, http://heyokamagazine .com/HEYOKA.4.FOTOS.ShirinNeshat.htm [accessed 7 May 2011]; Porter, *Word into art* (2006) p. 46.

61 Porter, *Word into art* (Dubai, 2008) pp. 116–17.

62 See the exhibition, *Unveiled – new art from the Middle East*, January–May 2009 at the Saatchi Gallery, London, http://www.saatchi-gallery.co.uk/ artists/ramin_haerizadeh.htm?section_name=unveiled [accessed 30 October 2010].

63 Robert Tait, 'Iran regime depicts male student in chador as shaming tactic', *The Guardian*, 11 December 2009, http://www.guardian.co.uk/world/2009/dec/ 11/iran-regime-male-student-chador [accessed 30 October 2010]; Christiane Hoffman, 'Die Tabus fallen wie Dominosteine', *Frankfurter Allgemeine Zeitung*, 15 December 2009, http://www.faz.net/artikel/C31325/iran-die -tabus-fallen-wie-dominosteine-30079365.html [accessed 30 October 2010].

64 http://iranian.com/main/albums/be-man [accessed 30 October 2010].

65 http://www.youtube.com/watch? v=xNgN1rbXjLc&feature=player_embedded [accessed 28 August 2011].

66 http://electronicintifada.net/

67 http://www.al-awda.org/ [accessed 3 November 2010].

68 http://liberationgraphics.com/home.html [accessed 3 November 2010]; http://liberationgraphics.com/ppp/Introduction.html [accessed 10 June 2012].

69 http://www.albasrah.net/index.php [accessed 3 November 2010]; see the video compilation by the Political Council of Iraqi Resistance, 'Hope and Challenge', 2009. http://www.archive.org/details/PCIR-HopeAndChallenge [accessed 26 August 2011].

70 http://edition.cnn.com/2004/WORLD/meast/09/20/iraq.beheading/ [accessed 26 August 2011].

71 For Zarqawi's video, see http://www.youtube.com/watch?v=pnuj5NrAQ64; for Mohamed Sidique Khan, see http://www.youtube.com/watch?v=jHXLai08G3I – broadcast by Al-Jazeera, 1 September 2005; the video of Ahmed Abdulla Ali, http://www.youtube.com/watch?v=9gVogfDsGRs; and Al-Qaeda in the Arabian Peninsula in 2009, http://www.youtube.com/watch?v=QtD2buzgyWM [all accessed 26 August 2011].

72 http://www.we-make-money-not-art.com/archives/2008/03/what-did-your -previous-project.php [accessed 4 November 2010].

73 http://www.flickr.com/photos/ganzeer/6540181269/?mid=55 [accessed 22 December 2011]. The extraordinary creativity of the street art of Egypt that has appeared since January 2011 has been well recorded on the website http://suzeeinthecity.wordpress.com/ [accessed 16 June 2012].

Conclusion

1 'Syrian official resigns over crackdown', Al-Jazeera online, 1 September 2011, http://english.aljazeera.net/news/middleeast/2011/08/ 2011831212956927978.html [accessed 5 September 2011].

2 Abdelmajid Hannoum, *Violent modernity: France in Algeria* (Cambridge, MA, 2010); see also Dan Neep, *Syria insurgent: occupation, space and violence under the French mandate* (Cambridge, 2012).

3 'Defiant Gaddafi vows to fight on', Al-Jazeera online, 23 February 2011, http://english.aljazeera.net/news/africa/2011/02/201122216458913596. html [accessed 6 September 2011].

4 http://knowyourmeme.com/memes/gaddafis-speech-zenga-zenga [accessed 27 August 2011].

5 The phenomenon is not confined to Asia and Africa, but for an extensive exploration of a particular African case, see William Reno, *Corruption and state politics in Sierra Leone* (Cambridge, 1995) pp. 21–7, 124–9, 177–88; for Iraq, see Charles Tripp, *A history of Iraq* (Cambridge, 2007) pp. 259–67.

6 In Arabic [*istada`afa/mustada`afin*], the word itself implies not simply people who happen to be weak or oppressed, but those who are deemed to be weak by others who behave arrogantly. This notion of 'the unconsidered' captures well the idea that the powerful have in fact created the very category of people who are now rising up to dispossess them.

7 Charles Tripp, '"In the name of the people": the "people's court" and the Iraqi revolution (1958–1960)', in Julia C. Strauss and Donal Cruise O'Brien (eds.), *Staging politics: power and performance in Asia and Africa* (London, 2007) p. 39.

8 Primo Levi, *The drowned and the saved* (tr. P. Bailey) (London, 1988) pp. 65–6.

9 As Philip Roth said of Primo Levi, his life and work after his liberation from Auschwitz had been 'his profoundly civilized and spirited response to those who did all they could to sever his every sustained connection and tear him and his kind out of history'. Philip Roth, *London Review of Books* 8/18, 23

October 1986, p. 17; Prof Hanna Yablonka, interview with *Haaretz*, 8 May 2011,http://www.haaretz.com/print-edition/features/identifying-the-unknown-soldiers-from-independence-war-1.360437; see also her article, 'Holocaust survivors in the Israeli army during the 1948 war: documents and memory', *Israel Affairs* 12/3 (2006) pp. 462–83.

10 Elizabeth Blair, 'Music of the Egyptian revolution', 9 August 2011, http://stealthishijab.com/2011/08/09/music-of-the-egyptian-revolution/ [accessed 30 August 2011].

Bibliography and Further Reading

Introduction

Asprey, Robert B., *War in the shadows: the guerrilla in history* (London, 1976).

Bayat, Asef, *Life as politics: how ordinary people change the Middle East* (Stanford, CA, 2010).

Beinin, Joel, and Frédéric Vairel (eds.), *Social movements, mobilization, and contestation in the Middle East and North Africa* (Stanford, CA, 2011).

Bourdieu, Pierre, *Acts of resistance – against the new myths of our time* (Cambridge, 1998).

Chalcraft, John, and Yaseen Nourani (eds.), *Counterhegemony in the colony and the postcolony* (Basingstoke, England, 2007).

Crooke, Alistair, *Resistance: the essence of the Islamist revolution* (London, 2009).

Darnton, Robert, *The great cat massacre and other episodes in French cultural history* (New York, 1985).

Forgacs, David (ed.), *The Antonio Gramsci reader – selected writings 1916–1935* (New York, 2000).

Foucault, Michel, *Power/knowledge: selected interviews and other writings 1972–1977* (tr. and ed. Colin Gordon) (Brighton, England, 1980).

Foucault, Michel, *Histoire de la sexualité*, Vol 1, *La volonté de savoir* (Paris, 1976) (English translation by Robert Hurley, *The history of sexuality* Vol 1 [London, 1981]).

Gills, Barry K. (ed.), *Globalization and the politics of resistance* (Basingstoke, England, 2000).

Goldman, Emma, *Anarchism and other essays* (Minneapolis, MN, 2005).

Harb, Mona, *Le Hezbollah à Beyrouth (1985–2005): de la banlieu à la ville* (Beirut, Lebanon, 2010).

Hollander, Jocelyn A., and Rachel L. Einwohner, 'Conceptualizing resistance', *Sociological Forum* 19/4 (2004) pp. 533–54.

Karatzogianni, Athina, and Andrew Robinson, *Power, resistance and conflict in the contemporary world* (London, 2008).

Lukács, Georg, *History and class consciousness* (Cambridge, MA, 1999).

Miller, Daniel, Michael Rowlands, and Chris Tilley, *Domination and resistance* (London, 1989).

Mitchell, Timothy, 'Everyday metaphors of power', *Theory and Society* 19/5 (1990) pp. 545–77.

Mutran, Khalil, *Diwan al-Khalil* (Beirut, Lebanon, 1967) 3 Volumes.

O'Brien, Kevin J., 'Rightful resistance', *World Politics* 49/1 (1996) pp. 31–55.

Pickett, Brent L., 'Foucault and the politics of resistance', *Polity* 28/4 (1996) pp. 445–66.

Polet, François (ed.), *The state of resistance: popular struggles in the global south* (London, 2007).

Scott, James C., *Weapons of the weak: everyday forms of peasant resistance* (New Haven, CT, 1987).

Scott, James C., *Domination and the arts of resistance: hidden transcripts* (New Haven, CT, 1990).

Selbin, Eric, *Revolution, rebellion, resistance* (London, 2010).

Thompson, Kevin, 'Forms of resistance: Foucault on tactical reversal and self formation', *Continental Philosophy Review* 36/2 (2003) pp. 113–38.

Wedeen, Lisa, *Ambiguities of domination – politics, rhetoric, and symbols in contemporary Syria* (Chicago, 1999).

Woodcock, George, *Anarchism* (Harmondsworth, England, 1971).

Chapter 1

Abbas, Ferhat, *Autopsie d'une guerre: l'aurore* (Paris, 1980).

Abd Allah, Umar, *The Islamic struggle in Syria* (Berkeley, CA, 1983).

Ageron, Charles-Robert, *Modern Algeria: a history from 1830 to the present* (London, 1991).

Amnesty International, *Israel/Gaza – Operation 'Cast Lead': 22 days of death and destruction* (London, 2009).

Amnesty International, *New order, same abuses – unlawful detentions and torture in Iraq* (London, 2010).

Bar, Neta, and Eyal Ben-Ari, 'Israeli snipers in the al-Aqsa intifada: killing, humanity and lived experience', *Third World Quarterly* 26/1 (2005) pp. 133–52.

Betts, Richard K., 'The soft underbelly of American primacy: tactical advantages of terror', *Political Science Quarterly* 117/1 (2002) pp. 19–36.

Bloom, Mia, *Dying to kill – the allure of suicide terror* (New York, 2007).

Brower, Benjamin C., *A desert named peace – the violence of France's empire in the Algerian Sahara 1844–1902* (New York, 2009).

Bulloch, John, and Harvey Morris, *No friends but the mountains* (London, 1992).

Chaliand, Gérard, *The Palestinian resistance* (London, 1972).

Chandrasekaran, Rajiv, *Imperial life in the emerald city: inside Iraq's green zone* (New York, 2006).

Clancy-Smith, Julia, *Rebel and saint: Muslim notables, popular protest, colonial encounters – Algeria and Tunisia* (Berkeley, CA, 1994).

Cockburn, Patrick, *The occupation: war and resistance in Iraq* (London, 2006).

Cockburn, Patrick, *Muqtada al-Sadr and the fall of Iraq* (London, 2008).

Cook, Michael, *Commanding the right and forbidding the wrong in Islamic thought* (Cambridge, 2000).

Cordesman, Anthony H., *Iraq's insurgency and the road to civil conflict* (Washington, DC, 2007).

Crenshaw, Martha, 'The causes of terrorism', *Comparative Politics* 13/4 (1981) pp. 379–99.

Etherington, Mark, *Revolt on the Tigris: the al-Sadr uprising and the governing of Iraq* (Ithaca, NY, 2005).

Fanon, Frantz, *The wretched of the earth* (London, 2001).

Gambetta, Diego (ed.), *Making sense of suicide missions* (Oxford, 2005).

Ghandour, Zeina B., *A discourse on domination* (London, 2010).

Gibson, Nigel C., *Fanon: the postcolonial imagination* (Cambridge, 2003).

Hannoum, Abdelmajid, *Violent modernity: France in Algeria* (Cambridge, MA, 2010).

Harb, Zahera, *Channels of resistance in Lebanon: liberation propaganda, Hezbullah and the media* (London, 2011).

Hashim, Ahmed S., *Insurgency and counter-insurgency in Iraq* (London, 2006).

Hasso, Frances, 'Discursive and political deployments by/of the 2002 Palestinian women suicide bombers/martyrs', *Feminist Review* 81 (2005) pp. 23–51.

Heiberg, Marianne, Brendan O'Leary, and John Tirman (eds.), *Terror, insurgency and the state* (Philadelphia, PA, 2007).

Herring, Eric, and Glen Rangwala, *Iraq in fragments* (London, 2006).

Hirst, David, *The gun and the olive branch* (London, 1977).

Hirst, David, *Beware of small states: Lebanon, battleground of the Middle East* (London, 2010).

Hoffman, Bruce, *Inside terrorism* (New York, 2006).

Hughes, Matthew, 'The banality of brutality: British armed forces and the repression of the Arab Revolt in Palestine, 1936–39', *English Historical Review* 124 (2009) 313–54.

Hughes, Matthew, 'From law and order to pacification: Britain's suppression of the Arab revolt in Palestine, 1936–39', *Journal of Palestine Studies* 39/2 (2010) pp. 1–17.

Human Rights Watch/Middle East, *Iraq's crime of genocide: the Anfal campaign against the Kurds* (New Haven, CT, 1995).

Kadi, Leila, *Basic political documents of the armed Palestinian resistance movement* (Beirut, Lebanon, 1969).

Kalyvas, Stathis, 'The ontology of "political violence": action and identity in civil wars', *Perspectives on Politics* 1/3 (2003) pp. 475–94.

Khader, Bishara, and Naim Khader (tr. and eds.), *Textes de la révolution palestinienne 1968/74* (Paris, 1975).

Khalidi, Rashid, 'The Palestinians and 1948: the underlying causes of failure', in Eugene Rogan and Avi Shlaim (eds.), *The war for Palestine* (Cambridge, 2007).

Khalidi, Walid (ed.), *From haven to conquest: readings in Zionism and the Palestine problem until 1948* (Washington, DC, 1971).

Klein, Menachem, *The Jerusalem problem: the struggle for permanent status* (Gainesville, FL, 2003).

Lia, Brynjar, *Architect of the global jihad: life of al-Qaida strategist Abu Mus'ab al-Suri* (London, 2007).

Mayer, Thomas, 'The Islamic opposition in Syria, 1961–1982', *Orient* 4 (1983) pp. 589–609.

McDougall, James, 'Savage wars? Codes of violence in Algeria, 1830s–1990s', *Third World Quarterly* 26/1 (2005) pp. 117–31.

Metzler, Jacob, *The divided economy of mandatory Palestine* (Cambridge, 1998).

Milton-Edwards, Beverley, and Stephen Farrell, *Hamas* (Cambridge, 2010).

Napoleoni, Loretta, *Insurgent Iraq: Al Zarqawi and the new generation* (London, 2005).

Naylor, Philip C., *France and Algeria: a history of decolonization and transformation* (Gainesville, FL, 2000).

Neep, Dan, *Syria insurgent: occupation, space and violence under the French mandate* (Cambridge, 2012).

Packer, George, *The assassins' gate: America in Iraq* (New York, 2006).

Pape, Robert A., *Dying to win – the strategic logic of suicide terrorism* (New York, 2005).

Ricks, Thomas, *The gamble: General David Petraeus and the American military adventure in Iraq 2006–2008* (New York, 2009).

Rosen, Nir, *In the belly of the green bird – the triumph of the martyrs in Iraq* (New York, 2006).

Rosen, Nir, *Aftermath* (New York, 2010).

Ruedy, John, *Modern Algeria: the origins and development of a nation* (Bloomington, IN, 2005).

Sayigh, Yezid, *Armed struggle and the search for state: the Palestinian national movement 1949–1993* (Oxford, 1997).

Shlaim, Avi, *Lion of Jordan – the life of King Hussein in war and peace* (London, 2007).

Shultz, Richard H., *Insurgents, terrorists and militias: the warriors of contemporary combat* (New York, 2006).

Stein, Leonard, *The Balfour Declaration* (New York, 1961).

Streatfield, Dominic, *A history of the world since 9/11* (London, 2011).

Todenhöfer, Jürgen, *Why do you kill?* (New York, 2009).

Townshend, Charles, 'The defence of Palestine: insurrection and public security, 1936–1939', *The English Historical Review* 103 (1988) 917–49.

Tripp, Charles, *A history of Iraq* (Cambridge, 2007).

Ullman, Harlan K., and James P. Wade et al. *Shock and awe: achieving rapid dominance* (Washington, DC, 1996).

Weinstein, Jeremy M., *Inside rebellion: the politics of insurgent violence* (Cambridge, 2007).

Young, Robert, *Postcolonialism: an historical introduction* (Oxford, 2001).

Chapter 1. Research and Further Reading

Algeria

Abbas, Farhat, *Guerre et révolution d'Algérie* (Paris, 1962).

Ait Ahmed, Hocine, *La guerre et l'après-guerre* (Paris, 1964).

Ben al-Hajj, `Uthman Sa`di, *Mudhakkirat* (Algiers, Algeria, 2000).

Bu`aziz, Yahya, *Thawrat al-jaza'ir fi al-qarnayn al-tasi` `ashar wa-l-`ishrin*, Vol. 3, *Min watha'iq jabahat al-tahrir al-watani al-jaza'iriyya 1954–1962* (Wahran, Algeria, 2004).

Centre des Archives d'Outre Mer, Aix-en-Provence, France. References to the relevant series dealing with Algeria from the 19th to the mid-20th century can be found in McDougall, James, *History and the culture of nationalism in Algeria* (Cambridge, 2006) pp. 239–40.

Darrar, Anisa Barakat, *Adab al-nidal fi al-jaza'ir min sana 1945 hatta al-istiqlal* (Algiers, Algeria, 1984).

Dusgate, Richard H., *O.A.S. – A report on the origins, formation, organization and operations of the OAS in Algeria, France and Spain 1961–1962* (Cheltenham, England, 2004).

Fanon, Frantz, *L'An V de la révolution algérienne* (Paris, 1959).

Le Front de Libération Nationale, *La plateforme de la révolution algérienne* (n.p., 1956).

Le Front de Libération Nationale, *La programme de Tripoli* (Tripoli, Libya, 1962).

Le Front de Libération Nationale, *La Charte d'Alger* (Algiers, Algeria, 1964).

Harbi, Mohammed, *Les archives de la révolution algérienne* (Tunis, Tunisia, 1981).

Harbi, Mohammed, *L'Algérie et son destin* (Paris, 1992).

Kafi, `Ali, *Mudhakkirat al-ra'is `Ali Kafi – min munadil al-siyasi ila al-qa'id al-`askari 1946–1962* (Algiers, Algeria, 1999).

Khudayr, Idris, *Al-bahth fi ta'rikh al-jaza'ir al-hadith 1830–1962* (Algiers, Algeria, 2006).

Musée d'Histoire Contemporaine – BDIC, *La France en guerre d'Algérie* (Paris, 1992).

Ouzegane, Amer, *Le meilleur combat* (Paris, 1962).

Sa`idani, al-Tahir, *Mudhakkirat – al-qa`ida al-sharqiyya, qalb al-thawra al-nabid* (Algiers, Algeria, 2001).

Service Historique de l'Armée de Terre, *La guerre d'Algérie par les documents*, Vol. 1, *L'avertissement 1943–1946* (Vincennes, France, 1990).

Service Historique de l'Armée de Terre, *La guerre d'Algérie par les documents*, Vol. 2, *Les portes de la guerre 1946–1954* (Vincennes, France, 1998).

Palestine

Pre-1948

The National Archives of the United Kingdom (Kew):
Colonial Office records, series:
CO 733 Palestine Original Correspondence
CO 765 Palestine Acts

CO 935 Confidential Print Middle East
War Office records, series: WO 32; WO 33; WO 191; WO 282

Al-Kayyali, `Abd al-Wahhab, *Watha'iq al-muqawama al-filastiniyya al-`arabiyya didda al-ihtilal al-britani wa-l-sahiyuni 1918–1939* (Beirut, Lebanon, 1968).

Al-Qawuqji, Fawzi, *Filastin fi mudhakkirat al-Qawuqji 1936–1948* (Beirut, Lebanon, 1975).

Al-Sakakini, Khalil, *Kadha ana ya dunya* (Jerusalem, Israel, 1955).

Qadri, Ahmad, *Mudhakkirati `an al-thawra al-`arabiyya al-kubra* (Damascus, Syria, 1956).

Sirhan, Nimr, and Mustafa Kabaha, *`Abd al-Rahim al-Hajj Muhammad – al-qa'id al-`am li-thawra 1936–1939* (Ramallah, West Bank, 2000).

Zu`ayter, Akram, *Yawmiyyat: al-haraka al-wataniyya al-filastiniyya 1935–1939* (Beirut, Lebanon, 1980).

Post-1948

Abu Hammam, *Al-muqawama `askariyyan* (Beirut, Lebanon, 1971).

Al-`Azm, Sadiq Jalal, *Dirasa naqdiyya li-fikr al-muqawama al-filastiniyya* (Beirut, Lebanon, 1973).

Dajani, Ahmad Sidqi, *Min al-muqawama ila al-thawra al-sha`biyya fi Filastin* (Cairo, Egypt, 1969).

Maktab al-Siyasi li-l-Jabha al-Dimuqratiyya li-Tahrir Filastin, *Al-muqawama al-Filastiniyya 1970 fi zill izdiwaj al-sulta* (Damascus, Syria, 2007).

Markaz Dirasat al-Mukhtar al-Islami, *Hamas wa-l-jihad: janiha al-muqawama al-islamiyya fi Filastin al-muhtalla: al-judhur, al-`amaliyyat, al-ib`ad* (Cairo, Egypt, 1993).

Markaz Dirasat al-Sharq al-Awsat, *Mafhum al-irhab wa-haqq al-sha`b al-Filastini fi al-muqawama* (Amman, Jordan, 2003).

Muhsin, Hashim `Ali, *Intifada hatta al-nasr* (Damascus, Syria, 1983).

Rabitat al-Shaghghila [Workers' League], *Azmat al-muqawama al-Filastiniyya* (Beirut, Lebanon, 1984).

Samarah, `Adil, *Musahama fi al-irhab: al-irhab tab`a min al-harb al-rasmiyya, wa-tab`a min al-muqawama al-sha`biyya* (Ramallah, West Bank, 2006).

Yasin, `Abd al-Qadir, *Hamas: harakat al-muqawama al-islamiyya fi Filastin* (Cairo, Egypt, 1990).

Iraq Post-2003

Ahmad, Rif`at Sayyid, *`Ala madhbah al-ihtilal fi al-`Iraq: dirasa watha'iqiyya fi milaffat, al-Islam, al-muqawama, al-ihtilal* (Cairo, Egypt, 2007).

Al-Baghdadi, Ahmad al-Hasani, *Hakadha takallama Ahmad al-Hasani al-Baghdadi: al-muqawama mustamirra wa-l-ihtilal ila al-zawal wa-sha`buna lan yamut* (Beirut, Lebanon, 2005).

Al-Dulaymi, `Abd al-Nasir, *Lamahat min al-muqawama al-i`lamiyya al-`Iraqiyya fi muwajaha al-ihtilal wa-l-dam-qratiyya* (Beirut, Lebanon, 2009).

Kubaysi, Muhammad `Ayyash Mutalli, *Min fiqh al-muqawama* (Amman, Jordan, 2005).

Islamist Insurgency in Syria

Al-Ikhwan al-Muslimun, Haut commandement de la révolution islamique en Syrie, *Déclaration et programme de la révolution islamique en Syrie* (n.p., 1980).
Rizq, Jabir, *Al-ikhwan al-muslimun wa-l-mu'amara `ala Suriya* (Cairo, Egypt, 1980).

Kurdish Iraq

Badi, `Arif Mivan `Abd al-Rahman, *Al-haraka al-qawmiyya al-kurdiyya al-taharuriyya fi Kurdistan al-`Iraq* (Dohuk, Iraq, 2005).
`Issa, Hamid Mahmud, *Al-qadiyya al-kurdiyya fi al-`Iraq – min al-ihtilal al-britani ila al-ghazw al-amriki 1914–2003* (Cairo, Egypt, 2003).
Kurdish Democratic Party, *Taqyim masirat al-haraka al-thawriyya al-kurdiyya wa-inhiyaraha* (n.p., 1977).
Patriotic Union of Kurdistan, *Hawl al-haraka al-tahririyya li-l-sha`b al-kurdi fi Kurdistan al-`Iraq* (n.p., 1977).

Chapter 2

Abrahamian, Ervand, *Iran between two revolutions* (Princeton, NJ, 1983).
Al Aswany, Alaa, *On the state of Egypt: what caused the revolution* (Edinburgh, Scotland, 2011).
Alexander, Jeffrey C., *Perfomative revolution in Egypt – an essay in cultural power* (London, 2011).
Anderson, Lisa, 'Demystifying the Arab Spring: parsing the differences between Tunisia, Egypt, and Libya', *Foreign Affairs* 90/3 (2011) pp. 2–7.
Andrain, Charles F., and David E. Apter, *Political protest and social change: analyzing politics* (New York, 1995).
Ansari, Ali (ed.) with Daniel Berman and Thomas Rintoul, *Preliminary analysis of the voting figures in Iran's 2009 presidential election*, Chatham House and Institute of Iranian Studies, University of St Andrews, 21 June 2009.
Ansari, Ali, *Crisis of authority: Iran's 2009 presidential election* (London, 2010).
Azar, George Baramki, *Palestine: a photographic journey* (Berkeley, CA, 1991).
Baramki, Gabi, *Peaceful resistance: building a Palestinian university under occupation* (London, 2010).
Barghouti, Omar, *Boycott, divestment and sanctions* (Chicago, 2011).
Batatu, Hanna, 'Iraq's underground Shi`i movements', *MERIP* 12/1 (1982) p. 6.
Bayat, Asef, 'The "street" and the politics of dissent in the Arab world', *Middle East Report* 226 (2003) pp. 10–17.
Bayat, Asef, *Life as politics: how ordinary people change the Middle East* (Stanford, CA, 2010).

Beinin, Joel, and Frédéric Vairel (eds.), *Social movements, moblilization and contestation in the Middle East and North Africa* (Stanford, CA, 2011).

Dahi, Omar S., 'Understanding the political economy of the Arab revolts', *Middle East Report* 259 (2011) pp. 47–53.

Denoeux, Guilain, *Urban unrest in the Middle East: a comparative study of informal networks in Egypt, Iran and Lebanon* (Albany, NY, 1993).

Gelvin, James, *The Israel–Palestine conflict: one hundred years of war* (Cambridge, 2007).

el-Ghobashy, Mona, 'The praxis of the Egyptian revolution', *Middle East Report* 258 (2011) pp. 2–13.

Hashemi, Nader, and Danny Postel (eds.), *The people reloaded: the green movement and the struggle for Iran's future* (Brooklyn, NY, 2010).

Hunter, F. Robert, *The Palestinian uprising: a war by other means* (Berkeley, CA, 1993).

Ismail, Salwa, 'Authoritarian government, neoliberalism and everyday civilities in Egypt', *Third World Quarterly* 32/5 (2011) pp. 845–62.

Ismail, Salwa, 'Epilogue', *Third World Quarterly* 32/5 (2011) pp. 989–95.

Jabar, Faleh, 'Le leviathan et le sacré: le Baas et les chiites', in C. Kutschera (ed.), *Le livre noir de Saddam Hussein* (Paris, 2005).

Johnston, Hank, and John A. Noakes, *Frames of protest: social movements and the framing perspective* (Lanham, MD, 2005).

Kennedy, R. Scott, 'The Druze of the Golan: a case of non-violent resistance', *Journal of Palestine Studies* 13/2 (1984) pp. 48–64.

Keshavarzian, Arang, *Bazaar and state in Iran – the politics of the Tehran marketplace* (Cambridge, 2007).

Khamis, Sahar, and Katherine Vaughn, 'Cyberactivism in the Egyptian Revolution: how civic engagement and citizen journalism tilted the balance', *Arab Media and Society* 13 (2011) http://www.arabmediasociety.com

King, Mary, *A quiet revolution – the first Palestinian intifada and nonviolent resistance* (New York, 2007).

Kurzman, Charles, 'The Qum protests and the coming of the Iranian revolution, 1975 and 1978', *Social Science History* 27/3 (2003) pp. 287–325.

Kurzman, Charles, *The unthinkable revolution in Iran* (Cambridge, MA, 2004).

Marzouki, Nadia, 'From people to citizens in Tunisia', *Middle East Report* 259 (2011) pp. 16–19.

Milani, Mohsen A., *The making of Iran's Islamic revolution* (Boulder, CO, 1994).

Moaddel, Mansour, *Class, politics and ideology in the Iranian revolution* (New York, 1993).

Osman, Tarek, *Egypt on the brink* (New Haven, CT, 2010).

Peteet, Julie, 'Male gender and rituals of resistance in the Palestinian intifada: a cultural politics of violence', *American Ethnologist* 21/1 (1994) pp. 31–49.

Polletta, Francesca, *It was like a fever: storytelling in protest and politics* (Chicago, 2006).

Poulson, Stephen C., *Social movements in twentieth-century Iran: culture, ideology, and mobilizing frameworks* (Lanham, MD, 2005).

Qubain, Fahim I., 'Social class and tensions in Bahrain', *The Middle East Journal* 9/3 (Summer 1955) pp. 269–71.

Qumsiyeh, Mazin, *Popular resistance in Palestine – a history of hope and empowerment* (London, 2011).

Randle, Michael, *Civil resistance* (London, 1994).

Roberts, Adam, and Timothy Garton Ash (eds.), *Civil resistance and power politics: the experience of non-violent action from Gandhi to the present* (Oxford, 2009).

Sadiki, Larbi, 'Popular Uprisings and Arab Democratization', *International Journal of Middle East Studies* 32/1 (2000) pp. 71–95.

Sadiki, Larbi, *Rethinking Arab democratization: elections without democracy* (Oxford, 2009).

Schock, Kurt, *Unarmed insurrections: people power movements in nondemocracies* (Minneapolis, MN, 2006).

Shami, Seteney (ed.), *Publics, politics and participation: locating the public sphere in the Middle East and North Africa* (New York, 2009).

Sharp, Gene, *The politics of nonviolent action* (Cambridge, MA, 1973–1985) 3 Volumes.

Sharp, Gene, 'The intifadah and nonviolent struggle', *Journal of Palestine Studies* 19/1 (1989) pp. 3–13.

Sharp, Gene, with J. Paulson, *Waging nonviolent struggle: 20th century practice and 21st century potential* (Manchester, NH, 2005).

Sowers, Jeannie, and Chris Toensing (eds.), *The journey to Tahrir – revolution, protest and social change in Egypt* (London, 2012)

Stein, Kenneth, 'The intifadah and the 1936–39 uprising: a comparison', *Journal of Palestine Studies* 19/4 (1990) pp. 64–85.

Stork, Joe, *Routine abuse, routine denial: civil rights and the political crisis in Bahrain* (New York, 1997).

Tilly, Charles, *Contentious performances* (Cambridge, 2008).

Volpi, Frédéric, 'Framing civility in the Middle East: alternative perspectives on the state and civil society', *Third World Quarterly* 32/5 (2011) pp. 801–6.

Wiktorowicz, Quintan (ed.), *Islamic activism: a social movement theory approach* (Bloomington, IN, 2003).

Workman, W. Thom, *The social origins of the Iran–Iraq war* (Boulder, CO, 1994).

York, Steve, *Bringing down a dictator* [DVD] (York Zimmerman, Washington DC, 2002).

Young, Michael, *The ghosts of Martyrs' Square: an eyewitness account of Lebanon's life struggle* (New York, 2010).

Zunes, Stephen, Lester R. Kurtz, and Sarah Beth Asher (eds.), *Nonviolent social movements: a geographical perspective* (Malden, MA, 1999).

Chapter 2. Research and Further Reading

Iran

International Institute of Social History, Amsterdam, The Netherlands, *Iranian political and social movements collection, 1950–1997.*

Kurzman, Charles, 'Historiography of the Iranian revolutionary movement 1977–79', *Iranian Studies* 28/1–2 (1995) pp. 25–38. See also Charles Kurzman's comprehensive list of mostly Iranian documentary sources in *The unthinkable revolution in Iran* (Cambridge, MA, 2004) pp. 239–42.

The National Archives of the United Kingdom (Kew) Foreign & Commonwealth Office records, series: FCO 8/3183–3190, 3351–3354

Bahrain

Bahrain Center for Human Rights, http://www.bahrainrights.org/en

Bahrain Youth Society for Human Rights, http://byshr.org/

Hammadah, Rashid, `Asifa fawq miyah al-khalij – qissat awwal inqilab `askari fi al-Bahrayn 1981* (London, 1990).

Human Rights Watch – Bahrain web page, http://www.hrw.org/middle -eastn-africa/bahrain

Al-Mahrus, Karim, *Jazira bila watan* (London, 2004).

Mudayris, Falah `Abd Allah, *Al-haraka wa-l-jama`a al-siyasiyya fi al-Bahrayn 1937–2002* (Beirut, Lebanon, 2004).

Palestine

Badil Resource Center for Palestinian Residency and Human Rights, http://www.badil.org

Bil`in village website, http://www.bilin-village.org

Boycott Divestment and Sanctions (BDS) Movement, http://www.bdsmovement.net/

The Electronic Intifada, http://electronicintifada.net/

Hamas: al-maktab al-i`lami, *Watha'iq harakat al-muqawama al-islamiyya* (n.p., 1990).

Ibrahim, Saad al-Din (ed.), *Al-muqawama al-madaniyya fi al-nidal al-siyasi* (Amman, Jordan, 1988).

Institute for Palestine Studies, http://www.palestine-studies.org/

International Solidarity Movement, http://palsolidarity.org/

Egypt

Arabawy (Hossam al-Hamalawy, ed.), http://www.arabawy.org/

Bashir, Muhammad Gamal, *Kitab al-Ultras* (Cairo, Egypt, 2011).

Ghonim, Wael, *Revolution 2.0* (London, 2012).

Mehrez, Samia (ed.), *Translating Egypt's revolution – the language of Tahrir* (Cairo, Egypt, 2012).

Watha'iq al-Tahrir (Tahrir documents), http://www.tahrirdocuments.org/

Chapter 3

Alexander, Anne, 'Leadership and collective action in the Egyptian trade unions', *Work, Employment and Society* 24/2 (2010), pp. 241–59.

Ansari, Hamied, *Egypt, the stalled society* (Albany, NY, 1986).

Arnold, Thomas C., 'Rethinking moral economy', *The American Political Science Review* 95/1 (2001), pp. 85–95.

Bayat, Asef, 'Populism, liberalization and popular participation: industrial democracy in Egypt', *Economic and Industrial Democracy* 14 (1993) pp. 77–8.

Bayat, Asef, 'Activism and social development in the Middle East', *International Journal of Middle East Studies* 34/1 (2002) pp. 1–28.

Beinin, Joel, 'Islam, Marxism and the Shubra al-Khayma textile workers: Muslim Brothers and Communists in the Egyptian trade union movement', in Edmund Burke and Ira Lapidus (eds.), *Islam, politics and social movements* (Berkeley, CA, 1988).

Beinin, Joel, 'The state, capital and labor in Nasserist Egypt', *International Journal of Middle East Studies* 21/1 (1989) pp. 71–90.

Beinin, Joel, *Workers and peasants in the modern Middle East* (Cambridge, 2001).

Beinin, Joel, 'Egyptian textile workers: from craft artisans facing European competition to proletarians contending with the state', in Lex Heerma van Voss, Els Hiemstra-Kuperus, and Elise van Nederveen Meerkerk (eds.), *The Ashgate companion to the history of textile workers, 1650–2000* (Farnham, England, 2010) pp. 172–97.

Beinin, Joel, *The struggle for worker rights in Egypt* (Washington, DC, 2010).

Beinin, Joel, 'A workers' social movement on the margin of the global neoliberal order, Egypt 2004–2009', in Joel Beinin and Frédéric Vairel (eds.), *Social movements, mobilization, and contestation in the Middle East and North Africa* (Stanford, CA, 2011) pp. 181–201.

Beinin, Joel, and Zachary Lockman, *Workers on the Nile* (London, 1988).

Berti, Benedetta, 'The economics of counterterrorism: devising a normative regulatory framework for the hawala system', *MIT International Review* (2008).

Binder, Leonard, *In a moment of enthusiasm: political power and the second stratum in Egypt* (Chicago, 1978).

Booth, William J., 'On the idea of the moral economy', *The American Political Science Review* 88/3 (1994) pp. 653–67.

Brown, Nathan, *Peasant politics in modern Egypt* (New Haven, CT, 1990).

Burke, Edmund, and Ira Lapidus (eds.), *Islam, politics and social movements* (Berkeley, CA, 1988).

Chalcraft, John, *The striking cabbies of Cairo and other stories: crafts and guilds in Egypt 1863–1914* (Albany, NY, 2004).

Colburn, Forrest D. (ed.), *Everyday forms of peasant resistance* (Armonk, NY, 1989).

Davis, Eric, *Challenging colonialism* (Princeton, NJ, 1983).

El-Mahdi, Rabab, and Philip Marfleet (eds.), *Egypt – the moment of change* (London, 2009).

El Qorchi, Mohammed, *Informal funds transfer systems: an analysis of the informal hawala system* (Washington, DC, 2003).

El Shafei, Omar, *Workers, trade unions and the state in Egypt 1984–1989*, Cairo Papers in Social Science, Vol. 18, Monograph 2, Summer 1995 (Cairo, Egypt, 1995).

Enayat, Hamid, *Modern Islamic political thought* (London, 1982).

Goldberg, Ellis, *Tinker, tailor, textile worker: class and politics in Egypt 1930–1952* (Berkeley, CA, 1986).

Hanson, Brad, 'The "Westoxication" of Iran: depictions and reactions of Behrangi, al-e Ahmad, and Shariati', *International Journal of Middle East Studies* 15/1 (1983) pp. 1–23.

Hashimoto, Kohei, 'Lebanese population movement 1920–1939', in A. Hourani and N. Shehadi (eds.), *The Lebanese in the world: a century of emigration* (London, 1992).

Henry, Clement M., and R. Wilson (eds.), *The politics of Islamic finance* (Edinburgh, Scotland, 2004).

IMF Monetary and Financial Systems Department, *Regulatory frameworks for hawala and other remittance systems* (Washington, DC, 2005).

Kazarian, Elias, *Islamic vs. traditional banking* (Boulder, CO, 1993).

Keddie, Nikki, *Religion and rebellion in Iran – the tobacco protest of 1891–92* (London, 1966).

Kienle, Eberhard, *A grand delusion: democracy and economic reform in Egypt* (London, 2000).

Kuran, Timur, *Islam and Mammon – the economic predicaments of Islamism* (Princeton, NJ, 2004).

Kuran, Timur, 'The economic system in contemporary Islamic thought: interpretation and assessment', *International Journal of Middle East Studies* 18/2 (1986) pp. 135–64.

Maimbo, Samuel M., *The money exchange dealers of Kabul: a study of the Hawala system in Afghanistan* (Washington, DC, 2003).

Maurer, Bill, *Mutual Life, Limited: Islamic banking, alternative currencies, lateral reason* (Princeton, NJ, 2005).

Mitchell, Richard, *The society of the Muslim Brothers* (Oxford, 1969).

Mitchell, Timothy, 'The invention and reinvention of the Egyptian peasant', *International Journal of Middle East Studies* 22/2 (1990) pp. 129–50.

Nomani, Farhad, and Ali Rahnema, *Islamic economic systems* (London, 1994).

Paul, Jim, 'Riots in Morocco', *MERIP Reports* 99 (1981) pp. 30–1.

Polanyi, Karl, *The great transformation* (Boston, MA, 2001).

Pratt, Nicola, *The legacy of the corporatist state: explaining workers' responses to economic liberalisation in Egypt* (Durham, England, 1998).

Pripstein Posusney, Marsha, 'Irrational workers: the moral economy of labor protest in Egypt', *World Politics* 46/1 (1993) pp. 83–120.

Pripstein Posusney, Marsha, *Labor and the state in Egypt: workers, unions and economic restructuring 1952–1996* (New York, 1997).

Quataert, Donald, *Social disintegration and popular resistance in the Ottoman Empire, 1881–1908: reactions to European economic penetration* (New York, 1983).

Razavy, Maryam, 'Hawala', *Crime, Law and Social Change* 44/3 (2005) pp. 277–99.

Rodinson, Maxime, *Islam and capitalism* (London, 1974).

Sadiki, Larbi, 'Popular uprisings and Arab democratisation', *International Journal of Middle East Studies* 32/1 (2000) pp. 79–85.

Sallam, Hesham, 'Striking back at Egyptian workers', *Middle East Report* 259 (2011) pp. 20–5.

Scott, James C., *The moral economy of the peasant – rebellion and subsistence in South East Asia* (New Haven, CT, 1978).

Scott, James C., *Weapons of the weak: everyday forms of peasant resistance* (New Haven, CT, 1987).

Seddon, David, 'Riot and rebellion: political responses to economic crisis in North Africa, Tunisia, Morocco and Sudan', in Berch Berberoglu (ed.), *Power and stability in the Middle East* (London, 1989).

Shari`ati, Ali, *Marxism and other Western fallacies: an Islamic critique* (Berkeley, CA, 1980).

Shehata, Samir, *Shop floor culture and politics in Egypt* (Albany, NY, 2009).

Thompson, Edwina, *Trust is the coin of the realm: lessons from the money men in Afghanistan* (New York, 2011).

Toth, James, 'Rural workers and Egypt's national development', *British Journal of Middle Eastern Studies* 21/1 (1994) pp. 38–56.

Toth, James, 'Beating plowshares into swords: the relocation of rural Egyptian workers and their discontent', in Nicholas S. Hopkins and Kirsten Westegaard (eds.), *Directions of change in rural Egypt* (Cairo, Egypt, 1998) pp. 66–87.

Toth, James, *Rural labor movements in Egypt and their impact on the state, 1961–1992* (Gainesville, FL, 1999).

Traugott, Mark, *Repertoires and cycles of collective action* (Durham, NC, 1995).

Tripp, Charles, *Islam and the moral economy – the challenge of capitalism* (Cambridge, 2006).

Van de Bunt, Henk, 'The role of hawala bankers in the transfer of proceeds from organized crime', in Dina Siegel and Hans Nelen (eds.), *Organized crime: cultures, markets and policies* (New York, 2008) pp. 113–26.

Vitalis, Robert, *When capitalists collide: business conflict and the end of empire in Egypt* (Berkeley, CA, 1995).

Warde, Ibrahim, *Islamic finance in the global economy* (Edinburgh, Scotland, 2009).

Waterbury, John, and Farhad Kazemi (eds.), *Peasants and politics in the modern Middle East* (Miami, FL, 1991).

Chapter 3. Research and Further Reading

Egyptian Workers

`Adli, Huwayda, *Al-`ummal wa-l-siyasa: al-dawr al-siyasi li-l-haraka al-`ummaliyya fi Misr min 1952–1981* (Cairo, Egypt, 1993).

Markaz al-ard li-huquq al-insan [Land Center for Human Rights (Egypt)], http://www.lchr-eg.org/

Al-markaz al-masri li-l-huquq al-iqtisadiyya wa-l-ijtima`iyya [Egyptian Center for Economic and Social Rights], http://ecesr.com/

MENA Solidarity Network, http://menasolidaritynetwork.com/

Mustafa, Ahmad Muhammad, *Al-idrab wa-l-ighlaq* (Cairo, Egypt, 2009).

Solidarity Center [AFL-CIO] Middle East Resources, http://www .solidaritycenter.org/content.asp?pl=407&sl=407&contentid=863

Tadamun [Egypt] http://tadamonmasr.wordpress.com/

Islamic Economic Alternatives

Al-Ahram al-Iqtisadi, *Al-fatawa al-islamiyya fi al-qadaya al-iqtisadiyya* (Cairo, Egypt, 1990).

Harb, Muhammad Tal`at, `*Ilaj Misr al-iqtisadi wa-mashru` bank al-misriyyin aw bank al-umma* (Cairo, Egypt, 2002).

Iqbal, Munawar, *Al-tahaddiyat allati tawajihu al-`amal al-masrafi al-islami* (Jeddah, Saudi Arabia, 1998).

Qanduz, `Abd al-Karim, *Al-handasa al-maliyya al-islamiyya bayna al-nazariyya wa-l-tatbiq* (Beirut, Lebanon, 2008).

al-Sadr, Muhammad Baqir, *Iqtisaduna* (Beirut, Lebanon, 1982).

Shudar, Hamzah al-Hajj, `*Alaqat al-bunuk al-islamiyya bi-l-bunuk al-markaziyya: fi zill nuzum al-raqaba al-naqdiyya al-taqlidiyya* (Amman, Jordan, 2009).

Al-Siba`i, Mustafa, *Ishtirakiyyat al-Islam* (Damascus, Syria, 1960).

Chapter 4

Abdulhadi, Rabab, 'The Palestinian women's autonomous movement: emergence, dynamics and challenges', *Gender and Society* 12/6 (1998) pp. 649–73.

Agnaou, Fatima, *Gender, literacy, and empowerment in Morocco* (London, 2004).

Ahmadi, Fereshteh, 'Islamic feminism in Iran: feminism in a new Islamic context', *Journal of Feminist Studies in Religion* 22/2 (2006) pp. 33–53.

Al-Ali, Nadje, and Nicola Pratt, *What kind of liberation? Women and the occupation of Iraq* (Berkeley, CA, 2009).

Allabadi, Fadwa, 'Secular and Islamist women in Palestinian society', *European Journal of Women's Studies* 15/3 (2008) pp. 181–201.

Amayreh, Khalid, *Islamist women's activism in occupied Palestine* (Conflicts Forum Monograph, 2010).

Baker, Alison, *Voices of resistance: oral histories of Moroccan women* (Albany, NY, 1998).

Brand, Laurie, *Women, the state, and political liberalization – Middle Eastern and North African experiences* (New York, 1998).

Buskens, Léon, 'Recent debates on family law reform in Morocco: Islamic law as politics in an emerging public sphere', *Islamic Law and Society* 10/1 (2003) pp. 70–131.

Dieste, Josep Lluis Mateo, '"Demonstrating Islam": the conflict of text and the Moudawanna reform in Morocco', *Muslim World* 99 (2009) pp. 134–54.

El Guindi, Fadwa, *Veil: modesty, privacy and resistance* (Oxford, 1999).

Elliott, Carolyn M. (ed.), *Global empowerment of women: responses to globalization and politicized religions* (New York, 2008).

Faier, Elizabeth, 'Looking in/acting out: gender, modernity and the (re)production of the Palestinian family', *Political and Legal Anthropology Review* 20/2 (1997) pp. 1–15.

Faqir, Fadia, 'Intrafamily femicide in defence of honour: the case of Jordan', *Third World Quarterly* 22/1 (2001) pp. 65–82.

Fisher, Sue, and Kathy Davis (eds.), *Negotiating at the margins: the gendered discourses of power and resistance* (New Brunswick, NJ, 1993).

Fleischman, Ellen, *The nation and its 'new women': the Palestinian women's movement 1920–1948* (Berkeley, CA, 2003).

Gerami, Shahin, and Melodye Lehnerer, 'Women's agency and household diplomacy: negotiating fundamentalism', *Gender and Society* 15/4 (2001) pp. 556–73.

Glavanis-Grantham, Kathy, 'The women's movement, feminism and the national struggle in Palestine – unresolved contradictions', in Haleh Afshar (ed.), *Women and politics in the third world* (London, 1996) pp. 171–85.

Gunning, Jeroen, *Hamas in politics: democracy, religion, violence* (London, 2009).

Haj, Samira, 'Palestinian women and patriarchal relations', *Signs: Journal of Women in Culture and Society* 17/4 (1992) pp. 761–78.

Halper, Louise, 'Law and women's agency in post-revolutionary Iran', *Harvard Journal of Law and Gender* 28/1 (2005) pp. 85–142.

Harrak, Fatima, 'The history and significance of the new Moroccan Family Code', Working Paper 09–002 March 2009, Institute for the Study of Islamic Thought in Africa, Buffett Centre, Northwestern University.

Hasso, Frances S., 'The "Women's Front": nationalism, feminism and modernity in Palestine', *Gender and Society* 12/4 (1998) pp. 441–65.

Hasso, Frances S., 'Discursive and political deployments by/of the 2002 Palestinian women suicide bombers/martyrs', *Feminist Review* 81 Bodily Interventions (2005) pp. 23–51.

Hasso, Frances S., *Resistance, repression, and gender politics in occupied Palestine and Jordan* (Syracuse, NY, 2005).

Herrera, Linda, 'Downveiling: gender and the contest over culture in Cairo', *Middle East Report* 219 (2001), pp. 16–19.

Holt, Maria, 'Palestinian women and the intifada – an exploration of images and realities', in Haleh Afshar (ed.), *Women and politics in the third world* (London, 1996) pp. 186–203.

Human Rights Watch, *At a crossroads: human rights in Iraq eight years after the US led invasion* (New York, 2011).

Husain, Sarah, *Voices of resistance: Muslim women on war, faith and sexuality* (Emeryville, CA, 2006).

Ismail, Salwa, *Political life in Cairo's new quarters: encountering the everyday state* (Minneapolis, MN, 2006).

Jad, Islah, 'Between religion and secularism: Islamist women of Hamas', in Fereshteh Nouraie-Simone (ed.), *On shifting ground: Muslim women in the global era* (New York, 2005) pp. 174–204.

Joseph, Souad, 'Women and politics in the Middle East', *MERIP Middle East Report* 138, Women and Politics in the Middle East (1986) pp. 3–7.

Kandiyoti, Deniz, 'Bargaining with patriarchy', *Gender and Society* 2/3 (1988) pp. 274–90.

Kandiyoti, Deniz, 'Gender, power and contestation – rethinking bargaining with patriarchy', in Cecile Jackson and Ruth Pearson (eds.), *Feminist visions of development* (London, 1998) pp. 135–54.

Kapchan, Deborah, *Gender on the market: Moroccan women and the revoicing of tradition* (Philadelphia, PA, 1996).

Khaled, Leila, *My people shall live – autobiography of a revolutionary by Leila Khaled as told to George Hajjar* (Toronto, Canada, 1975).

Khalidi, Rashid, *Palestinian identity: the construction of modern national consciousness* (New York, 1997).

Khalili, Laleh, *Heroes and martyrs of Palestine* (Cambridge, 2007).

Macleod, Arlene E., *Accommodating protest: working women, the new veiling and change in Cairo* (New York, 1991).

Maddy-Weitzman, Bruce, 'Women, Islam and the Moroccan State: the struggle over the Personal Status Law', *Middle East Journal* 59/3 (2005) 393–410.

Maghraoui, Abdeslam, 'Political authority in crisis: Mohammed VI's Morocco', *Middle East Report* 218 (2001) pp. 12–17.

Mernissi, Fatima, *Beyond the veil: male–female dynamics in modern Muslim society* (London, 1985).

Mernissi, Fatima, *Doing daily battle: interviews with Moroccan women* (London, 1988).

Milton-Edwards, Beverley, *Islamic politics in Palestine* (London, 1996).

Mir-Hosseini, Ziba, 'Women and politics in post-Khomeini Iran: divorce, veiling and emerging feminist voices', in Haleh Afshar (ed.), *Women and politics in the third world* (London, 1996) pp. 145–73.

Mir-Hosseini, Ziba, 'The conservative–reformist conflict over women's rights in Iran', *International Journal of Politics, Culture and Society* 16/1 (2002) pp. 37–53.

Mir-Hosseini, Ziba, 'How the door of ijtihad was opened and closed: a comparative analysis of recent family law reforms in Iran and Morocco', *Washington and Lee Law Review* 64/4 (2007) pp. 1499–511.

Mitchell, Timothy, 'Everyday metaphors of power', *Theory and Society* 19/5 (1990) pp. 545–59.

Moghadam, Valentine, *Modernizing women: gender and social change in the Middle East* (Boulder, CO, 2003).

Moghadam, Valentine (ed.), *From patriarchy to empowerment: women's participation, movements, and rights in the Middle East, North Africa, and South Asia* (Syracuse, NY, 2007).

Mohan, Rajeswari, 'Loving Palestine: nationalist activism and feminist agency in Leila Khaled's subversive bodily acts', *Interventions* 1/1 (1998) pp. 52–80.

al-Nowaihi, Magda M. 'Resisting silence in Arab women's autobiographies', *International Journal of Middle East Studies* 33/4 (2001) pp. 477–502.

Othman, Norani (ed.), *Muslim women and the challenge of Islamic extremism* (Petaling Jaya, Selangor, Malaysia, 2005).

Peteet, Julie, *Gender in crisis: women and the Palestinian resistance movement* (New York, 1991).

Rubenberg, Cheryl A., *Palestinian women: patriarchy and resistance on the West Bank* (Boulder, CO, 2001).

Sabbagh, Suha (ed.), *Arab women – between defiance and restraint* (New York, 1996).

Salih, Ruba, *Gender in transnationalism: home, longing and belonging among Moroccan migrant women* (London, 2003).

Sasson-Levy, Orna, and Tamar Rapoport, 'Body, gender, and knowledge in protest movements: the Israeli case', *Gender and Society* 17/3 (2003) pp. 379–403.

Shaaban, Bouthaina, *Both right and left handed: Arab women talk about their lives* (London, 1991).

Shalhoub-Kervorkian, Nadera, 'Re-examining femicide: breaking the silence and crossing "scientific" borders', *Signs: Journal of Women in Culture and Society* 28/2 (2002) pp. 581–608.

Sharoni, Simona, 'The myth of gender equality and the limits of women's political dissent in Israel', *Middle East Report* 207 (1998) pp. 24–8.

Sherkat, Shahla, *Zanân: le journal de l'autre Iran* (Paris, 2010).

Skalli, Loubna, 'Women and poverty in Morocco: the many faces of social exclusion', *Feminist Review* 69 (2001) pp. 73–89.

Strum, Philippa, 'West Bank women and the intifada: revolution within the revolution', in Suha Sabbagh (ed.), *Palestinian women of Gaza and the West Bank* (Bloomington, IN, 1998) pp. 63–77.

Tillion, Germaine, *The republic of cousins: women's oppression in Mediterranean society* (London, 1983).

Yeganeh, Nahid, 'Women, nationalism and Islam in contemporary political discourse in Iran', *Feminist Review* 44 (1993) pp. 3–18.

Chapter 4. Research and Further Reading

`Adnani, Samirah, *Thawra hadi'a min mudawwanat al-ahwal al-shakhsiyya ila mudawwanat al-usra: majmu`a min al-ikhtisasin* (Rabat, Morocco, 2004).

Dizeyi, Shahbal Ma`ruf, *Al-`unf didda al-mar'a bayna al-nazariyya wa-l-tatbiq* (Irbil, Iraq, 2007).

Kurdish Women's Rights Watch, http://www.kwrw.org/

Palestinian Women's Research and Documentation Center, http://www.pwrdc.ps/

La Revue Marocaine d'Administration Locale et de Développement, *Le Nouveau Code de la Famille: avec les textes d'application/al-Mudawwanah jadidah li-l-usrah* (Rabat, Morocco, 2006).

Wizarat al-`Adl (Morocco), *Al-ayyam al-dirasiyya hawla al-mudawwana da`ama li-l-usra al-Maghribiyya al-mutawazina* (Rabat, Morocco, 2006).

Women Against Violence, http://www.wavo.org/?LanguageId=1

Zaki, Ahmad, Nifin Sulayman, and Huwayda al-Rifa`i (eds.), *Al-`unf didda al-mar'a fi Misr* (Cairo, Egypt, 2007).

Zalzal, Marie Rose, *Al-`unf al-qanuni didda al-mar'a fi Lubnan* (Beirut, Lebanon, 2008).

Chapter 5

Abu-Lughod, Lila, and Ahmad Sa`idi (eds.), *Nakba: Palestine, 1948 and the claims of memory* (New York, 2007).

Arkoun, Mohammed, 'Langues, société et religion dans le Maghreb indépendant', in Marial-Angels Roque (ed.), *Les cultures du Maghreb* (Paris, 1996) pp. 83–109.

Benrabah, Mohamad, 'Language in education planning in Algeria: historical development and current issues', *Language Policy* 6 (2007) pp. 225–52.

Ben-Raphael, Eliezer, 'Critical vs non-critical sociology: an evaluation', *Israel Studies* 2/1 (1997) pp. 175–89.

Chaker, Salem, 'Langue et identité berbères (Algérie/émigration): un enjeu de société', in Jean-Robert Henry (ed.), *Nouveaux enjeux culturels au Maghreb* (Paris, 1986) pp. 173–80.

Chaker, Salem, *Berbères aujourd'hui* (Paris, 1989).

Finkelstein, Norman, 'Myths, old and new', *Journal of Palestine Studies* 21/1 (1991) pp. 66–89.

Flapan, Simha, *The birth of Israel – myths and realities* (New York, 1987).

Gelber, Yoav, *Palestine 1948: war, escape and the emergence of the Palestinian refugee problem* (Brighton, England, 2001).

Goodman, Jane E., 'Imazighen on trial: human rights and Berber identity in Algeria, 1985', in Katherina E. Hoffman and Susan Gibson Miller (eds.), *Berbers and others: beyond tribe and nation in the Maghrib* (Bloomington, IN, 2010) pp. 103–25.

Gouméziane, Smaïl, *Algérie, l'histoire en héritage* (Paris, 2000).

Gutwein, Daniel, 'Left and right post-Zionism and the privatization of Israeli collective memory', *Journal of Israeli History* 20/2 (2001) pp. 9–42.

Harkabi, Yehoshafat, *Arab attitudes to Israel* (London, 1972).

Harkabi, Yehoshafat, *The Bar Kochba syndrome* (Chappaqua, NY, 1983).

Harkabi, Yehoshafat, *Israel's fateful decisions* (London, 1988).

Hill, Jonathan, 'Identity and instability in postcolonial Algeria', *Journal of North African Studies* 11/1 (2006) pp. 1–16.

Hoffman, Katherine E., and Susan Gilson Miller (eds.), *Berbers and others: beyond tribe and nation in the Maghrib* (Bloomington, IN, 2010).

International Crisis Group, *Algeria: unrest and impasse in Kabylia*, Report 15, 10 June 2003.

Karsh, Efraim, *Fabricating Israeli history: the 'new historians'* (London, 2001).

Khalili, Laleh, *Heroes and martyrs of Palestine: the politics of national commemoration* (Cambridge, 2007).

Likhovski, Assaf, 'Post-post-Zionist historiography', *Israel Studies* 15/2 (2010) pp. 1–23.

Lissak, Moshe, '"Critical" sociology and "Establishment" sociology in the Israeli academic community: ideological struggles or academic discourse', *Israel Studies* 1/1 (1996) pp. 247–94.

Lowi, Miriam R., *Oil wealth and the poverty of politics* (Cambridge, 2009).

Maddy-Weitzman, Bruce, *The Berber identity movement and the challenge to North African states* (Austin, TX, 2011).

Maddy-Weitzman, Bruce, and Daniel Zisenwine, *The Maghrib in the new century: identity, religion and politics* (Gainesville, FL, 2007).

Martinez, Luis, *The Algerian civil war 1990–1998* (London, 2000).

McDougall, James, *History and the culture of nationalism in Algeria* (Cambridge, 2006).

Morris, Benny, *The birth of the Palestinian refugee problem* (Cambridge, 1987).

Morris, Benny, 'Review: refabricating 1948', *Journal of Palestine Studies* 27/2 (1998) pp. 81–95.

Morris, Benny, *The birth of the Palestinian refugee problem revisited* (Cambridge, 2004).

Olick, Jeffrey K., *States of memory: continuities, conflicts and transformations in national retrospection* (Durham, NC, 2003).

Pappé, Ilan, *The making of the Arab–Israeli conflict* (London, 1994).

Pappé, Ilan, 'Post-Zionist critique on Israel and the Palestinians: part I: the academic debate', *Journal of Palestine Studies* 26/2 (1997) pp. 29–41.

Pappé, Ilan, 'Post-Zionist critique on Israel and the Palestinians: part III: popular culture', *Journal of Palestine Studies* 26/4 (1997) pp. 60–9.

Pappé, Ilan, 'The Tantura case in Israel: the Katz research and trial', *Journal of Palestine Studies* 30/3 (2001) pp. 19–39.

Pappé, Ilan, *The ethnic cleansing of Palestine* (Oxford, 2006).

Pappé, Ilan, 'Histories and historians in Israel and Palestine', *Transforming Cultures* 1/1 (2006) http://epress.lib.uts.edu.au/journals/TfC

Podeh, Elie, *The Arab–Israeli conflict in Israeli history textbooks, 1948–2000* (Westport, CT, 2002).

Ram, Uri, *The changing agenda of Israeli sociology* (New York, 1995).

Ram, Uri, 'Postnationalist pasts: the case of Israel', in Jeffrey K. Olick (ed.), *States of memory* (Durham, NC, 2003) pp. 236–50.

Raz-Krakotzkin, Amnon, 'History textbooks and the limits of Israeli consciousness', *JIH* 20/2 (2001) pp. 155–65.

Renan, Ernest, 'What is a Nation?', in Geoff Eley and Ronald Suny (eds.), *Becoming national: a reader* (Oxford, 1996) pp. 41–55.

Rogan, Eugene, and Avi Shlaim (eds.), *The war for Palestine: rewriting the history of 1948* (Cambridge, 2001).

Sands, Shlomo, *The invention of the Jewish people* (London, 2009).

Sayigh, Rosemary, 'Palestinian camp women as tellers of history', *Journal of Palestine Studies* 27/2 (1998) pp. 42–58.

Seliktar, Ofira, '"Tenured radicals" in Israel: from New Zionism to Political Activism', *Israel Affairs* 11/4 (2005) pp. 717–36.

Shafir, Gershon, 'Israeli Society: a counterview', *Israel Studies* 1/2 (1996) pp. 189–213.

Shapira, Anita, 'Politics and collective memory: the debate over the "new historians" in Israel', *History and Memory* 7/1 (1995) pp. 9–40.

Shapira, Anita, 'The strategies of historical revisionism', *The Journal of Israeli History* 20/2 (2001) pp. 62–76.

Sheffer, Gabriel (ed.), *Dynamics of a conflict: a re-examination of the Arab–Israeli conflict* (Atlantic Highlands, NJ, 1975).

Shenhav, Yehuda, 'Jews from Arab countries and the Palestinian right of return: an ethnic community in the realms of national memory', *British Journal of Middle East Studies* 29/1 (2002) pp. 27–56.

Shlaim, Avi, *The politics of partition: King Abdullah, the Zionists and Palestine* (Oxford, 1990).

Shlaim, Avi, 'The debate about 1948', *International Journal of Middle East Studies*, 27/3 (1995) pp. 287–304.

Shlaim, Avi, *The iron wall: Israel and the Arab world* (London, 2001).

Shlaim, Avi, 'La guerre des historiens israéliens', *Annales* 59/1 (2004) pp. 161–9.

Silberstein, Laurence, *The postzionism debates: knowledge and power in Israeli culture* (London, 1999).

Slyomovics, Susan, *The object of memory – Arab and Jew narrate the Palestinian village* (Philadelphia, PA, 1998).

Smith, Rogers, *Stories of peoplehood: the politics and morals of political membership* (Cambridge, 2003).

Tahi, Mohand Salah, 'The struggle for linguistic rights and democratic pluralism: the case of the Kabyle Berbers in Algeria', in Bo Isaksson and Marianne Laanatza (eds.), *About the Berbers: history, language, culture and socio-economic conditions* (Uppsala, Sweden, 2004) pp. 207–26.

Troen, Selwyn K., 'De-judaizing the homeland: academic politics in rewriting the history of Palestine', *Israel Affairs* 13/4 (2007) pp. 872–84.

Trouillot, Michel-Rolph, *Silencing the past – power and the production of history* (Boston, MA, 1995).

Waxman, Chaim I., 'Critical sociology and the end of ideology in Israel', *Israel Studies* 2/1 (1997) pp. 194–210.

Weingrod, Alex, 'How Israeli culture was constructed: memory, history and the Israeli past', *Israel Studies* 2/1 (1997) pp. 228–37.

Zertal, Idit, *Israel's holocaust and the politics of nationhood* (Cambridge, 2005).

Zerubavel, Yael, *Recovered roots: collective memory and the making of Israeli national tradition* (Chicago, 1995).

Chapter 5. Research and Further Reading

Israel

Ben Gurion University website documenting the case of Teddy Katz's Haifa University Masters thesis on the massacre at Tantura in 1948, http://www.ee .bgu.ac.il/~censor/katz-directory/

Israel-Academia-Monitor website, http://www.israel-academia-monitor.com/

Zochrot ['remembering'] website, http://www.zochrot.org/en/

Algeria

http://www.amazigh-voice.com/index.html
http://www.berberes.com/
Colonna, Fanny, *Les versets de l'invincibilité* (Paris, 1995).
Madjeber, Smaïl, *ABC Amazigh: une expérience éditoriale en Algérie 1996–2001* (Paris, 2005).
Mu'assasa Thaqafiyya Amazighiyya website, http://www.tawalt.com/

Chapter 6

Al-Ali, Naji, *A child in Palestine – the cartoons of Naji al-Ali* (London, 2009).
Baker, Raymond, 'Combative cultural politics: film art and political spaces in Egypt', *Alif: Journal of Comparative Poetics* 15 (1995) pp. 6–38.
Balaghi, Shiva, and Lynn Gumpert (eds.), *Picturing Iran: art, society and revolution* (London, 2002).
Baron, Beth, *Egypt as a woman: nationalism, gender and politics* (Berkeley, CA, 2005).
Becker, Cynthia, 'Exile, memory and healing in Algeria', *African Arts* 42/2 (2009) pp. 24–31.
Berger, John, *The sense of sight* (New York, 1985).
Boullata, Kamal, 'Artists re-member Palestine in Beirut', *Journal of Palestine Studies* 32/4 (2003) pp. 22–38.
Boullata, Kamal, 'Art under siege' *Journal of Palestine Studies* 33/4 (2004) pp. 70–84.
Boullata, Kamal, *Palestinian art – from 1850 to the present* (London, 2009).
Bourdieu, Pierre, *The field of cultural production* (Cambridge, 1993).
Chelkowski, Peter, and Hamid Dabashi, *Staging a revolution: the art of persuasion in the Islamic Republic of Iran* (London, 2000).
Clark, Toby, *Art and propaganda in the twentieth century: the political image in the age of mass culture* (London, 1997).
Egrikavuk, Isil, 'Interview with Halil Altindere', *Boot Print* 1/2 (2007) p. 22.
Fyfe, Gordon and John Law (eds.), *Picturing power: visual definition and social relations* (London, 1988).
Gamboni, Dario, *The destruction of art – iconoclasm and vandalism since the French revolution* (London, 1997).
Gröndahl, Mia, *Gaza graffiti – messages of love and politics* (Cairo, Egypt, 2009).
Hallaj, Muhammad, 'Palestine – the suppression of an idea', *The Link* 15/1 (1982) pp. 1–16.
Held, Jutta, and Alex Potts, 'How do the political effects of pictures come about? The case of Picasso's "Guernica"', *Oxford Art Journal* 11/1 (1988) pp. 33–9.
Isaak, Jo Anna, *Feminism and contemporary art: the revolutionary power of women's laughter* (London, 1996).

Issa, Rose, 'Weapons of mass discussion', in *Reorientations – contemporary Arab representations* (Brussels, 2008) pp. 10, 24–31.

Jowett, Garth, and Victoria O'Donnell, *Propaganda and persuasion* (Thousand Oaks, CA, 2006).

Khalaf, Samir, *Cultural resistance: global and local encounters in the Middle East* (London, 2001).

Khalil, Karima (ed.), *Messages from Tahrir – signs from Egypt's revolution* (Cairo, Egypt, 2011).

Kosova, Erden, 'An extra struggle', *Bidoun* (2005) pp. 70–1.

Laidi-Hanieh, Adila, 'Arts, identity and survival: building cultural practices in Palestine', *Journal of Palestine Studies* 35/4 (2006) pp. 28–43.

Maasri, Zeina, *Off the wall – political posters of the Lebanese civil war* (London, 2009).

Massad, Joseph, 'Permission to paint: Palestinian art and the colonial encounter', *Art Journal* 66/3 (2007) pp. 126–33.

Mir-Hosseini, Ziba, 'Iranian cinema: art, society and the state', *Middle East Report* 219 (2001) pp. 26–9.

Mitter, Partha, *Art and nationalism in colonial India 1850–1922* (Cambridge, 1994).

Mouffe, Chantal, Rosalyn Deutsche, Branden W. Joseph, and Thomas Keenan, 'Every form of art has a political dimension', *Grey Room* 2 (2001) pp. 99–125.

Parry, William, *Against the wall – the art of resistance in Palestine* (London, 2010).

Peteet, Julie, 'The writing on the walls: the graffiti of the intifada', *Cultural Anthropology* 11/2 (1996) pp. 139–59.

Porter, Venetia, *Word into art – artists of the modern Middle East* (London, 2006).

Porter, Venetia, *Word into art – artists of the modern Middle East – Dubai 2008* (Dubai, 2008).

Ram, Haggai, 'Multiple iconographies: political posters in the Iranian revolution', in Shiva Balaghi and Lynn Gumpert (eds.), *Picturing Iran* (London, 2003) pp. 89–101.

Safawi, Azarmi D., *Revolution and creativity: a survey of Iranian literature, films and art in the post-revolutionary era* (New Delhi, 2006).

Schnapp, Jeffrey T., *Revolutionary tides: the art of the revolutionary poster 1914–1989* (Milan, 2005).

Shammout, Ismail, and Tamam al-Akhal, *Jadariyyat al-sira wa-l-masira al-filastiniyya/Palestine: the Exodus and the Odyssey* (Amman, Jordan, 2000).

Silem, Ali, 'Mouvement Aouchem: signes et résistance', in Noureddine Sraieb (ed.), *Pratiques et résistance culturelles au Maghreb* (Paris, 1992) pp. 197–202.

Weber, Samuel, 'War, terrorism, and spectacle, or: on towers and caves', *Grey Room* 7, On 9/11 (2002) pp. 15–23.

Chapter 6. Further Reading

Abu Rashid, `Abd Allah, *Fann al-taswir al-Filastini: hiwariyat al-ard, al-turath, al-Quds, al-muqawama, al-intifada, namadhij mukhtara* (Damascus, Syria, 2007).

Altindere, Halil, 'When ideas become crime' exhibition Depo Istanbul, http://www.depoistanbul.net/en/activites_detail.asp?ac=37

Bidoun – arts and culture from the Middle East (magazine published in New York since 2004) http://www.bidoun.org/

'Egypt's Protest Art', *Foreign Policy*, 4 August 2011, http://www.foreignpolicy.com/articles/2011/08/04/protest_art?page=0,0 [accessed 25 August 2011]

Jadaliyya, Culture page, http://www.jadaliyya.com/pages/index/Culture

Nashashibi, Salwa Mikdadi, *Forces of change – artists of the Arab world* (Washington, DC, 1994).

Zoghbi, Pascal, and Don Karl Stone, *Arabic graffiti* (Berlin, 2011).

Conclusion

Hannoum, Abdelmajid, *Violent modernity: France in Algeria* (Cambridge, MA, 2010).

Levi, Primo, *The drowned and the saved* (tr. P. Bailey) (London, 1988).

Neep, Dan, *Syria insurgent: occupation, space and violence under the French mandate* (Cambridge, 2012).

Reno, William, *Corruption and state politics in Sierra Leone* (Cambridge, 1995).

Tripp, Charles, *A History of Iraq* (Cambridge, 2007).

Tripp, Charles, '"In the name of the people": the "people's court" and the Iraqi revolution (1958–1960)', in Julia C. Strauss and Donal Cruise O'Brien (eds.), *Staging politics: power and performance in Asia and Africa* (London, 2007) pp. 31–48.

Yablonka, Hannah, 'Holocaust survivors in the Israeli army during the 1948 war: documents and memory', *Israel Affairs* 12/3 (2006) pp. 462–83.

Index